Japan and Russia

Japan and Russia

The Tortuous Path to Normalization, 1949–1999

Edited by Gilbert Rozman

St. Martin's Press
New York

ISBN 0-312-22877-5

Library of Congress Cataloging-in-Publication Data
Japan and Russia : the tortuous path to normalization, 1949–1999 / edited by Gilbert Rozman.
p. cm.
Includes bibliographical references and index.
ISBN 0-312-22877-5 (cloth)
1. Japan—Foreign relations—Soviet Union. 2. Soviet Union—Foreign relations—Japan.
3. Japan—Foreign relations—20th century. 4. Soviet Union—Foreign relations—1945–1991. 5. Japan—Foreign relations—Russia (Federation) 6. Russia (Federation)—Foreign relations—Japan. I. Rozman, Gilbert.
DS849.S65 J36 2000
327.52047—dc21 99–047763

Design by Letra Libre, Inc.

First edition: April, 2000
10 9 8 7 6 5 4 3 2 1

CONTENTS

Acknowledgments

This book became a reality only with the support of the Center for Global Partnership (CGP) of The Japan Foundation, the International Research & Exchanges (IREX), and the Social Science Research Council (SSRC). Together IREX and the SSRC funded a planning conference at which this project was developed. Then the CGP plus IREX provided funding for a full-scale conference where almost all of the papers in this volume were presented. Their generosity made possible a productive exchange of experiences and ideas crossing national boundaries and essential for the study of relations between Japan and Russia, which are so often viewed from only one side.

I also want to express my appreciation to Shigeki Hakamada, Tsuyoshi Hasegawa, and Konstantin Sarkisov, who assisted in the organization of the project. They were instrumental in arranging for the participation of other authors, in working for a balanced and objective volume, and in sharing their unparalleled knowledge and insight with me. Hasegawa agreed to write a second chapter when a gap in coverage became clear. Hakamada and Sarkisov brought the book's coverage up-to-date for 1998 and the first part of 1999 as bilateral relations intensified.

Finally, I must thank the diplomats and ex-diplomats who joined this academic pursuit. On the Japanese side Ambassador Sumio Edamura and Akio Kawato shared their personal experiences in Russia at critical times in the 1990s. On the Russian side Ambassador Oleg Troyanovsky added his reminiscences at the conference and Deputy Foreign Minister Georgi Kunadze recounted his experience in the early 1990s.

Gilbert Rozman
January 2000

Acronyms

APEC	Asia-Pacific Economic Corporation
APR	Asia-Pacific Region
CIS	Commonwealth of Independent States
ERINA	Economic Research Institute of Northeast Asia
IMEMO	Institute of World Economy and International Relations
JCP	Japanese Communist Party
JSP	Japanese Socialist Party
KOR	Congress of Russian Communities
MID	Ministry of Foreign Affairs
NPT	New Political Thinking
WTO	World Trade Organization

Japanese names: We present Japanese names with the surname first except when we are referring to Japanese authors writing in English, including the authors of this book.

Japan and Russia

Introduction

Gilbert Rozman

IN 1999, RELATIONS BETWEEN JAPAN AND RUSSIA were poised between the troubled century past and the unknown century ahead. Begun in war and long mired in cold war, prolonged by an unresolved territorial dispute, Russo-Japanese relations in the twentieth century rank poorest among the great powers. Whereas other bilateral ties may have briefly sunk to a more intense antipathy, Russo-Japanese relations have sustained a mood of abnormality and irreconcilability for a longer time. Over the second half of the century they remained continuously troubled despite flashes of hope. In the 1990s, of the great powers, only Japan and Russia have yet to "normalize" relations. This means not only that they cannot agree on territorial boundaries and sign a peace treaty left in abeyance since World War II, but also that they do not feel free to conduct business as usual. Intense bursts of interest in overcoming the past keep ending in disillusionment. This record of the past 50 years stands in the way of plans for the twenty-first century.

In 1997 and 1998, negotiators from the two countries stepped up the pace of bilateral contacts with the goal of leaving the problems of the twentieth century behind. Hopes for building a new, forward-looking relationship for the twenty-first century soared, but a downturn followed in 1999. The strategies each side had adopted to overcome the past themselves proved to be excessively rooted in bygone days. With bilateral relations again at an impasse the challenge looms of looking back for lessons about what has gone wrong. This book presents a chronology of half a century of Japanese-Russian relations, with emphasis on the eventful final decade. It shows the patterns in the repeated search for a breakthrough in relations and the enduring barriers. It sheds light on relations by evaluating how the two sides perceived each other and by comparing their respective struggles for national identity. By adding new understanding of the sustained failures of the past, the authors look ahead toward a realistic foundation for moving Japanese-Russian ties forward and for refocusing on their role as partners in an evolving world order suitable for the century ahead.

At first glance, the years 1949 and 1999 do not stand out as milestones in the history of Japanese-Russian relations. Unlike other years of high drama when long-anticipated summits or international events occurred, these years showed little outward sign of setting relations on a new course. Yet, from the long-term perspective of bilateral ties, the two years stand as bookends marking the opposite sides of an era. In 1949, as China turned socialist and the cold war intensified between the United States and the Soviet Union, officials in Washington, D.C., and Tokyo were laying the groundwork for territorial demands that would remain in the forefront for half a century. After the decisions advanced in 1949 were confirmed in the San Francisco Treaty of 1951 and at negotiations to restore diplomatic relations between Japan and the Soviet Union in 1956, Japanese fixated on the "legal" and "just" return of what became known as the "Northern Territories" and Russians responded dismissively, seeing Japanese claims as "arrogant" assertions against one of the world's mightiest powers. For half a century the same mindset locked bilateral relations into a time warp no matter how much global geopolitical and geoeconomic currents pressed for reconsideration.

Without waiting for the wisdom of historical hindsight, we hazard to suggest that the year 1999 has special significance too as the end of an era. After the most dizzying climb yet toward normalization, the realization rapidly sunk in early in 1999 that Japan and Russia had reached a full-blown impasse. The old approach, in its manifold disguises, could no longer be resurrected. Already in the 1990s three variations had been tried—at the Gorbachev "cherry blossom" summit in Tokyo in April 1991, at the Yeltsin "parliament burning" summit in Tokyo in October 1993, and finally at the troika of Hashimoto-Yeltsin-Obuchi "no-necktie" and "sanatorium sickbed" summits in Krasnoyarsk, Kawana, and Moscow successively in November 1997, April 1998, and November 1998. As the results of the supposedly secret Japanese Kawana and Russian Moscow plans respectively leaked to the public, a sense of hopelessness spread. Together they offered no basis for moving forward. The year 1999 signifies the dead end of the past. At year end, the two sides kept the façade of improving ties, obscuring the lack of substantive talks.

Attention to relations between Tokyo and Moscow has paled in comparison to the importance of these two capitals in world affairs. The Soviet Union was a military juggernaut with the status of a superpower for over four decades until its collapse in 1991, while Japan emerged in the 1970s as an industrial powerhouse and has remained so through the 1990s. In the second half of the twentieth century these were the top two rivals, each in its own one-sided way, to the United States. Moscow's significance for security and Tokyo's for economics placed them in two distinct spheres of the global compass, but as those spheres have drawn together in the 1980s and 1990s, the impact of Russo-Japanese relations in world affairs has risen. As architects of global relations think about ways of balancing U.S. unipolarity and great power multipolarity, of fostering regional integration in Northeast Asia that engages China rather than contains it, and of nursing unstable states away from threatening postures, success is hard to envision without Japan and Russia joining forces.

Although Russian political turmoil and economic decline destroyed much of what had made the Soviet Union strong, and Japanese political immobility coupled with economic stagnation and the Asian financial crisis have reduced Japan's global stature in the second half of the 1990s, relations between Moscow and Tokyo have not lost their newfound importance. After all, uncertainty about Russia's path raises a profound question mark for the international order as a whole, and Japan's status as the world's largest creditor nation and a neighbor and determining force in the development of Asiatic Russia indicates Japan's potential role in Russia's future. Russia's need to become integrated into Asia without undue dependence on China leads naturally to Japan. Meanwhile, as Japan struggles with its continued dependency on the United States and its complex relations with China, Russia looms as one key to Japan's rise on the global stage as a political power and its "reentry into Asia" as an all-around power and champion of regionalism.

While relations between Tokyo and Moscow have gained added importance, they also have had an enduring quality. Whether Moscow was riding high, the two countries were roughly in balance,

Tokyo was overtaking Moscow, or both were in decline, the same set of issues kept driving bilateral relations. At the forefront was a territorial dispute over four islands, and in the background were concerns about political status, national dignity, economic development, and the great power balance. By examining the various dimensions of relations between Japan and Russia over half a century we can appreciate the continuities. Paying heed to the sharp oscillations of the late 1980s and 1990s in this relationship, we can make better sense of impending challenges of our new era.

From the 1950s through the 1990s, the focus of Russo-Japanese relations kept returning to the question of how to put the conflict of August 1945 (when Moscow went to war in Asia as Tokyo's aggression was ending) behind them and sign a peace treaty. What must they do to resolve their territorial dispute? At times progress was so slow that any initiative appeared useless. At other times interest intensified in how to draw the attention of national leaders and to advance relations through a bilateral summit. Whenever attention focused on this relationship, the two sides were challenged to reexamine their foreign policy priorities and demonstrate their diplomatic finesse. As the cold war receded, public opinion increasingly entered the picture. At stake was the challenge of finding a shared vision of the future that would induce both sides to cooperate. When a sudden upsurge in negotiations and summitry occurred in 1997–98, these concerns again rose to the forefront.

At Krasnoyarsk in November 1997, Prime Minister Hashimoto Ryutaro of Japan and President Boris Yeltsin of Russia agreed to accelerate efforts to resolve the political and economic problems between their countries by the end of the twentieth century. Each side gave a favorable evaluation to this informal summit, agreeing that it symbolized the arrival of a new era for the Japan-Russia relationship. Despite some skepticism, press coverage in both countries was generally positive, and in many Japanese newspapers it was downright exuberant. But sharp differences in interpretation could be detected in the media coverage in Moscow and Tokyo. On the Russian side, hopes soared that now a peace treaty could be discussed without the return of territory; the thorny issue of the disputed islands could be shelved for the next generation. Meanwhile, the door would be opening wide to large-scale Japanese investment in the Russian economy. On the Japanese side, success in including a reference to the 1993 "Tokyo Declaration" in the summit agreement was taken as a sign that a territorial solution would be a prime goal in accelerated negotiations. While details of timing remained vague, agreement to base a solution on the principles of "law" and "justice" signaled a positive outcome to Japan's insistence that all four disputed islands be returned by Moscow. If Russia were to put its economic system in order, the Japanese government would not be adverse to encouraging investment too, but there was little confidence that Russia would act and no sense of urgency that Japan's own economic development would benefit much from tapping the natural resources in Siberia and the Russian Far East until well into the next century. Some economic assistance would smooth any agreement, but this would not pose an undue burden, the Japanese assumed.

Once again global observers could see how difficult it is for Japan and Russia to agree on an agenda to resolve differences lingering from the end of World War II and to set a firm course for cooperation, vital to a new world order, in the twenty-first century. Whether in criticism of setbacks to relations or in praise of agreements to negotiate further, the two sides had mastered the art of talking past each other. Such differences arose at critical moments, such as: 1949–1951, during the buildup to the San Francisco Peace Treaty; 1955–56, in talks to normalize relations that in fact led to the restoration of diplomatic ties; 1960, when Moscow unilaterally renounced the 1956 agreement to return two islands; 1973, when a rare summit occurred in Moscow; 1978, when Japan signed a treaty with China that offended Russia; 1986–91, when intensified negotiations explored the meaning of glasnost and new thinking for bilateral relations; and 1992–99, as both sides struggled to accommodate each other in a suddenly transformed domestic and world order. High officials, informed elites, and mass opinion share in the bewilderment about how to temper what the other side perceives as arrogance with encouragement in order to redirect relations to serve national interests.

Japanese have long sought to end the abnormal state of their postwar passive diplomacy and political obscurity on the global stage. They have become accustomed to identifying their country's relation with the Soviet Union and Russia as a symbol of this abnormality. In their new weak state, Russians have had trouble accepting Japan's claims to global status commensurate with economic power. Having lost their superpower identity, Russians want recognition as a meaningful partner of Japan. Questions of political status continue to plague bilateral relations.

Both nations link this bilateral relationship to national dignity. Surveys of public opinion and the rhetoric of many publications indicate that a high degree of emotionalism is involved. Efforts to boost relations acknowledge the need to overcome negative stereotypes. There is frequent reference to building a foundation for good relations based on respect, trust, and mutual understanding. It is important to consider the social psychological side of Russo-Japanese relations along with the diplomatic, economic, and great power dimensions.

From the 1960s, Tokyo and Moscow began to cooperate to develop the natural resources of Eastern Siberia and the Russian Far East. Troubled political relations, and a shift in Japan's economic development model after the first oil shock led to resource conservation, kept early plans from being realized, but hopes did not die for regional economic integration in Northeast Asia. As many Japanese spoke in the late 1980s of reentering Asia and creating a Sea of Japan rim economic sphere, interest rose in macroprojects to extract energy and other resources from Russia. Soon, Russians were proposing development programs for their Asian regions to draw on Japanese capital and technology above all. In their calculations on how to improve relations Japanese counted on Russian determination to open their economy and recover from the severe downslide after the disintegration of the Soviet Union. Any vision of a future of cooperation must make joint economic development the centerpiece.

Japanese-Russian relations have been overshadowed by U.S. and Chinese relations with both Japan and Russia. This was true during the cold war, when the United States and China often tried to pressure Japan in its relations with Russia, and it has remained true in the headlines after the end of the cold war. Throughout the 1990s, jockeying for influence by China, Japan, Russia, and the United States has taken for granted that of the six bilateral relations among these powers the weakest link is Japanese-Russian relations. When a pair of these powers met, this imbalance often figured into their deliberations, whether it was the United States cajoling Japan to further assist Russia, China seeking Russia's support for more pressure on Japan and the U.S.-Japan security alliance, or Russia complaining of one-sided U.S. support for Japan's territorial demands. The problematic nature of relations between Japan and Russia was a given to be adjusted in the interest of other powers, not a source of leverage for either of these countries. Suddenly a timetable was set on the Yenisei River to conclude a peace treaty and achieve a huge increase in economic cooperation over just three years. Japan and Russia began to address their bilateral problems directly, while anticipating a new balance in great power relations. The potential impact could be far-reaching, but the great power context was slipping into the background from the summer of 1998 in the midst of the Asian financial crisis and Russia's terrible domestic problems. Meanwhile, misunderstandings about what the other side was thinking produced superficial signs of a relationship on the verge of a breakthrough that could not be sustained. The story of bilateral relations from 1996 to 1999 adds but one more chapter to the saga of the most consistently troubled relationship among the world's powers in the second half of the twentieth century.

In this book we seek to understand the history of Russo-Japanese relations, while drawing attention to what has been lost by the long periods of stalemate and what might be gained by normalization. The history of relations since 1949, when efforts began in earnest to situate Japanese-Russian ties within the postwar order, is not just a series of failed or partially inconclusive negotiations. It is also a process of gradual, if halting, realization of what difference a breakthrough in relations might make.

The four organizers of the project from which this book derives are not newcomers to the subject of Japanese-Russian relations. They have written on the topic before but are convinced that a more comprehensive, multinational assessment from the perspective of the end of the century following the Hashimoto-Yeltsin burst of negotiations will serve a different purpose. For those who want the fullest history of the Northern Territories dispute as well as a rich chronology on bilateral relations, we recommend Tsuyoshi Hasegawa's two volumes.[1] And readers who are interested in delving further into relations in the second half of the 1980s as seen through internal debates, are directed to Gilbert Rozman's book.[2] Those who read Japanese or Russian will no doubt recognize the names of Shigeki Hakamada and Konstantin Sarkisov as the experts who have most knowledgeably interpreted the course of bilateral relations over the past two decades, encouraging better understanding among officials and the public. Too bad that so few of their publications have appeared in English. This collective work builds on what these four authors as well as the other contributors have written elsewhere.

Part I retraces a familiar topic: the origins of the postwar division between the two countries. It covers familiar ground from the end of the 1940s to the late 1950s to set the stage for the rest of the half century, and offers something new. What is new is best revealed in the opening paper by Haruki Wada, drawing on recent archival research, to show the inside story of how on the Japanese side with the strong hand of the United States the territorial dispute emerged after the war and became a preoccupation. This is followed by a review by Boris Slavinsky, which also draws heavily on archival records to give us some of the inside story on the Soviet side. Completing the trio of papers on the 1950s is an analysis by Alexei Zagorsky that extensively refers to sources on both the Soviet and Japanese sides to spell out the logic of Soviet decision making in the 1950s. The legacy of the end of the 1940s and 1950s in relations between Japan and Russia, more than relations between any other great powers, endures a half century later. This mix of papers should fix in our minds the real meaning of the incomplete postwar peace settlement between the two countries.

This volume devotes only two chapters to the two decades of Soviet-Japanese relations prior to the start of the Gorbachev era. These are years that have been well covered elsewhere and for which we have not found very much new to say. But we do find it necessary for purposes of understanding what follows to reinforce and further explain two of the most compelling images of the times: Moscow's stubborn diplomatic continuity and Japan's deepening sense that relations were sinking lower and lower. Peter Berton offers one explanation for continuity, pointing to the extraordinarily enduring role, to the second half of the 1980s, of Andrei Gromyko on the Soviet side. Ambassador Oleg Troyanovsky, who served in Tokyo for a decade under Gromyko, reminded the contributors to this volume that Gromyko was a first-rate diplomat who had mastered the art of extracting every possible advantage from a situation. Yet, Troyanovsky acknowledged that by overstressing relations with the United States, Gromyko failed to appreciate all of the policy options available in improving relations with countries that he saw as operating in the shadow of the United States. The ambassador added that at decisive moments in bilateral relations the Soviet leadership was preoccupied with other matters. For example in August 1973, when Prime Minister Tanaka Kakuei came to Moscow, war had broken out in the Middle East. Obsessed with China and angered by Japanese talks with China that would lead to a friendship treaty with wording targeted against "hegemonic" Soviet foreign policy, Moscow overreacted in 1976–78. The mood of optimism with which Troyanovsky began his tenure in the late 1960s turned to frustration in dealings with Japan. Hiroshi Kimura adds a stark depiction of the low point in relations in the late 1970s and the first half of the 1980s. Aroused by one sign after another of the dreadful state of ties with the Soviet Union, the Japanese people succumbed to a mood of hopelessness. Together the Berton and Kimura chapters show us how troubled this bilateral relationship had become on the eve of the Gorbachev era.

Part II offers perspectives on relations in the Gorbachev period, during Yeltsin's early years in power, and finally on the years at century's end when hopes rose and then fell. These perspectives range from decision making in Moscow and Tokyo to cross-border relations between neighboring regions. The great uncertainty of the Gorbachev era is captured in the two papers by Nobuo Shimotomai and Lisbeth L. Tarlow. Shimotomai faults the Japanese side for the delay in overcoming the legacy of stagnation and its bad timing. He traces the problem to the decision-making process in Japan without hesitating to draw attention as well to complications on the Russian side. Tarlow delves more deeply into the conditions that made it possible for Gorbachev to contemplate a shift in policy toward Japan and the reasons why he ultimately abandoned the possibility of a breakthrough in relations. Together the two papers on the final years of the Soviet Union suggest the possibilities that might have been, while accentuating the powerful obstacles on both sides.

Part II next juxtaposes the recollections of Ambassador Sumio Edamura with those of Deputy Foreign Minister Georgi Kunadze of the turbulent first two years of relations between the new Russian government and Japan when ties were emboldened by the end of the cold war. After striving to work together at a time of heightened opportunity, the two sides ended up disputing who was to blame for the breakdown in relations that was symbolized by the decision of Yeltsin to cancel his planned visit in September 1992. These chapters help us to understand too the limits of the repair work that led to a summit in October 1993 and the "Tokyo Declaration." The same period figures into Tsuyoshi Hasegawa's chapter that draws on both sides' perspectives as he explains why no rapprochement was achieved and my chapter that shows the illusory hopes of building improved ties from the bottom up, starting with cross-border relations. Both of these chapters carry the story forward until the second half of the 1990s, when a new round of accelerated contacts began to normalize relations.

Perhaps the most dramatic story to be told about Japanese-Russian relations in the second half of the twentieth century is the roller-coaster ride of rising hopes in 1997–98 and dashed dreams in late 1998 and 1999. Konstantin Sarkisov and Shigeki Hakamada update the coverage, carrying the story of bilateral relations forward from the time of Yeltsin's reelection in 1996 and showing the precarious nature of the exhilarating steps that for a short time suggested that normalization was just around the corner. Sarkisov concentrates on the upswing in relations, while Hakamada concludes with a stark picture of the downswing.

In the late 1980s both sides gained a new appreciation of the possibilities of a normalized relationship. The upbeat mood of the Krasnoyarsk summit only became possible after each side became newly aware of its own opportunities in a changing era and newly conscious of the other side's distinct role in great power and regional relations. Yet, hopes had risen before, and neither Russians nor Japanese were sufficiently focused on the positive prospects of their relations to have much confidence that the year 2000 would become a milestone separating two contrasting centuries. The countdown that was initiated in 1997 exposed the discrepancy between newly shared hopes and entrenched separate points of view. Its shortsightedness confirms the lessons we draw from the previous decades of ups and downs in Japanese-Russian relations.

The chapters that trace the history of bilateral relations over 50 years point to 3 conclusions about what went wrong. First, they highlight the adverse interrelationship between domestic priorities and foreign policy flexibility. Without calibrating their responses to policymaking in the other country, Japanese and Russian officials spoke to domestic priorities at the expense of foreign relations. This resulted from skewed perceptions of the political process and interests on the other side and from other foreign policy priorities that stood in the way of normalization. Second, the history of Russo-Japanese relations illustrates how the conduct of diplomacy can fail to advance negotiations. While much attention focused on the goal of diplomacy, little concern was shown for steering talks past a series of hurdles through a multistage approach. The two sides did not build relations of trust essential to solving the problems before them. Third, Japan and Russia became so absorbed with the legacy of their past relations, they missed the opportunity to develop a shared vision of the future. They neglected to identify how much could be gained.

The chapters in Part III show that when public opinion mattered neither government had an effective strategy for taking it into account or shaping it. They misperceived opinion abroad and helped to shape domestic opinion in ways that later limited policy flexibility. They did not prepare the public at home or abroad for the compromises that were required through normalization. Semyon Verbitsky draws on his many years as a Soviet Japanologist to analyze how views of Japan were shaped. Tsuyoshi Hasegawa provides parallel coverage of Japanese views, extending his coverage through the mid-1990s. Then Akio Kawato looks back on his years as the Japanese diplomat in charge of cultural relations with Russia to describe the public relations campaign to change Russian thinking and its limitations. Without understanding the role of public opinion and entrenched stereotypes, it would be difficult to appreciate how intractable the problems in Japanese-Russian relations have been.

The final two chapters present comparisons of national identity in Russia and Japan and its consequences for bilateral relations. Tadashi Anno depicts the transformation of nationalism in each country over a long time frame. Gilbert Rozman carries the story forward through the 1990s with a discussion of great power identities in the context of internal social structure in each country. To understand mutual influences it is helpful to probe through comparisons into deep-seated domestic forces that can help to shape the course of bilateral relations.

Our goal is to be objective without insisting on evenhandedness. The list of authors is divided quite evenly among Americans, Japanese, and Russians, including current and past foreign ministry officials of the latter two countries. These are experts with in-depth knowledge of the course of bilateral relations, through firsthand involvement or extensive research. They recognize that the purpose of this undertaking was not to ruffle as few feathers as possible in a search for the least common denominator to boost Russo-Japanese relations, but rather to find lessons from the past as a step toward finding solutions for the future.

This book can best be read as a series of linked papers. The Wada, Slavinsky, and Zagorsky chapters combine perspectives on the formative postwar period in the 1950s, each reflecting the fruits of individual scholarship rather than the conventional views often heard in the author's country. The Berton and Kimura chapters, supplemented by the views of Ambassador Troyanovsky reported above, concentrate on the deterioration of relations in the Brezhnev era. They are followed by the Shimotomai and Tarlow perspectives on the Gorbachev era. The book's most pointed match-up occurs in the Edamura and Kunadze chapters covering the opening years of the Yeltsin era. The following two chapters by Hasegawa and Rozman are not a pairing in themselves, but rather serve to link the chapters by the two diplomats to the final chronological contributions by the well-placed academic experts, Sarkisov and Hakamada. Each combination of authors provides a balance of thematic concerns and national viewpoints.

At the end of the 1990s Russia is again in transition and Japan faces a transition of its own. Prolonged economic problems in the 1990s followed by the Asian financial crisis have forced each country to shift direction, but the path ahead remains unclear. This may seem like an inauspicious time to solve problems in bilateral relations that could not be settled previously. But each side may also gain new appreciation for the need to move forward, leading to a more realistic approach for addressing their relations in order to concentrate elsewhere.

As elements of such an approach, we want to highlight three ideals that would speed good relations. First, for cooperation to become the keystone in relations Japan and Russia should become "normal" countries in their national identity and priorities. This means no special suspicions of the outside world, no excessive protectionism, a suitable balance of economic and military interests, and a growing embrace of internationalist attitudes. Russia must traverse a greater distance to reach these goals; Japanese policies should be sensitive to the arduous nature of this transition.

Second, Japan and Russia will turn to each other more to the extent that they recognize the wisdom of balance-of-power politics in a period of U.S. supremacy mixed with multipolar maneuvering. If the United States played a large role in keeping Japan and the Soviet Union apart during the cold war while China reinforced this separation as a result of the Sino-Soviet split, then China is likely to exert a large influence in bringing Japan and Russia together in coming decades while the United States reinforces this tendency. Prudence in balancing the rise of China is sufficient impetus for closer relations without outright deterioration of bilateral relations on either side.

A third force that favors improved relations is economic regionalism in Northeast Asia. This is a desperate need of the Russian Far East. It represents the ardent wishes of provinces in northeast China and areas along the Japan Sea coast away from Japan's prosperous Pacific urban agglomerations. Nonetheless, apart from criminalized exports by Russia of crabs and fish to Hokkaido and imports from Japan of used cars, there is little to show for hundreds of delegations and conferences planning for regionalism. North Korea forsook regionalism at the cost of famine and isolation. Sino-Russian cross-border trade, rooted in primitive barter, fell precipitously in 1994 amid civilizational accusations. Japanese plans came to naught to develop agricultural exports in northeast China. And even energy projects—the lynchpin of most regional planning—have, with the exception of offshore Sakhalin, floundered before Russia's stalemated decision making. But however elusive regionalism may be, hopes centering on Russian natural resources and Japanese investment survive. This match has the potential to catapult bilateral relations forward, and to reshape an entire region.

Some advances in the 1990s toward normalcy in each country, balance-of-power politics, and economic regionalism give cause for heightened optimism. Yet, other setbacks, especially in Russia, result in uncertainty. A half century of missed opportunities in bilateral relations leaves grounds for caution. The countdown to the end of this century started with insufficient energy to allow the positive forces to prevail. As diplomats redoubled their efforts in 1998, the public in neither country reflected sufficiently on what had gone wrong before or on what could be achieved through compromise. Relations between Japan and Russia stand at a crossroads. By looking closely at the past, we can gain a better idea of how to shape the future.

As the year 2000 began Vladimir Putin, who was suddenly thrust into the position of acting president, addressed the need to strengthen relations with countries in Asia. Although he naturally would give priority to China and India, Japan also figured as a target. A vigorous president working with a newly elected Duma may succeed in passing legislation that opens the way to foreign investment. If so, Putin would be likely to press Japan's leaders to expand economic ties. They, in turn, would again seek concessions on the territorial dispute. New leadership in Moscow means another chance to raise hopes, despite little preparation of public opinion in each country for a mutually acceptable solution. At least, this time Moscow should know how difficult it is to accomplish an economic transition and bring investment into the Far East and Siberia that would decrease its vulnerability in Asia, and Tokyo should realize how limited is its leverage as a great power able to win cooperation in dealing with North Korea and China. Despite the impasse in relations, possibilities persist for a new realism and vision for bilateral ties.

NOTES

1. *The Northern Territories Dispute and Russo-Japanese Relations*, vol. 1, *Between War and Peace, 1697–1985*, vol. 2, *Neither War Nor Peace, 1985–1998* (Berkeley: University of California at Berkeley, International and Area Studies, Research Series Publications, 1998).
2. *Japan's Response to the Gorbachev Era: A Rising Superpower Views a Declining One* (Princeton: Princeton University Press, 1992).

PART I

Relations: 1949–1984

CHAPTER 1

The San Francisco Peace Treaty and the Definition of the Kurile Islands

Haruki Wada

IN JAPANESE-SOVIET AND JAPANESE-RUSSIAN NEGOTIATIONS over the territorial question, the Japanese government has demanded the return of the "Northern four islands," shaking off the fetters resulting from its decision to abandon the Kurile Islands in the San Francisco Peace Treaty. For the purpose it high-handedly redefined the Kurile Islands. In other words, it insisted that not only Habomai and Shikotan, but also Etorofu and Kunashiri were originally not included in the Kurile Islands (*Chishima,* in Japanese). The governments of the Soviet Union and Russia have not accepted this new definition, and the negotiations over the territorial question long were at a deadlock. But at present, the Japanese government is no longer conducting negotiations of the territorial question based on this definition.[1] Thus the question raised in this chapter has become a matter for the past. In order to finally leave this question behind us it is necessary to clarify its contents and their import. In this way, we can free ourselves once and for all from the logic of confrontation that characterized those negotiations of the cold war period and, irrevocably, shift to the logic of dialogue.

On this issue several Japanese scholars have worked energetically. They have explored in detail all four of the foundations for redefining the Kurile Islands: the Japanese-Russian Treaty of 1855, the Japanese-Russian Treaty of 1876, the secret Yalta agreement of 1945, and the San Francisco Peace Treaty of 1951. The late Murayama Shichiro and I studied two treaties of 1855 and 1875 and came to the conclusion that these treaties did not give any foundation for redefining the Kurile Islands.[2] Tsuyoshi Hasegawa gave us strong support in his new book.[3] Recently, Hara Kimie made a notable contribution by discovering in the Australian Archives an unpublished Japanese Foreign Ministry pamphlet of 1946. This pamphlet should put an end to the debates over the definition of the Kurile Islands, since it shows that Murayama's and my interpretations were correct. Moreover, concerning the draft prepared by the United States in preparation of the San Francisco Treaty, Tsukamoto Takashi made an important contribution based on research in the National Archives of the United States. This chapter draws on the findings by Hara and Tsukamoto with the perspective of further analysis.

Japan's Peace Preparations

The Japanese Foreign Ministry in November 1945 set up a Peace Problems Research Board (*heiwa mondai kenkyu kanjikai*), which consisted mainly of members of the Treaty Bureau and Political Affairs Bureau. Preparations were begun for peace. While materials prepared by this board were assembled in a Foreign Ministry archival file, "Relevant to the Preparatory Research Concerning the Japan Peace Treaty," almost everything on territorial relations has not been declassified.

Thirty-six pamphlets compiled by this board were sent to the U.S. government, among which seven treated the territorial question. Prime Minister Yoshida Shigeru asserted in his *Ten-Year Reminiscences* that the explanatory materials in these seven pamphlets described in detail why historically, geographically, ethnically, and economically a number of islands are Japan's inseparable territory.[4] However, only the pamphlets on the Ryukyu Islands and Tsushima were declassified. The three pamphlets on the northern territories problem presented in November 1946 and January and April 1949 were kept away from public disclosure. The reason, I surmise, is that the Foreign Ministry's official notion of the Kurile Islands later contradicted the description of these pamphlets of the earlier time.

That my conjecture is correct has been proven by the discovery of Hara Kimie (now an Assistant Professor at Calgary University). While a Ph.D. candidate at Australian National University, Hara in 1994 found in the National Archives in Canberra the first of the above-mentioned three pamphlets, "The Kurile Islands, the Habomais and Shikotan."[5] This pamphlet identifies Etorofu and Kunashiri as the South Kuriles. It divides the Kuriles into two sections based on climate and vegetation, noting that the southern zone of Kunashiri and Etorofu is closer to Hokkaido. And it explains that in the treaty of 1875, "Japan gave up entirely its rights on Saghalien and accepted in exchange the northern portion of Kuriles."[6] The accurate translation of the text of the treaty of 1875 is cited. At the end of the first chapter, "The Kurile Islands" (*Chishima*), it is stated that "Japanese sovereignty over the Kuriles was never disputed since then."[7] Hinting that at the time the Kurile Islands and southern Sakhalin were under the occupation of the Soviet army, this is a position in support of sovereignty over the entire Kurile chain.

Chapter 2 notes that the Habomai Island group and Shikotan island "are to be considered topographically and geologically as an extension of the Nemuro promontory of Hokkaido," and adds, "In some cases the group of Habomais and Shikotan are included in the Kurile Islands."[8] The pamphlet cites the following assertion from *Lippincott's Gazetter of the World:* "The South Kurile group compromises Kunashiri, Yetorohu and Shikotan, but the Habomais are not included among the islands of the Kuriles."[9] In conclusion it says that the Habomais and Shikotan "constitute the economic unit of Hokkaido."[10] The reason for keeping this pamphlet long hidden, which presented the shared consciousness to that time of Japan, Russia, and the world, can easily be understood. Before long Japan's official position would define the Kuriles very differently.

The Start of American Peace Preparations

In the State Department's Far Eastern Bureau at the end of the World War II, a Japan experts group intensified criticism of the Yalta Agreement, arguing that the southern group of the Kuriles should be kept in Japan. Their criticisms were expressed in their preparation for the Japan Peace Treaty. Tsukamoto Takashi, a research specialist of the National Diet Library, studied preparations for the peace treaty, found a number of variants of it in the National Archives in Washington, D.C., and traced the process of their change.[11] But he did not show keen interest in the definition of the Kurile Islands. Guided by his findings, I myself examined the Washington archives too. Here I will study variants from the standpoint of the definition of the Kurile Islands.

By March 1947, Hugh Borton, head of the Far Eastern Bureau, Department of State, drafted the first variant of a peace treaty in accord with the Yalta Agreement. It says, "Japan hereby cedes to the Soviet Union in full sovereignty the Kurile islands, lying between Kamchatka and Hokaido."[12] However, after his visit to Japan in March and April,[13] Borton prepared the second draft on August 5, 1947, in which it was asserted that the Habomai Islands, Shikotan, Kunashiri, and Etorofu are within Japan's territorial limits, saying, "Japan hereby cedes to the Union of Soviet Socialist Republics in full sovereignty the Kurile Islands, comprising the islands northeast of Etorofu Strait . . . from Urup . . . to Shumshu inclusive, which were ceded by Russia to Japan by the Treaty of 1875."[14]

Thus, the redefinition of the Kuriles was done to save for Japan the southernmost islands. The Kuriles came to be defined as a chain of islands north from Uruppu. At that time inside Japan local residents of Hokkaido were talking about the northern territories problem and calling for the return of precisely these islands south of Uruppu, but the argument had not yet appeared that Etorofu and Kunashiri were not part of the Kuriles. Thus the Far Eastern Bureau's idea of redefinition of the Kuriles went beyond what the Japanese were thinking in judging why the islands should be returned to Japan. But the State Department did not support this redefinition. In September, a memorandum entitled the "Southern Kuriles" was prepared.[15] In a paper of October 14, George Kennan, Director of the Policy Planning Staff, advocated that the southernmost islands of the Kurile archipelago be retained by Japan. Although the influence of the cold war in resisting the Soviet Union and revising the Yalta Agreement can be seen, Kennan remained with the standard definition of the Kuriles.[16]

On January 30, 1948, Borton prepared a new draft for a Japan peace treaty. Although the text itself was not found in the archives, he noted in a paper of annotations on the draft, "In reference to the Kuriles, they are not defined in the Yalta Agreement. . . . If the United States proposes a narrow interpretation of the 'Kurile Islands,' the southernmost islands of Kunashiri and Etorofu, the Habomai group and Shikotan would be retained by Japan."[17] Despite opposing views in the Department of State, Borton stuck to his new interpretation.

In the spring of 1948, with the crisis of the Guomindang regime deepening in China, U.S. policy toward Japan changed decisively under George Kennan's initiative. Now he placed the stress on economic recovery rather than democratization of Japan in order to make Japan a stronghold of the United States against communist forces in Asia. He argued that a peace treaty with Japan should not be punitive. From this viewpoint, stronger support was given to the course of giving four islands to Japan. But redefining the Kurile Islands was not part of Kennan's idea.[18] Cloyce Huston, the chargé in Japan sent a position paper on June 27, 1949, asserting, "The Habomai Islands and Shikotan Island have been traditionally regarded as an island group distinct from the Kurile archipelago, and under Japanese control had a local administration as a political subdivision of Hokkaido separate from the Kurile islands," while Etorofu and Kunashiri are recognized as "the two southernmost Kurile Islands." He recognizes that the Yalta Agreement "afforded ample justification for the invasion and occupation of this area by Soviet forces," but adds that since historically these islands were always Japanese territories, all four islands should be returned to Japan.[19]

Therefore in 1949 all officials of the State Department agreed that the four islands should be given to Japan, while they were still divided over the definition of the Kuriles. In April of that year the Japanese government sent a pamphlet, "South Kuriles, Habomais and Shikotan," to the United States government.[20] Realizing that it would be hopeless to seek the return of all of the Kuriles and grasping the atmosphere in the State Department, it argued for the return of four islands. But this time too Japan's Foreign Ministry did not dare to redefine the Kuriles. Etorofu and Kunashiri were recognized as part of the Kuriles, but Japan wanted their return.

At this time in the local movement on Hokkaido the argument was put forward that Etorofu and Kunashiri were not part of the Kuriles. On June 14, 1949, the Hokkaido association of municipalities and villages took this position in a letter to the Foreign Ministry, making the same case for redefinition, as had Borton.[21]

A Big Change in the American Position

In October 1949, the British Foreign Minister, A. Bevin, visited Washington and asked for a draft of the peace treaty with Japan in time to present it, if London was in agreement, for examination by the British Commonwealth at its Ceylon meeting in January 1950. In the hope of gaining British approval the State Department prepared a new draft on October 13, which provided that all four disputed islands belong to Japanese territory.[22] According to the research of Tsukamoto, in the paper of annotations on this draft, it is recognized that there was a discussion on whether the four islands were a part of the Kuriles, which had been promised to the Soviet Union at Yalta. Yet, the drafter judged that the islands should remain with Japan for "political, economic, and strategic" reasons, noting that "we do not expect that the Soviet Union will let go of them," and "if this is the case, we will gain the goodwill of the Japanese people and the Soviets will be held in bad repute.[23] This clearly reveals that the United States challenged the Yalta Agreement in its plan to incorporate the Japanese sovereignty of the four islands into the peace treaty with Japan.

In the upper reaches of the State Department, however, there was doubt that this draft could be shown at a conference with Great Britain. We have already noted the view inside the State Department and the Tokyo embassy that the logic that Etorofu and Kunashiri are not included in the Kuriles could not withstand formal examination. A new draft was ordered, and it was finished on November 2. It excluded all four islands from Japanese territory, although saying in a note that a "decision whether the U.S. should propose the retention by Japan of Etorofu, Kunashiri, and the Lesser Kuriles (the Habomais and Shikotan) has not been finally made" and that "present thinking is that the U.S. should not raise the issue but that if it is raised by Japan we might show a sympathetic attitude."[24]

In a paper of annotations on this draft it is said, "the territorial dispositions in Chapter iii follow the terms of the Cairo, Yalta, and Potsdam Agreements and of previous U.S. Governmental studies relating to their implementation. The U.S. position with respect to the implementation of some of the terms of these Agreements is under recurrent review."[25] As for the possibility of making the four islands Japanese territory, there are "economic, political and strategic reasons which would make that disposition desirable," but the present view is that the United States "should not propose this." "Irrespective of the Japanese records which can be advanced to show that these islands are not part of 'the Kurils', it is believed that the U.S., in view of its commitments and actions to date, would expose itself to charges of bad faith by the Soviets which it would be difficult to refute." Adding that Truman agreed with Stalin to include all of the Kuriles to the zone of Soviet military occupation, and that Soviet forces have remained on the islands for four years "without challenge or objection by the U.S.," the paper concludes "there would seem to be no advantage to our advancing a proposal which is almost certain to be rejected."[26]

Why was the U.S. policy about to make a 180-degree turn from four islands for Japan to zero? Was it the result of being driven by the feeling that a draft had to be able to persuade the British? This point remains a puzzle; however if there was respect for the Yalta Agreement, then would this not have been the way matters would have turned out?

When this draft was sent to William Sebald, the Acting Political Adviser in Japan, he was naturally dissatisfied. In the telegram he sent on November 14 after he and Douglas MacArthur conferred, he said that "Japan will unquestionably advance a strong claim to Etorofu, Kunashiri, Habomai, and Shikotan" and that he believed "the United States should support such a claim."[27] And further, in his letter of November 19, he proposed the following instead: "it is suggested that the draft . . . contain a provision for the 'ceding to the Soviet Union . . . of the Kuril Islands, being those islands eastward and northeastward from the mid-channel line between Etorofu Island and Uruppu Island,' and this be accompanied by a footnote to the effect that 'it is the hope of the United States that the Soviet Union will not seek to annex Etorofu, Kunashiri, Shikotan, or Habomai Islands. The claim of their forming a part of the Kuril Islands is historically weak, and they are of far greater navigational and fishing importance to Japan than to any other possessor.'"[28] Sebald urged adoption of a redefinition of the Kurile Islands, allotting to Japan four islands.

And this time Maxwell M. Hamilton of the Far Eastern Bureau requested a legal examination by Adrian S. Fisher, the Legal Advisor on Political Affairs. Although political advisor Sebald's comment introduced no new factors, Hamilton said, "it emphasizes the necessity for full study of all aspects of the problem, since it seems clear that it will come up prominently at the peace conference."[29] In response, Conrad E. Snow, the Assistant Legal Advisor for Political Affairs, on November 25 answered, "it is believed that there is sound basis for the legal contention that the Habomai and Shikotan are not properly part of the Kurile Islands," but he added, "there seems to be no sound legal reason for claiming that Kunashiri and Etorofu are not part of the Kurile Islands. While . . . they have never been under Russian sovereignty since the Treaty of 1855, both that Treaty and the Treaty of 1875 indicate that they were considered to be part of the Kurile Islands."[30] This analysis, which supported the foundation of the November 2 draft, became the basic position of the State Department.

On December 29 the year's third peace treaty draft was prepared. It continued to allot the Kurile islands to the Soviet Union, but included the Habomai group and Shikotan in Japanese territory. The commentary paper on this draft repeated the November 2 logic that the United States would "expose itself to charges of bad faith by the Soviets which it would be difficult to refute were it to claim that the Kuriles did not include those islands. Moreover, U.S. assumption of control over the Ryukyus will place the United States in a poor position to suggest to the Soviets that they renounce the two islands to the Japanese simply in response to Japanese interests and desires." It added, "significant advantages would be derived by Japan from the retention of the Habomais and Shikotan even without the southern Kuriles. U.S. sponsorship of Japan's claim to the Habomais and Shikotan would indicate to the Japanese our desire to support their claim in this area to the maximum feasible extent."[31] This was the final position of the U.S. government on the Japanese territory in the north that was formed in preparing drafts of a Japan peace treaty.

At this time in Japan a Hokkaido member of the Diet introduced before the Foreign Affairs Committee of the Lower House an interpretation that the name "Kuriles" should be reserved for the islands from Uruppu northward. The Ministry of Foreign Affairs answered that "while the Yalta Agreement had used the Kuriles (*Chishima*), we think that this includes the southern and northern Kuriles. But we think that the Habomais and Shikotan which are close to Hokkaido are not included."[32]

When the mainstream in the State Department retreated from the attempt to redefine the Kuriles, in Japan the Ministry of Foreign Affairs had never had an idea of redefinition of the Kuriles.

Dulles's Rise

In April 1950, John Foster Dulles was appointed State Department counsel, and U.S. preparations for a Japan peace treaty began in earnest. Tsukamoto's 1991 article covered the period of preparation before Dulles's appearance. So from here I am to trace the process without his help.

As Dulles was engaged in preparations on the peace treaty, the Korean War broke out in June. This brought a dramatic change to the environment surrounding Japan. The United States saw Soviet intent behind North Korean behavior. Dulles then pigeonholed the draft peace treaty of late 1949, and from August to September 1950 worked out the skeleton of a simple peace treaty draft. Already the Korean War had turned into a war between the United States and Communist China when on November 24 Dulles's skeleton was issued as "Seven Principles for Peace with Japan." Point C stated that Japan would "accept the future decision of the U.K., USSR, China and the U.S. with reference to the statues of Formosa, the Pescadores, South Sakhalin and the Kuriles. In the event of no decision within a year after the Treaty came into effect the U.N. General Assembly would decide."[33] Dulles clearly demonstrated a willingness to revise radically the attitude of his government toward the Yalta Agreement. But for the time being it was a bluff. As early as October 25, an interpretation had been added to Point C stating that, "if the Japanese Peace Treaty were multilateral, and the Soviet Union a party thereto, Japan, would, by the Treaty, cede South Sakhalin and the Kuriles to the Soviet Union."[34]

In January 1951, when Dulles visited Japan, Prime Minister Yoshida in a position paper presented to Dulles asked that the decision to place the Ryukyus and Bonin islands under U.S. trust control be reconsidered. The Okinawa question was treated in the context of discussions that reached an agreement on the Japan-U.S. Security Treaty. But Yoshida did not touch on the Kurile question in his talks of January 29 with Dulles.[35] And Dulles did not want to talk about it, either.

On February 3, a "Provisional memorandum" was prepared by the Dulles mission to hand to the Japanese government, in which the problem of South Sakhalin and the Kuriles was dropped from the paragraph on territory.[36] On the other hand, when Dulles met with the British ambassador in Tokyo and then Australia's Foreign

Minister in Canberra, he heard from them unanimously that according to the Yalta Agreement Southern Sakhalin and the Kuriles should be handed to the Soviet Union, which occupied them.[37]

On the basis of the progress reached in Tokyo, Dulles returned to Washington and drafted his first version of a peace treaty with Japan on March 1, 1951. Article 5 of this draft treated the territory problem in the North as follows: "Japan will return to the Union of Soviet Socialist Republics the southern part of Sakhalin as well as all the islands adjacent to it and will hand over to the Soviet Union the Kurile islands, as they may be defined by bilateral agreement or by judicial decision pursuant to Article 19 of the present Treaty."[38] By a concerted pressure from the governments of the Commonwealth, Dulles was forced to return to the position of the last draft of 1949, respecting the Yalta Agreement. But he avoided a definition of the Kurile Islands, while pointing in the text that this is the very problem. According to Article 19, one could seek a treaty interpretation at the International Court of Justice. Such precision about Habomai and Shikotan as set in the draft of December 29, 1949, was omitted. Anyway, what was expected here was to rescue for Japan these two islands from the Kuriles.

However, it was not the case that Dulles simply agreed to respect the Yalta Agreement. He wished to keep a condition that if the Soviet Union were not a party to the treaty, Japan would not cede the Kuriles to it. The ideas behind the draft of March 1 were transmitted from the State Department to the British ambassador on March 13, with the explanation that if the Soviet Union participated in the peace treaty Japan should be prepared to cede South Sakhalin and the Kuriles to it, but the precise definition of the extent of the Kurile Islands should be a matter for bilateral agreement between Japan and the Soviet Union or for judicial determination by the International Court of Justice.[39] At the same time a memorandum was handed to the Japanese government, in which Article 5 of the March 1 draft was conveyed with a comment that the "provision would be operative only if the Soviets sign and ratify the treaty."[40]

When a revised draft was prepared on March 16, Article 5 remained basically unchanged. But a new Article 19 was interpolated, by which the Soviets would be denied any benefits if it were not a party to the treaty.[41] The Japanese government responded to the memorandum of the U.S. government on March 16 as follows: "Proposed provision for return of South Sakhalin and handing over of Kuriles to the Soviet Union under assumption it will participate in peace treaty is agreeable. However, it is desired to have the passage in question read: "as they may be defined by the powers concerned, including Japan.' . . . In case the Soviet Union goes definitely out of picture, it is hoped such stipulation regarding South Sakhalin and Kuriles will be omitted."[42]

Although Japan agreed to give up the Kuriles, it wished that some islands should be excluded from the Kuriles. It would be inconvenient if the decision was settled by a bilateral agreement or by the Court of Justice. It wanted the United States also to join in the decision making, expecting that allied countries would agree to rescue Habomai and Shikotan from the Kuriles. To this time the Japanese government had yet to raise the idea of Etorofu and Kunashiri not belonging to the Kurile Islands.[43]

Dulles could not agree with the Japanese government's response. To the fullest extent possible, the United States wanted to stand aloof. Although it held that Habomai and Shikotan should be saved from the Kuriles, it did not want to define the Kuriles in the treaty since it secretly plotted to leave a seed that would expand into a grievance between Japan and the Soviet Union. As Dulles explained on March 19 to the Far East Subcommittee of the Senate Foreign Relations Committee, since the Soviet Union already occupied Southern Sakhalin and the Kuriles the problem of these islands did not amount to much. "It had therefore been thought worthwhile to hang out a certain amount of bait," Dulles said. But what was most important in his mind was disclosed, when he said, "the issue of exactly what constitute the Kuriles was a further detracting factor."[44]

Dulles, in the name of Dean Acheson, answered the Japanese government on March 20 that his government now thought it necessary to omit any reference to a definition of the Kurile Islands, leaving this automatically to the International Court of Justice. If the Soviet Union did not participate, the article on Sakhalin and the Kuriles would be completely expunged.[45] Dulles made up his mind to make the Habomai problem vaguer, because it was the more convenient to him. So the first draft of a peace treaty with Japan, which was sent to the allied countries on March 28, contained Article 6 as follows: "Japan will return to the Union of Soviet Socialist Republics the southern part of Sakhalin as well as all the islands adjacent to it and will hand over to the Soviet Union the Kurile Islands."

And Article 19 stated that the present Treaty shall not confer any rights, title or benefits to or upon any State unless and until it signs and ratifies, or adheres to, the Treaty.[46]

Yoshida wrote in his memoirs that when Dulles visited Japan in April he proposed to Dulles that the Southern Kuriles not be included in the Kuriles. Memos from both sides describe their meeting.[47] Although there are omissions in the public version of Nishimura's memo, the American records allow us to fill them in. Both memos never supported Yoshida's assertion.[48] Moreover, on August 24, 1956, when Foreign Minister Shigemitsu Mamoru met with Dulles, then Secretary of State, in London, Dulles said clearly, "at the time of the San Francisco treaty the Yoshida government sought that we take the position that Habomai and Shikotan are not part of the Kuril Islands, but they made no request of this kind about Etorofu and Kunashiri."[49] Accordingly, we can conclude that out of later political considerations, Yoshida's memoirs present false evidence.

The British government had stood on the position that the Soviet Union should be given South Sakhalin and the Kuriles unconditionally, whether it was a part of the treaty or not. Therefore in the negotiations between the British and U.S. governments Article 19 of the U.S. draft became most controversial.[50] But the British government accepted the U.S. stand. On May 3, 1951, a joint U.S.-British draft was prepared based on an agreement of both governments. Article 4 stated "Japan cedes to the Union of Soviet Socialist Republics the Kurile islands and that portion of South Sakhalin and islands adjacent to it over which Japan formally exercised sovereignty." And Article 25 repeated Article 19 of the U.S. draft.[51]

About the limits of the Kuriles the British government had had a clear position. Its former drafts of a Japan peace treaty contained the provision that Habomais and Shikotan should belong to Japan.[52] And a new study in the Foreign Office that was made in the beginning of May also recognized Japan's de jure sovereignty over the Soviet Union's de facto occupation of Habomais, while on Shikotan there should be talk of gathering the opinions of experts about whether it was part of the Kuriles.[53] But here too the British government accepted the U.S. government's omission of the definition of the Kuriles.

Among the opinions on the joint draft, New Zealand agreed with the old British draft that the longitude and latitude of Japan's territory should be made precise, adding that of the territory occupied by the Russians, Habomai and Shikotan should remain with

Japan. The U.S. side commented, however, that it would be realistic not to separately specify the return of Habomai and Shikotan to Japan.[54] France repeated the same demand and got the same answer.[55] The U.S. March draft and the U.S.-British joint draft were premised on the Soviet Union participating in the peace conference and signing the treaty. But as early as May 7, correspondence indicated that the Soviets would not participate. With the Japan-U.S. Security Treaty to be concluded at the same time as the peace treaty, the United States gave thought to its obligation to defend Japanese territory. It would bring trouble to American-Soviet relations if the Soviet Union occupied what the United States agreed is Japanese territory. With the goal of leaving the return of territory unclear, a new draft was completed on June 14. Article 2 (c) stated, "Japan renounces all right, title, and claim to the Kurile Islands, and to that portion of Sahkhalin and the islands adjacent to it over which Japan acquired sovereignty as a consequence of the Treaty of Portsmouth of September 5, 1905."[56]

In his memoirs Yoshida remarked on the big difference between the March draft and the final draft, with the former specifying the transfer of Southern Sakhalin and adjoining islands as well as the Kuriles (*Chishima*) archipelago to the Soviet Union. He said that Japan had strongly opposed this and that in the end the allies had tacitly incorporated what Japan had advocated, thinking ahead to future negotiations.[57] This was also false testimony. The revised U.S.-British draft was explained to the Japanese government on June 24.

The Peace Conference

On September 4, 1951, in the San Francisco Opera House, the peace conference opened. On the next day Dulles in his speech stated, "Some question has been raised as to whether the geographical name 'Kurile Islands' mentioned in Article 2 (c) includes the Habomai Islands. It is the view of the United States that it does not. If, however, there were a dispute about this, it could be referred to the International Court of Justice under Article 22."[58]

In fact contrary to expectations, the Soviet representative attended the conference, and the possibility remained that he would sign. If this were the case, with Soviet agreement it would have been possible to go to the court. But since other parties clearly expected the Soviet Union not to sign, this part was only a smokescreen to camouflage the lack of preparation of a draft item. Dulles clearly wanted not to include in the treaty the definitional question.

Andrei Gromyko, the Soviet representative, spoke on September 5. He did not give historical grounds why Southern Sakhalin and the Kurile islands "currently under Soviet sovereignty" should be transferred, insisting that there had been no room for discussion about Soviet sovereignty over these territories. He criticized the fact that the peace treaty did not specify the obligation to recognize Soviet sovereignty as a plot to infringe on that sovereignty and a violation of the Yalta Agreement, and he proposed an amendment to the draft. Using the term "currently under Soviet sovereignty," he aimed to include the Habomai islands in the Kuriles.[59] But the Soviet position was isolated. Under Stalin's instructions, Gromyko did not sign the treaty. Along with Communist China, the Soviet Union rejected the Japan peace treaty advanced by the United States. Stalin encouraged Japanese Communist leaders to start violent attacks against the U.S. armed forces in Japan. It is certain that if the Soviet Union had signed, it would have been advantageous for the Soviets in future negotiations with Japan, but Stalin preferred to defend the "cause of revolution."[60]

In comparison to the speeches of the U.S. and Soviet representatives, Japan's representative Yoshida Shigeru's speech naturally touched more precisely on the Kuriles problem. Yoshida spoke in Japanese, and it was translated into English. What he intended was to protest the loss of Southern Sakhalin and the Kurile Islands and to retain the sovereignty over Shikotan and the Habomai islands. But it should be noted that Yoshida stood on the orthodox definition of the Kuriles by saying "Both Sakhalins and the North and South Kuriles were placed under Soviet occupation as of September 20, 1945, shortly after Japan surrendered."[61]

Conclusion

In the cold war, the United States and the Soviet Union did not hesitate to choose any method they could to serve them in their conflict with each other, dragging other countries into becoming allies and making a sharp contrast between partners and opponents. The "northern territories" problem was precisely one of these methods. The definitional problem of the Kurile Islands was an offshoot of this.

My study showed that a redefinition of the Kuriles based on the Treaty of 1875 was started first by officials of the Department of State in 1947 and that it was finally rejected by the Department in 1949. The Japanese government hesitatingly adopted this redefinition of the Kuriles in 1956 and the U.S. Department of State suddenly readopted it in 1957 to support the Japanese stand against the Soviet Union. The logic of redefinition was intrinsically one of confrontation.

If we abandon the logic of this kind of confrontation and turn to the logic of dialogue, we should completely forget a redefinition that defies common sense on the Kurile Islands. In spite of the San Francisco Peace Treaty, for the sake of friendship between Japan and Russia, Japanese today hope sincerely that the Russian people give the four islands to them.

NOTES

1. Wada Haruki, *Hoppo ryodo mondai: rekishi to mirai* (Tokyo: Asahi shimbunsha, 1999).
2. Murayama Shichiro, *Kuriru shoto no bunkengakuteki kenkyu* (Tokyo: San'ichi shobo, 1987); Wada Haruki, *Hoppo ryodo mondai o kangaeru* (Tokyo: Iwanami shoten, 1990).
3. Tsuyoshi Hasegawa, *The Northern Territories Dispute and Russo-Japanese Relations,* Vol. 2, *Neither War Nor Peace, 1985–1998* (Berkeley: International & Area Studies Research Series #97, University of California, Berkeley, 1998), pp. 515–19.
4. Yoshida Shigeru, *Kaiso junen,* Vol. 3 (Tokyo: Shinchosha, 1957), p. 26.
5. Hara wrote about this first in "New Light on the Russo-Japanese Territorial Dispute," *Working Paper* (Canberra: Australian National University, Department of International Relations), No. 1, 1995. Her doctoral dissertation is now published as Kimie Hara, *Japanese-Soviet-Russian Relations Since 1945: A Difficult Peace* (London: Routledge Press, 1998). See pp. 24–33.
6. "Minor Islands Adjacent to Japan Proper. Part I. The Kurile Islands, the Habomais and Shikotan," Foreign Office, Japanese Government, November 1946, pp. 5–6.
7. Ibid., p. 6.
8. Ibid., p. 8.
9. Ibid., p. 9.

10. Ibid., p. 10.
11. Tsukamoto Takashi, "Beikokumusho no tainichi heiwa joyaku soan to hoppo ryodo mondai," *Refaransu,* No. 482, March 1991, pp. 113–20.
12. Tsukamoto, p. 114. *National Archives* (hereafter *NA*), RG59, Decimal File 1945–49, Box 3513, 740.0011PW (PEACE)/3–2047, p. 4.
13. See Borton's memoirs published only in Japanese, *Sengo nihon no sekkeisha: Boton kaikoroku* (Tokyo: Asahi shimbunsha, 1998), Ch. 15.
14. Tuskamoto, pp. 114–15. *NA,* 740.0011PW (PEACE)/8–647, pp. 3–4.
15. This title can be found in the list of materials attached to the letter of Hamilton to Fisher on November 22, 1949. *NA,* 740.0011PW (PEACE)/11–2249, p. w.
16. *Foreign Relations of the United States* (hereafter *FRUS*), 1947, Vol. VI, pp. 538–39.
17. *FRUS,* 1948, p. 657. Tsukamoto, p. 115.
18. Igarashi Takeshi, *Tainichi kowa to reisen* (Tokyo: University of Tokyo Press, 1986), pp. 102–24.
19. *FRUS,* 1949, Vol. 3, pp. 787–91.
20. Nishimura Kumao, *San Furanshisuko heiwa joyaku* (Tokyo: Kashima kenkyusho shuppanbu, 1971), p. 46.
21. *Foreign Ministry Archives, Japan,* B4001, *Tainichi heiwa joyaku kankei junbi kenkyu kankei,* Vol. 7, p. 17.
22. Tsukamoto, p. 115, *NA* 740.0011PW (PEACE)/10–1449, p. 3.
23. Tsukamoto, pp. 115–16.
24. Tsukamoto, p. 116. *NA,* 740.0011PW (PEACE)/11–249, pp. 5–6.
25. Tsukamoto, p. 116. *NA,* 740.0011PW (PEACE)/11–749, p. 2.
26. *NA,* 740.0011PW (PEACE)/11–749, pp. 3–4.
27. *FRUS,* 1949, Vol. 7, part 2, p. 900.
28. Tsukamoto, p. 117. *NA,* 740.0011PW (PEACE)/11–1949, pp. 2–3.
29. Tsukamoto, p. 117. *NA,* 740.0011PW (PEACE)/11–2249, p. 1.
30. *FRUS,* 1949, Vol. 7, part 2, pp. 904–906.
31. Tsukamoto, p. 118. Draft treaty of peace with Japan (December 29, 1949) and Commentary, *NA,* RG 59, Lot 54D423 JAPANESE PEACE TREATY FILES, Box 12, Treaty Drafts 1949–March 1951.
32. *Daishichikai kokkai shugiin gaimuiin kai kaigiroku,* No. 7 (Tokyo: Shugiin, 1950), p. 13.
33. *FRUS,* 1950, Vol. 6, p. 1296.
34. Ibid., pp. 1332–36.
35. Kajiura Atsushi, "Hoppo ryodo mondai o meguru Beikoku no seisaku," *Kokusai seiji,* No. 85, 1987, p. 101.
36. *FRUS,* 1951, Vol. 6, p. 850.
37. Ibid., pp. 831, 886.
38. "Provisional Draft of a Japanese Peace Treaty, March 1, 1951," *NA,* Lot 54D423, Box 12.

39. *FRUS,* 1951, Vol. 6, part 1, p. 921.
40. Ibid., p. 908.
41. "Provisional Draft of a Japanese Peace Treaty, March 16, 1951," *NA,* Lot 54D423, box 12. The March 1 draft was first amended on March 12.
42. *FRUS*, 1951, vol. 6, part 1, p. 929.
43. Several scholars have contended that the Japanese government had already adopted a two-tier policy, reasoning that even if the Soviet Union participated, Japan would be able to get support from allied countries for its definition of the Kuriles that excluded Etorofu and Kunashiri. Tanaka Takahiko, *Nisso kokko kaifuku no shiteki kenkyu* (Tokyo: Yuhikaku, 1993), p. 31; Tsuyoshi Hasegawa, *The Northern Territories Dispute, Vol. 2,* p. 90.
44. *FRUS,* 1951, Vol. 6, part 1, p. 933.
45. Ibid., p. 935. In the file of the National Archives there is a copy of the March 20 draft, Article 5 of which does not any longer contain the phrase "as they may be defined by bilateral agreement . . ." *NA,* Lot 54D428, box 12.
46. Ibid., pp. 945, 949.
47. Yoshida Shigeru, *Kaiso junen,* p. 61.
48. *FRUS,* 1951, Vol. 6, part. 1, pp. 985–89, 1006–1009. *Foreign Ministry Archives, Japan,* B4005, pp. 13–37, 53–66.
49. *FRUS, 1955–1957,* Vol. 23, part 1, pp. 208–09.
50. Tanaka Takahiko, *Nisso kokko kaifuku no shiteki kenkyu,* pp. 21–23, 34–38.
51. *FRUS,* 1951, Vol. 6, part 1, pp. 1026, 1035.
52. Tanaka Takahiko, *Nisso kokko kaifuku no shiteki kenkyu,* p. 37.
53. Minutes by R. S. Milward, "Sovereignty over the Habomai Islands, May 2, 1951," *Foreign Office* 371/92546, Public Records Office. I saw this thanks to Kibata Yoichi.
54. *FRUS,* 1951, Vol. 6, part 1, p. 1061.
55. Ibid., p. 1114.
56. Ibid., pp. 1119–21.
57. Yoshida Shigeru, *Kaiso junen,* pp. 61–62.
58. U.S. Department of State, *Conference for the Conclusion and Signature of the Treaty of Peace with Japan: Record of Proceedings* (Washington, DC: 1951), pp. 78–79.
59. Ibid., pp. 102–22.
60. Haruki Wada, "The Korean War, Stalin's Policy, and Japan," *Social Science Japan Journal,* Vol. 1, No. 1, April 1998, pp. 23–26.
61. U.S. Department of State, *Conference for the Conclusion and Signature of the Treaty of Peace with Japan: Record of Proceedings,* pp. 278–79.

CHAPTER 2

The Soviet-Japanese Postwar Peace Settlement in Retrospect

Boris Slavinsky

ONE UNSOLVED PROBLEM—A DISPUTE ESSENTIALLY over four islands—exerted an enormous impact on postwar relations between the USSR and Japan and has passed by right of succession to Russia. Prolonged discussions among experts and in commissions headed by deputy foreign ministers of the two countries have repeatedly failed to reach a mutually acceptable solution on the territorial disagreement and to produce a peace treaty. Agreement is required to fix the transfer to Russia of Southern Sakhalin and to define which of the Kurile Islands occupied by the Red Army in August-September 1945 should be passed to the jurisdiction of Russia and which are to be returned to Japan. As the search for a solution has gained new momentum, we can benefit by returning to the history of the San Francisco Peace Treaty to appreciate the root of the present problem and to reflect on how present realities may have altered the barriers that took shape around that time.

On the Southern Kurile problem or, according to Japanese terminology, the Northern Territories problem, hundreds of books and articles have appeared in Russian, Japanese, and English. While the bulk of them side fully with either the longstanding official Soviet position that Japan has no right to any of the islands, or the unchanging official Japanese position that the four islands of Kunashiri, Etorofu, Shikotan, and the Habomai group must be returned to Japan, since the late 1980s ideas for resolving the dispute have become quite varied. A cartoon in one Russian newspaper on the eve of Boris Yeltsin's visit to Japan in 1993 captured the current flux when it showed a group of advisors surrounding the Russian president and whispering in his ears 14 variants for solving the Kurile problem! Yet, even in the midst of widely floating ideas about linking the territorial issue to a broadened agenda, shifting from political pressure to appeal to mutual interests, and talking about unusual stratagems such as joint development and residual sovereignty, the fundamental problem has not changed. Will Moscow agree to return zero, two, or four islands, and will Tokyo agree to a temporary arrangement of zero or two islands if it does not get Moscow's consent for more? The same problem existed in the 1950s.

The Legacy of War

As is well known, the political conditions for the entry of the USSR into World War II with Japan were adopted in Yalta at the conference of Stalin, Roosevelt, and Churchill on February 11, 1945, in a secret protocol. In order to bring clarity and provide the public with accurate information on this matter, the governments of the United States, the USSR, and England decided to publish the secret protocol exactly one year later on February 11, 1946, at 5:00 P.M. (Moscow time) simultaneously in Moscow, Washington, and London.[1] Furthermore, in all statements of Soviet officials in the first postwar years, the Soviet Union adhered to the position that the question of the Kurile Islands and Southern Sakhalin, as far as the USSR was concerned, had been conclusively resolved at Yalta on the basis of the Crimean accords. At the outset there was no ambiguity, no territorial issue.

In the second half of the 1940s, various difficulties unfolded in Soviet-American relations. Along with conflicts between the two countries in Eastern and Central Europe was added Manchuria, where the Soviet Union in defiance of promises it had given at the Yalta conference supported the Chinese Communist Party in the unfolding Chinese Civil War and transferred to its troops the weapons that had been seized from the Japanese. As for relations with Japan, clashes between the USSR and the United States occurred on practically all questions at the meetings of the Far Eastern Commission in Washington and the Allied Council on Japan in Tokyo. Without going into other causes of dispute, we want to draw attention here to how the Kurile problem appeared in the context of Soviet-American relations. This question arose after the start of the Korean War. Since the United States was interested in close cooperation with the Japanese leadership in the use of Japanese territory, it began preparations for a peace treaty with Japan.

In September 1950 the United States prepared and distributed among its closest allies an American memorandum consisting of seven points concerning peace regularization with Japan. Only in October 1950, at the initiative of the American side, did there occur a meeting of John Foster Dulles, who was undertaking this work on behalf of the State Department, and the chief Soviet representative at the UN, Jacob Malik, at which this document was handed to the Soviet government.[2] Wada Haruki quoted from this document (on page 23), explaining that this was regarded as an attempt to revise radically the U.S. attitude toward the Yalta agreement. After two years of internal discussion in the United States, and exchanges with Japan, the issue was brought before the Soviet Union.

What was the reaction of the Soviet government? In a memorandum to the U.S. government from November 20, 1950, it asked to clarify, especially, an interpretation of the sentence in the memorandum on the question regarding the status of Formosa, the Pescadore islands, Southern Sakhalin, and the Kurile Islands to a new decision of the United States, Great Britain, China, and the USSR, and in case these states did not reach agreement in the course of a year, to a decision of the UN General Assembly. Indeed, it is well known, stated the memorandum, that the question of the return to China of Formosa and the Pescadore islands was already decided by the Cairo Declaration of December 1, 1943, signed by the United States, Great Britain, and China, and the Potsdam Declaration of July 26, 1945, signed by these same countries and the Soviet Union. In the same manner, the Yalta Declaration signed by the United States, Great Britain, and the USSR, decided the question of the return to the Soviet Union of the southern part of Sakhalin with the adjoining islands and on the transfer to the USSR of the Kurile Islands.[3]

In connection with the Soviet memorandum, the majority of Western researchers asserted the opinion that the character of the questions posed in the form of answers to the seven-point plan by

Dulles in its essence cast doubt on the entire program of Japanese peace regularization. They asserted that the Soviet questions had the goal of "pouring water" on the plan and reflected the unwillingness of Moscow to go forward with working out a peace treaty with Japan. In fact, in 1950–51, Soviet-American relations sharply deteriorated. The Korean War was under way. Political processes in the United States made it improbable that the Senate would ratify a treaty that recognized the Yalta concessions to the Soviet Union in the Far East. Therefore, the USSR did not participate in drawing up a peace treaty with Japan.

On March 30, 1951, the Soviet embassy in Washington received a note from the State Department dated March 29 that contained a secret memorandum with a proposal related to a peace treaty with Japan. In the documents it was pointed out that this is a preliminary draft of the peace treaty with Japan (only in the form of recommendations) for the examination of the Soviet government. It consisted of 22 points, including several related to territorial questions.

> 3. Japan renounces all rights, legal foundations and pretensions to Korea, Formosa and the Pescadore islands and the rights and legal foundations to the mandated territories and Antarctica . . .
> 5. Japan will return to the USSR the southern part of Sakhalin and also all islands belonging to it, and transfer to the Soviet Union the Kurile islands.[4]

To this we can add some important details that became known after the release of secret documents of the U.S. State Department in 1976. In a memorandum to the headquarters of the higher command of the allied powers (VGKSD) there was mention of the desire for the participation of the Soviet Union in the process of drawing up a peace treaty with Japan, and also to the United States' agreement to the return of Southern Sakhalin and the Kurile Islands to it. However, further in the telegram one can read, "This situation will be realized only if the Allies sign and ratify the treaty."[5]

The territorial question was discussed on March 19 at a meeting of Dulles with senators of the Foreign Affairs Committee of the U.S. Congress. To a question of Senator Alexander Smith on what benefits Americans would gain from their agreement to transfer to the USSR the southern part of Sakhalin and the Kuriles, Dulles clarified that the Department of Defense wanted the Soviets to conclude peace with

Japan and in that way to limit their rights as a belligerent. He underlined that the draft had a special article in which the USSR would be deprived of any benefits from the treaty if it would not be a participant. Dulles called this coordination "bait," although he declared that its value was not great since these territories were already occupied by the Soviet Union. Answering the question of what rights as a belligerent the Soviet Union would have if it did not sign the peace treaty, Dulles said that from a technical point of view the USSR could not, according to existing agreements, station its armed forces in Japan other than only under the authority of the American command. And this, no doubt, was unacceptable for it. Although, of course, Dulles added, hinting at the war in Korea, that the Soviets could at any time provoke military actions if they wanted to do so.[6] This is how an English newspaper commented on the question: "If Russia refuses to sign the Japanese peace treaty and remains in a state of war with Japan, then it can formally insist on its right to send occupation forces into Japan when the American occupation will end."[7]

Relations of the United States to the Soviet Union on the question of peace regularization with Japan can be well seen in Dulles's March 31, 1951, presentation in Los Angeles. He asserted that in "the course of the last three months representatives of the Soviet Union have participated together with us in full and open discussions (of this question). But now, when peace with Japan seems actually close, Soviet leaders, apparently, are gripped by fear. The Soviet government publicly declared that it will not renew negotiations with us."[8]

Unfortunately, however, participation of the Soviet Union was not so essential that there was no possibility to proceed without it. The Soviet Union had no legal right to assert a veto. In moral relations it had no demands that had to be satisfied, since the great booty that it had taken in Manchuria, Port Arthur, Dalian, Sakhalin, and the Kurile Islands was compensation ten thousand fold for its nominal participation in military action over six days.[9]

It is interesting to note also the position of the prime minister of Japan on the territorial question, which he set forth in a telegram to Dean Acheson on March 16, 1950, through G. Bond, who was carrying out the duties of political advisor to VGKSD.

> a) The proposed article to return Southern Sakhalin and to transfer the Kuriles to the Soviet Union on condition that it will be a

> participant in the peace treaty, is acceptable. However, it is desirable to have for the question this entry, "How they (the Kuriles) will be defined by the interests of the powers, including Japan."
> b) In case the Soviet Union definitely leaves the game one can hope that this condition concerning Southern Sakhalin and the Kuriles will be omitted.[10]

The American administration had to consider also the position of Great Britain, which was set forth in a memorandum that was given to Dulles by the English ambassador to Washington on March 12. It consisted of the following,

> 2) As was written in the Livadiiskii (Crimean) agreement of February 11, 1945, Japan should concede Southern Sakhalin and the Kuriles to the Soviet Union.[11]

In mid-April 1951, Great Britain finished work on its own draft for a peace treaty with Japan, which, as the American version, was distributed to the other countries of the Far Eastern Commission. However, between these two drafts there were notable differences. Thus, in the preamble to the treaty China was mentioned as one of the allied powers, and article 23 directly referred to the central people's government, i.e., the People's Republic of China. Also in the preamble it was noted that the Japanese military regime "shares responsibility for the unleashing of war." In accord with article 4 of the draft Japan should cede Formosa and the Pescadores to China, while in the American variant loss of Japanese sovereignty over these islands was simply mentioned. There were also other differences connected to English demands to prohibit "undesirable associations" in Japan, and questions were raised about the payment of reparations, problems of fishing, Japanese gold reserves, etc.

It is necessary to recall that at this time the White House made the decision to replace MacArthur as commander of the UN forces fighting in Korea. With this step the United States attempted somewhat to soften the disappointment of Great Britain and some other countries with the course of events in the Korean War. At the same time for the American administration it was important to demonstrate that this action did not signify any softening in its policies toward Communist China, which because of its assistance to North Korea was accused of aggression by the United Nations. Therefore, the English proposal to offer Beijing the opportunity to participate in the regularization of peace in Japan was rejected. The same thing occurred with the proposal that Formosa be returned to "China" and not the "Chinese Republic" as it had been fixed in the Cairo Declaration. The American administration insisted that the government of Chiang Kai-shek be one of the principal participants that would sign the peace treaty with Japan. Let us note that Nationalist (*Guomindang*) China, commenting on the American proposal for a peace treaty with Japan, expressed concern that at the same time that the USSR was receiving Southern Sakhalin and the Kuriles after Japan renounced them, China did not receive Formosa and the Pescadore Islands. Therefore, nationalists insisted that an equal status should be established, that is, it should be indicated that Formosa and the Pescadores were transferred to China "or the position of this article should be changed to simple renunciation by Japan of Southern Sakhalin and the Kurile islands."[12]

To resolve the growing disagreement between the United States and England, negotiations were held in Washington from April 24 to May 4 between the director of the British department of Japanese affairs and countries of the Pacific Ocean, Charles Johnston, and Dulles's deputy, Allison. However, even this round of negotiations did not lead to an agreement on the future status of Formosa and on the participation of the Chinese government in negotiations over a peace treaty. It was decided to transfer discussion of these questions to a higher level.

On May 3 the two sides did agree on the key question for our discussion: "Article 4. Japan cedes to the Union of Soviet Socialist Republics the Kurile islands and that part of Southern Sakhalin and the islands adjoining it over which Japan earlier possessed sovereignty."[13] Nevertheless, the position of England gradually softened. The Minister of Foreign Affairs Herbert Morrison, speaking in the House of Commons, declared that the question of Formosa must never be allowed to delay discussion of a peace treaty with Japan. In this connection *The Times* of London wrote on May 17 that it was reasonable to suppose that England and the United States would agree that "as long as the operations in Korea continue it is worth avoiding any attempt to provide in the treaty a final decision on the question of Formosa."

Meanwhile on July 3, as special representative of the American president, Dulles arrived in London for negotiations with the minister of foreign affairs of Great Britain. On that date, wrote James Reston, the well-informed commentator for *The New York Times,* Dulles had "strict instructions to insist that the Guomindang representative sign the peace treaty with Japan, and the representative of the PRC be excluded from participation in the negotiations over the peace treaty until it stops its aggression in Korea." Since England considered that the government of the PRC should be allowed to participate in the negotiations and signing of the peace treaty, Reston observed, England and the United States diverged in their opinions about the fate of Formosa. The United States insisted that Japan renounce for the future all pretensions to Formosa, but it be left open which China is to receive Formosa. We have at our disposal a document that sheds some light on the subject under discussion. On July 5 the U.S. ambassador in London telegraphed the Secretary of State: "in the end of the discussions the British delegation was clearly disposed to accept the proposal of the United States that the treaty must simply demand the renunciation by Japan of sovereignty over Formosa, leaving discussion of its future status to a later time. Acceptance of this decision was eased for Great Britain by the fact that the United States earlier proposed that Sakhalin and the Kuriles be in an analogous way ceded to the USSR by treaty."[14] When agreement came, neither government of China was mentioned in the final text of the treaty. However, in it was a separate article that allowed an independent and sovereign Japan after the treaty took effect to decide itself which Chinese regime should be given precedence. As for Formosa and the Pescadore Islands, the treaty notes that Japan is renouncing all rights, legal foundations, and pretensions to these territories, that is not indicating to whom they will be transferred. For a balanced approach to China and the Soviet Union the question of Southern Sakhalin and the Kurile Islands was handled analogously. (In this decision, it is obvious, the opinion of Chiang Kai-shek was taken into account.) On June 14 the working language was set as explained by Wada Haruki (on page 27), this draft left the return of territory, from Japan to the Soviet Union, not clearly identified. In this way an agreement was reached for the first time between the United States and Great Britain that then was reflected in the final text of the peace treaty.

Although the editors of the 1993 book from which many of our quotations are taken asserted that "there is no clear explanation" for the change in the territorial articles of principal importance to

Russia related to Sakhalin and the Kuriles from March 30 to June 14, 1951,[16] the juxtaposition of the above documents brings clarity to this question. The editors appear to be wrong that the United States decided not to sanction the official transfer of the islands to the Soviet Union when it became clear that the Soviet government did not intend to sign the peace treaty. Although Moscow sent Washington notes on May 7 and June 10 with all sorts of questions and criticisms of the American approaches, it did not follow that it would not become a participant in the peace conference. It is worth considering the Soviet position more closely.

At this time the Soviet Union clearly did not strive to speed the course of events in the regularization of peace in Japan. Its answer to the December 1950 U.S. memorandum was worked out over more than four months. Moscow tried to distance itself from the impetuous activity of Dulles, who was traveling from one capital to another with the aim of working out a consensus on Japanese peace regularization. At the beginning of March 1951, in response to Dulles's assertion that he was informing Jakob Malik about his activities, came an official denial: the Soviet Union would take no part in the work under way by Washington, all of which were one-sided actions of the United States.

Only on May 7, 1951, to the American ambassador in Moscow was delivered "Remarks of the government of the USSR regarding the draft of the USA of a peace treaty with Japan." Since the Soviet argumentation in this document almost word-by-word repeated the fundamental position of Moscow on the question of the peace treaty with Japan, let's look at it in some detail.

> The American draft of a peace treaty with Japan . . . contains positions that are not in correspondence with international agreements, especially the Cairo declaration of 1943, the Yalta agreement of 1945 and the Potsdam declaration of 1945, and ignores the obligations assumed by the governments of the USA, Great Britain, China, and the USSR . . . in these international documents . . . in regard to territorial questions. For example, in the Cairo declaration it says directly that Taiwan and the Pescador islands must be returned to China. The American draft foresees only Japan's renunciation of all rights to these islands, remaining silent on their transfer to China.[17]

In order to proceed to the preparation of a peace treaty with Japan, the Soviet government again proposed to convene a session of the Council of Foreign Ministers, to draw into the preparatory work representatives of all states that participated with their armed forces in the war with Japan, and then to place the draft of the treaty for examination by a peace conference.

The world press with the exception of the pro-communist press evaluated the Soviet May 7 remarks as the unwillingness of Moscow to reach a mutual understanding with the United States on questions of peaceful regularization with Japan. In the Soviet argumentation there was not even a hint of possible compromise. One can suppose that there was fear in the Kremlin that the Soviet Union, because its support for North Korean aggression against South Korea had left it in a state of practically complete isolation on the international arena, including in the UN and the Far Eastern Commission, had little chance for support of its rights to territorial acquisitions (Southern Sakhalin and the Kurile Islands) and also for consideration of its strategic interests linked to China. Precisely these thoughts were at the base of Soviet behavior, when it insisted that the question be presented to the Council of Foreign Ministers where the USSR had the right of a veto. No doubt also, here a negative role was played by the notorious suspicion of Stalin to Western, especially American, leaders.

Meanwhile, events developed swiftly. As a result of its persistent energies, Washington succeeded in reaching a joint understanding in problems of security with Australia, New Zealand, and the Philippines, which feared the possible rearmament of Japan, and then also with Great Britain on the problem of China, thus leading on July 3, 1951, to a joint American-English draft of a peace treaty with Japan. On July 6 this document was given to the Soviet side through the embassy of the USSR in Washington.

Presenting on July 18 directly to Stalin for affirmation of the draft of a note of the USSR's response to the U.S. memorandum of July 6, the Foreign Ministry (Gromyko) remarked that "in contrast to the American draft of March 30 (1950) where it says that Japan will return to the Soviet Union the southern part of Sakhalin with the islands belonging to it and transfer the Kurile islands, the draft of July 3 speaks only of Japan's renunciation of rights, legal foundations and pretensions to these territories and says nothing about the transfer of these territories to the Soviet Union."[18]

Despite the fact that the interests of the USSR were practically not considered in the peace treaty prepared by the United States and Great Britain, Moscow decided to participate in the San Franciso conference. The reasons were set forth in a telegram in cipher that the Foreign Ministry sent to the Soviet ambassador in Beijing, N. B. Roshchin. "Visit Zhou Enlai and inform him that you have been instructed to inform the government of the PRC that the Soviet government has decided to send its delegation to the September 4 San Francisco conference on a peace treaty with Japan. The Soviet government considers that it would be difficult for the Soviet Union to refuse to participate in the indicated conference since such a refusal could be assessed by public opinion as the unwillingness of the Soviet Union to have normal relations with Japan. The Soviet representatives will take part in the San Francisco conference and will strive for the proposals of the Soviet Union to be adopted."[19]

The USSR was prepared to present its own draft for a peace treaty with Japan. By this time it was edited and all interested departments of the Ministry of Foreign Affairs had agreed. Most relevant to this discussion is Article 7. Japan recognizes the full sovereignty of the Union of Soviet Socialist Republics to the southern part of Sakhalin with all islands belonging to it and to the Kurile Islands and renounces all rights, legal foundations, and pretensions to these territories.[20] However, when it later became apparent that the conference would not examine the Soviet draft, the Kremlin decided to put forward Soviet amendments to the Anglo-American draft.

When First Deputy Foreign Minister Gromyko spoke on the second day of the conference on September 5, he paid special attention to territorial questions that, in the opinion of the Soviet authorities, had earlier been settled by the allied powers. He pointed to the agreements that gave the rights to China, now the People's Republic of China, to Taiwan, the Pescadores, the Paracel Islands, which should be returned to the PRC. He also insisted that the rights of the Soviet Union to the southern part of Sakhalin and the Kuriles, now under Soviet sovereignty are indisputable. And the Soviet delegation proposed a series of amendments that only needed to be punched in. After its proposals had been ignored, the Soviet side refused to sign the document. This fatal step of Soviet diplomacy brought the consequences of a territorial problem between the USSR and Japan that even to the present exerts an extremely negative effect on the entire specter of bilateral relations.

During the years 1952–56 relations were very complicated. They proceeded in an atmosphere of uncertainty, but not without some expectations of a turn for the better. In September 1955 in London, official negotiations of delegations from the two governments began on the subject of peaceful regularization. As a result of about twenty meetings they achieved agreement on 95 percent of a text for a peace treaty. Only the territorial article remained in dispute. If the Soviet Union asserted its readiness to return to Japan the islands of Habomai and Shikotan, then Tokyo would have still insisted on the return of Kunashiri and Iturup (Etorofu). As a result, in March 1956 the negotiations were broken off. In these circumstances Premier Hatoyama Ichiro took the initiative, proposing to end the state of war and establish diplomatic relations in order later to continue bilateral negotiations on the territorial problem. Premier Nikolai Kosygin quickly accepted this offer. On October 19 in Moscow, a joint declaration on the normalization of Soviet-Japanese relations was signed, which read in part, "The USSR, meeting the wishes of Japan and considering the interests of the Japanese state, agrees to the transfer to Japan of the islands of Habomai and the islands of Shikotan with the proviso, however, that in fact the transfer of these islands to Japan will occur after the conclusion of a peace treaty between the USSR and Japan."

The signing of the joint declaration opened the way for broad development of good neighbor ties between the two countries. Especially impressive was the development of trade, the volume of which doubled almost yearly. In the mid-1960s were established national committees on trade and economic cooperation, which approved a series of big projects: exploitation of the timber resources of Siberia and the Soviet Far East; construction of a port in Vostochnoi Bay (near Nakhodka); exploitation of the deposits of coking coal in South Yakutia; prospecting for deposits of oil and gas on the Sakhalin shelf, and others. As a result of this, Japan firmly occupied first place among the developed capitalist foreign trade partners of the USSR. But the unresolved business of 1951 left its mark, and when relations deteriorated in the 1970s, the territorial problem became Japan's foremost preoccupation. The linkage between politics and economics intensified. In 1997–99 the leaders of Japan and Russia were at last approaching the territorial question with renewed determination and increased flexibility. The tough decisions, however, remain to be made.

NOTES

1. *Vneshniaia politika Sovetskogo Soiuza. 1946. Dokumenty i materialy* (Moscow: Gospolitizdat', 1952), pp. 89–91.
2. Foreign Ministry of the USSR, *Sbornik not i zaiavlenii pravitelstv SSSR, SShA, Kitaia, Anglii i drugikh stran po voprosu mirnogo uregulirovaniia dlia Iaponii, July 1947-July 1951* (Moscow: 2nd Far Eastern Department, Foreign Ministry of the USSR, 1951), pp. 41–42.
3. Ibid., pp. 14–17.
4. AVP RF, *Fond of A. Ya. Vyshinsky,* opis 24, portsiia. 371, papka 32, delo 193, tom 1, L. 11–18.
5. *FRUS.* 1951, Vol. 6, part 1 (Washington, DC: 1977), p. 908.
6. Ibid., p. 933.
7. *Daily Telegraph and Morning Post,* March 9, 1951.
8. *FRUS,* 1951, Vol. 6, pt. 1, pp. 944–50.
9. *TASS,* March 31, 1951, L. 76-o.
10. *FRUS,* 1951, Vol. 6, part 1, p. 929.
11. Ibid., p. 910
12. Ibid., pp. 1055–1104, as cited in *Ot kholodnoi voiny k trekhstoronnemu sotrudnichestvu v Aziatsko-tikhookeanskom regione* (Moscow: Nauka, 1993), p. 222.
13. *Ot kholodnoi voiny k trekhstoronnemu sotrudnichestvu,* p. 146.
14. Ibid., p. 147.
15. Ibid.
16. Ibid., p. 148.
17. Boris Slavinskii, "San-Frantsiskii mirnyi dogovor s Iaponiei i sovetskiaia diplomatiia (novye dokumenty iz arkhiva MID Rossii), *Znakom'tes' Iaponiia,* no. 6, 1994, pp. 50–58
18. AVP RF, *Fond of A. Ia Vyshinsky,* op. 24, por. 371, papka 32, delo 193, tom 1, L. 22–23.
19. Ibid., L. 6.
20. Ibid., L. 91–116.

CHAPTER 3

Reconciliation in the Fifties: The Logic of Soviet Decision Making

Alexei V. Zagorsky

THE LIST OF BOTH PRIMARY SOURCES AND SECONDARY descriptive and analytical publications on the history of normalization of Soviet-Japanese relations in the 1950s is really quite abundant in languages of the nations concerned, as well as in English. This gives the impression that very little may be added, at least until Russian archival documents for the second half of the fifties and the early sixties are declassified and opened for access (the current legislation on archival documents preserves a 50-year freeze, assuring that even the earliest documents on Soviet-Japanese relations dating from just after the death of Stalin may not be available before the twenty-first century). Available primary sources are mostly Japanese, including abundant memoirs by the top decision makers of the time (Prime Minister Hatoyama Ichiro,[1] Minister of Agriculture and Fisheries Kono Ichiro),[2] and direct participants in the negotiations (chief negotiator Matsumoto Shunichi,[3] Shigemitsu Akira)[4] or observers at the time (Kubota Masaaki).[5] Yet, documentary sources in Japanese remain limited to the appendix in Matsumoto's publication, presenting major Soviet and Japanese draft documents exchanged through the negotiating process.

Soviet/Russian primary sources remain astonishingly scarce. Very few Soviet participants in the negotiations have left any reminiscences. Until recently the only available Russian primary source had been Nikita Khrushchev's memoirs.[6] Andrei Gromyko's memoirs, though he was not a key figure in Soviet-Japanese talks at the time (being a first deputy foreign minister in 1953–57, he did not cover East Asian issues, leaving them to Nikolai Fedorenko, then the deputy foreign minister responsible for Far Eastern affairs), could have shed some light, especially in relation to the exchange of letters between him and Matsumoto in 1956. Yet, in accord with established Soviet practice, Gromyko carefully evaded any discussion of a controversial issue of Soviet foreign policy in the early post-Stalin period. As far as Soviet policy toward Japan is concerned, he does not even describe it, limiting his comments to praise of Hatoyama's efforts "to conduct an independent foreign policy," and adding that "in time, however, this independence plainly declined and became subordinated to America's global interests" as an explanation of the following stalemate.[7] Forthcoming memoirs of Dmitrii Shepilov, foreign minister in 1956–57 and Shigemitsu Mamoru's partner in 1956, written presumably in 1969–70, are now advertised in the Russian mass media,[8] but only an extract on Soviet-Chinese relations has so far been published. The only Russian documentary source available is the recent publication of archival materials related to the elaboration of the 1956 Soviet-Japanese Joint Declaration.[9] The only author who has enjoyed nearly unlimited access to the archives related to this period, Dmitrii Volkogonov, writer of the fundamental biography of Khrushchev,[10] concentrated his presentation on domestic affairs, leaving Khrushchev's foreign policy outside his focus and not mentioning Japan.

Descriptive and analytical publications on the issue in English, Russian, and Japanese seem quite abundant. Yet, anything that has appeared in Russian was published in the late fifties or early sixties,[11] and fails to go beyond mere propaganda advocating the Soviet official interpretation, and therefore adds very little to deeper understanding of the issue. The classical monograph in English by Donald Hellmann[12] basically relies on Japanese domestic sources for the formulation of policy toward the USSR without contributing much to understanding Soviet behavior. The later publication by Savitri Vishvanathan[13] presents a broader picture, but mostly confines itself to a description of the situation not probing deeply into Soviet logic.

Japanese analytical publications include the already mentioned work by Shigemitsu Akira combining both the analysis of a Japanese diplomat and the narrative of a junior participant in the negotiations, a detailed description of events in *History of Postwar Japanese Foreign Policy* edited by Ishimaru Kazuto and others,[14] and the most recent analysis by Tanaka Takahiko,[15] which may be evaluated as the most all-encompassing publication. Yet again, the bias in available sources and author's dependence on English sources in aspects concerning the Soviet Union, could not prevent an imbalance between deeper insight into the Japanese process of decision making and coverage of Soviet motivations that is largely guesswork.

The purpose of the current chapter is to fill in part of this gap by analyzing the logic of the sudden change of the Soviet approach to Japan after Stalin's death, especially the reasons for Moscow's large concessions both in abandoning previous political and security demands as conditions to normalize relations and taking a softer approach to the territorial dispute, as well as the reasons for the Soviet reverse course toward Japan in 1960. Sources are essentially those used in previous publications, and conclusions still require conjecture; nevertheless, placing Soviet policy toward Japan in the wider framework of the elaboration of a new foreign policy during the transitional period of 1953–57 may provide grounds for better understanding Moscow's overtures.

The Soviet Motivation: Reappraisal of Earlier Explanations

Earlier studies of Soviet-Japanese relations in the fifties (Matsumoto, Hellmann) tended to explain the shift in the Soviet policy toward Tokyo not by specific calculations or expected gains from the change of the line, but rather by the general revision of Stalinist foreign policy and the emergence of a new Soviet strategy for the cold war, referring to withdrawal of Soviet troops and signing the State Treaty with Austria, normalization of relations with West Germany, the Geneva agreement on Indochina, etc.[16] Donald Hellmann adds to the equation the changing international atmosphere in the Far East and Asia in general after the Korean and Indochinese truces and the increasingly "neutralist" and cooperative tendencies in the world vision by major Asian nations, as demonstrated by the Bandung conference in 1955. He adds that, "by this time it was also evident to Moscow that little profit would accrue from continuing the policy of almost complete isolation from the Japanese, and this further encouraged moves toward reconciliation."[17]

Supported by obvious evidence of crucial changes in Soviet policy toward wartime enemies and conflicts in Asia, the thesis still fails to explain the scope of concessions proposed to Tokyo during the talks, implying not only the abandonment of strategic conditions for normalization of relations (which would have been natural under the new line), but also an unprecedented Soviet flexibility on a territorial dispute. One may note that in the mid-fifties Khrushchev had not yet announced his notion of "peaceful coexistence" addressing Western nations in general,[18] and changes in the Soviet line affected only former enemies, while an attempt to elaborate a larger cooperative framework at the "Big Four" conference at Geneva in 1955 failed to produce any effective reconciliation.

Besides, Hellmann's reference to changing international conditions in Asia would imply anything but the USSR compromising in its overtures to Japan. Asian neutralism was largely regarded in Moscow as a chance to expand her influence in the third world, an opportunity to challenge the West in new geographic areas when the balance of power and general situation in Europe seemed little prone to further change. This phenomenon later made possible a situation where "Khrushchev's foreign policy rested on the two pillars of peaceful coexistence and a far from peaceful national liberation struggle."[19] Analyzing Soviet policy in 1953–57, Martin McCauley notes tendencies in Asia going clearly against the spirit of cooperation and reconciliation, indicating that "American efforts in 1954–55 to widen the ring of containment around the Soviet Union by recruiting countries on its southern periphery—Pakistan, Iran, and Iraq—made Moscow very nervous. The Soviets were very encouraged by the hostile reception that US policy encountered in much of the Third World and this encouraged Moscow to cultivate countries there."[20]

The publication of Nikita Khrushchev's memoirs[21] added more confusion about the driving forces behind the Soviet decision to normalize relations with Japan. His main thesis is that it was Stalin's large mistake to refuse to sign the San Francisco Peace Treaty to the advantage of the West and the isolation of the Soviet Union from Japan. He interpreted the basic disadvantages as follows: "If we had signed we would have had an embassy there. We would have had access to Japanese public opinion and influential circles. We would have established trade relations with Japanese firms."[22] The nature of this interpretation makes the conclusion very ambiguous. Certainly, in the mid-fifties Japanese trading companies would not have been a major interest for the Soviet economy due to their weakness at the time and the general Soviet orientation to a self-sustaining economy. One may note, for instance, Khrushchev's disdain for expanding trade relations with the United States during his visit in 1959, when he remarked at his last press conference at Camp David: "Russia is not a colony in need of your sausages. We are a great industrial nation able to satisfy the demand of our population."[23] It seems that the vision presented in his memoirs was largely determined by later impressions.

Khrushchev's reference to the absence of Soviet representatives in Tokyo and lack of access to Japanese public opinion is not correct; from the time of the establishment of the Far Eastern Commission and Allied Council for Japan in 1946, each allied nation had a representative office in Japan, which was eventually transformed into an embassy after the conclusion of the San Francisco Treaty. The USSR maintained a representative office in Tokyo, although it was not recognized by the Japanese government and was limited in personnel, until 1956 when it was reorganized into the embassy. The beginning of Soviet-Russian contacts in 1954 demonstrated that Soviet representatives had quite satisfactory contacts with influential political circles in Japan. Khrushchev's reference to the problem may be explained by his lack of information on Japan at the time, which may have resulted from the fact that he was not the most important leader in discussing the issue (a possibility evaluated later in the chapter). Thus, the whole passage is unreliable for the interpretation of Soviet decisionmaking on Japan in 1954–56. Conspicuous as it was, Khrushchev's version was largely adopted by Japanese analysts, such as Shigemitsu Akira, Kubota, and Tanaka,[24] although paying more attention to Soviet isolation in Asia.

But how could normalization of Soviet-Japanese relations improve Moscow's position in the region? The generally accepted answer says that Moscow saw a chance to capitalize on Hatoyama's more nationalistic rhetoric and his desire to put a greater distance between Japan and the United States. For the Soviet Union it was an opportunity to open a wedge between Tokyo and Washington,[25] a notion strongly supported by Gromyko's memoirs.

It is interesting that Tanaka Takahiko discovers the first hints of change in the Soviet approach to Japan even earlier than any attempt to use Asian nationalism, and traces them back to an assumed revised vision of the international role of wartime enemies as presented in Stalin's *Economic Problems of Socialism in the USSR*, published in 1952. He refers to Stalin's comment: "To speak about nations defeated in the war, Japan and Germany. Now these nations are constrained by American imperialism. Their industry, agriculture, foreign and domestic policies, i.e., all their lives are constrained by American occupation. They should liberate themselves."[26] Tanaka interprets this in the following way: "The USSR was waiting for contradictions between the capitalist states to become aggravated and set as the basis of her policy toward the West increasing these contradictions. She recognized that promoting Japanese self-determination vis-à-vis the United States and separating Japan from the US is an important option for her policy toward Japan."[27]

It is beyond dispute that in the mid-fifties one of the most important Soviet strategies in confronting the West, primarily the United States, was to make use of growing third world nationalism. Then evaluated in the USSR as a semicolonial nation under the "dominance of American imperialism," Japan could easily have fallen into the category from a theoretical standpoint, and Hatoyama certainly could have been assessed as a figure suitable for the game. Even more, judging from the essence of the first Soviet overtures in 1953–54, there is little doubt that Moscow attempted to play with rising Japanese nationalism and anti-Americanism to revise the San Francisco system as seen in the fact that Soviet conditions for normalization of bilateral relations basically coincided with Gromyko's demands at the San Francisco peace conference. Commenting on Soviet-Chinese negotiations in October 1954, Dmitrii Shepilov, a rising star in Khrushchev's group who was deeply involved in international negotiations and became foreign minister after Vyacheslav Molotov was ousted, indicated: "Both governments spoke against the San Francisco Peace Treaty imposed on Japan by the United States and keeping Japan in the situation of a semi-occupied nation; for normalization of relations with Japan and development of trade or cultural ties."[28] As foreign minister, Molotov clearly stated in his interview to the editor-in-chief of the *Chubu Nihon shimbun* that "the nature of Japanese-American relations is an important obstacle for the establishment of normal Soviet-Japanese ties."[29]

Yet, the thesis seems valid only for the period to the end of 1954, when *Izvestiia* published an article stating that the USSR did not insist on changing the nature of American-Japanese relations as a condition for restoring diplomatic ties.[30] It should be noted that at the London negotiations between Jakob Malik and Matsumoto Shunichi in 1955 the USSR rather easily withdrew proposed clauses infringing on the nature of the U.S.-Japan security alliance. The next attempt to bring the topic to the table is attributed to Khrushchev in 1956 at negotiations with Hatoyama and Kono, when he tried to link the problem of Shikotan and Habomai with the issue of Okinawa, but finally this effort was dropped. In general, the course of Soviet-Japanese negotiations in 1955–56 testifies to the fact that undermining US-Japan ties was not Moscow's major purpose (if any at all except a card to gain a strong negotiating position). Therefore, reference to the broader Soviet policy in Asia hardly explains the USSR's approach at the time.

Another explanation provided by Japanese researchers stresses an alleged Soviet need to legitimize the acquisition of Southern Sakhalin and the Kurile Islands through Japanese recognition of the fact bypassing the United States and Great Britain.[31] Looking at the logic in Moscow, this assumption cannot withstand scrutiny. In the Soviet view, Japan at that time was a nation deprived of any important international role and voice, and therefore her opinion could not improve the international situation for newly acquired territories. The USSR traditionally referred to the Yalta agreement as the legal background to justify the incorporation of Southern Sakhalin and the Kuriles. The Soviet interpretation went further, stressing that through joint occupation (i.e., the American-led occupation) the Allied Powers and the United States were to accept the surrender on the Japanese territory and Directive No. 1 of the Office of the Supreme Commander for the Allied Powers clearly indicated that the Soviet zone of responsibility would be "Manchuria, Korea North of 38 degrees North latitude, Karafuto, and the Kurile Islands."[32] That the islands of Etorofu, Kunashiri, Shikotan, and Habomai were excluded from the American zone is the legal grounds for including all four islands in the range of the Kuriles renounced by Japan at San Francisco, an argument repeated in the London negotiations. It was specifically stressed by Khrushchev to Kono that the USSR considered even Habomai and Shikotan as her integral land, and was ready not to "return," but to transfer them meeting Japan's "desire," but not its claims.[33] After all, it was a Soviet initiative after the London negotiations had reached a stalemate to adopt a "German formula" for the final document, implying that the restoration of diplomatic relations should precede the solution of the territorial dispute, and therefore the signing of a peace treaty. The remaining questionable status of all Soviet territorial gains in the Pacific never posed a problem for the Soviets, and even for Russians (after 1991).

In the end Tanaka's conclusion that "the most important Soviet task at the negotiations was not the solution of unresolved issues, but the mere fact of the restoration of diplomatic relations"[34] seems to be most plausible. An explanation of the fact demands a deeper incursion into the course of the decision-making process.

Whose Initiative?

The initial change in the Soviet approach toward the normalization of relations with Japan represents a great enigma hard to explain in the context of the early political struggle in Moscow after Stalin's death and the general revision of Soviet policy toward the West. Japanese sources largely view the origin of the process in an overall change of Soviet policy taken in the fall of 1954 with respect to West Germany and Japan.[35] Kubota Masaaki even stresses Japan's initiative as the first step, citing an early statement by Hatoyama Ichiro in September 1952 soon after his comeback to political activities, claiming his major political priorities to be revision of the 1947 Constitution and an end to the state of war with the Soviet Union and China.[36] Kubota stresses that the direction was shaped by a clear message soon after the establishment of the first (coalition) Hatoyama cabinet in 1954 when Foreign Minister Shigemitsu Mamoru stated: "Japan is thinking about restoration of political relations with the USSR and China under mutually acceptable conditions unless Japan's basic policy of cooperation with free nations is jeopardized." Under this interpretation, Molotov's clear statement in December 1954 stressing Soviet desire to enter negotiations with Japan was a mere response to an overture by Shigemitsu.[37]

There is no doubt that Hatoyama Ichiro was the first politician in either nation to raise the issue. Yet, his position in 1952 cannot be interpreted as an initiative of the Japanese government. A leading figure of the conservative opposition in Japan, he could be expected by Moscow to gain power eventually, but any estimation of his potential role in meeting Soviet foreign policy goals would be premature before late 1954. Yet, visible changes in the Soviet approach can be traced to as early as 1953 soon after Stalin's death.

The first apparent sign of a new Soviet approach to Japan can be attributed to the resumption of the return of detained prisoners of war (halted in 1951–52) with 798 persons going home in 1953 and 420 following in 1954.[38] The remarkable feature of the move is in the fact that it was taken much ahead of the release of German POWs,[39] while at least parallelism in the policy to Germany and Japan with a stronger stress on the obviously more important issue of Germany would have seemed more natural. The step lacks any logic if Moscow was supposed to capitalize on the new line of Hatoyama, who had used the problem of POWs as a major justification for his call for early restorations of ties with the USSR. Release of POWs at a time when the uncooperative Yoshida cabinet was still in power could be nothing but counterproductive.

The first direct Soviet step clearly aimed at establishing relations with Tokyo was taken as early as August 8, 1953, when Soviet Premier Georgii Malenkov said at a session of the Supreme Soviet that the Soviet government was ready to restore diplomatic ties with Japan, forcing Japanese Foreign Minister Okazaki Katsuo (still of a Yoshida cabinet) to respond at a session of the House of Councilors that if the USSR recognized the San Francisco Peace Treaty and the U.S.-Japan Security Treaty, the government would not mind discussing peace with the Soviet Union.[40] In fact, the meaning of Okazaki's statement did not differ from Shigemitsu's statement a year later, a fact that should at least raise doubts about the Soviet desire to play the Hatoyama card. It seems that the Japanese response did not discourage Moscow very much, as the call was repeated by First Deputy Foreign Minister Andrei Vyshinsky in July 1954, then by Vyacheslav Molotov in September 1954, and later in the Soviet-Chinese Joint Communiqué in October, and then by a second statement by Molotov in December. Obviously, all these initiatives assumed hard criticism of the system of U.S.-Japan cooperation born as a result of San Francisco, and hardly could be welcomed by any Japanese cabinet, be it under Yoshida or Hatoyama. Nevertheless, the constant Soviet offensive in reiterating the move irrespective of the figure in power in Tokyo and Japan's cautious response are indicative of the fact that a radically new policy toward Japan was under consideration in Moscow from 1953.

The reference to 1953 is also important for further analysis of the case. In fact, dating the first Soviet initiatives to 1953 means that Japan turned out to be the first wartime enemy subject to reconsideration in the public Soviet diplomacy, preceding even the cases of West Germany and Austria (closely connected to the German issue), the major sources of the origin of the cold war as viewed by the new Soviet leadership and certainly a more important concern. There is no explanation in terms of the value of Japan for any possible Soviet strategic goal to explain the initiative in revising the structure of the cold war from the Japanese angle.

The Scope of Soviet Concessions

The scope of concessions agreed to by the USSR to meet the Japanese demands for the restoration of diplomatic relations may also look very enigmatic, as they contradict any logic described by analysts. Judging by the relative value of the issue from the Japanese and Soviet perspectives, especially with the high stake set by Prime Minister Hatoyama on the restoration of ties with Moscow (in the end, among his three major political goals declared in 1952, it was the only one he finally achieved), one would more easily suppose a much softer Japanese approach and a rather hard Soviet response. Yet the Hatoyama government, under the restraint of domestic political conditions, turned out to preserve most of its initial demands until final negotiations in 1956, while the USSR was rather eager to create basic conditions for a deal, and even resorted to open pressure to ensure greater Japanese flexibility.

In fact, during 1955 the USSR revoked every previous demand presented as a precondition for the restoration of diplomatic relations, which were basically related to an attempt to undermine the U.S.-Japan strategic alliance. According to Matsumoto Shunichi, even the first proposal by the Soviet representative in Tokyo, Andrei Domnitsky, to Hatoyama Ichiro in January 1955 did not imply any disruptive acts toward the San Francisco system. His ideas assumed only an end to the state of war, establishment of diplomatic relations, and exchange of ambassadors as the first steps, and negotiations on existing problems (the territorial issue, trade, U.N. membership etc.) at the second stage.[41] It was the Japanese side that insisted on negotiations on the full list of issues (for the quite understandable reason of its fear of satisfying the only valid Soviet desire to establish diplomatic relations and gaining nothing in response) leading to the London talks in 1955.

The exchange of draft peace treaties at London presented the USSR with a new chance to reiterate its ideas to drive a wedge between Tokyo and Washington, proposing articles 2.2 and 6.b. Article 2 stressed that "Japan agrees not to be a party to any alliance or military alliance directed against any of the countries which had participated in the war against her," leaving Moscow and Beijing the chance to interpret the U.S.-Japan Security Treaty as directed against them and therefore contradicting the Soviet-Japanese agreement. Article 6.a read: "The contracting parties agree not to restrict the free navigation in Soya Strait, Nemuro Strait, Notsuke Strait and Goyomai Strait. Japan also agrees not to restrict free navigation in Tsugaru Strait and Tsushima Strait. The above straits will be open for free commercial navigation of all countries," a text acceptable to Japan if not appended by the clause 6.b stating "The above-mentioned straits will be open to warships only belonging to countries bordering the Japan Sea,"[42] implying that the Seas of Okhotsk and Japan should acquire the same status as the Black Sea and available for warship activities by the USSR, China, North Korea, and Japan, barring the United States and its allies, a provision obviously undermining the U.S.-Japan security cooperation.

Yet, both clauses were withdrawn by the USSR rather easily, the issue of alliances suspended in August 1955 as a proposal to find a compromise basically on Japanese conditions,[43] and the issue of straits never mentioned after the end of the London talks. At least the Soviet resume on negotiations for normalization of Soviet-Japanese relations prepared by the Foreign Ministry on the eve of the Bulganin-Hatoyama talks in 1956 indicates that "the Japanese did not accept our proposal and insisted on withdrawing this article [on straits–A. Z.]. Later we hinted that the article may be withdrawn if they accept our proposal on the territorial issue."[44] Though the Soviet proposal on the territorial dispute was never accepted by Japan in full, neither the issue of alliances nor the issue of straits was ever raised by the USSR after London.

No doubt, later in 1956 Nikita Khrushchev tried again to introduce an anti-American clause into the Joint Declaration linking the issue of the return of Shikotan and Habomai to the return of Okinawa during his meetings with Kono Ichiro on October 16 and

17, with Nikolai Bulganin and Anastas Mikoyan repeating the offer at their meeting with Hatoyama and Kono on October 17. Nevertheless, the initiative may be considered Khrushchev's impulsive move and not discussed beforehand (Khrushchev proposed the idea to the Presidium of the Central Committee of the Communist Party of the Soviet Union [CPSU CC] only after his second discussion with Kono), and the problem was dismissed by Khrushchev himself at the third meeting with Kono on October 18.[45] Even more, recent information found by the Japanese journalist Nagoshi Kenro in the archives of the Soviet fishery ministry (minutes of the Ishkov-Kono talks) shows that the whole idea of linking the solution of the Northern Territories problem with the return of Okinawa initially came from Kono. Talking with Ishkov on October 16, 1956, the day before his first meeting with Khrushchev, Kono had raised a new initiative proposing: "In the future we will not push the problem of the islands of Kunashiri and Etorofu unless the United States returns Okinawa and the Ogasawara islands. We will raise the issue of these two islands only in case the United States returns Okinawa and Ogasawara. Though we want to indicate in the text of the Declaration other territorial problems to be considered in the future, it is nothing but just a pose to be shown to the public. We want the Declaration to say that territorial problems other than Habomai and Shikotan should be considered in due time. Or it may declare that the territorial issue in full scope will be discussed after the return of Okinawa and Ogasawara."[46] Without doubt, Ishkov informed Khrushchev about Kono's proposal to provoke him into linking the issue of Shikotan and Habomai with the return of Okinawa as he did at the next day's meeting with Kono. Therefore Khrushchev's sudden reference to Okinawa represented rather a deviation from an agreed approach, and not a demonstration of a strong Soviet intention to damage the Japanese-U.S. partnership.

In the end, if the Soviet leadership really had the intention to undermine the American-Japanese security cooperation, every concession in 1955 seems to have lacked any logic and deprived the USSR of any imaginable leverage on the U.S.-Japan relationship, and even meant a tremendous retreat from positions advocated in 1953–54 without any important gain except the mere fact of establishing diplomatic relations.

The discussion of the territorial dispute also did not bring the USSR any important achievement if one assumes that the Soviet goal was in legalizing its postwar territorial aggrandizement in the Pacific. It is worth noting that the USSR was first to propose a compromise on the territorial dispute in parallel with withdrawing the alliances clause, while the Japanese side still stuck to a rather unrealistic demand for the right to interpret the issue of sovereignty over Southern Sakhalin (*Karafuto*) and the Kuriles (*Chishima*). It was the USSR that was first to drop the idea to gain Japanese recognition of its rights over the territories renounced by Japan at San Francisco, and to propose the transfer of Shikotan and Habomai, precisely in line with what was advocated by the Japanese representative at the time of the signing of the San Francisco treaty, i.e., recognition of Kunashiri and Etorofu as a part of the Kuriles renounced by Japan, but strong insistence on Habomai and Shikotan being part of Hokkaido, and therefore referred to at that time as the Northern Territories (*hoppo ryodo*) separate from North and South Chishima.[47]

Finally, it was a Soviet initiative to move the negotiations from the framework of the peace treaty to a looser agreement along the lines of the "Adenauer formula," i.e., leaving the territorial issue aside. According to Tanaka, the notion of accepting the Adenauer formula was initially proposed by Andrei Domnitsky in Tokyo at his meeting with the president of the "Hokuyo seisan" fishing company as early as January 1956,[48] even before the Shepilov-Shigemitsu talks in Moscow. Kono also indicates that the idea was presented by the Soviet side, initially at his meeting with Nikolai Bulganin during Kono's fishery negotiations in May 1956.[49] It should be noted that Soviet understanding of the Adenauer formula implied that the issue of territories should not be mentioned at all, therefore leaving the USSR without any additional legal justification for its claims over Southern Sakhalin and the Kuriles except previous references to the Yalta agreement. It was only on the insistence of the Japanese side that the territorial issue was even debated in 1956, giving Khrushchev the new opportunity to link it with Okinawa.

In the end, Soviet behavior at the negotiations in 1955–56 testifies that legitimizing postwar territorial gains was not Moscow's objective. If we discard both explanations, the attempt to divert Japan from cooperation with the US and the desire to support Soviet territorial claims, then the only reason for Soviet initiatives and various concessions, as well as a resort to direct pressure imposing the "Bulganin fishery line" in 1956, seems to have been the goal of establishing diplomatic relations, a goal certainly not matching the intensive character of Soviet diplomacy at that time and the unjustified level of priority of Japan in Soviet policymaking. The answer certainly should be sought in a broader explanation of Soviet foreign policy in 1953–56.

Who Defined Soviet Policy toward Japan?

The question may look quite academic, lacking a distinct answer. A very peculiar feature may be found in examining existing analysis of the Soviet foreign policy in 1953–56: with all the importance of the Japanese issue for Moscow at the time, the topic is literally silenced in analytical publications by experts on Soviet affairs and no important information is available from recently published Soviet sources, though they cover a wide range of Soviet internal debates on policymaking toward other nations.

The only testimony on the Soviet decision on Japan belongs to Khrushchev, and the presentation is very simple:

> After Stalin's death I spoke to Mikoyan, Bulganin, and Malenkov about it. We all agreed that we needed to find a way to sign the treaty and end the state of war with Japan. That way we could send an ambassador to Japan who would carry out proper work. But Molotov showed the same fierce stubbornness, the same obtuseness, that he did when the question of concluding a peace treaty with Austria was discussed.[50]

After extended description of disagreement with Molotov, he adds:

> We finally did adopt a resolution to take some diplomatic steps that would allow us to establish contact with the Japanese government—and, more important, with the United States over the matter of protocol.[51]

The situation looks very simple: a broad-minded group of new leaders bring new ideas and have to overcome the stubbornness of the only remaining old Stalinist. Yet, a lot of inconsistency may be discovered in the paragraph. The first question unanswered is the timing of "Khrushchev's first initiative." With Beria not even mentioned, it should be after summer 1953, when Beria was already ousted. If it were between late 1953 and 1954, then, why is Bulganin mentioned? The person had nothing to do with the foreign policy issues before he became the prime minister in February 1955, replacing Malenkov. A reference to the Austrian treaty seems indicative of early 1955 when secret negotiations with Chancellor Karl Raab began in Moscow preceding London negotiations with Japan. But then, the whole list of Soviet appeals in 1953–54 and new initiatives brought to Hatoyama by Domnitsky in January 1955 are omitted. Would it imply that a "resolution to take some measures" was adopted after more than a year of intensive appeals to Tokyo?

Additional suspicions are caused by Khrushchev's complete ignorance of the Soviet policy toward Japan in 1954–55, as manifested by his memoirs. Thus, he mentioned that Hatoyama has visited the Soviet Union *after* "we did establish an embassy in Tokyo" to discuss the peace treaty.[52] It seems unbelievable that a national leader who has taken the initiative to revise the line toward Japan *in order to establish an embassy,* as he claims, does not remember all, (presumably his own) efforts to put aside the issue of the peace treaty and concentrate on establishing a formal relationship, even if the aberration of time is supposed. One may assume that Khrushchev never paid attention to the reasons behind the Japanese territorial claim to say that "there was no historical basis at all for Japan to claim that territory, since Japanese imperialists had seized the islands by force at a time when Russia was weak and unable to defend its own territory."[53] Nevertheless, it is impossible for an involved leader to say that the condition for ceding islands under dispute was that "the U.S. troops no longer be stationed in Japan" and to state that "we told Japanese, any discussion about transferring the islands to Japan could only take place when the Japanese-U.S. military alliance aimed against the Soviet Union was no longer in force."[54] The statement rejects the whole logic of London and Moscow negotiations in 1955–56, and the very nature of an alleged difference in Khrushchev and Molotov's views, as Molotov defended in 1954 the exact policy that Khrushchev presents in the memoirs. One can assume that with time passing, the author forgets some details, may mix dates, places, and names, but no political leader may be as forgetful as to not remember his own basic line and the essence of his major opponent over the issue, especially to the extent that he remembers the facts of the disagreement, but finally advocates the opposite view.

Paying attention to the severe inconsistency in Khrushchev's memoirs and real Soviet foreign policy at the time, one should assume that the story presented is a fake one and in reality Khrushchev had very little to do with the elaboration of the Soviet approach to Japan, emerging as an important negotiator only at the 1956 talks with Hatoyama and Kono.

Understanding that the Soviet approach to Japan began changing soon in 1953, one may assume that Khrushchev had little say in the issue. His prior goals in 1953 should have been securing his rise within the post-Stalin hierarchy rather than challenging priorities in foreign policy. During the short period in March 1953 he was only one of ten full members of the Presidium of the CPSU Central Committee and the last of its secretaries, while his major adversaries, Beria, Malenkov, and Molotov were much more important. He was de facto first secretary after March, but received the full title only in September after ousting Beria, to enter a new stage of competition with Prime Minister Georgii Malenkov.[55]

Among four newly emerging Soviet contenders for ultimate power, Khrushchev understood nothing of foreign policy issues, his only exposure outside USSR being a short wartime stay in occupied Poland and Germany. On the other hand, Molotov was Stalin's long-time foreign minister and a major architect of both the wartime alliance and the cold war. Both Beria and Malenkov, along with Molotov, Zhdanov, and Mikoyan used to be members of special Politburo commissions dealing with particularly troubling and complex issues of security, defense, and foreign policy.[56] Besides, according to policy imposed by Malenkov, only those who headed the state structures could take part in substantive discussions of foreign policy, defense, and security issues, removing four CC secretaries including Khrushchev.[57] Khrushchev simply lacked the knowledge and experience to intrude into the area of his rivals' expertise.

Besides, his position within the post-Stalin hierarchy did not offer him much voice in foreign affairs. He did not have any position in the government, remaining a pure party man, while foreign policy remained the domain of the state bureaucracy, therefore in the hands of Malenkov, Beria, and Molotov. Therefore, the only way to the top leadership available to him was, according to Martin McCauley, in undermining the role of the state in general decision making to boost the importance of the party institution, with the first natural priority in domestic issues.[58] His first intrusions into the area of foreign policy are noticed only in 1954 with his visits to China and Yugoslavia, excluding Foreign Minister Molotov from his team. It is noticeable that initial steps were taken toward socialist nations, more easily included under party guidance within the notion of the priority of party-to-party relations over interstate relationships. His first important personal involvement in relations with the West was at secret negotiations with Austrian Chancellor Raab over the State treaty.[59]

These circumstances indicate that the earliest time Khrushchev had any chance to intervene in the making of Soviet policy toward Japan was around the beginning of the London negotiations. Yet, the course was obviously set earlier, and his complete lack of understanding of Soviet initiatives in 1955 hints that his role in Japanese affairs was not important.

Then, where may be found the origins of the sudden Soviet revision of Japanese policy? No objective proof may be presented, but as an hypothesis the broad framework for a new Soviet foreign policy advocated by Beria and Malenkov in 1953–54 should draw our attention. By the end of the nineties the assumption of an overwhelming revision of Stalin's cold war policy conceived by Lavrenti Beria and supported by Georgii Malenkov seems dominant, with the interpretation initially introduced by Amy Knight and based on recently declassified Soviet archive documents.[60] As a large part of these sources derives from Beria files, classified materials of the Beria trial accusing him of espionage much in the style of notorious Stalinist trials of thirties, the interpretation may be not very reliable in important details, but more evasive general data certainly hint that the overall image of Beria and Malenkov trying to revise Soviet foreign policy soon after Stalin's death is correct.

It is noteworthy that Georgii Malenkov declared a "Soviet peace initiative" at Stalin's funeral, stating that "there are no contested issues in the U.S.-Soviet relations that cannot be resolved by peaceful means."[61] The same day Malenkov and Molotov spoke to Chinese envoy Zhou Enlai about ways to stop the Korean war. As Vladislav Zubok and Constantine Pleshakov remark, "Stalin was the main obstacle to a compromise between the West, Peking, and Pyongyang on the Korean armistice. But his death unleashed the peace process." The whole affair was handled by Malenkov, Beria, and Molotov.[62] Besides, the earliest moves included the restoration of diplomatic relations with Israel, Yugoslavia, and Greece, as well as the abandonment of territorial claims to Turkey (the Kars and Ardagan area in Turkish Armenia).

A new conciliatory policy toward the Austrian peace treaty as well as reconciliation with Yugoslavia is to be noted for this period (since 1953), advocated by Malenkov and Beria and rejected by Molotov. It would be natural to assume that a cornerstone of the new policy was the radical revision of approaches to Germany under the premise of the demolition of the socialist state in GDR and reunification of Germany[63] prevented by Beria's arrest in July 1953.

Despite doubts about certain details, especially related to Germany and Yugoslavia heavily cited in the final verdict at Beria's trial, it is obvious that there was a strategic reconsideration of the whole paradigm of Soviet foreign policy at the time when Khrushchev's role in this area was nonexistent. At rare occasions when he had a chance to express his views, he is known to have sided with the conservative Molotov. To a large extent, the policy was ameliorated after Beria's arrest, at least in its most radical parts (Germany, Austria, Yugoslavia). A broad reconciliation with the West, however, was still strongly advocated by Malenkov on the grounds of catastrophic suicidal aftereffects of a new world war under conditions of nuclear competition.[64] The policy became one (though not the most important) of the reasons of Malenkov's fall in early 1955.

There is no evidence that the issue of Japan ever attracted the attention of Beria and Molotov. Yet, the mere fact that the reassessment of Stalin's policy toward Tokyo was started precisely at the time of their strong influence on Soviet foreign policymaking, as well as a certain recession in the radicalism of Soviet overtures since 1954 (a return to the demands to eliminate the U.S.-Japan cooperation system always advocated by Molotov), may be indicative. It seems possible to assume that Moscow's policy toward Tokyo simply followed the general pattern, though Japan was not that important to the Beria-Malenkov line to be specifically mentioned, as Germany, Austria, or Yugoslavia were. At the same time, the lesser importance of the Japanese case turned out to help prevent the early abandonment of innovation after Beria's fall, as had happened in all the most important cases.

One more important point to note: after the ousting of Beria in 1953 and Malenkov in 1955, the only important rival to

Khrushchev was Molotov, and it is precisely at the time of Malenkov's decline that Khrushchev began his intrusion into foreign affairs, pushing Molotov aside and promoting the less radical part of an earlier Beria-Molotov line (Austria, Finland, Big Four summit at Geneva, etc.) as the strongest challenge to the foreign minister's authority. The situation provides an easy explanation of a softer Soviet line to Tokyo from January 1955 (according to the Domnitsky letters). It seems that the turn was sanctioned by Khrushchev as a matter of general change without deep insight into a matter of lower importance. This explains the profound ignorance demonstrated by his memoirs.

In the end, the hypothesis proposed implies that the change of Soviet vision of Japanese affairs represented a less important issue in the general revision of Stalin's policy by Beria and Malenkov. As a minor issue it did not arouse enough controversy after Beria's arrest to give Khrushchev a chance to use it, along with other cases, in his competition with Molotov, finally resulting in his notion of "peaceful coexistence," also largely derived from Malenkov's views.

Origins of the Reverse Course

The proposed hypothesis seems valid to explain a sudden change of Soviet policy to Japan and its turn to a hostile vision accompanied by new attempts to undermine the U.S.-Japan Security Treaty. In fact, the Soviet decision in 1960 to repudiate the promised transfer of Shikotan and Habomai islands as retaliation for the signing of a revised U.S.-Japan Security Treaty could be logical only if the explanation presented by Khrushchev's memoirs is accepted. If it were really a fact that the transfer of islands was promised under condition of withdrawal of American troops from Japan, as Khrushchev insists, then the new treaty certainly should have caused in Moscow a feeling of betrayal. Yet, Khrushchev's explanation definitely does not match the reality, as demonstrated above.

The 1960 U.S.-Japan treaty in any of its aspects changed the security environment around the USSR, and a decrease of the number of American troops accompanied with a stronger Japanese voice should rather have been welcomed by Moscow. No trends in Soviet-Japanese relations would invite any strong retaliation. Though bilateral relations were not expanding much, at the same time Tokyo did not press either for discussing the peace treaty, nor the unsolved issue of Kunashiri and Etorofu, a status quo apparently accepted by Moscow in 1955–56. Then, what are the reasons for a harsh act?

Again, it seems that the changing international environment and Soviet global priorities were the major factors. By 1960 Soviet relations with the West, especially with the United States, entered a difficult stage. The U-2 incident, Eisenhower's failure to visit Moscow, the break-up of the Paris summit on the German issue, all contributed to increasing strain and confrontation. At the same time Khrushchev had started his shift from rational "peaceful coexistence" to the revolutionary paradigm of stronger support for national liberation movements as a challenge to Western dominance in the third world. His stake on Cuba substantially added to the atmosphere of uneasy Soviet-American relations. It should be added that events in Tokyo in 1960, the massive campaign against the new U.S.-Japan treaty, were largely viewed in Moscow as a manifestation of national liberation bringing Japan to the verge of a "revolutionary situation."[65]

The defeat of the anti-treaty offensive was evaluated as a setback in the liberation movement, largely contradicting broad Soviet goals in Asia and an indisputable success of American policy to be challenged and rebuked. As Japan per se had no important value in Soviet priorities, and therefore no substantial damage for Soviet interests was anticipated from more strangled relations, a kind of punishment for Tokyo and pressure on Washington in the form of repudiating the obligation to transfer two islands could be interpreted as the only response Moscow could imagine at the time, and fully compatible with Khrushchev's spontaneous style. With the international environment changing, Japan turned out to be an acceptable sacrifice for other goals and purposes.

Though no official documents concerning the 1960 decision are available, the usually well-informed Moscow weekly *Novoe vremia* directly stated in 1990 that the signing of the new American-Japanese security treaty was only a pretext, but not the real motivation for the Soviet Union to abrogate the pledge to give up Shikotan and Habomai. The weekly explains the decision by the changing domestic context of Soviet politics and international environment, referring to the tendency for curbing "the spirit of the 20th party congress" with its criticism toward Stalin, and increasing tension in Soviet-American relations. It says that Khrushchev was advised that under such conditions the prospect of the return of two islands to an American ally would demonstrate the weakness of his leadership, thus pushing him to abrogate the pledge.[66]

The Paradigm of Soviet/Russian-Japanese Relations

Ups and downs in Soviet-Japanese relations in the Khrushchev era (1953–64) are indicative of the later pattern of their development. For both sides initial rapprochement was largely motivated by goals and purposes outside the value of direct bilateral cooperation. For Japan, the major reason was in Hatoyama's domestic and foreign political ambitions, with the issue of a peace treaty and restoration of diplomatic relations with Moscow serving as very important instruments to secure his alternative to the Yoshida line. For the USSR, the case of Japan simply matched the much broader general framework of building a new relationship with the West and formulating a new strategy for the cold war. It was not Japan as such that was important for the new policy, but the legacy of Stalin's policy becoming a liability under new conditions that had determined a sudden Soviet shift.

At the same time, improved relations seriously lacked an internal rationale, making them a hostage of broader international perceptions. With the outside environment or national strategies going through significant changes and transformation, an initial cooperative stand became not important enough to be preserved and vulnerable to the temptation of sacrificing it even for certain tactical considerations. The failure to create a viable backbone of a bilateral relationship has defined a pattern of an up and down curve heavily influenced by incidental outside factors.

It seems that the pattern turned out to be repeated through the decades. At least the model of early Russian-Japanese relations during the Yeltsin administration looks very close to it. Initial rapid rapprochement in late 1991 and early 1992 also was basically motivated by outside considerations. For Japan the emergence of a new democratic Russia presented a historic chance to assure the return of the Northern Territories, certainly an issue of bilateral relations, but still within the confines of a broader Japanese notion of "settling postwar accounts," where further Russian-Japanese cooperation was not assigned high importance. In reality, Japanese policy toward Russia in 1991–92 was a one-issue phenomenon oriented to the settlement of the old unpleasant legacy but not offering the grounds for a new start.

For Russia in its turn, Japan also grew in importance due to outside problems and calculations. Moscow badly needed a more cooperative Japan to assure a much hoped G-7 economic assistance plan, with Japan being its most severe and important critic. Intentions to go beyond Gorbachev and achieve success in the only field of foreign policy where the Soviet president had failed were instrumental to build Yeltsin's positive image in the West and overcome a Gorbymania effect. But again, the major goal was the West at large with a major stress of Russian expectations put on the United States and Western Europe. Improved relations with Japan were not anything more than an instrument in the Atlantic orientation of Russian policy.

Therefore, quite like the case of 1953–60, the emerging Russian-Japanese cooperation strongly lacked an internal backbone, and when the stake in improving relations with Tokyo began to jeopardize the much more serious problems of domestic political stability and the survival of the Yeltsin administration, the orientation toward an accommodation with Japan was easily replaced in late August 1992 in the rudest manner without any thought of possible future implications.

The strong similarity in the patterns of development of Russian-Japanese relations during the Khrushchev and Yeltsin periods suggests that temporary considerations of the moment fail to provide a solid ground for understanding mutual accommodations. Any attempts to improve relationships remain very vulnerable and easy to revise. Unless a solid basis of overlapping long-standing mutual interests is found, each nation will remain a very complicated partner for the other. The search for new grounds of the relationship was demonstrated by the "no necktie" Yeltsin-Hashimoto summit at Krasnoyarsk in early November 1997, but still the motivation and sincere efforts of both sides need to be tested by time.

NOTES

1. Hatoyama Ichiro, *Hatoyama Ichiro kaisoroku.* (Tokyo: Bungei shunju sha, 1957).

2. Kono Ichiro, *Ima da kara hanaso: Kono Ichiro kaisoroku.* (Tokyo: Shun'yodo shoten, 1958).
3. Matsumoto Shunichi, *Mosukuwani kakeru niji: Nisso kokko kaifuku kiroku.* (Tokyo: Asahi shimbunsha, 1966). The book is also available in English: Shunichi Matsumoto, *Northern Territories and Russo-Japanese Relations.* (Tokyo: Northern Territories Policy Association, 1970). Further citations refer to the Japanese edition.
4. Shigemitsu Akira, *"Hoppo ryodo" to Soren gaiko.* (Tokyo: Jiji tsushinsha, 1983).
5. Kubota Masaaki, *Kuremurin no shisetsu: Hoppo ryodo kosho 1955–1983.* (Tokyo: Bungei shunju sha, 1983).
6. Nikita Khrushchev, *Khrushchev Remembers: The Glasnost Tapes* (Boston: Little, Brown, and Co, 1990).
7. Andrei Gromyko, *Memoirs* (New York: Doubleday, 1989), p. 256.
8. *Nezavisimaia gazeta,* November 11, 1997.
9. "'Soglashaetsia na peredachu Iaponii ostrovov Habomai i Sikotan': Kak gotovilas' sovetsko-iaponskaia deklaratsiia 1956 g." *Istochnik,* No. 6, 1996, pp. 107–36.
10. Dmitri Volkogonov, *Sem' vozhdei: Galereia liderov SSSR,* 2 vols. (Moscow: Novosti, 1995).
11. Kh.T. Eidus; *SSSR i Iaponiia: Vneshnepoliticheskie otnosheniia posle Vtoroi Mirovoi Voiny.* (Moscow: Nauka, 1964); L. N. Kutakov; *Istoriia sovetsko-iaponskikh diplomaticheskikh otnoshenii.* (Moscow: Izdatel'stvo mezhdunarodnykh otnoshenii, 1962); L. N. Kutakov, *Moskva-Tokio: Ocherki diplomaticheskikh otnoshenii.* (Moscow: Mezhdunarodnye otnosheniia, 1988); D. V. Petrov, *Vneshiaia politika Iaponii posle Vtoroi Mirovoi Voiny.* (Moscow: Mezhdunarodnye otnosheniia, 1965).
12. Donald C. Hellmann, *Japanese Foreign Policy and Domestic Politics: The Peace Agreement with the Soviet Union.* (Berkeley: University of California Press, 1969).
13. Savitri Vishvanathan, *Normalization of Japanese-Soviet Relations 1945–1970* (Tallahassee, FL: The Diplomatic Press, 1973).
14. Ishimaru Kazuto, et al., eds., *Sengo Nihon gaiko,* vol. 2, *Ugokidashita Nihon gaiko.* (Tokyo: Sanseido, 1983, pp. 3–171).
15. Tanaka Takahiko, *Nisso kokko kaifuku no shiteki kenkyu.* (Tokyo: Yuhikaku, 1993).
16. Matsumoto Shunichi, *Op. Cit.,* pp. 156–57; Donald C. Hellmann, *Op. Cit.,* pp. 31–32.
17. Donald C. Hellmann, *Op. Cit.,* p. 31.
18. Martin McCauley notes that "Khrushchev had evolved his own 'new political thinking' in foreign affairs." Martin McCauley, *Khrushchev Era 1953–1964.* (London: Longman, 1995), p. 41. His

first notion of anything that may be interpreted as "peaceful coexistence" is dated to November 1955, when he said in Bombay that "the socialists and the capitalists have to live side by side on the planet" (*Pravda,* November 26, 1955), at the time when new approaches to the wartime enemies had already gained substantial pace, and Japan remained the only subject of the new policy not yet accommodated.

19. Harry Hanak, "Foreign Policy," in Martin McCauley, ed., *Khrushchev and Khrushchevism.* (Bloomington and Indianapolis, IN: Indiana University Press, 1987), p. 184.
20. Martin McCauley, *Khrushchev Era 1953–1964,* p. 40.
21. Current publication refers to the last and most complete edition of 1990. The first abridged version with his presentation of the case of Japan appeared at Little, Brown and Co. in 1970, making it available to all further commentators.
22. Nikita Khrushchev, *Op. Cit.,* p. 85.
23. Cited in K. S. Karol, *Khrouchtchev et l'Occident.* (Paris: René Julliard, 1960), p. 101.
24. Shigemitsu Akira, *Op. Cit.,* p. 47; Kubota Masaaki, *Op. Cit.,* p. 31; Tanaka Takahiko, *Op. Cit.,* p. 300.
25. Kubota Masaaki, *Op. Cit.,* p. 32; Tanaka Takahiko, *Op. Cit.,* p. 65.
26. Joseph Stalin, *Economic Problems of Socialism in the USSR.* (New York: International Publishers, 1952), p. 39.
27. Tanaka Takahiko, *Op. Cit.,* p. 61.
28. Dmitri Shepilov, "Khrushchev, Mao i atomnaia bomba" *Nezavisimaia gazeta,* November 11, 1997, p. 5.
29. Tanaka Takahiko, *Op. Cit.,* p. 74.
30. *Izvestiia,* December 22, 1954.
31. Shigemitsu Akira, *Op. Cit.,* pp. 61–63; Tanaka Takahiko, *Op. Cit.,* p. 127; Watase Shukichi, *Hoppen kokkyo kosho shi.* (Wakayama: Kaiten hakkosha, 1976), p. 249.
32. Division of Special Records, Foreign Office, Japanese Government, *Documents Concerning the Allied Occupation and Control of Japan,* vol. 1. (Tokyo: Gaimusho seimukyoku tokubetsu shiryo ka, 1949), p. 35.
33. "Protokol'naia zapis' besedy mezhdu N. S. Khrushchevym i I. Kono, 16 oktiabria 1956 g." *Istochnik,* No. 6, 1996, p. 116.
34. Tanaka Takahiko, *Op. Cit.,* p. 154.
35. See for example Shigemitsu Akira, *Op. Cit.,* p. 47.
36. Cf. Kubota Masaaki, *Op. Cit.,* p. 11. See also Hatoyama Ichiro, *Op. Cit.,* p. 117.
37. Ibid., pp. 12–13.
38. Shigemitsu Akira, *Op. Cit.,* p. 47.

39. The release of German POWs was first mentioned in a "strictly confidential" letter by Khrushchev to Ulbricht only on July 14, 1955 (Martin McCauley, *Khrushchev Era,* p. 40), i.e., more than two years after the process of release of Japanese POWs had ended with a few exceptions.
40. Tanaka Takahiko, *Op. Cit.,* pp. 52–63, 65.
41. Matsumoto Shunichi, *Op. Cit.,* p. 24. Letters by Andrei Domnitsky are known only from Japanese sources and reproduced in the book by Matsumoto. There is no reference to them in any Soviet/Russian publications, and related archival materials are still classified and unavailable for any verification.
42. The English translation is cited in Savitri Vishwanatan, *Op. Cit.,* pp. 73–74.
43. Matsumoto Shunichi, *Op. Cit.,* pp. 42–43.
44. "Peregovory o normalizatsii sovetsko-iaponskikh otnoshenii (spravka)" *Istochnik,* No. 6, 1996, p. 112.
45. "Protokol'naia zapis' besedy mezhdu N. S. Khrushchevym i I. Kono, 16 oktiabria 1956 g." "Zapiska N. S. Khrushcheva v Prezidium TsK KPSS, 17 oktyabrya 1956 g." "Protokol'naia zapis' besedy N. S. Khrushcheva s I. Kono, 17 oktiabria 1956 g." "Zapis' besedy N. A. Bulganina i A. I. Mikoyana s I. Khatoyama i I. Kono, 17 oktiabria 1956 g." "Protokol'naia zapis' besedy N. S. Khrushcheva s I. Kono, 18 oktiabria 1956 g." *Istochnik,* No. 6, 1996, pp. 118, 121, 123, 126, 128.
46. Nagoshi Kenro, *Kuremurin himitsu bunsho ga kataru: Yami no Nisso kankei shi.* (Tokyo: Chuko shinsho, 1994), pp. 218–219.
47. At the San Francisco conference Japanese plenipotentiary Yoshida Shigeru stressed that "at the time of the opening of Japan two southern Kurile islands, Etorofu and Kunashiri, were the territory of Japan," but described Shikotan and Habomai as "a part of Hokkaido, the basic territory of Japan." In a later session of the special committee of the House of Representatives the head of the Treaties Department of the Japanese Foreign Ministry Nishimura Kumao interpreted the situation in the following way: "As far as the scope of the Kurile islands mentioned in the treaty, both the northern Kuriles and southern Kuriles are included in the notion." Shigeta Hiroshi and Suezawa Shoji, eds., *Nisso kiso bunsho: Shiryo shu.* (Tokyo: Sekai no ugoki, 1988), pp. 111, 121.
48. Tanaka Takahiko, *Op. Cit.,* p. 212.
49. Kono Ichiro, *Op. Cit.,* p. 40.
50. Nikita Khrushchev, *Op. Cit.,* p. 85.
51. Ibid., p. 87.
52. Ibid., p. 88.

53. Ibid., pp. 88–89.
54. Ibid., p. 89.
55. Martin McCauley, "Khrushchev as a Leader," in Martin McCauley, ed. *Khrushchev and Khrushchevism,* pp. 9–10.
56. Cf. Vladislav Zubok and Constantine Pleshakov, *Inside the Kremlin's Cold War: From Stalin to Khrushchev.* (Cambridge, MA and London: Harvard University Press, 1996), p. 146.
57. Ibid., p. 156.
58. Martin McCauley, "Khrushchev as a Leader," pp. 17–18.
59. Vladislav Zubok and Constantine Pleshakov, *Op. Cit.,* p. 171; Joseph L. Nogee and Robert H. Donaldson, *Soviet Foreign Policy Since World War II,* third edition. (New York: Pergamon Press, 1988), p. 44.
50. Amy Knight, *Beria: Stalin's First Lieutenant.* (Princeton, NJ: Princeton University Press, 1993).
61. *Pravda,* March 12, 1953.
62. Vladislav Zubok and Constantine Pleshakov, *Op. Cit.,* p. 155.
63. For details see Amy Knight, *Op. Cit.,* p. 195; Vladislav Zubok and Constantine Pleshakov, *Op. Cit.,* pp. 157–62.
64. For details see Vladislav Zubok and Constantine Pleshakov, *Op. Cit.,* pp. 163–69.
65. Cf. S.I. Verbitskii, *Iapono-amerikanskii voenno-politicheskii soiuz, 1951–1970.* (Moscow: Nauka, GRVL, 1972.)
66. *Novoe Vremia,* June 29, 1990.

CHAPTER 4

Two Decades of Soviet Diplomacy and Andrei Gromyko

Peter Berton

POSTWAR SOVIET POLICY TOWARD JAPAN IS ONE of the least successful achievements of Soviet diplomacy. And one of the main reasons for this fiasco is that basically it was a hard-line policy punctuated by a few short periods of softening and reappraisal. The broad outlines of four decades of Soviet policy toward Japan from the 1951 San Francisco Peace Conference, and its ratification when Japan regained its sovereignty, to the dissolution of the Soviet Union in 1991, will confirm the essentially hard-line approach, interrupted by three periods of relative softening. The first occurred in the mid-1950s, as part of Nikita Khrushchev's peaceful coexistence campaign; the second arose from the Nixon-Kissinger diplomacy of American opening to China, which forced the Soviets to put on a "smile diplomacy" toward Japan; and the third was part of the "new thinking" of Mikhail Gorbachev in the mid-1980s. The soft line of the mid-1950s, which saw the signing of the Soviet-Japanese Joint Declaration in 1956, came to an abrupt end with the conclusion of a revised U.S.-Japanese Security Treaty in Washington in 1960 and Foreign Minister Andrei Gromyko's immediate and unilateral renunciation of the 1956 Soviet offer to return two of the disputed northern islands to Japan. The "smile diplomacy" of the early 1970s, initiated at the time of Gromyko's second visit to Japan in January 1972 and culminating in Prime Minister Tanaka Kakuei's visit to Moscow in October 1973, ended a few years later when Japan began negotiating a peace treaty with Communist China that would include opposition to hegemonism (a Chinese code word for the Soviet Union). The positive approach of Soviet policy toward Japan initiated under Gorbachev continued to the end of his rule, and may be said to be continuing under Boris Yeltsin.

This chapter highlights Soviet-Japanese relations in the 1960s and most of the 1970s, the roughly two decades that began with Gromyko's initiation of a hard-line approach to Japan at the beginning of 1960, and which included the Soviet foreign minister's three trips to Japan: in 1966, 1972, and 1976. The first trip occurred during the hard-line period, while the second and third trips symbolized the changing approaches in Soviet policy toward Japan. Gromyko's faulty perceptions of Japan to a large extent reflected the views of Politburo members. Thus, one can better understand the perceptions and motives of Soviet policymakers through the eyes of the long-time Soviet foreign minister and senior foreign policy advisor and toward the end of his career an important foreign-policy decision maker in his own right as a member of the ruling Politburo. After a description and analysis of each of Gromyko's three trips to Japan, I shall portray Gromyko's perceptions of Japan and of Soviet-Japanese relations, and draw some conclusions regarding Soviet policy toward Japan during the period under discussion, as well as some observations about its abysmal record in general.

Gromyko's First Visit to Japan, July 1966

In anticipation of Foreign Minister Gromyko's first visit to Japan (the first ever by a Soviet foreign minister), Prime Minister Sato Eisaku told the Diet that the Japanese government would renew Japan's claim to the Soviet-held islands in the northern Pacific and would also try to settle the issue of safe fishing operations. He said that he also hoped that Gromyko's visit would be successful and pave the way for Sato's visit to Moscow.[1]

Gromyko arrived at Tokyo International Airport on Sunday, July 24, 1966, for a seven-day goodwill visit at the invitation of the Japanese government. In a statement issued at the airport, he voiced the usual optimism, but also remarked that "the current international situation is not normal and in a sense it is critical" (probably a reference to the American escalation in Vietnam. On other occasions in Japan, Gromyko attacked the U.S. policy in Vietnam).[2]

On Tuesday, July 26, Gromyko paid a courtesy call on the governor of Tokyo (from whom he received a key to the Tokyo metropolis), attended a luncheon given in his honor by the Tokyo Chamber of Commerce and Industry, went to the top of Tokyo Tower, visited Toshiba Corporation's television assembly plant in Kawasaki, went on a tour of the NHK broadcasting center and the national gymnasium at Yoyogi (the site of the 1964 Tokyo Olympics), and hosted a reception at the Soviet Embassy in the evening. At the Toshiba plant Gromyko saw a small computer assembly and inquired whether the computers were being exported to the Soviet Union. He was told that they were not.[3] Gromyko knew the answer perfectly well, because the United States had imposed strict regulations on all its allies (with the so-called COCOM agreement) insofar as what could and what could not be exported to the Soviet Union for strategic reasons. But Gromyko's question was a not-so-subtle hint that if it were not for the Americans, Toshiba could substantially increase its sales.

On Wednesday Gromyko spent about an hour and a half with Prime Minister Sato and after lunch (hosted by the prime minister), the Soviet party took the superexpress to Kyoto. There the Gromyko party visited the Nijo palace, took part in a tea ceremony, inspected the Hitachi shipbuilding facilities, and met with the governor of Osaka Prefecture and business leaders in the Kansai area.[4]

On Friday the Soviet delegation returned to Tokyo. After an imperial audience that lasted about forty minutes, Gromyko went back to the Foreign Ministry to sign a consular treaty with Japan that had been negotiated in Moscow. The treaty called for the opening of a Japanese consulate in the Soviet port of Nakhodka in the Far East and a Soviet consulate in Osaka. The two countries also agreed to exchange visits by foreign ministers on a regular basis.

The main purpose of Gromyko's first visit to Japan was, naturally, to hold a series of discussions with his counterpart, Foreign Minister Shiina Etsusaburo. The first issue taken up was fishing operations in the northwestern Pacific, and some progress was made building on previous negotiations held in Tokyo with Fisheries Minister Aleksandr Ishkov. The conferees also discussed future bilateral relations; economic relations, including Japanese participation in the projected development of Siberia; commercial air service between the two countries; and, most importantly, the territorial issue.

In response to Japanese entreaties, Gromyko "in frank terms" essentially slammed the door shut and reiterated the familiar Soviet stand that the issue had already been settled.[5] At a dinner party in Gromyko's honor that evening Foreign Minister Shiina again brought up the question of the northern territories; Gromyko was unmoved.[6]

Prime Minister Sato, in his meeting with Gromyko, also raised the territorial issue, but the Soviet Foreign Minister's reply was that he had no intention of changing present Soviet policy. The two statesmen, however, did agree on initiating regular foreign minister meetings on an annual basis.[7] The final communiqué noted only that "the two sides recognized the need for concluding a peace treaty," but Gromyko objected to any mention of the territorial issue.[8]

Thus, the first postwar visit by a Soviet foreign minister to Japan led to an agreement to initiate regular foreign minister meetings. But after a return visit by Foreign Minister Miki Takeo to Moscow in 1967, it would be almost five years until Gromyko would return to Japan, in January 1972. One reason why Gromyko was avoiding Japan was undoubtedly his reluctance to listen to incessant demands to return the northern territories. It is also clear that Gromyko decided to visit Japan only after the Kissinger overture to China, and the fear that Japan might follow suit. Gromyko's next visit to Japan definitely proved the importance of the Moscow-Peking-Tokyo triangle.

Gromyko's Second Visit to Japan, January 1972

Japanese Ambassador to Moscow Niizeki Kinya described Gromyko's 1972 visit as "Gromyko's Smiling Diplomacy." The Soviet ambassador in Tokyo, Oleg Troyanovsky, confirmed to Foreign Minister Fukuda Takeo that Foreign Minister Gromyko would visit Japan, beginning January 23, 1972. The Soviet ambassador expressed his dissatisfaction that Prime Minister Sato Eisaku had asked President Richard Nixon at their meeting at the Western White House in San Clemente, California, to intercede with the Soviets on behalf of Japan with regard to the return of the northern territories, when the American president would visit Moscow in May.[9]

This was Gromyko's second visit to Japan. He arrived at Haneda airport on January 23 and stayed in Japan for about a week. It was five years since Foreign Minister Miki Takeo's visit to Moscow, when an agreement was reached to exchange foreign minister visits on a regular basis. And it was the first time that such a "regular" meeting was held in Japan. Gromyko met with Foreign Minister Fukuda Takeo three times and once with Prime Minister Sato Eisaku. The topics of discussion included the peace treaty, fisheries, economic cooperation, and cultural exchange. Opinions were also exchanged on U.S.-Soviet, Sino-Soviet, and Sino-Japanese relations, Vietnam, Mongolia, Bangladesh, the Near and Middle East, and Europe.[10]

On the territorial issue, Gromyko said that it was "a difficult question," but he did not reject the Japanese demand as "a problem which had already been solved," as in the past. As a goodwill gesture, Gromyko agreed to the release of 14 Japanese fishermen held in the Soviet Union. He urged the Japanese Government to provide aid to establish a pipeline from Irkutsk to Nakhodka, to develop continental shelf oil resources in northern Sakhalin, and to provide loans for financing development projects in Siberia. In considering Soviet proposals, the Japanese government, of course, had to not only study the economic feasibility of these projects, and take into account the Soviet willingness to compromise on the territorial issue, but most importantly weigh the Chinese reaction.[11]

While the following is the official public account of negotiations between Gromyko and the Japanese foreign minister and prime minister, it became clear after the collapse of the Soviet Union and the opening of Soviet archives that in his talk with Prime Minister Sato, Gromyko hinted that the Soviets would be willing to consider again their offer to return Shikotan and Habomai to Japan, which Gromyko unilaterally withdrew in 1960. Sato did not directly respond to Gromyko's gesture.[12]

The fact that Gromyko was accompanied by Mikhail Kapitsa, head of the First Far Eastern Department of the Foreign Ministry (in charge of Chinese affairs) was proof that the Soviets also attached great importance to Sino-Japanese relations.[13] Of course, the Soviets were obviously upset by the fact that the Chinese Prime Minister Zhou Enlai issued a statement on the occasion of Gromyko's visit to Japan in which he supported the "just" Japanese demands for the return of the northern territories.

Gromyko visited Sony's Shinagawa plant (shown around by Sony Chairman Ibuka, and where Mrs. Gromyko kept saying "marvelous" when shown color video), the Toyota automobile works near Nagoya, and the pearl industry off the Shima peninsula. Also on the day of his arrival in Tokyo, Gromyko went to Rikugi Park in Komagome Ward to meet with Tokyo Governor (and former professor) Minobe Ryokichi. The socialist governor (Mayor) of Tokyo prided himself on conducting foreign policy and was heavily involved in Japan's rapprochement with Communist China. But the Soviet authorities did not appreciate his leaning toward China, and reportedly cancelled an invitation to visit Moscow. This meeting, however, was at Governor Minobe's request and Gromyko accepted the invitation. An invitation to visit Moscow was renewed at that meeting.[14]

The joint communiqué issued at the conclusion of Gromyko's visit included an agreement to open negotiations for the conclusion of a peace treaty. Although the territorial issue was again not mentioned in the communiqué, the Japanese Foreign Ministry announced that the agreement implied that the two sides would discuss the northern territorial issue. (Another issue absent in the final communiqué was the China problem.)

The statement also included an agreement to exchange visits by the Japanese prime minister and the Soviet premier. Prime Minister Sato resigned from office before he could take advantage of the Soviet invitation and it fell to his successor, Tanaka Kakuei, to visit Moscow in the fall of 1973. As for a visit by a Soviet premier or CPSU general secretary, the Japanese had to wait until 1991, when Mikhail Gorbachev visited Tokyo. In his final press conference, Gromyko said that the two countries had agreed to begin negotiations on "various problems concerning the conclusion of a peace treaty," again avoiding specifically mentioning the territorial issue. He said that the Soviet Union would not oppose moves by any country, including Japan, to normalize relations with China, but he warned that normalization should be conducted in such a way so as not to impair the "security and interests" of the Soviet Union. He took the opportunity to blame China for the deterioration of Sino-Soviet relations, but added that Moscow wanted to improve them.[15]

Gromyko's Third Visit to Japan, January 1976

The Soviet-Japanese talks began on Saturday, January 10, 1976, between the Soviet delegation headed by Gromyko and the Japanese hosts led by Foreign Minister Miyazawa Kiichi. The talks were held in two rounds (lasting six hours) at the Foreign Ministry, with the first session devoted to the thorniest problem in the relations between the two countries—the territorial issue.[16]

But even before the formal meetings, at the welcoming dinner held at the Foreign Ministry reception building the day before, after Gromyko's arrival at Tokyo's Haneda Airport on board a special government plane, the atmosphere of confrontation became evident.[17] The formal discussions were heated, with Miyazawa persistently reiterating the Japanese demand for the package reversion of four Soviet-held islands off Hokkaido, on the ground that the islands were inherently Japan's proper territory. He emphasized that the islands' return was the most important prerequisite for concluding the proposed Russo-Japanese peace treaty.[18]

Gromyko, on the other hand, renewed the Soviet proposal that the two countries conclude a "treaty of good neighborliness and friendship," as a step toward conclusion of a full-fledged peace treaty. However, Gromyko added that the Soviet Union had no intention of forcing upon Japan the Soviet-proposed pact.

At Gromyko's request, Miyazawa explained the Japanese Government's basic position on the proposed peace and friendship treaty between Japan and China, which, in Moscow's view, was directed against the Soviet Union. Gromyko's main purpose of visiting Japan was to try to prevent Japan from concluding a treaty that would include opposition to "hegemony," a Chinese code word for the Soviet Union.

Miyazawa reiterated the standard Japanese line that China's "anti-hegemony clause" under negotiation for inclusion in the Tokyo-Peking pact was not directed against any country, including the Soviet Union. In fact, the final text of the treaty, which was concluded in August 1978, has a separate Article V that says in so many words that the "anti-hegemony" Article II is not directed against any third country.

Gromyko, however, warned the Japanese against negotiations with the Chinese, in an apparent attempt to drive a diplomatic wedge between the two countries.[19] He argued that even though Japan's attitude toward the Sino-Japanese Treaty was as explained to him, no one knew what the Chinese attitude was. Miyazawa's reply was that this was of no concern, and that Japan could not influence Sino-Soviet relations. If Japan were to get into a quarrel with the Soviet Union because of deepening friendly ties with China, it would be in violation of its peace constitution. Gromyko kept arguing that even though this was Japan's position, China's position was different.[20]

In the second round of talks, bilateral problems related to fishing in Soviet and Japanese waters were discussed. To compensate for his tough stand on the territorial issue, Gromyko announced that the Soviets were planning to release shortly the 32 Japanese fishermen whose boats had been seized by Russian patrol boats on charges of violating Soviet laws.[21]

On Monday, January 12, Gromyko met with Prime Minister Miki Takeo, and the one-hour meeting was extended to two hours. The territorial issue and Sino-Japanese relations again became the focus of much acrimony, and at one point Gromyko openly threatened the Japanese: "If you conclude a peace treaty with China, the Soviet Union will have to reconsider its relations with Japan." Miki was not intimidated. For one thing, he had met with Gromyko in the past in the capacity of foreign minister. Now he was Prime Minister of Japan and he treated Gromyko somewhat condescendingly, telling him to convey Miki's views to General Secretary Brezhnev.[22] Analysts at the American Embassy in Tokyo thought that Gromyko's threats were most counterproductive, as they convinced Prime Minister Miki that he should immediately pursue negotiations with the Chinese.[23]

After the stormy visit with the Japanese prime minister, Gromyko again met with Foreign Minister Miyazawa to discuss international affairs in general, the meeting of the seven advanced industrial democracies in France, and President Ford's new Pacific Doctrine.[24]

Prior to his departure for Moscow, Gromyko held a press conference at the Hotel New Otani. On the subject of the territorial issue, Gromyko was uncommunicative, but when questions touched on China, he would repeatedly go on the attack, often wildly gesticulating.[25]

Why did Gromyko behave so aggressively in Tokyo? My colleague, Professor Rodger Swearingen, a specialist on Soviet-Japanese relations, happened to be visiting Moscow in the summer of 1976. Talking to Dr. Leonid Kutakov, a former high-ranking Soviet diplomat and author of works on Soviet-Japanese relations, he remarked that it was rather undiplomatic of Foreign Minister Gromyko to threaten the Japanese on the territorial issue. Kutakov smiled and said, "You don't understand. This was not intended for Japanese ears. This was a message for the Chinese."[26]

Thus, the seemingly unproductive visit of Gromyko to Tokyo had some positive value to the Japanese. Gromyko's efforts to block the conclusion of the Sino-Japanese Peace Treaty may be said to have had the opposite effect. The Japanese felt that by carefully explaining their motives toward the conclusion of a peace treaty with China to Gromyko, they were now in a position to pursue their negotiations with China without fear that the Soviet Union might misinterpret this rapprochement.

Perceptions of Japan in Gromyko's Memoirs

In 1988, Gromyko published two volumes of his memoirs. In the second volume, he devotes half of Chapter 12 (a total of 17 pages) to Japan. The subheadings in the section on Japan are revealing: a not very original "The Land of the Rising Sun" and "Here She is Fujiyama," as well as a tourist's "Kyoto and the Tea Ceremony." Political discussions are tackled in "The Prime Minister's Apologies," "Some Opinions about Japanese Public Figures," and "Watching the Zigzags of Thought." Finally, a page is devoted to "The Japanese Phenomenon."[27]

In Gromyko's mind, it was the exotic Japan, the Land of the Rising Sun, Mount Fuji, the tea ceremony, and not the Japan that had the world's second largest economy, very advanced world-class technology, and financial clout that affected all markets in the world. This seems to have been the prevalent Soviet view. A 1984 survey in the popular journal *Novoe vremia,* entitled "Present-Day Imperialism," identifies Japan as one of its three centers. Although, the cover shows a cluster of skyscrapers in downtown Manhattan symbolizing the United States, a massive multiwing, multistory headquarters building for the European Economic Community in Brussels, and, incongruously, a dainty Torii gate of a Shinto shrine for industrial Japan.[28]

Gromyko on the Japanese Phenomenon

What does Gromyko say about the "Japanese Phenomenon?" First, he asserts that there are few people who are not interested in Japan, which in a sense constitutes a phenomenon in the contemporary world. After World War II the country made a real jump in economics and technology. And there are many interpretations and explanations so that people sometimes are so fascinated that there is little objectivity in their discussions.

They say, for example, that Japan's successes can be explained by the fact that the Japanese are people of a special character, that they approach everything scrupulously, and that they are inclined to exact and painstaking work. Hence, they say, their attraction to electronics and other branches of industry that require special precision.

But Gromyko does not accept these explanations. He credits Japan's success to the fact that after its defeat in war, Japan kept its military expenses to a minimum, and that almost everything it produced was for peaceful purposes. And he asks a rhetorical question: Would other states, who in the postwar period for a variety of reasons put a huge share of their material resources into military production, be much behind Japan if they too developed instead only those branches of their economy that are devoted to peaceful purposes?"

And he answers his question in a way that acknowledges his own uneasiness that the Soviet Union fell behind Japan: Quite possibly, and I take upon myself to assert boldly that they would not be behind at all. And if they would be behind, then not to a great degree.[29]

While it is true that Japan's minimal expenditures on defense did contribute to the development of Japan's economy, how would Comrade Gromyko explain the South Korean and Taiwanese "economic miracles," when the two countries devoted an extraordinary percentage of their GNP to defense? As far as the efficacy of a market economy is concerned, Gromyko seems to have been as blind as the rest of the aging Soviet leaders.

Gromyko on Soviet-Japanese Relations

Soviet-Japanese relations since 1945 developed unevenly: periods of relative thaw changed into lengthy phases of stagnation, and often periods of cooling and even tension. This was never our fault, stated Gromyko. We have always stood and stand for good neighborliness and cooperation on the basis of mutual benefit.

According to Gromyko, the unevenness of Soviet-Japanese relations is the direct result of zigzags in Japanese policy, the unwillingness of Tokyo to take into account realities that came about as a result of World War II. During these years, Japanese policy had elements of reason and falsehood. But the tendency was that the periods of reason grew shorter, and there was more and more falsehood.

The joint Soviet-Japanese declaration on the termination of the state of war and restoration of diplomatic and consular relations contained practically all of the questions that normally constitute the basis of a peace treaty. But a peace treaty as such has not yet been concluded because of the Japanese side's unrealistic approach that does not consider the situation that came about as a result of World War II.[30]

Gromyko published his memoirs after the advent of perestroika and "new thinking," but his analysis of Soviet-Japanese relations betrays all the formulations of "old thinking." "The situation (or realities) that came about as a result of World War II" is, of course, a reaffirmation of Soviet territorial conquests, of the Yalta accords, and an unwillingness to meet Japan's demands even halfway.

Gromyko continues: "As time went on, the level of independence in Japanese foreign policy diminished and the subordination of Japan to the global interests of the United States grew stronger. Tokyo began to find all kind of pretexts to slow down and even turn around relations with the Soviet Union."[31] Here is another blind spot. Gromyko saw Japan only as an extension of the United States.

Conclusions

Andrei Gromyko's three visits to Japan represent three phases in Soviet-Japanese relations. In 1966, he was tough, "hardboiled," unsmiling Mr. Nyet [Mr. No]. In 1972, trying to drive a wedge between Japan on the one hand, and the United States and China on the other, he came smiling. The Japanese press used two English-based Japanese expressions, "imeji chenji" [image change] and "sofuto muudo" for the change in Gromyko's image and his "soft mood."[32] Gromyko even made an informal hint that the Soviet Union would return to Japan two of the disputed islands that had been conditionally offered by Khrushchev in 1956. In 1976, Gromyko came again smileless, this time trying to break up the impending conclusion of a Sino-Japanese peace treaty. He threatened dire consequences if the Japanese were to proceed with their plans vis-à-vis China.

All three visits were counterproductive. The 1966 visit, with its tough stance, especially on the territorial issue, did not bring about any appreciable Japanese response. The 1972 visit did not prevent Prime Minister Tanaka Kakuei from traveling to Peking and normalizing relations with China. And the 1976 visit, likewise, did not prevent the conclusion of the Sino-Japanese Treaty of Peace and Friendship two and a half years later with that dreaded "hegemony" word in the text.

Gromyko's misperceptions and neglect of Japan stem from three sources. First is the image of Japan as the exotic Land of the Rising Sun and Mount Fuji, and not of Japan that is a member of the Group of Seven most advanced industrial powers. Second, to quote Arkady Shevchenko, a senior Soviet diplomat who defected to the United States and who worked closely under Gromyko in the Soviet foreign policy apparatus, "In Gromyko's approach to world affairs there exists a good deal of classic balance-of-power politics."[33] This classic balance-of-power politics is concerned primarily with military power and strategic balance, rather than economic, technological, or financial power, which is Japan's forte. In some ways, we are reminded of Stalin's remark when the discussion turned to the position and power of the Catholic Church. He is reputed to have made a rather stupid statement, "And how many divisions does the Pope have?" Third, while Gromyko's *Realpolitik* approach to the United States had merit (compared to some orthodox dogmatists on the Politburo), the trouble was that he saw the entire international system through the prism of Soviet-American relations and was obsessed with superpower relations. He never visited any Black African nation, despite countless invitations, and with the exception of Cuba, he had never been to a Latin American country. China interested him primarily through the prism of the Moscow-Washington-Peking triangle. But Japan seemed to have been neglected not only because it was unimportant when compared to superpower relations, but also because it was seen as simply an appendage to the United States. In the Soviet view, the situation in the Asia/Pacific was a strategic triangle in which Japan was part of the American pole, while Western analysts were conceptualizing the situation in the Pacific as a quadrangle including Japan.

Soviet leaders relied primarily on the military instrument, and except for brief periods of détente, used hard-line tactics. This was particularly true vis-à-vis Japan. As a rule, the Soviets threatened Japan, used fishery permits as a weapon, constantly tested Japan's defenses by deliberate intrusions into Japanese airspace, and in the early post-Occupation period tried to destabilize the Japanese government by covert support of the Japanese communists, socialists, and left-leaning labor unions. The carrot was to entice Japanese business to participate in the development of natural resources in Siberia, but always on Soviet terms. Soviet foreign policy that stressed the military instrument of power was basically flawed. In the case of Japan, the hard-line, confrontational, in-your-face Soviet approach only helped solidify Japanese-American relations, including greater acceptance by the Japanese public of the U.S.-Japan Security Pact, and of the Japanese Self-Defense Forces, surely the very opposite of Soviet goals and objectives for Japan.

NOTES

1. *The Japan Times,* July 15, 1966, p. 1.
2. *The Japan Times,* July 25, 1966, p. 1.
3. "Tonai wa niko-niko rekiho: Guromuiko gaisho ni to no kagi" and "Shikicho totemo azayaka: Guromuiko gaisho TV koba e," *Asahi shimbun,* July 26, 1966, pp. 7 and 14.
4. "Soren gaisho honichi nittei kimaru," *Asahi shimbun,* July 19, 1966, evening edition, p. 2. "Nisso ryoji joyaku ni choin: Guromuiko gaisho no rainichi," *Fuoto,* August 15, 1966, pp. 52–57.
5. *The Japan Times,* July 26, 1966, pp. 1 and 4.
6. *The Japan Times,* July 26, 1966, p. 4.
7. *The Japan Times,* July 28, 1966, p. 1.
8. *The Japan Times,* July 31, 1966, p. 1.
9. *The Japan Times,* January 12, 1972, p. 1.
10. Niizeki Kinya, *Nisso kosho no butai ura: Aru gaikokan no kiroku* (Tokyo: Nihon Hoso Shuppan Kyokai, 1989), p. 82.
11. *The Japan Times,* January 25, 1972, pp. 1 and 5.
12. Interview with Mikhail Kapitsa, International House of Japan, Tokyo, 1993.
13. Niizeki Kinya, *Nisso kosho no butai ura,* p. 82.
14. Seeing some parallels with Henry Kissinger, some reporters called him Minobenger. *The Japan Times,* January 24, 1972, p. 1.

15. *The Japan Times,* January 28, 1972, pp. 1 and 5; and January 29, 1972, pp. 1 and 5.
16. Yoshihiro Nishimura, "Japan Sees Hard Prospect Ahead in Islands Impasse," *The Japan Times,* January 11, 1976, p. 1.
17. Hirano Minoru, *Gaiko kisha nikki: Miyazawa gaiko no ninen* (Tokyo: Gyosei tsushinsha, 1979), Vol. 2. Chap. 1, "Shuonrai shusho no shi to Guromuiko gaisho no rainichi," pp. 9–39.
18. Yoshihiro Nishimura, "Japan Sees Hard Prospect Ahead in Islands Impasse," p. 1.
19. *The Japan Times,* January 11, 1976, pp. 1 and 3.
20. Hirano Minoru, *Gaiko kisha nikki,* p. 24.
21. Ibid., p. 22.
22. Ibid., pp. 22–23; *The Japan Times,* January 13, 1976, p. 1.
23. Hirano Minoru, *Gaiko kisha nikki,* p. 26.
24. Ibid., pp. 22–23.
25. Ibid., p. 25.
26. Professor Rodger Swearingen, University of Southern California, interview, Los Angeles, July 14, 1989.
27. A. A. Gromyko, *Pamiatnoe* (Moscow: Izdatel'stvo politicheskoi literatury, 1988), Vol. 2. Chap. 12, "More About Neighbors and Friends," pp. 138–55.
28. "The Three Centres of Present-Day Imperialism: U.S.A., E.E.C., Japan: A Survey," Supplement to *New Times,* 1984, cited in Peter Berton, "Soviet Perceptions of Japan: Foreign and Defense Policies, and Relations with the Strategic Triad," Chapter 7 in Ilpyong J. Kim (ed.), *The Strategic Triangle: China, the United States, and the Soviet Union* (New York: Paragon House Publishers, 1987), pp. 124–46.
29. A. A. Gromyko, *Pamiatnoe,* pp. 150–51.
30. Ibid., p. 140.
31. Ibid., p. 141.
32. "'Noruma ijo' ni waratta 'warawanu otoko' ga nokoshita hamon," *Shukan Asahi,* February 11, 1972, pp. 130–32.
33. Arkady N. Shevchenko, *Breaking with Moscow* (New York: Alfred A. Knopf, 1985), pp. 151–52.

CHAPTER 5

Japan-Soviet Political Relations from 1976–1983

Hiroshi Kimura

GENERALLY SPEAKING, SINCE THE END OF WORLD WAR II, relations between Japan and the former Soviet Union have remained cool. However, the period from the late Brezhnev era to the Andropov era (1976–1983), which is to be covered in this chapter, could be described as the coldest and most difficult period in the entire postwar history of Japan-Russian relations. During this period, except for the attendance of Japanese Prime Minister Suzuki Zenko at Leonid Brezhnev's funeral, no official visits were made to either country by the top leaders of these two neighboring nations. During the same period of time, Japanese Foreign Minister Sonoda Sunao paid only one visit to Moscow, and his Soviet counterpart, Andrei A. Gromyko, long refused to come to Tokyo, making his visit in 1976 his last one. The Soviets officially admitted this deterioration in their relations with Japan after the mid-1970s, which, of course, they claimed was primarily caused by Japanese misconduct. In the Soviet yearbook *JAPAN: 1981,* O. V. Vasil'ev wrote: "From the mid-1970s, unfavorable tendencies have begun to develop, through no fault of the Soviet side, in relations between the USSR and Japan."[1]

First, let me simply identify the series of incidents and events that contributed to make this period the lowest ebb in bilateral relation between these neighboring countries:

-the MiG-25 incident (1976)
-the 200-nautical-mile fishing zone negotiations (1977)

-Japan's signing of the Treaty of Peace and Friendship with the PRC (1978)
-Soviet redeployment of troops on the "Northern Islands" (1979)
-the Soviet military invasion into Afghanistan (1979)
-Japan's participation in the U.S.-sponsored sanction policy against the USSR (1980)
-Suzuki Zenko's decisions to undertake the "1,000 mile sea lane defense" and to establish "the Northern Territories Day" (1981)
-Tokyo's acceptance of deployment of U.S. advanced F-16 fighter-bombers at Misawa (1982)
-The Soviet threat to transfer their SS-20s from Europe to Asia (1982–83)
-Nakasone Yasuhiro's statement on Japan being an "unsinkable aircraft carrier" (1983)
-The shooting down of KAL 007 by a Soviet MiG-23 fighter (1983)

Why, then, did Japan-Soviet relations worsen to such a low level in this period? Before trying to answer this important question, it is worthwhile mentioning an interesting attempt by the Soviet Union to discern two stages in this period of deterioration.

Some Soviet specialists[2] on Asian and Japanese affairs divide this period of deterioration into two stages, one stage being the latter half of the 1970s and the other the early 1980s. According to these specialists, the difference between these two periods is as follows. In the latter half of the 1970s, Soviet-Japanese relations deteriorated due to "isolated, individual actions."[3] However, attempts were also made in these years not only to prevent relations from further deteriorating but also to normalize and even improve relations. In the early 1980s, however, Soviet-Japanese relations steadily worsened, and neither country showed any willingness to make efforts to improve them. In his speech to the Central Committee at the 26th CPSU's Party Congress on February 23, 1981, the General Secretary Leonid Brezhnev thus noted that (in Soviet relations with Japan) "negative factors are becoming stronger."[4] The difference between these two stages can be summarized by the following words : While in the mid-1970s, signs of decline were apparent only in isolated, or individual, actions carried out by the Japanese ruling circles, in the early 1980s the cooling of relations with the Soviet Union seemed to stem from "a political line," which has taken on a "systematic" character, according to Vasil'ev.[5]

From a theoretical point of view, the aforementioned incidents and events that contributed to cooling of Japan-Soviet bilateral relations in the latter half of the 1970s and early 1980s may be divided into the following five categories: (1) those that stemmed from the exasperation of the overall international environment, particularly *global* confrontation between the Western and the Eastern camps; (2) those that were related to the *regional* power configuration in the Asia-Pacific region; (3) those that were mainly an outcome of *bilateral* interactions between Japan and the Soviet Union; (4) those whose causes were ascribable to *domestic* factors in either or both Japan and the USSR; and (5) those that occurred almost *accidentally* as one-time incidents or at least independently from those factors described above.

However, in practice, it is difficult and sometimes even inappropriate to make such a distinct classification; most of these incidents and events were a result of a combination of two or more factors. Let me elaborate on this.

East-West Confrontation

The MiG-25 incident: Can this incident be regarded as a purely accidental, one-time incident? To a certain extent it was, but not exclusively so. In fact, as long as the Soviet system continued to be a totalitarian one and constrain freedom of speech and other human rights, it would have been unable to prevent other daring attempts at defection by high-ranking military officers. Moreover, without the global confrontation between the West, headed by the United States, and the East, headed by the USSR, the impact of the MiG-25 incident upon Japanese-Soviet relations would not have been so great. Because of this *global* confrontation and Japan's association with the Western side of the two opposing camps, Japan had no choice but to let the United States completely disassemble the body of the MiG-25, which further contributed to the worsening of Japan's relationship with the Soviet Union.

The Korean Air Lines (KAL) Flight 007 incident is another example that was not a purely one-time accident. As long as the Soviet system and ideology remained as they were, one can assume that Soviet frontier coastal guards would have done the same thing again under the same circumstances, as illustrated by the so-called Murmansk incident on April 20, 1978, the forced downing of another Korean commercial airliner, KAL 902, by a Soviet fighter over another militarily sensitive area, the Murmansk (Kola) peninsula. The Soviet siege mentality, and the obsessed feeling of being encircled by, and the concomitant xenophobia against, the corrupted, wicked bourgeois imperialists were so strong that the Soviets did not hesitate to resort to physically coercive means to protect their sacred, inviolable national borders.[6] Moreover, the military-strategic value of the Sea of Okhotsk area increased in the late 1970s and early 1980s period, due not only to the Soviet deployment there of SLBMs (Submarine-Launched Ballistic Missiles), discussed below, but also to the deteriorated relations between the two superpowers.[7]

Likewise, the Soviet military buildup on the disputed islands (1978–79), Japan's acceptance of U.S. deployment of F-16s at Misawa airbase (1982), and Nakasone's statements that Japan is an "unsinkable aircraft carrier" and that "[Japan's] security is indivisible [with other Western nations]" (1983) should be interpreted not only in the light of purely bilateral Japan-Soviet relations but also on a much broader, multilateral, and even *global* framework of East-West confrontation. This was the case at least in the Soviet perception of the world power constellation, in which the United States occupied a far more important position than did Japan—so much so that Soviet leaders did not consider it necessary for them to formulate a policy oriented specifically toward Japan. Underlining that Soviet policy was nothing other than a function, or almost automatic extension, of Soviet global strategy. Professor Basil Dmytryshyn at Portland State University wrote in 1979 that the Soviets simply did not have a clear, distinct, positive policy toward Japan. Offers made by the Soviets toward Japan were only "spinoffs" of Soviet policy toward the United States and/or toward China.[8] Iurii Bandura, former Tokyo correspondent and then deputy director of the International Department of *Izvestia,* wrote in 1982 the following in an article he contributed to the Japanese periodical *Jiyu:* "The title prepared for my article by the Japanese editor, 'What Does the Soviet Union Want from Japan?' is misleading and somewhat perplexes me. There is nothing that can be specifically called a Soviet policy aimed solely at Japan among Soviet policy goals. . . . Even when concrete questions regarding Japan are being considered, they are based on the general line of foreign policy adopted for the party and government."[9]

Even the signing of the Sino-Japanese Peace Treaty (1978) should be interpreted not simply as a regional affair in Asia but rather as an international one. To put it bluntly, the conclusion of this treaty was a part of the U.S. global strategy, promoted and pressed by the Carter-Brzezinski team.[10] Sonoda, then Japanese foreign minister, made a slip of the tongue in saying that the treaty was considered to be "one facet of U.S. global strategy."[11] It is therefore understandable that Oleg N. Bykov, one of the deputy directors of the Institute of World Economy and International Relations (IMEMO), Soviet Academy of Sciences, viewed U.S.-Soviet relations as "the foundation upon which, for example, quadrilateral relations among the U.S.S.R.–the U.S.A.–the P.R.C.–Japan in Asia depended."[12]

The foregoing line of logic leads us to suspect that the Soviets had a *Weltanschauung* that world affairs are basically determined by U.S.-Soviet global confrontation. In 1959, at the height of the cold war, Nikita S. Khrushchev remarked : "The case of international tension is like a cabbage. If you tear off the leaves one by one you come to the heart. And the heart of this matter is relations between the Soviet Union and the United States."[13] Andrei Gromyko, the veteran Soviet foreign minister for 28 years, expressed a similar bipolar perception of the world in his statement: "International situations depend largely upon Soviet-U.S. relations."[14]

I agree with the above-mentioned view, held primarily by the Soviets, that the most important reason why Soviet-Japanese relations deteriorated so greatly in the threshold between the late 1970s and the early 1980s lies in the further exasperation of the overall international environment, i.e., confrontational relations between the two superpowers—that is to say, the situation that, some observers too prematurely concluded, was "the End of Détente" or "the Arrival of the New Cold War Era."[15] This is not, however, to be taken to mean that I consider that all of the causes of deterioration in Japan-Soviet relations in this period are ascribable to the cooling of U.S.-USSR relations. In other words, I believe that Japan-Soviet relations were strongly influenced but not completely controlled by U.S.-Soviet relations. What, then, are the other factors besides the U.S.-Soviet relations that contributed to the worsening of Japanese-Soviet relations in this period? There are many factors, but the following two factors are particularly worth mention: the *regional* environment in Northeast Asia, and the *domestic* environments of both Japan and the Soviet Union.

China Factor and Regional Power Configuration

The single most important factor among the *regional* environments in Northeast Asia influencing Japan-Soviet relations is the China factor. Put simply, in the 1975–79 period the PRC moved closer to the United States and Japan, which led to the formation of the Washington-Beijing-Tokyo triangle against Moscow.[16] Then, in the early 1980s the People's Republic of China (PRC) began to back away from the U.S. embrace, and tilted toward the USSR.[17] Due to such a permutation of the PRC, the Kremlin, first, strengthened a feeling of isolation and, later, regained its self-confidence in these respective periods. Let me elaborate briefly on these two periods.

The conclusion of the Sino-Japanese Peace and Friendship Treaty in August 1978 was obviously a diplomatic loss for the Soviet Union, which had been opposing the treaty, particularly because the treaty contained the "antihegemony" clause.[18] The treaty in itself did not constitute a significantly serious threat to Soviet security, and yet both the symbolic and political significance of the treaty-signing at that time cannot be easily underestimated.[19] Its negative impact upon the Soviet Union was eminent.

In politico-diplomatic fields, the rapprochement of the PRC and Japan, accompanied by the blessing of the United States, meant almost automatically a tremendous blow to the remaining power, the USSR. The impact upon the USSR was more than doubled by another diplomatic blow immediately thereafter, the Sino-U.S. normalization in January 1979. The Sino-Japanese treaty-signing clearly marked a Chinese victory over the Soviets in their bitter rivalry to court the Japanese.[20] Japan and China had begun their efforts to improve relations far later than Japan and the USSR, but they had been able to move quickly. Japan's signing of a peace treaty with China signaled a manifestation of Tokyo's decision of "let us do first what we can do now, leaving other matters until later," but by the same token meant that the Tokyo government de facto discarded one of its foreign policy principles, i.e., "equidistance diplomacy" toward two Communist rivals.

In economic fields, China and the Soviet Union were in a position of competing against each other in a not necessarily completely but at least partially mutually exclusive fashion, particularly given the fact that Japan's capital and other economic capabilities were not unlimited. In this regard, the Chinese success meant a loss for the Soviet Union. There is no need to add that cultural, academic, and athletic exchanges between Japan and China have greatly increased since 1978. To top it off, the regular ministerial meetings, aside from economic ministers' conferences between the two governments, have been formally established so that bilateral problems, matters of common interest, and the methods for promoting further cooperation are to be constantly discussed.

The largest benefit that the treaty-signing brought to Japan is that the military threat from the PRC to the security of Japan was largely reduced. In addition, the treaty negotiations and conclusion brought another no less significant benefit to Japan, that is, the Chinese pledge to abrogate the 1950 Sino-Soviet Treaty of Friendship, Alliance and Mutual Assistance, which was directed specifically against "Japan and any states allied with it." Deng Xiaoping told Japanese Foreign Minister Sonoda Sunao that China was ready to take the necessary steps to annul the treaty with the USSR and in fact within a year, in April 1979, carried out this promise.

It is debatable whether the signing of a peace treaty with Beijing contributed to the enhancement of Tokyo's diplomatic leverage with regard to Moscow. Some observers of international affairs argue that this is not necessarily the case. In their view, compromise, or what the Soviets call "capitulation,"[21] made by the Japanese side to the Chinese demand to include the "antihegemony" clause in the main body of the treaty helped make the Japanese position vulnerable vis-à-vis the Soviet Union, who wanted in turn to take full advantage of such a compromise or "capitulation" in the Soviet favor. Others, including the Tokyo government, argued that it was China that made a concession in the end, because it agreed to insert in the treaty the so-called third countries clause, which states expressly that the treaty shall not affect "the position of either contracting party regarding its relations with third countries" (Article 4). Since Japan made such a painstaking effort to include this provision in the main body of the treaty simply in order to mollify Soviet apprehension, the Tokyo government did not have to feel—they argue—a strong sense of guilt toward one of the third countries, the Soviet Union.

What is also indicated by some, including Soviet spokesmen,[22] is that Japan's signing of a peace treaty shelving the issue of the Senkaku (*Diaoyu* in Chinese) Islands, which are claimed by Tokyo, Beijing, and Taipei, has provided the Soviet Union with a pretext to follow the same formula as well in Japan-Soviet peace treaty negotiations. Others, however, point out that the factual situations are so different in the two territorial disputes that the same formula cannot be automatically applied from the one to the other. Regardless of which of these arguments may be correct, one quite clear byproduct of the conclusion of the Sino-Japanese treaty is the fact that, after the concluding of the treaty, the Japanese have appeared with more self-confidence than before in their dealings with the USSR. Having done fairly well in dealing with one of the two communist powers, the Japanese in general appear to feel that one more *Vergangenheitbewältigung* (overcoming of the past) would not be very difficult if they would concentrate their entire diplomatic effort on the only remaining job—a new phenomenon in which some observers detect the birth of Japanese nationalism.

The early 1980s period, however, saw another twist of the power configuration in Northeast Asia, at least in the Soviet perception. The Soviets entertained an idea that Sino-Soviet relations would be improved in the very near future, which they believed inevitably would help greatly enhance their bargaining position vis-à-vis Japan. Already in the last days of Brezhnev's rule, the Kremlin had offered a number of olive branches to both China and Japan, illustrated by Brezhnev's addresses at the 26th CPSU Party Congress in February-March 1981[23] and at Tashkent in March 1992.[24] Particularly, Brezhnev's Tashkent speech recognized China as a "socialist" country and called for talks with China without any preliminary conditions. True, these speeches also called for improved relations with Japan, but it was not Japan but China that responded positively toward the Soviet overtures.[25]

Even within months of the euphoria of Sino-U.S. normalization that took place in January 1979, China began to feel disappointed in the United States's diplomatic behavior, particularly in the U.S. passivity toward, or even criticism against, China's handling of the Vietnam problem, and also in the United States's continued Taiwan policy.[26] For its part, the United States was also disillusioned with its new partner, the PRC, whose value and role as a restraint on Soviet expansionist behavior the United States found of limited use.[27]

Due to those respective sides' serious reconsiderations on their "marriage of convenience," by 1981 both the PRC and the United States began to feel not very comfortable in their quasi-allied relationship with each other.

Encouraged by the far more receptive responses from Beijing, the Soviets seemed to have decided to work first with China, leaving Japan until later, which was clearly manifested by Brezhnev's speech at Baku in September 1982.[28] Andropov, who succeeded Brezhnev in November 1982, also demonstrated that he would not only continue, but would also pursue with greater boldness and at a quicker pace than his predecessor, this strategy of normalizing relations with China with the aim of breaking the so-called anti-Soviet Sino-Japanese-American entente formulated in the latter half of the 1970s, and hopefully even isolating Japan and the United States.[29]

The reconciliation of differences with the PRC brought a number of benefits to the Soviet Union. In the field of diplomacy, it greatly improved the Soviet position in the world and particularly in Northeast Asia. A Sino-Soviet rapprochement would end the possible or actual formation of the Washington-Tokyo-Beijing triangle targeted against Moscow, thereby providing Moscow a way out of its awkward isolation in Asia. In addition, it would enable the Soviet Union to increase its bargaining power vis-à-vis Japan and the United States. In the military-strategic field, accommodation with Beijing would also provide Moscow great relief and help. If the presence of one million Soviet troops along the Sino-Soviet border[30] ceased to be necessary and the number were reduced, it would help the USSR lessen its military burden and financial costs. The Soviet Union could have threatened the West, including Japan, since the troops and SS-20s formerly stationed on the Sino-Soviet border could have been transferred in Asia.[31] It is also possible that a Sino-Soviet détente would deprive Japan of economic profit and that the USSR could use this possibility as a threat.

"Globalization" Trend of Japan

So far I have examined the significant influence that international circumstances, particularly the *global* confrontation between the United States and the USSR, exerted upon the relationship between

Japan and the Soviet Union. I have also stressed that *bilateral* relations between the PRC and the United States and between the PRC and Japan, for example, have also greatly influenced Japanese-Soviet relations. Finally, in this section, I would like to point out that the domestic environments of *individual* countries (Japan and the USSR) also played a large role in shaping the bilateral relations between Japan and the Soviet Union.

Japan's domestic and foreign policies are an important determining factor in Japan-Soviet relations. Domestically, for example, Japan's successful shift in its economic structure from predominately smokestack industries to an economic structure that consumes less energy in the mid-1970s and early 1980s has greatly decreased her need to cooperate with the Soviet Union in Siberian and other economic development projects. This has contributed to an improvement in Tokyo's political bargaining position vis-à-vis Moscow. Due to the recent "high yen–cheap dollar" phenomenon, Japan has surpassed not only the USSR in terms of GNP but also the United States in terms of per capita income. Though very few Japanese feel they are richer than Americans, it is true that the majority of Japanese have started to look down upon the materially poor living standard of the Soviet Union, thus increasing their self-confidence over the Soviet type of inefficient socialist economy. Increasingly more Japanese have begun to feel that Japan can get along well without the Soviet Union, whereas the Soviet Union will need Japan even more.

Having achieved an economic miracle and overcome two oil crises in the 1970s, however, the Japanese became self-confident and even began to demonstrate a strong sense of nationalism. Gradually, the Japanese began to realize that their national security and economic prosperity are dependent on their alliance with the Western camp, particularly with the United States. In order to keep this alliance alive and workable, the Japanese began to consider the need to make their own contribution to the Western community. This process, which has been labeled by some as "Japan's awareness of its global role" or "globalization of Japan" was advancing at a very slow but steady pace.

Let me present an example reflecting this gradual change in Japanese psychology and behavior. In 1977, in fishing negotiations with the Soviet Union, the Fukuda Takeo cabinet showed a very low-profile negotiating behavior, which was labeled as "beggar or kowtow diplomacy."[32] In 1978, however, the same Fukuda cabinet decided to ignore the strong opposition and pressure exerted by the USSR, thereby going ahead with the Chinese to conclude a peace treaty.[33] In 1980, the Ohira Masayoshi cabinet showed no hesitation in joining the U.S.-sponsored sanctions against the Soviet Union for its military incursion into Afghanistan.[34] In 1982–83, the Nakasone Yasuhiro cabinet made it clear that "security is indivisible" and that Japan was thus ready to become an "unsinkable aircraft carrier" for the defense of the Western community against the Soviet Union.[35]

The change in Japanese psychology and behavior described above is illustrated best by a statement made by the Japanese Prime Minister Suzuki Zenko in 1980: "If the Soviet Union wants to improve its relations with Japan, it must fulfill Japan's two requests for a withdrawal of Soviet troops from Afghanistan and the reversion of the Northern Territories."[36] Suzuki went so far as to say: "As long as the Soviet Union remains unchanged in its policy with regard to Afghanistan and the Northern Territories, any improvement in Japan-Soviet relations will be impossible."[37] Previously "the Soviet return of the Northern Territories" had been the only condition, but now "the Soviet withdrawal from Afghanistan" and later the removal of SS-20s from the Russian Far East were added, and, as indicated by the order of listing in Suzuki's speech, the latter two demands were considered to be more important than the first one.

Soviet Opposition without Compromise ("The Carrot")

For its part, the Kremlin made strenuous attempts, through both criticism and action, to block Japan's trend toward "globalization" and "remilitarization." Japan's "globalization" involves a growing awareness of its membership in the world, or, to be more exact, the Western community, and a readiness to accept responsibility for defense commensurate with its economic capability. As the Soviets perceived it, Japan intended to become a power with interests throughout the world.[38] The transition of Tokyo's principles of foreign policy conduct from the "Yoshida doctrine," which concentrated on the economic welfare of the Japanese people, to the "doctrine of 'globalism'"[39] was a "very substantial, qualitative change."[40] The Kremlin had good reason not to welcome such a "transformation."[41] Tokyo's transition to a position of "global diplomacy" was, according to Soviet judgment, dictated "not so much by Japan's individual national interests as by its 'membership in the club' of imperialist states,"[42] thereby taking "a course of confrontation with the Soviet Union."[43]

With the hope that Japan will forever remain in her immediate post–World War II status, whose concern was confined strictly to her own narrowly defined interests and particularly to the defense of her own territories, Moscow tried hard to persuade Tokyo not to get interested in the affairs of "third countries, such as Afghanistan and Poland," which, in the Soviet view, "do not have anything in common with the interests of the Japanese people."[44] It was also unnecessary and even dangerous to the security of Japan, according to the Soviets, for Japan to participate in such joint naval maneuvers as the joint U.S.-Australian-New Zealand exercises, conducted in the Pacific Ocean basin, "thousands of miles away from the Japanese coast, far beyond the boundaries of the Far East."[45] What was likewise intensified was the Soviet campaign against the Japanese plan to undertake a so-called 1,000-mile sea-lane defense. Referring to these exercises, Dmitrii V. Petrov, a noted Soviet Japanologist, said, "This means an essential expansion of the function of the Japanese 'Self-Defense Forces.' It would mean that Japan's navy is going to act thousands of miles away from the coast of its own country."[46]

One of the major reasons why the Kremlin was concerned about Japan's "globalization" tendency is that this is in practice almost inevitably accompanied by what the Soviets refer to as the "remilitarization" of Japan. Except for the unlikely case in which Japan would move away from the United States and/or closer to the USSR, Moscow, of course, did not welcome at all what they term "remilitarization" of Japan.[47] This proved to be the case, particularly since Japan's effort to increase its defense force was targeted almost exclusively against the threat from the Soviet Union. As the Soviets saw it, "anti-Sovietism and militarism [in Japan] were intertwined into a single mass."[48] On the other hand, the Soviets were also probably correct to observe that the United States did not like to see Japan overly strong militarily either. What the United States persistently wants to see is Japan remaining as its faithful, junior partner with a reasonable, but never exceedingly large amount of armament and, more importantly, supporting the framework of the American global strategy.[49]

However, it seemed to Soviet observers an almost inevitable and irreversible trend that Japan would accelerate its rearmament drive in the future toward the development of independent military forces. Factors that drove Japan in that direction were, in the Soviet view, the "weakening of the American guarantee for the security of Japan and U.S. credibility as perceived" and "shifting the focus of American attention to Western Europe and the Middle East."[50] Whatever the reasons, according to Petrov, "The [Japanese] proponents of militarization state that Japan should rely on her own forces and build up her 'defensive capabilities', i.e., her military potential."[51] While stressing the potential power of Japan,[52] the Soviets did not place much trust in the intentions of the Japanese government[53] to keep its potential within a reasonable, limited scale. According to the Soviets, the existence of potential capabilities are almost automatically identified as the threat itself. In short, what worried the Soviets was the *direction* in which Tokyo was moving and the traditional rapid *speed* of transformation once Japan set its course. Lest they should counter such a transformation of Japan too late, the Soviets seemed quite determined to nip in the bud what they refer to as the "resurgence of Japanese militarism."

Continued Soviet Military Buildup ("The Stick")

The most important single factor leading to, or at least accelerating, Japan's "globalization" was the Soviet worldwide military buildup and particularly that in the vicinity of Japan.[54] It is difficult and perhaps impossible to say precisely how much the enhancement of Soviet military forces contributed to this transition in Japan, but there is no question that, without the rapid, massive Soviet armament efforts, the aforementioned shifts in Japan would not have occurred. Frequent Soviet allegations of "a resurgence of militarist tendencies" in Japan merely criticized a situation for which the USSR was at least partly responsible.[55]

Thus, the Soviet Union's domestic and foreign policies were certainly a principal determinant of Japan's foreign policy and Japanese-Soviet relations. The most important domestic factor influencing Soviet-Japanese relations in this period was the Soviet mindset or proclivity to rely upon military means for solving international conflicts. It is well known that the Soviets regarded the "correlation of forces" (*sootnoshenie sil*) as the key concept in their view on international relations.[56] It is true, that "force" (*sila)* involves more than simply military power; it also includes political, economic, social, scientific-technological, and even mental powers.[57] Yet, it is obvious that Soviet authorities regarded the military component as the most vital factor. Andrei Grechko, Soviet defense minister, bluntly stated that: "the military might of the USSR is one of *the most important factors assuring favorable conditions to countries*" (emphasis added by H. K.).[58] Upon his assumption of the CPSU's General Secretarial post on November 12, 1982, Yurii Andropov also emphasized immediately the role of military might, by stating: "We know that one cannot yet make peace by begging the imperialists for it. It can be upheld *only by relying on the invincible might (tol'ko opiraias' na nesokrushimyiu moshch')* of the Soviet armed forces" (emphasis added by H. K.)[59]

The foregoing Soviet conviction resulted in the following consequences. Firstly, there was a further beefup of Soviet military forces in the Far Eastern part of the Soviet Union. Of particular importance was rapid modernization of the Soviet SSBNs (ballistic missile submarines, nuclear-powered) in the 1970s and 1980s, from the Golf and Hotel classes through Yankee class to Delta class.[60] Moreover, by the middle of the 1970s, Soviet SLBMs (submarine-launched ballistic missiles) had developed to the point where in the foreseeable future all U.S. targets would be within range of launch points within Soviet home waters.[61] But U.S. advanced antisubmarine warfare technology is capable of detecting Soviet SSBNs. This engendered a "special zone (bastion)" strategy,[62] in which the Soviet SSBNs operate from relatively enclosed seas, protected from U.S. or U.S. allied antisubmarine forces by a combination of minefields, radars, seabed sonars, attack submarines, surface warships, and aircraft.[63] The two bastions are the Barents Sea in the northwest and the Sea of Okhotsk. In the late 1970s the latter leapt from almost total strategic insignificance to being the second most important sea area[64]—namely, such a "bastion strategy" made the Sea of Okhotsk a sanctuary for the Soviet SSBNs. This strategic leap naturally applied also to the importance of the islands that separate the Sea of Okhotsk from the Pacific Ocean. In short, such a situation in the late 1970s made the reversion of the islands to Japan almost out of the question. Without appreciating this increased military-strategic significance of the region to the Soviet Union, one could never fully comprehend the reason as well why the Soviets brutally and ruthlessly shot down the KAL 007 that strayed into the Soviet airspace over Kamchatka and Sakhalin in September 1993.

Secondly, there was a firm conviction among Soviet leaders that military force was the utmost important determinant in international affairs, tempting them to overestimate the role that military power plays as an effective means for achieving Soviet political and diplomatic objectives. Based on this inaccurate assumption the Brezhnev leadership redeployed Soviet troops on the disputed islands and the Andropov leadership tried to threaten Japan by disclosing its possible scheme of transferring mobile SS-20s from Europe to Asia, thereby targeting Japan as well as China. Thirdly, the corollary of excessive Soviet emphasis upon physical muscle was a proclivity to underestimate other nonmilitary factors such as Japan's economic, scientific-technological clout, and concomitant Japanese psychology.

In summary, in the period from the late 1970s to the early 1980s, Japan-Soviet relations reached their lowest ebb. The Soviet Union and Japan both became so concerned about their own national security problems that they tended to view the territorial dispute as an issue of secondary importance. In this regard, this period may be concluded as a unique period in the entire postwar history of Japan-Soviet relations.

NOTES

1. O. V. Vasil'ev, "Nekotorye problemy vneshnei politiki Iaponii v 1980 g.," in *Iaponiia 1981: Ezhegodnik* (Moscow: Nauka, 1982), p. 63.
2. Ibid. and V. Dal'nev, "Chto meshaet razvitiiu sovetsko-iaponskikh otnoshenii," *Mezhdunarodnaia zhizn'*, No. 1, 1981, p. 51.
3. Vasil'ev, "Nekotorye problemy vneshnei politiki Iaponii v 1980 g," p. 63.
4. *XXVI s'ezd Kommunisticheskoi Partii Sovetskogo Soiuza, 23 fevralia–3 marta 1981 goda: stenograficheskii ochet,* Vol. 1 (Moscow: Politizdat, 1981), p.42.
5. Vasil'ev, "Nekotorye problemy vneshnei politiki Iaponii v 1980 g.," pp. 63–64.
6. Soviet Foreign Minister Andrei Gromyko reportedly stated in Madrid on September 7, 1982 that "Soviet territory, the borders of the Soviet Union are sacred."

7. Explaining the Soviet stand over the KAL incident to *TASS,* Marshal Nikolai V. Ogarkov, chief of the Soviet general staff, candidly acknowledged that Kamchatka and Southern Sakhalin were the locations of "a major base of the Soviet Union's strategic nuclear forces" and "important military installations" (*Pravda,* September 7 and 10, 1983). Prime Minister Nakasone Yasuhiro also confessed in the Japanese Diet session that "the Sea of Okhotsk has now become more important strategically and tactically than he had previously thought" (*Japan Times,* September 10, 1983).
8. Basil Dmytryshyn, "Current Trends in Soviet Foreign Policy," a paper read at the Japan-U.S. Society in Sapporo, on February, 1979, p. 12.
9. Iurii Bandura, "Soren wa Nihon ni nani o nozomu ka?" *Jiyu,* (January 1982), p. 158.
10. Dr. Zbigniew Brzezinski, the then national security adviser to Jimmy Carter, candidly writes about pressure that he himself exerted upon the Japanese government concerning the Treaty issue:

> I was struck in the course of my conversation with Hua Guofeng, and the issue also arose with Deng [Xiaoping] and Huang [Hua], that the Chinese were frustrated by the lack of progress in negotiating the Chinese-Japanese friendly treaty. The obstacle was Japanese unwillingness to offend the Soviets by including in the treaty the so-called anti-hegemony clause. . . .
>
> Accordingly, and on my initiative, when briefing Prime Minister Fukuda in Tokyo, immediately after my departure from Beijing, on the substance of the American-Chinese talks, I made it a point to urge both him and Foreign Minister Sonoda to go ahead with the treaty, with the clause in it. I pointed out to the Japanese that the clause mentioned no state, and it could, theoretically, apply to China, to the United States, or anyone else. More important, I made it clear to them that the United States did not object to the inclusion of that clause and that it favored an expeditious conclusion of the treaty.
>
> I believe this statement, including more than subtle encouragement, did impress the Japanese, and shortly thereafter they acceded to the treaty, with the clause included in it. I subsequently reported on my initiative to the President, and he approved. Till then, the State Department had been leery about it. (all emphases added by H. K.)

Zbigniew Brzezinski, *Power and Principle: Memoirs of a National Security Advisor, 1977–1981* (New York : Farar, Straus & Giroux, 1983), p. 218.

11. Sonoda Sunao revealed candidly, perhaps more than he intended to, at the Foreign Relations Committee of the Liberal Democratic Party (LDP) on January 26, 1978: "Japan's close cooperation with the U.S. is the basic pivot of Japanese foreign policy. In this context, the Sino-Japanese Peace Treaty is not to be regarded as a simple bilateral agreement, but rather as a more advanced form of cooperation with the U.S. That is, we consider the treaty as *one facet of the U.S. world strategy*" (emphasis added by H. K.). *Asahi shimbun,* January 26, 1978.
12. Oleg N. Bykov, "Vneshnopoliticheskaia strategiia SShA v aziatsko-tikhookeanskom regione," in D. V. Petrov, ed., *Mezhdunarodnye otnosheniia v aziatsko-tikhookeanskom regione* (Moscow : Nauka, 1979), p. 53.
13. New York Times, May 11, 1959, cited by Dan Caldwell, *American Soviet Relations : From 1947 to the Nixon-Kissinger Grand Design* (Westport, Connecticut : Greenwood Press), 1981, p. 3.
14. *Pravda,* November 7, 1984.
15. Andrei G. Bochkarev and Don L. Mansfield, eds., *The United States and the USSR in a Changing World: Soviet and American Perspectives* (Boulder, Colorado: Westview Press, 1992), p. 42.
16. A few days after the signing of the Sino-Japanese Treaty of Peace and Friendship in August 1978, *TASS* stated that "there is a possibility in the near future of the strengthening of the planned Washington-Beijing-Tokyo axis with a clear anti-Soviet direction." *TASS,* August 16, 1978. In September 1979, *Pravda* wrote that the U.S. and Japanese ruling circles tried to strengthen "the trend of knocking together a tripartite Washington-Tokyo-Beijing alliance." *Pravda,* September 28, 1979. See also Dmitrii Petrov, "Japan's place in U.S. Asian Policy," *International Affairs,* No.10, October 1978, pp. 52–59.
17. Lowell Dittmer, *Sino-Soviet Normalization and Its International Implications, 1945–1990* (Seattle: University of Washington Press, 1992), p. 195. For a different view, see Peter Berton, "The Asian Strategic Balance and China," in James C. Hsiung, *Beyond China's Independent Foreign Policy: Challenge for the U.S. and Its Asian Allies* (New York: Praeger Publishers, 1985). pp. 13–79.
18. Dagmar Ahrens-Thiele, "Moscow's Opposition to Chinese-Japanese Peace Talks," *Radio Liberty Research Bulletin,* No. 48178 (March 1, 1978), pp. 1–10.
19. John Stephan, "Asia in the Soviet Conception," in Donald S. Zagoria, ed., *Soviet Policy in East Asia* (New Haven: Yale University Press, 1982), p. 47.
20. Hong N. Kim, "The Fukuda Government and the Politics of the Sino-Japanese Peace Treaty," *Asian Survey,* Vol. 19, No. 3 (1979), p. 310.

21. *Foreign Broadcasting Information Service* (Soviet Union), August 28, 1978, p. M1.
22. Ibid., May 31, 1979, p. C1 and June 22, 1979, pp. C1–2; *Mainichi shimbun,* February 4, 1975; V. M. Mazurov, *SShA—Kita—Iaponiia: perestroika mezhgosudarstvennykh otnoshenii: 1969–1979* (Moscow: Nauka, 1980), p. 151.
23. *XXVI s'ezd . . . ,* Vol. 1, pp. 27–28, 46.
24. *Pravda.,* March 25, 1982.
25. Donald S. Zagoria, "The Moscow-Beijing Detente," *Foreign Affairs,* Vol. 61, No. 4, (Spring 1983), pp. 854, 856–858; Robert G. Sutter, *Future Sino-Soviet Relations and Their Implications for the United States* (Congressional Research Service Paper No. 83–10F) (Washington, D.C.: Library of Congress, 1982), pp. 17, 19.
26. Lowell Dittmer, *Sino-Soviet Normalization and its International Implications: 1945–1995,* p. 216.
27. Ibid.
28. *Pravda,* September 27, 1982.
29. Donald S. Zagoria, "Gauging the Sino-Soviet Thaw," *The New Leader,* Vol. 65, No. 22 (November 29, 1982), p. 4; Vladimir Petrov, "China Goes It Alone," *Asian Survey,* Vol. 23, No. 5 (May 1983), p. 588.
30. The Soviet Union devoted an estimated 25 percent of its military budget to the "China factor," 52 of its 184 divisions are along the Sino-Soviet (including the Outer Mongolian) border. Lowell Dittmer, "The Strategic Triangle: A Critical Review," in Ilpyong J. Kim, ed., *The Strategic Triangle: China, the United States and the Soviet Union* (New York: Paragon House Publishers, 1987), p. 32.
31. It was estimated that 135 of 378 Soviet SS-20s were based in the Soviet Far East, putatively with Chinese targets. Dittmer, *loc.cit.*
32. Hiroshi Kimura, "Soviet and Japanese Negotiating Behavior: The Spring 1977 Fisheries Talks," *Orbis,* Vol. 24, pp. 43–67.
33. Hiroshi Kimura, "The Conclusion of the Sino-Japanese Peace Treaty (1978): Soviet Coercive Strategy and Its Limits," *Studies in Comparative Communism,* Vol. 18, Nos. 3 and 4 (Autumn/Winter 1985), pp. 151–80.
34. Hiroshi Kimura, "The Impact of the Afghanistan Invasion on Japanese-Soviet Relations," in Roger E. Karnet, ed., *Soviet Foreign Policy and East-West Relations* (New York: Pergamon Press, 1992), pp. 144–54 and Hiroshi Kimura, "Recent Japan-Soviet Relations: From Clouded to 'Somewhat Crystal'," *Journal of Northeast Asian Studies,* Vol. 1, No. 1 (March 1982), pp. 3–22.
35. Nakasone Yasuhiro, *Tenchiujo: gojunen no sengo seiji o kataru* (Tokyo: Bungei shunju, 1996), pp. 430, 439–40.

36. See the three newspapers *Asahi shimbun, Sankei shimbun,* and *Hokkaido shimbun,* July 19, 1980.
37. Ibid.
38. D. V. Petrov, "Vozrozhdenie iaponskogo ekspansionizma," in S. N. Morozova, ed., *Gegemonizm: s epokhoi v konflikte* (Moscow: Progress, 1982), pp. 186–90.
39. Ibid.
40. *Izvestiia,* August 16, 1980.
41. *Pravda,* January 19, 1982.
42. *Izvestiia,* August 16, 1980.
43. D. V. Petrov, "Vozrozhdenie iaponskogo ekspansionizma," p. 198.
44. D. V. Petrov, "Vneshnaia politika Iaponii na rubezhe 70–80-kh godov," *Iaponiia 1980: Ezhegodnik* (Moscow: Nauka, 1981), pp. 71–72.
45. D. V. Petrov, "Vozrozhdenie iaponskogo ekspansionizma," p. 199; *Pravda,* February 2, 1982; Modenov, "Tokio v farvatere politike Vashingtona," *Mezhdunarodnaia zhizn',* no. 4 (1981), p. 62; Petrov, "Militarizatsiia Iaponii—ugroza miry v Azii," *Problemy Dal'nego Vostoka,* No. 1 (1981), p. 61.
46. Petrov, "Militarizatsiia Iaponii," p. 58; *Krasnaia zvezda,* November 25, 1979; *Pravda,* July 21, 1982.
47. I. I. Ivkov, "Iaponskii militarizm podnimaet golovu," *Problemy Dal'nego Vostoka,* No. 3 (1978), p. 46.
48. *Pravda,* May 5, 1979.
49. For example, L. P. Pinaev noted in his book *Evolution of the Military Policy of Japan* (1982): "It would be dangerous to encourage Japan to rearm beyond these limits, because it would yield consequences contrary to the interests of the U.S.A. From the vantage point of American global military strategy, Japan should play not an independent, but an auxiliary role." L. P. Pinaev, *Evoliutsiia voennoi politiki Iaponii: 1959–1980 gg.* (Moscow: Nauka, 1982), p. 32. See also pp. 31, 22–30, 148–149.
50. D. V. Petrov, "Militarizatsiia Iaponii," p. 52.
51. Ibid.
52. Ibid., p. 46; Modenov, "Tokio v farvatere politike Vashingtona," p. 60; *Krasnaia zvezda,* October 25, 1981: Dmitrii Petrov, "Militarizatsiia Iaponii," p. 52; Paul F. Langer, "Soviet Military Power in Asia," in Zagoria, ed., pp. 260–261.
53. Ivkov, "Iaponskii militarizm podnimaet golovu," p. 47.
54. D. V. Petrov, "Militarizatsiia Iaponiia," p. 51.
55. For a more detailed discussion of this part, see Hiroshi Kimura, "The Soviet Military Buildup: Its Impact on Japan and Its Aims," in Richard H. Solomon and Masataka Kosaka, eds., *The Soviet Far*

East Military Buildup: Nuclear Dilemmas and Asian Security (Dover, Mass.: Auburn House Publishing Company, 1986), pp. 106–22.

56. G. Shakhnazarov, "K probleme sootnosheniia sil v mire," *Kommunist,* No. 3 (February 1974), p. 86.
57. V. Gantman, "Politika, preobrasuiushchaia mir: O roli vneshnei politiki SSSR v sovremenykh mezhdunarodnykh otnosheniiakh," *Kommunist,* No. 5 (May 1973), p. 35.
58. A. A. Grechko, *Na strazhe mira i stroitel'stva kommunizma* (Moscow: Voenizdat, 1971), pp. 16–17.
59. *Pravda, Izvestiia, Krasnaia zvezda,* November 13, 1982.
60. Derek da Cunha, *Soviet Naval Power in the Pacific* (Boulder, Colorado: Lynne Rienner Publishers, 1990), pp. 18, 90.
61. Geoffrey Jukes, *Russia's Military and the Northern Territories Issue* (Working Paper No. 277) (Canberra: Strategic & Defence Studies Centre, Australian National University, 1993), p. 7.
62. Derek da Cunha, *Soviet Naval Power in the Pacific.*
63. Geoffrey Jukes, *Russia's Military and the Northern Territories Issue.*
64. Ibid.

PART II

Relations: 1985–1999

CHAPTER 6

Japan-Soviet Relations under Perestroika: Perceptions and Interaction between Two Capitals

Nobuo Shimotomai

THE RELATIONSHIP BETWEEN JAPAN AND THE SOVIET UNION was transformed significantly between 1985 and 1991. At the least, both sides changed their perceptions of each other dramatically. Nonetheless, the two failed to settle the "unresolved question." This result sharply contrasts with the German situation, where West Germany succeeded in accomplishing its historical task of uniting a divided country. This discrepancy between German "success" and Japanese "failure" needs explanation. This chapter tries to meet this need by concentrating on bilateral relations between Moscow and Tokyo, following a chronological approach from the legacy of stagnation to the years of "non-decision" and on to the new phases in 1989–90 and then in 1990–91 during the buildup and aftermath of Gorbachev's visit to Tokyo.[1]

In the cold war era, Japan-Soviet relations generally depended on U.S.-USSR relations. Only when the superpower "coldness" began to dissipate could Japanese-Soviet relations start to thaw. This was the case in 1956 when the USSR and Japan agreed to diplomatic relations and jointly declared their intent to conclude a peace treaty in which two islands (the Habomai group and Shikotan) would be handed over to Japan. It was also true in 1973, at the peak of détente, when Tokyo and Moscow briefly recognized jointly that there existed an "unresolved issue." However, as Hiroshi Kimura explains in the preceding chapter, there was no significant movement afterwards, especially after 1979 when a new wave of the cold war began.

Before 1985 diplomatic relations between the two countries bore a resemblance to theological discussions about whether "God exists or not." One side claimed the return of the occupied islands of the Northern Territories, while the other categorically denied the very existence of the problem. Conflicts were ritualized, communications could not proceed, and even in the debates on each side there were few interests with a reason to air the case for broadening contacts with the other side. Some foreign countries took sides, but they did not necessarily remain constant. China supported Japan tactically in the 1970s, then it withdrew its support. In both Japan and Russia the masses were scarcely involved in consideration of the dispute; they were excluded by esoteric language and a lack of direct interests. But they, along with the elites, were moved by stereotypes and prejudices against the other side.

By 1991 the relationship between the two countries had dramatically changed its level and character. Public images on both sides improved greatly. The Japanese people had become more interested in Moscow politics than had their own government. Mikhail Gorbachev became more popular as a politician in Japan than in his own country. For a time in Japanese elections a photograph of the candidate with Gorbachev even became a ticket for a National Diet seat.

The changing character of the relationship was all the more salient in Moscow. Before 1985, few, apart from a handful of specialists, knew the essence of Soviet-Japanese relations or could say what the Northern Territories problem was. By 1991, however, the "Japan problem" had become one of the hottest topics because it touched on the most sensitive theme in Soviet political discourse, namely sovereignty at both the union and republic levels. This did not mean that a full-fledged rational policy debate over national interests and foreign policy options ensued. On the contrary, the issue became emotionally charged. Thus, Soviet-Japanese relations fell hostage to chaotic democratization in the Soviet Union, which is still true in Russia.

On the Japanese side only a tiny number of people in the Ministry of Foreign Affairs had actually been deeply involved in this issue, although the National Diet had voted overwhelmingly for the return of the Northern Territories. By 1991, in contrast, policy toward the Soviet Union had become more open, and wide-ranging debates buffeted Japanese public opinion. The Japanese Foreign Ministry found it difficult to deal with public opinion and seldom took it into account.

In Moscow this territorial issue had been a theme for sporadic geopolitical theorizing, which at first only the general secretary and his advisers were trusted to handle. In the cold war days, the territorial issue might have been solved quite easily once the top leadership had made up its mind about the geopolitical implications without dwelling over the implications for Soviet domestic politics. By 1991, however, even the most popular and seemingly powerful Kremlin leader could not even take a clear public stance affirming the existence of this problem and its historical background. Perestroika had ambivalent consequences: it both created an unprecedented chance to solve this lingering problem and diminished the possibility that the leadership of the country would dare to do so. This chapter traces this paradox, paying attention to the domestic dimension of bilateral relations in both capitals and especially in Tokyo.[2]

The Japanese response to perestroika and its impact on Soviet-Japanese relations may be divided into two stages. The first stage was 1985–88, when the initial consequences were felt but both capitals essentially remained silent. The second stage proceeded from 1989 to 1991, when the first official visit of the Soviet President, Mikhail Gorbachev, became the centerpiece in the agenda. Even as expectations heightened, it was becoming too late, given internal conditions in the Soviet Union, for Gorbachev to commit to this issue seriously. These two stages correspond to the Reagan and Bush administrations in the U.S. leadership.

The Legacy of Stagnation

The legacy for bilateral relations of the "stagnation period" was enormous in both capitals. After the visit of Prime Minister Tanaka

Kakuei in 1973, Japan's top decision maker never visited Moscow for close to 25 years, apart from ritual visits at the funerals of the general secretaries. In their turn, Soviet high officials rarely came to Japan for a decade after Gromyko's 1976 visit.[3] The Russian ambassador to Japan in the late 1990s, Aleksandr Panov, has pointed out that the top leadership had little notion of Japan.[4] The reverse was also true. The Japanese had little concept of the real Soviet Union, and political changes there were not well anticipated, to Japan's detriment.

Between 1985 and 1991 Japan had four prime ministers, all from the LDP, namely Nakasone Yasuhiro (Nov. 1982-Nov. 1987), Takeshita Noboru (Nov. 1987-June 1989), Uno Sosuke (June 1989-July 1989), and Kaifu Toshiki (Aug. 1989-Nov. 1991). Within LDP factional politics, both Nakasone and Takeshita were bosses of their own factions, while Uno and Kaifu were not and were controlled by, among others, the largest Takeshita faction. Among them, only Nakasone and Uno had some experience in dealing with the Soviet Union.[5] The role of Nakasone has been exaggerated somewhat in the West. His foreign policy dynamism was partly a response to his weak position in domestic politics. Although his group was one of the five factions, it was not as well organized as Takeshita's.

In the Gorbachev era there were also five Japanese foreign ministers, belonging to either the Nakasone faction or the Abe Shintaro faction. This high turnover contrasts with the relative stability on the Soviet side as Eduard Shevardnadze replaced Gromyko and stayed in office until the beginning of 1991. In the Japanese political system foreign ministers play little role in foreign policy because their stay in office is normally short and all the important decisions are prepared and de facto made by the staff of the ministry.[6] The case of Abe Shintaro at a time when bilateral relations were beginning to feel the effects of "new thinking" is somewhat an exception. As the boss of his own faction and a frontrunner for succeeding first Nakasone and then Takeshita as prime minister, Abe aspired to more. He had his own view on diplomacy with the Soviet Union and after his formal departure as foreign minister, he still wielded some influence, as discussed below.[7] It was a worsening illness that prevented him from playing his desired role.

The LDP also did little in the role of the governing party as an initiator of policy toward the Soviet Union. In the cold war, Japan's policy toward the Soviet Union had long been settled. Rarely were there signs that things might change. As far back as the time of Joseph Stalin's death in 1953 there was some historical chance, and nationalist politicians such as Hatoyama Ichiro and Kono Ichiro played a brief role as advocates of change.[8] They did not follow the mainstream of the Foreign Ministry and proved more independent in their decisions than those from central bureaucratic origins.[9] This potential for daring diplomacy was partly repeated by Nakasone and Abe in the Gorbachev era. Later it was Ozawa Ichiro, general secretary of the LDP from 1990, who showed signs of boldness. Before he was to break up the LDP government after almost four decades in power, he showed his spirit by taking the initiative to solve the impasse in Japanese-Soviet relations in 1990–91, though it proved to be too late and his personal approach lacked the right context, as will be discussed later.

The role of opposition parties in public debate also deserves mention. In the late 1980s Doi Takeo became a familiar figure as head of the Japan Socialist Party (Social-Democrats). She organized a public debate on perestroika, inviting political scientists and Sovietologists, before she visited Moscow in April 1988.[10] This became the first policy debate on a public level. Communist leader Fuwa Tesuzo, whose party had been more critical on perestroika and "new thinking," sought to seize the advantage by flying to Moscow one day before Ms. Doi.

By far the most important actor in formulating Soviet policy was the Foreign Ministry. Among others, a group called the Roshiaha (Russian school) had monopolized Japanese policy toward Russia. They were career diplomats who had been trained in the U.S. or UK on Soviet problems and had a strong professional commitment to the Soviet Union and security issues. Their esprit de corps was mostly anti-Soviet, though there were a few exceptions. Policy toward the Soviet Union was largely in the hands of three officials: the vice minister, the chief of the Eurasian department, and the head of the Soviet desk. However, in the process of perestroika, the appointment policy was changed deliberately to exclude prominent Russian school figures from key positions. Ambassadors to Moscow came from the European School.[11] This was particularly true of Ambassador Sumio Edamura, a former ambassador to Spain and Indonesia, who led in public relations to change the image of Japan in Moscow.[12]

A Time of Nondecision (1985–1988)

At the time of Gorbachev's advent to the top Soviet post, Japanese appeared less interested compared to the responsiveness in Western capitals. Tardy recognition of this historical chance was one of the reasons for Japan's diplomatic failure and exacted a price later. Japanese reactions at the first stage were basically negative or, to be more exact, indifferent. Prime Minister Nakasone was an exception. He dared to go to Moscow when the funeral of Konstantin Chernenko took place in March 1985, keen to use this chance to size up the new leader who welcomed him. However, he had to cope with the resistance of the Japanese Foreign Ministry. Nakasone bided his time as Shevardnadze visited Tokyo in January 1986, then Foreign Minister Abe went to Moscow in May, and finally Gorbachev made his historic speech at Vladivostok in July outlining important policy changes in international affairs, including a new cooperative spirit linked to the assertion that the Soviet Union is one of the Asian powers. Reportedly Nakasone sent a secret mission to Moscow to sound out the possibilities for the return of the four islands.[13] Not only was his initiative premature, his thinking can be seen as traditional in an effort to exploit new opportunities for an old cause.

A similar situation unfolded in Moscow. Before the official visit of Abe in May 1986, Shevardnadze was bold enough to propose in high-level Kremlin discussions a new policy of "going back to 1956," that is, recognition of the territorial issue and the return of two islands (Habomai and Shikotan). According to the memoirs of Mikhail Kapitsa, vice minister of the Soviet Foreign Ministry with responsibility for eastern countries, he, along with N. N. Soloviev, the ambassador to Japan, spoke against the proposal. Although they were not against the proposal in principle, they thought that circumstances were not yet ripe. At the highest level, Shevardnadze's position was criticized by Gromyko, whom he had replaced, and could not gain the support of Gorbachev himself. The Politburo decided to maintain the position that a peace treaty be concluded on the basis that the territorial problem had been solved.[14] Party-to-party relations also continued to remain hampered. While the International Department of the Communist Party of the Soviet Union had proposed a plan for widening contacts with the nonsocialist parties in Japan, including the LDP, this belated interest produced few fruits.

In Soviet policy circles, there were two competing tendencies. One was Gromyko's traditional U.S.-oriented policy. The other was Aleksandr Yakovlev's new approach toward Europe and Japan, or what was called the "three centers of the capitalist system." Yakovlev's new position was still weak, and Gromyko remained a Politburo member until 1988. As far as Japan was concerned, the emerging "new thinking" was still only "thinking."

In 1987 the gap between the two capitals was highlighted. Any chance for an official visit by the general secretary was postponed. Even visits by the foreign ministers became rare. Both capitals stuck to their traditional views. In the midst of these problems relations were set back by the Toshiba incident in April 1987, in which advanced technology had been leaked to the Soviets. Inside Japan only a few Sovietologists were beginning to take perestroika seriously.[15] The Japanese government took a wait and see approach.

After Takeshita became prime minister in October 1987, more time was wasted.[16] Soon the Reagan administration ended and the Bush administration took power, slowing the U.S. reaction to Moscow for a time as the Bush team consulted with allies. Meanwhile, the situation in Moscow changed more drastically than conventional wisdom and traditional Sovietology had anticipated. Tokyo and Moscow had lost an opportunity to set relations on a new course.

Open Politics and Diplomatic Stirrings

In 1989 a new phase began in Japanese-Russian relations, marked by a new dynamism in each capital. Closed politics gave way to open politics, especially in Moscow. While this meant that new possibilities emerged for dealing with Japan, it also meant that "institutional pluralism" turned to "institutional antagonism" and resulting chaos. Meanwhile, diversification spread in Japan over policy toward the Soviet Union, reducing coordination. What is worse, the Japanese side postponed its decisions (*atomawashi*), not knowing that the time horizon for dealing with Gorbachev was limited.

In this period, information breakthroughs preceded policy changes. Whereas high-level discourse still suffered from stalemates, at the academic level many initiatives surfaced—a first in Soviet rethinking of Japan. From 1988 Soviet scholars specializing in Northeast Asia made public new ideas on Japan. Such scholars as Vladimir Ivanov, Georgi Kunadze, Konstantin Sarkisov, and Vladimir Zaitsev took a fresh slant on bilateral relations.[17] By 1990 articles in Soviet publications were quite common and the position of the advocates of change was becoming more optimistic. Japanese followed closely their views about how many islands might be transferred from "two plus alpha" (Kunadze), to three (Zaitsev), and eventually four (Alexei Zagorsky).

The range of alternatives aired in Tokyo was more limited, but some prominent international scholars such as Nakajima Mineo and a few Sovietologists made their views known. Above all, they pressed for a foreign policy of more active engagement. In May 1989 Foreign Minister Uno finally announced that the Japanese government was replacing the cold war approach of the "inseparability of economics and politics" with a new approach of "expanded equilibrium." This looked like a positive-sum game, using Japanese economic leverage in exchange for political goals. In retrospect, however, we can detect two weak points. First, politics, i.e., the return of four islands, stood as a prerequisite for normalization. Second, economic leverage did not have the anticipated strength because of growing Soviet economic difficulties. A vicious circle ensued: the worsening economic situation damaged political leadership, and in turn the political situation undermined the chances for economic cooperation.

The number of actors involved in discussions of improving bilateral relations increased. This did not replace the dominant role of the ministries in both countries, but it did begin to supplement it. Conceptualization of the problems and prospects for Japanese-Soviet relations changed most decidedly. This was an overdue reaction to the perception of radical changes in the West as the cold war was ending and socialism was collapsing in Eastern Europe. Delegations talked of new approaches to problems in relations. Among others, the Supreme Soviet delegation in November 1989 produced a call by Yakovlev for solving the problems by finding a "third way."

On the Japanese side, the LDP began to play a role. This was due to the initiative of Shevardnadze in January 1989, who proposed to Abe, then general secretary of the LDP, to advance party-to-party contact with the Communist Party of the Soviet Union. By the end of the year Abe's visit to Moscow was decided. He saw his agenda in the LDP as scaling down the territorial issue and broadening the scope of bilateral relations. In his talk with Gorbachev in January 1990, Abe even avoided the term "territorial issue" and proposed to solve the "headache problem with wisdom."[18] It should be noted that this wording contradicted the approach of the Japanese Foreign Ministry, and, aware of this, Abe avoided seeing Ministry officials and wanted to exclude them from the LDP delegation. Instead, officials of the Ministry of Finance and MITI were invited. Abe's approach differed from the traditional "territory first" approach and was highly appreciated by Gorbachev.[19]

The diversification of Japanese political actors corresponded with the pluralization of Soviet actors. Boris Yeltsin, the leader of the radical opposition and of the Soviet parliament, came to Japan in January 1990 and proposed his "five-stage solution."[20] This was cautiously interpreted by some as a sign of a tactical maneuver from the Soviet side, although it was, in fact, a departure by new political forces from the Soviet/Gorbachev tutelage. These forces were growing rapidly, and by the beginning of 1991 they had become a real threat to Gorbachev and the Soviet leadership.

Abe died soon after his trip to Moscow, and his approach was carried further by his successor as LDP secretary general, Ozawa Ichiro. Ozawa, an ambitious politician from the Takeshita faction, began to depart from the postwar consensus based on harmony in the golden triangle of bureaucrats, business, and the conservative party. He advocated the supremacy of politics in the post–cold war era. Concerning the Soviet Union, his mentor, the powerful LDP politician Kanemaru Shin, dared to call for the return of two islands in April 1990. Before long Ozawa was taking the initiative in Soviet affairs, coupling the territorial issue with other issues such as economic cooperation.[21] His original idea was not a naive plan to "buy islands by economic means," as others charged later.[22] He was assisted by Kumagai Hiroshi, an LDP Diet representative and former MITI bureaucrat, and Sugimori Koji, a specialist on the Soviet Union with a social democratic orientation.[23] Kumagai and Sugimori contacted the CPSU with the proposal that the Japanese side would develop an economic plan, while the Soviet side prepared a political proposal. In short, it was meant to be a plan for "Japanese economic cooperation in return for Soviet political initiatives." This formula depended on the political clout and goodwill of Gorbachev and his associates.

The Japanese approach was indirectly echoed in the Shatalin "500-day program" in the summer of 1990. In its original version, the Shatalin program planned to solve Soviet economic difficulties by drawing on foreign money, although this was dropped in the final version. By the middle of 1990 both sides began to share a cautious optimism. But the timing was bad, and a backlash was developing in Moscow. The conservative reaction to perestroika was already intense by the time the Japanese took perestroika seriously. The interactions that started to boost Soviet expectations from Japan led before long to negative repercussions.

Gorbachev Is Coming

The Soviet side began preparations for the first official visit of a Soviet leader to Japan in the fall of 1990. The trip had been planned earlier and then postponed, with the new date set for the spring of 1991. However, the political climate in Moscow had shifted by the fall of 1990. Gorbachev failed to adopt the "500-day program," and as the political weight of reformers declined, that of the conservatives and statists such as Anatolii Lukyanov and Gennadii Yanaev rose. By November Gorbachev was siding with the conservatives. Thus, the Presidential Council, where the reformers had their power base, was disbanded, and Yakovlev's role was downgraded. The departure of Shevardnadze from the Foreign Ministry in December exposed the changing winds in Kremlin politics. A more professional diplomat, Aleksandr Bessmertnykh, was appointed foreign minister, and Yanaev became vice president, a move welcomed by some Japanese with whom he had met as a secretary of the Soviet trade unions. But he was a more conservative leader, eventually becoming a nominal leader of the coup against Gorbachev in August 1991. The reign of the CPSU was over, but the presidential system did not function well. "Institutional pluralism" inherent in the Soviet political system turned into "institutional chaos," devoid of the leading role of the CPSU or presidential initiative.[24] This tendency was also felt in foreign policy. This pluralization, as the hold of the once powerful and united Politburo slipped, led to ad hoc and disparate actions. It was coupled with growing private or divergent initiatives from foreign partners. Andrei Kozyrev emphasized this phenomenon with regard to the "Japan problem" between 1990 and 1993.[25]

He may have exaggerated the extent of confusion within the state apparatus to diminish his own responsibility, but there is truth to this interpretation.

According to Kozyrev, there emerged several policy centers regarding Japan. Yakovlev was first appointed as chairman of the preparatory commission for the official visit of Gorbachev. He invited several economic institutions to prepare to respond to plans for economic cooperation. However, after the shift in power in November 1990 Yanaev was assigned as the real chairperson of the preparatory commission without instructions from Gorbachev.[26] The new foreign minister, Bessmertnykh, was also assigned to coordinate Soviet policy toward Japan. Thus, a chaotic situation developed, contrary to the Japanese conventional image of the Soviet political system or of presidential rule under Gorbachev.

Original materials were prepared by the Foreign Ministry, the Ministry of Economic Relations, banks, the KGB, the Ministry of Defense, and scientific institutions.[27] Diametrically opposed viewpoints were voiced. According to Aleksandr Panov, there were originally two options for the island problem raised in the ministerial level preparations. One option was the formula of "back to 1956," calling for handing over two islands to Japan. The other was more cautious without the return of any territory.

Matters grew more complicated as the issue of Russian "sovereignty" rose to the foreground. Relations between the USSR under Gorbachev and the Russian Federation under Boris Yeltsin grew increasingly strained, and the Russian side insisted that it had to approve any territorial agreement with Japan. When the Soviet government used force against the Baltic republics in January 1991, opposition to Gorbachev intensified. Now he had to cope with two strong opposing sources: growing "Soviet statist" opposition among his advisors and intensifying "Republican democratic" opposition. Although Gorbachev characterized his policy by February as the "middle course," he openly collided with Yeltsin's radical approach. This domestic configuration kept Gorbachev from taking substantial initiatives on the part of the Soviet leadership.

This was the background for the official visit of the Soviet president to Japan. Military leaders such as Sergei Akhromeev were categorically opposed to any concessions to Japan, while foreign policy experts such as Andrei Kozyrev and Georgi Kunadze, who were emerging as spokesmen for the Russian Federation, also spoke against a Gorbachev initiative with regard to Japan. Among the official delegates traveling to Japan, Yanaev was to become the nominal leader of the August State Committee for the Emergency Situation, while Vladimir Lukin (of the Russian Supreme Soviet and International Commission) and Kozyrev represented Russia, and Valentin Fedorov (governor of Sakhalin) was outspoken in opposition to Japan's position.

On the Japanese side, the increasing number of actors was exemplified by the visit to Moscow of Ozawa Ichiro in March 1991, when ties with Yanaev were activated. Bypassing official channels, Ozawa reportedly proposed a deal for $28 billion in return for the islands. He met with Gorbachev twice, and at the second session he bluntly called for "massive economic aid in return for the islands."[28] The Soviet president was in no position to make such a deal even if Ozawa had been persuasive. The mission took place at the worst possible time, and turned out to be counterproductive.[29]

When Gorbachev finally went to Japan in April, the visit was important, but it was not as substantial as expected. Gorbachev opened a new page in the history of the two countries: he offered the Japanese long-sought lists of the detainees after the end of World War II, and he agreed to visa-free visits of former residents on the disputed islands. Moreover, the two sides agreed to continue discussions aimed at a peace treaty, using "positive elements of former agreements." There was even open discussion of the applicability of the 1956 joint declaration and of the relationship between the Kurile Islands and the "four islands." Nonetheless, heightened hopes on the part of the Japanese were not met by the cautious, if positive, moves of Gorbachev. Thus, the visit was all but forgotten in a short time, especially after it was overshadowed by the dramatic political events in Moscow beginning in August. Events would have to await a stable political situation.

Japan-Soviet relations failed to accomplish what German-Soviet relations did. For the German people, the Soviet hold over East Germany was of overwhelming importance. For the Japanese, the claim to four islands was not necessarily marginal, but it did not rise to the level of a life-or-death issue. The islands were inherently marginal even if they were often treated as a central concern. Having become a symbol of mutual distrust and, above all, ignorance, the islands cannot simply be neglected. Yet, the lessons of 1985–91 also demonstrate that they must not become the centerpiece if bilateral relations are to improve substantially.

NOTES

1. Officials active in bilateral negotiations have produced a significant literature on the period. See Aleksandr Panov, *Ot nedoveriia k doveriiu* (Tokyo: Saimaru, 1992); and Edamura Sumio, *Teikoku hokai zengo* (Tokyo: Toshi shuppan, 1997). On memoirs in the perestroika period in general, I have a forthcoming book.
2. Gilbert Rozman, *Japan's Response to the Gorbachev Era: A Rising Superpower Views a Declining One* (Princeton: Princeton University Press, 1992).
3. We now know from various memoirs that this stereotype is not totally correct. A. Aleksandrov-Agentov, foreign policy adviser to the general secretary, had sent a memorandum to Iu. Andropov in 1978 that in order to prevent "US-China" unity, a more balanced policy toward Japan should be elaborated. Andropov replied as follows: "Regarding Japan . . . in general pragmatically use their orientation to 'incline toward us' (for us this is a useful thing from them). This is better for us than silence." A. M. Aleksandrov-Agentov, *Ot Kollontaya do Gorbacheva* (Moscow: 1994), p. 276.
4. Aleksandr Panov, *Ot nedoveriia k doveriiu*, p. 16.
5. Uno had been in Siberia as a war detainee in the 1940s. He stayed in office for only two months because of a sex scandal. His main role in bilateral relations occurred while he served as foreign minister under Takeshita when the Japanese Foreign Ministry proposed a new approach to the Soviet Union known as "expanded equilibrium."
6. The Japanese prime minister has several assistant secretaries, among them one who represents the Foreign Ministry. Under Takeshita and Kaifu, diplomats from the Soviet desk served as personal and formal representatives. Even powerful LDP politicians could do little without the prior consensus of the Foreign Ministry.
7. J. Goodby, V. Ivanov, and N. Shimotomai, "*Northern Territories" and Beyond* (Westport, CN: Praeger, 1995), pp. 83–91.
8. Postwar conservatives were of two types. One type was recruited from the state bureaucrats and normally was inclined, as part of the mainstream in the tradition of the Yoshida school, to support the alliance with the United States. The other type was seen as traditional and nationalistic and was recruited from professional local politicians.

9. Kono Ichiro's meeting with Nikita Khrushchev was criticized as bypassing the diplomats or the "head" (*atama gonashi* diplomacy). According to the logic of the Japanese bureaucracy, even the minister should be subordinated to diplomats as the "head." See Kubo Koshi, *Tanaka Kakuei to kare no deshitachi* (Tokyo: 1995), p. 125.
10. See *Shakai shimpo,* No. 5, 1988. Under her leadership the Socialist Party became more nationalist than leftist. On Soviet policy both socialists and communists had been maximalists insisting on the return of all 22 islands in the Kuriles, instead of the four islands demanded by the government. Ms. Doi scaled the number down to four.
11. Reportedly, esprit d'ecole among Japanese diplomats originates from the first assignment. In addition to the "Russian School" and "European School," there was also an "American School."
12. Edamura Sumio, *Teikoku hokai zengo.*
13. According to one source, this envoy was Sejima Ryuzo.
14. Ivan Kovalenko, p. 209.
15. A bipartisan discussion on perestroika among U.S. and Japanese diplomats and scholars occurred from May 1987 until 1989. In the first discussion, the U.S. position was rather soft while the Japanese Foreign Ministry took a hard view.
16. Reportedly, Nakasone personally chose Takeshita as his successor and intended to keep watch over foreign policy. This was exemplified by Nakasone's visit to Moscow in July 1988, where Gorbachev hinted at a two-island compromise.
17. At a summer 1988 NIRA symposium, many Soviet specialists aired their ideas, including Kunadze, who proposed a kind of joint control over the islands, a special international status, and other alternatives.
18. According to Isomura Junjiro, political adviser to Abe, Abe had had a "bad" experience in his ministerial ties to the Soviet Union and sensed their limits. Already sick, he had instructed Isomura to meet an official of the CPSU. Before Abe's meeting with Gorbachev, the German ambassador suggested to Isomura that the territorial issue be scaled down.
19. According to Isomura, the aims of the Abe delegation were not fully appreciated by the Soviet Foreign Ministry, but they were understood by the International Department of the CPSU and others.
20. Although Yeltsin's gradualist approach was not generally taken seriously, some Japanese scholars including the present author praised it highly. See *Novoe vremia,* No. 6, 1990, p. 20.
21. Ozawa's subordinate Kumagai Hiroshi, a former MITI official, drafted, with the aide of one Soviet expert, a plan for $28 billion in cooperation.
22. Mikhail Gorbachev, *Zhizni i reformy,* Vol. 2, (Moscow, 1995), p. 264; Andrei Kozyrev, *Preobrazhenie,* (Moscow: Mezhdunarodnye otnosheniia, 1995), p. 295.

23. Sugimori had collaborated with Fukuda Takeo, who as prime minister had entertained thoughts of approaching the Soviet Union in 1977–78. In 1990 Kumagai and Sugimori contacted the International Department of the CPSU and ended up negotiating with Arkady Volsky. Kumagai and his associates at MITI were enthusiastic about big energy projects, while Vol'sky was associated with Soviet economists. Soviet liberal Japanologists played a role in these discussions too. (Interview with Sugimori on September 24, 1997.)
24. According to the memoirs (only the Japanese edition) of Anatolii Chernyaev, Gorbachev complained that "the LDP in Japan is more effectively governing the country than our CPSU." See p. 429.
25. Andrei Kozyrev, *Preobrazhenie,* (Moscow: Mezhdunarodnye otnosheniia, 1995), p. 294.
26. G. Yanaev, *Moia zhizn'* (unpublished manuscript). The author wishes to thank Hakamada Shigeki for access to this memoir. According to it, Yanaev wanted a lively discussion among various institutions and viewpoints. But, in fact, according to one participant, Yanaev's leadership was "nothing but smoking."
27. Position papers on Japan as on other important foreign policy issues were prepared by the "five institution commission" comprised of the Central Committee (the conservative A. Koshikin and the progressive Vasilii Saplin), the Ministry of Foreign Affairs (Igor Rogachev and Aleksandr Panov), the Ministry of Defense, the KGB, and the scientific institutions of the Academy of Sciences (the director of IMEMO Vladlen Martynov and Konstantin Sarkisov from the Institute of Oriental Studies).
28. *Asahi shimbun,* March 26, 1991.
29. On Gorbachev's loss of power and orientation, see Anatolii Chernyaev, *1999 god: dnevnik pomoshchnika presidenta SSSR* (Moscow: 1997), p. 127.

CHAPTER 7

Russian Decision Making on Japan in the Gorbachev Era

Lisbeth L. Tarlow

MIKHAIL GORBACHEV, WHETHER BY DESIGN, incremental opportunism, or both, was a reformer, whose goal was the revitalization of the Soviet regime. By pursuing the policies of perestroika and glasnost, he advanced a reorganization of the political system and introduced elements of democratization and pluralism into a society that had known neither for seven decades.

In foreign policy, Gorbachev pursued policies equally unprecedented for a nation whose very legitimacy was derived from its adherence to Marxist-Leninist ideology. He pushed détente with the United States to previously unimaginable levels. He agreed to deep cuts in strategic nuclear forces. He made the difficult decision to withdraw the Soviet military presence from Afghanistan. He sought to improve relations with China and to settle outstanding border issues with Beijing. And, perhaps most importantly, he refrained from using force to prop up the communist regimes of Eastern Europe and thereby virtually encouraged the public uprisings against these governments that led to their demise.

The one notable foreign policy issue on which Gorbachev seemingly made no progress was in Soviet relations with Japan. The Kurile Islands issue was not resolved, even though arguably its resolution could have led to significant Japanese economic assistance for the Soviet Far East—a policy goal fully consistent with Gorbachev's overall strategy. Evidence exists that attempts were made by Gorbachev's advisers, in anticipation of the Moscow-Tokyo summit in April 1991, to craft a compromise that would break the impasse in Soviet-Japanese relations.

This paper seeks to illuminate just how seriously Gorbachev considered offering a compromise that would satisfy Tokyo.[1] In so doing, it will examine the conditions that made it possible for him to contemplate a policy option long anathema to Moscow's foreign policy establishment, and the reasons why he ultimately abandoned that option.

Ideas, Politics, and Policy Imperative

In order for Gorbachev to embrace and implement successfully a radically new policy initiative concerning the Kurile Islands, three conditions had to be satisfied: first, the absorption and official articulation of ideas that would produce a different conceptual paradigm about Japan; second, a "propitious political environment" in which both domestic and international political spheres would be conducive to the adoption and implementation of a major policy shift; and, third, a "policy imperative," a sufficiently compelling reason to justify an initiative contrary to traditionally perceived Soviet and Russian interests. Without a convergence of these factors, no radical change in Soviet policy toward the Kuriles was sustainable.

It will be argued that for a brief period of time during Gorbachev's tenure, these variables did indeed converge. During that time, Gorbachev empowered his advisers to recommend policy options geared toward breaking the impasse. Although he always retained the prerogative to make his own decision, the fact that he considered a spectrum of options, including the most radical, suggests how far he had come in his willingness to consider real compromise.

New Political Thinking

Perceptions about Soviet domestic political requirements and international developments had led, in the 1985–87 period, to a new conceptualization of traditional Marxist-Leninist ideological concepts. The pressing need to shift resources from the defense to the civilian sector, combined with the acknowledgment of a history of failure to accomplish foreign policy objectives, resulted in the adoption by the end of 1987 of a set of principles that came to be known as New Political Thinking (NPT). Most important among those principles were the following:

1. Peaceful coexistence can no longer be seen as a breathing space before a renewed assault by capitalism, but must be viewed as a permanently operating condition.
2. National interests and general human values, and not class interests, are to be the basis for relations between states.
3. Capitalism's instinct to destroy socialism has been overridden by the need to avoid nuclear war; therefore militarism and a clash with socialism are not inevitable; moreover, capitalism will not necessarily collapse, and indeed its economic prognosis is very favorable.
4. The precedence of national interests renders obsolete the traditional analysis of the correlation of forces; a "zero-sum" concept of international relations must give way to an "expanding sum." The struggle between two opposing systems is no longer the determining factor in international relations.

The logic of NPT led to a new way of thinking about Japan, both as an international actor and as a potential partner of the USSR. Gorbachev's major foreign policy speeches concerning Asia during the period 1986–88 reflected several important changes in perspectives on Japan: (1) references to Japan as a militarily insignificant puppet of the United States gave way to a description of Japan as a "power of front-ranking significance"; (2) warnings of Japan's reemerging militarism were replaced by complimentary references to its (along with Germany's) success in achieving high levels of economic development without resorting to militarism; and (3) the importance of improved Soviet-Japanese relations, especially economic relations, was stressed with unprecedented urgency as necessary for the twin goals of jump-starting Soviet Far Eastern economic development and for establishing the Soviet Union as a qualified and active member of the Asia-Pacific region.[2]

Although Gorbachev came to realize that any improvement in relations with Japan required, at the very least, the acknowledgment of the existence of the territorial dispute, it was only when a policy imperative intersected with a propitious political environment that

Gorbachev began to consider seriously a possible solution to the problem. Until then, Gorbachev was still under the mistaken impression that he could improve relations without tackling the territorial issue. Consequently Japan continued to withhold from the Soviet Union economic and financial aid and to veto efforts by the major industrialized powers to develop a collaborative economic plan for the Soviet Union.

Political Environment

A propitious political environment emerged between mid-1988 and the end of 1990 as a result of the combination of several factors: (1) Gorbachev's personnel and institutional changes that increasingly shifted decision-making power and authority away from the Party toward new or reconstructed government institutions, a reform that resulted in an initial political vacuum that Gorbachev filled with a small network of close advisers; (2) the temporary reduction of influence on policymaking by the institution traditionally most adamant in its opposition to giving up any territory, including the Kuriles—the military; (3) the strengthening of formerly marginal players in policymaking, in particular, academics and parliamentarians, many of whom spoke publicly of the need to settle the issue and vigorously and publicly entered into the debate; (4) certain developments in the international arena, which resulted from Gorbachev's foreign policy initiatives; and (5) a political environment in Japan that encouraged the emergence of politicians eager to pursue a breakthrough with the Soviet Union.

Policy Imperative

To date, it remains impossible to confirm exactly when and why Gorbachev began to consider the prospect of transferring to Japan some, if not all, of the disputed territory. A strong case can be made, however, based upon numerous interviews with those close to the problem, that around late summer 1990, Gorbachev had become persuaded by some advisers that in exchange for a territorial concession, Tokyo could be induced to compensate Moscow with substantial, and desperately needed, financial and economic benefits.

A precipitous economic collapse in the Soviet Union "began in 1988, deepened in 1989 and had increasingly negative consequences in 1990–1."[3] By 1990 the social, political, and economic system was on the verge of collapse. Moreover, with a society newly informed about and able to debate issues, such an ominous condition could not but exacerbate public fears.

The economic crisis of 1990 emerged as the all-important policy imperative that thrust the territorial issue directly onto Gorbachev's agenda. Both the lessons drawn from recent negotiations over German unification and Gorbachev's search for a solution to economic reform provided important links between the crisis and a compromise with Japan. Roald Sagdeev, former head of the Soviet Space Agency and special adviser to Gorbachev on science and disarmament from 1988 to 1990, identified these links.[4] Sagdeev stated that in late 1989 and early 1990 Gorbachev saw that "something was not working with structural perestroika," that there was something fundamentally flawed with the type of economic reform he had implemented. Up until that time, there was economic growth and it looked like the Soviet Union was prospering. With the harsh realization that the economy not only was not prospering, but was on the verge of a crisis, Gorbachev began to look desperately to economic aid as a solution.

On the advice of some of his closest advisers, Gorbachev came to the conclusion that in order for the country to survive in the short term, he needed to collect foreign credits quickly. Thus, as Sagdeev stated, "Gorbachev [first] took a lot [of credits] from Helmut Kohl [as the quid pro quo for German unification and entry into NATO]. Then he was looking for Japan."[5] Sagdeev's impression was that Gorbachev "was ready to have a deal around the Kurile Islands" some time in 1990. Moreover, Sagdeev believed that Gorbachev did not even care about the specific disposition of the islands, but was worrying only about the quid pro quo. Sagdeev believed that "Gorbachev would have been willing to accept any one of [the ideas circulating] if it would bring him even temporary financial relief."[6]

Back-Channel Diplomacy

Soviet-Japanese discussions on the territorial issue took place in three distinct but intersecting spheres of Soviet policymaking. The first level was the official diplomatic arena, in which the territorial issue was discussed in open negotiations among top leaders and analyzed in the press. Gorbachev and Shevardnadze directly acknowledged that the conclusion of a peace treaty would require at the very least a specific recognition of the territorial dispute. Concerning Moscow's willingness and intention to reach some compromise on the issue, however, official statements alternated between the vague and the negative. The territorial issue was being directly discussed, however, especially after 1989, at a second level—in an ever-broadening circle of nonofficial or semi-official political observers, academic specialists, and journalists. Here a debate emerged concerning not if, but how, to settle the dispute. Finally, discussions about the islands were taking place on a third level—through an officially sanctioned back-channel, initiated by certain faction leaders within Japan's powerful Liberal Democratic Party (LDP).

It was in the back-channel arena where real progress toward an agreement occurred. In this sphere, negotiations on an "islands-for-cash" agreement began to take shape in late 1990 between highly placed representatives from both sides. While details of the negotiations have never been officially published, a general picture can be drawn with some confidence. The principal player on the Soviet side was Arkady Volsky, veteran Party official and former aide to Andropov and Chernenko. His Japanese counterpart was Ozawa Ichiro, general secretary of the LDP.

Based on his political credentials and personal relationship to both Gorbachev and high-level Japanese, Volsky was uniquely positioned to play this delicate role. Along with Aleksandr Yakovlev, Ergenii Primakov, and Anatolii Chernyaev, Volsky was one of a handful of people who enjoyed direct access to Gorbachev. With a background in industrial administration, Volsky had headed the Central Committee department responsible for the machine-building industry from 1985 until 1988. In that capacity, he made a visit to Nagorno-Karabakh in March 1988 to address the problem of malfunctioning factories. As an indication of Gorbachev's confidence in him, several months later Gorbachev appointed Volsky to remain in Nagorno-Karabakh to help ease tension between the Azeris and Armenians. Subsequently, Volsky spent almost a year and a half there, from July 1988 to November 1989, serving as head of the Committee of Special Administration, which governed the territory on behalf of Moscow.

With a strong Party leadership background in the industrial sector, Volsky was elected in June 1990 president of the Union of Science and Industry of the USSR *(Nauchno-promyshlennyi soiuz)*, one of the new voluntary associations established under perestroika. Volsky had a keen interest in the Soviet Union expanding relations with Japan. His knowledge of Japanese business successes stemmed from his wide contacts with Japanese leaders of the *Keidanren*. He looked to Japan as both an example of a successful capitalist economy and a potentially crucial partner in the long-overdue economic reform of the Soviet economy and the development of the Soviet Far East. It is not unlikely that he was positioning himself for lucrative business relations with the Japanese.

In September 1990, Volsky was approached by someone acting on behalf of Ozawa about a possible deal. Both Gorbachev and Yakovlev, whom Volsky had informed, were in favor of Volsky pursuing such negotiations. From the Japanese point of view, Volsky could successfully open a back channel, since he had many ties with Japanese business and government leaders as well as direct access to Gorbachev. From Gorbachev's perspective, as well, Volsky was an ideal choice as mediator. He was knowledgeable about Japan and the Japanese economy, and he was someone Gorbachev trusted. Moreover, Volsky was a safe envoy because he was in transition between official positions. Since Gorbachev certainly did not know how this affair would end, it was important to have the option of distancing himself from Volsky should that be necessary.

Volsky made two trips to Tokyo in 1990 to talk with Ozawa, one in October and the second in December. On the first trip he brought with him two people. The first was Gennadii Yanaev, Politburo member in charge of international affairs (having replaced Yakovlev in the summer of 1990). As former vice president of the Friendship Association, he had frequently visited Japan, where he was quite well connected. The second person accompanying Volsky was Vasilii Saplin of the International Department. Saplin had been recommended to Volsky when the latter was looking for someone both trustworthy and knowledgeable about Japan. Saplin had also spent time at the Friendship Association and was very much in favor of a territorial settlement. Moreover, he had been a member of Yakovlev's parliamentary delegation to Tokyo in 1989 and was known to have good relations with Chernyaev. In December 1990, Volsky made his second trip accompanied only by Saplin. This time the two sides came to a general agreement, involving the exchange of territory for something in the range of $26 billion in aid and investment.

"Draft Plan and Schedule for the Visit of the President of the USSR to Japan"

This author was able to obtain a copy of an original document that identifies the various territorial positions that important decision makers were recommending to Gorbachev for the summit. Upon Chernyaev's request, the document, entitled "Draft Plan and Schedule for the Visit of the President of the USSR to Japan" *("Skhema podgotovki i provedeniia vizita prezidenta SSSR v Iaponiiu")* had been coordinated by Saplin, then serving as *otvetstvennyi sekretar'* (executive secretary), with responsibility for working with the Preparatory Commission for the Japan Summit.[7] Toward the end of December the draft was given to Chernyaev for his editing. Above the title of the final version, in Chernyaev's handwriting, it was noted that the document had been "discussed with Yanaev on 19 January 1991," and "sent to M[ikhail] S[ergeevich Gorbachev], [Karen] Brutents [First Deputy Head of the International Department], [and Gennadii] Yanaev on 21 January 1991."

The document is noteworthy on several accounts. First, it provides an authoritative account of an emerging consensus on the territorial issue among the salient policy-making individuals and institutions on the eve of Gorbachev's visit to Japan. Second, it specifically confirms the existence of the back-channel negotiations involving an "islands-for-cash" deal among representatives of the two sides. Finally, the document suggests that Gorbachev himself was probably at least toying with the idea of bringing to Japan some form of compromise on the issue. Given decision makers' desire to please the leader and pick up signals indicating parameters of decisions, one can conclude that at the time this document was written, its authors and contributors believed there was at least a reasonable chance that Gorbachev would adopt a formula involving some transfer of territory.

The document begins with the statement that the main aim of the visit to Tokyo is to lay the foundations for radical changes in Soviet-Japanese relations. The importance of improvement in those relations for Moscow's Asia-Pacific initiatives is compared to that of the settlement of the German problem in Europe. Since "Japan holds the key position in the integration processes evolving in the APR," Moscow will be "unable to join and participate in the processes without cooperation on behalf of Japan." To develop relations, primarily economic ones, with Japan is "of great importance given the future social and economic development of Eastern Siberia and the Far East."[8]

The document recognizes the "territorial issue" as the "key" issue remaining between Moscow and Tokyo, and that "success or failure" of the Presidential visit will depend mainly on finding a formula that would meet the following conditions:

> -it will not contain a promise to turn over to Japan any one of the islands prior to the peace treaty;
> -at the same time it will open up perspectives for future initiatives;
> -it will be viewed in Japan as a real step forward leading to talks on the subject. [To demonstrate to Tokyo Moscow's seriousness,] the parameters of the formula will demonstrate readiness to work towards a peace treaty, will admit the existence of the territorial issue as an obstacle to it, will point out previous reassuring steps in this field.[9]

The document goes on to outline a variety of initiatives and solutions. First, it summarizes the two versions promoted by the Ministry of Foreign Affairs:

> First. Return to the conditions of the Joint Soviet-Japanese Declaration of 1956 ratified by the Supreme Soviet of the USSR, i.e., reiterate the pledge to return the islands of Habomai and Shikotan to Japan on signing the peace treaty (not discuss the problem of the two other islands).
>
> Second. Just recognize the territorial issue, but not go beyond. Express eagerness to develop economic, scientific and cultural activities in that region, and give visa-free treatment to Japanese citizens. But say that to settle the territorial issue, a new environment of trust is required.[10]

The document points out that this second version was very "close to the proposal submitted by the International Department of the

Central Committee, [namely to] take a flexible stand that will not preclude future initiatives. Demonstrate readiness to discuss the territorial issue but try to tie its solution to the evolution of relations."[11]

In his book on Soviet-Japanese relations, Aleksandr Panov, then deputy foreign minister, explains that these two plans had been drawn up between the end of November and the beginning of December. It was Panov's idea "to propose the two plans to the President and leave the choice to him."[12]

The document describes a third proposal, which it says is explained in a note by Gorbachev's economic adviser, Nikolai Petrakov. This option, the most radical of all, suggests that Moscow "recognize 'unconditionally and immediately' the sovereignty of Japan over all four islands." The document articulates the argument behind this position:

> Japanese demands are "fully legal and just," since they proceed from the *Russian-Japanese Agreements of 1855 and 1875*. Stalin annexed the islands. The fact of the annexation should be recognized and condemned which will ensure a breakthrough in relations. Japan and its grateful responsive public will open up towards the Soviet Union. Its economic assistance will help the Soviet state solve its numerous problems. Japan alone is able to provide "real money" on such a scale to insure serious help to the economy ($40–70–120 billion in the near future).[13]

The actual compromise contained in this third approach could be either of two options:

> . . . sign the peace treaty recognizing the sovereignty of Japan over the "northern territories" during the visit, while a special protocol should stipulate that actual submission will take place 10 years later, in the year 2000.
>
> Or: agree on the intentions of the parties to begin negotiations on the ways and timing of the actual transfer to take place at the end of the period of mutual utilization of the four islands, and on ensuring property and human right guarantees to the inhabitants of the islands even if they decide to relocate to Russia.[14]

Closely related to the third proposal was the fourth, identified in the document as coming from the Institute of World Economy and International Relations (IMEMO). It proposes returning to

Japan the Habomais and Shikotan (based on the 1956 Joint Declaration), with options concerning how to deal with Kunashiri and Etorofu:

> After recognition of the Soviet pledge on the Joint Declaration of 1956 concerning the return of the islands of Habomai and Shikotan to Japan, also agree to discuss the islands of Kunashir and Iturup in the course of the talks on the peace treaty or after signing it.
>
> Depending on the course of the talks, a variety of versions of the islands' status become a possibility, even submission of the latter two to Japan under specific conditions and with an obligatory time-span between transfers and, naturally, material compensation on the part of Japan.[15]

Proposal five is identified as that submitted by the participants in a situation analysis held at the Institute of Oriental Studies on December 13, 1990. This proposal suggests that Gorbachev:

> Reiterate the pledge in the Joint Declaration of 1956 and at the same time declare that Soviet rights to Kunashir and Iturup logically derive from the provisions of *the Yalta Conference and the San Francisco Treaty.*
>
> In case Japan begins to insist on the transfer of the islands, it is important to develop a framework for a joint Soviet-Japanese forum that will accommodate discussions of the issue and lead to its solution within the framework of the peace treaty.[16]

This section of the document ends with the statement that all of these proposals "contain elements of the formula that is most effective for Soviet interests, and which might satisfy, according to preliminary discussions, the Japanese side as well." It suggests that the formula might develop in the following way:

1. our [Soviet] recognition of the territorial question and readiness to discuss it;
2. recognition in principle of Japan's legitimate right to sovereignty over the four islands with the understanding that it does not mean the revision of the terms of World War II (the Japanese side will have to confirm the renunciation of its rights to the [rest of the] Kurile

Islands which Japan had received according to the terms of the treaty of 1875);

3. the transfer of the islands will require the consent of the inhabitants of the islands as well as that of the people of the Russian Federation; special conditions will have to be created to this end which will take some time, while the Japanese side should be prepared to provide significant material compensation and take responsibility for the development of wide-scale Soviet-Japanese economic cooperation;
4. the return of the islands should take place in stages, extending to the year 2000;
5. the concrete terms and status for the islands to be returned to be the subject of negotiations and special agreements.[17]

In short, this document is remarkable in the overall endorsement of the 1956 formula at the very least, as well as significant support for eventual return of all four islands.

The Summit: The Cherry Blossoms Wilt

The now well-known results of the long-awaited Tokyo summit between Gorbachev and Kaifu in April 1991 were a major disappointment for any who still hoped for a breakthrough in Soviet-Japanese relations. It was the breakdown of the "propitious" Soviet political environment that precluded any significant initiative on the territorial issue. By the time Gorbachev arrived in Tokyo, his political strength was at the lowest point since he took office. He believed, probably correctly, that any suggestion of giving away Soviet territory would be used by his political opponents as grounds for his removal from office. His opponents were at the two ends of the political spectrum: at one end, the military and civilian reactionaries, including the military-industrial complex, the KGB, and the Party hard-liners; at the other end, the new democrats, especially Boris Yeltsin.

Attack from the Right

The conservative forces had been the first to form a coalition, in the fall of 1990. Their grievances against Gorbachev were many, foremost among them being: the almost complete loss of power of the Communist Party and subsequently of their own status and perquisites; the substantially unilateral dismantling of the Soviet military; the growing economic crisis; the loss of Eastern Europe; the collapse of the Warsaw Pact; a united Germany in NATO; and the growing separatist sentiments in the Soviet republics. The first bold sign of Gorbachev's capitulation to these conservatives had been his decision to reject the Shatalin Plan in November. In the process, he betrayed his two most important allies in reform, Shevardnadze and Yakovlev, both of whom had been so important for the crafting of a new Japan policy, and both of whom resigned in December. The second sign of his growing dependence on the reactionaries was the decision to use force in Vilnius, Lithuania, on January 13, 1991, against a peaceful demonstration. The brutal killing of ten unarmed civilians was an astonishing act of Stalinism. Where these reactionaries stood on the question of the Kuriles had been blatantly revealed in the one-page letter to Gorbachev in March, signed by Vladimir Kriuchkov and Dmitrii Yazov, outlining all the reasons he must not give any territory back to Japan.

Attack from the Left

As severe as the attack from the conservatives had been, Gorbachev had weathered it by compromising and giving in to their demands. On the left, the liberal and reformist groups were outraged that Gorbachev had betrayed the Shatalin Plan, which they considered to be the only hope for the Soviet economy. Moreover, they saw through Gorbachev's attempt to hide behind a veil of ignorance and dodge responsibility for the bloodshed in Lithuania. Disgusted with Gorbachev's indecisiveness, weakness, and capitulation to the reactionaries, these democrats embraced Yeltsin as the new hero, the new promise for a democratic Russia.

Yeltsin had reemerged in political life fully recovered from his humiliation by Gorbachev at the Party plenum in 1987. He had campaigned for, and been elected, people's deputy, then president of the Supreme Soviet of the RSFSR, and finally the only leader in Russian history to ever stand for popular election, an achievement that stood in stark contrast to Gorbachev's failure to do the same.

Yeltsin was increasingly feeling the strength of his popularity and legitimacy, and was determined to block any initiative on Gorbachev's part that would help Gorbachev politically. Yeltsin challenged the legal authority of Moscow to transfer sovereignty of the islands, and stated on several occasions that any agreement negotiated by Gorbachev would not be acceptable without the participation of the Russian Republic government. For that reason, Gorbachev had invited Russian Foreign Minister Andrei Kozyrev and four other Russian Republic officials to accompany him to Tokyo. In January 1990 Yeltsin went to Japan and made a five-stage proposal concerning the islands. In August 1990, he visited Kunashiri, listened to the opposition of its residents, and then loudly opposed the return himself.

Having discovered that Gorbachev was close to making a deal with Ozawa over the Kurile Islands, Yeltsin was concerned that an infusion of Japanese aid would provide the safety net that Gorbachev needed. He thus enflamed Russian nationalist sentiments with statements exposing Gorbachev's intention to "sell Russian territory." He even went on television calling for Gorbachev's resignation. Some have suspected a direct link between Yeltsin and Anton Tarasov, a shady entrepreneur and people's deputy of the Russian congress, who published an inflammatory article in *Sovetskaia Rossiia* in 1991, claiming Gorbachev was about to sell the Kurile Islands for $200 billion.

Of all the factors constraining Gorbachev, most people who were close to the scene assert with confidence that Yeltsin was the most important. By April 1991, with the threat of the dissolution of the Soviet system and Soviet empire growing every day, Gorbachev was barely holding on to his own power. The one person who could claim popular legitimacy was clamoring to usurp what remained of Gorbachev's power. Any territorial concession on Gorbachev's part in April 1991 would surely have been the excuse Yeltsin was looking for.

Back to the Future

Gorbachev and his closest advisers had learned to look at Japan in a new way. Moreover, Gorbachev had encountered a sufficiently compelling reason to reverse the long-standing policy prohibiting ceding any Soviet territory. What he had lost was the political environment able to support and implement that policy reversal. In the process of dismantling a totalitarian system and establishing a more democratic one, Gorbachev no longer had in place a system he could control.

In the wake of the Tokyo summit, the state of the territorial issue between Moscow and Tokyo remained virtually unchanged, save for the fact that it had now been officially acknowledged by Moscow. Once again, Japan slipped off Gorbachev's agenda. The last Soviet leader turned his attention to more pressing matters, such as the question of the preservation of the Soviet Union, not to mention that of his own political power.

NOTES

1. For a fuller examination of this topic, see Lisbeth Tarlow Bernstein, "On the Rocks: Gorbachev and the Kurile Islands," (Ph.D. diss., The Fletcher School of Law and Diplomacy, 1997).
2. Gorbachev's new thinking on the Asia-Pacific region was expressed in what was considered at the time a major policy statement, his speech in Vladivostok on July 26, 1986. In addition, he included statements on the APR in several other official statements, including his Political Report to the 27th Party Congress on February 25, 1986; his Government Report of April 24, 1986; and his interview with the Indonesian newspaper *Merdeka* on July 21, 1987. Also, his book *Perestroika,* published in 1987, devoted four pages to "The Asia-Pacific Knot."
3. Vladimir Kontorovich and Michael Ellman, eds., *The Disintegration of the Soviet Economic System* (New York: Routledge, 1992), p. 1. See also Gertrude Schroeder, "The Soviet Economy and the Fate of the USSR," June 1997, unpubl.
4. Interview with Roald Sagdeev, July 9, 1993.
5. Ibid.
6. Ibid.
7. Preparatory Committee for the Presidential Visit to Japan, "Skhema podgotovki i provedeniia vizita prezidenta SSSR v Iaponiiu," unpublished manuscript
8. Ibid., p. 1.
9. Ibid.
10. Ibid., p. 2.
11. Ibid.
12. Aleksandr N. Panov, *Beyond Distrust to Trust: Inside the Northern Territories Talks With Japan,* [translation from the Japanese provided to the author by Futoshi Ogo], (Tokyo: Simul, 1992), p. 82.

Panov noted in his book that it was the second plan which was the one Gorbachev ultimately adopted at the summit.

13. Preparatory Committee for the Presidential Visit to Japan, "Skhema podgotovki i provedeniia vizita prezidenta SSSR v Iaponiiu," unpublished manuscript, pp. 2–3.
14. Ibid., p. 3.
15. Ibid. Identified by Alexei Zagorsky (interview November 1997) as the "Kunadze line."
16. Ibid. Identified by Alexei Zagorsky (interview November 1997) as the "Sarkisov line."
17. Ibid., p. 4.

CHAPTER 8

A Japanese View of Japanese-Russian Relations between the August 1991 Coup d'Etat and President Yeltsin's State Visit to Japan in October 1993

Ambassador Sumio Edamura

THIS REVIEW OF JAPANESE AND RUSSIAN RELATIONS during a critical period is based mainly on my personal experience as the Japanese ambassador in Moscow from June 1990 to January 1994. The history can be divided into several periods according to the vicissitudes seen in the relations. For each period I record in chronological order the important developments that took place and then add my comments on these.

Period prior to the Dissolution of the Soviet Union

Although the breakup of the Soviet Union did not occur until December 1991, I focus on the Russian Federation in the preceding two years in order to note continuities with later policies. The logical starting point is Yeltsin's proposal for "A Five-Stage Solution of the Northern Territorial Issue." Yeltsin visited Japan as a people's deputy of the Soviet Union in January 1990. On January 16, 1990, Yeltsin made a speech at the Asian Affairs Research Council in which he proposed to settle the territorial issue in five stages: (1) official recognition by the Soviet side of the existence of the dispute; (2) the four islands to be made a free enterprise zone open to the Japanese; (3) demilitarization of the four islands; (4) conclusion of a peace treaty as a concession by the Japanese side; and (5) a final resolution to be left to the next generation. Three possible alternatives were mentioned for the ultimate dispensation, offered without prejudice to a wiser solution by the coming generation: (1) a condominium would be formed by the Soviet Union and Japan; (2) the four islands would be made free and autonomous; and (3) their transfer to Japan would not be excluded.

This proposal was never given official status, even after Russia succeeded the Soviet Union. For example, it is not included in the collection of historical documents on the territorial issue jointly edited by the Japanese and Russian Foreign Ministries published in September 1992. But it was often referred to in meetings between Yeltsin and Japanese officials, and Yeltsin used it frequently as a point of reference to measure the progress in the negotiations on the territorial issue. The common Japanese reaction was that the major weak point of the proposal was deferral of the solution to the next generation. To this Yeltsin sometimes admitted that with improved circumstances the timing could be advanced.

In September 1991, after the failed August coup d'etat, Mr. Khasblatov, the acting speaker of the Supreme Soviet, visited Japan with President Yeltsin's personal letter dated September 4. While requesting Japan to extend contingency economic aid, this letter contained remarkably positive passages such as the following: "The positive changes in the world lead us all to a new international order where the distinction between the victorious nations and the defeated ones in the Second World War no longer exists. The Russian leadership is well aware how serious an obstacle the absence of a peace treaty has been for us all, and also how intolerably slow have been the steps taken in the past by both sides for its conclusion."

"The Russian people, who stood up to defend democracy, legality and justice in the days of the coup d'etat, shall act also according to those permanent values when they seek to resolve the difficult problems in relations with Japan."

Mr. Khasblatov's report on his visit to the Presidium of the Supreme Soviet contained interesting views regarding the relationship between the territorial issue and Russian public opinion. It mentioned that while the Soviet government referred to public opinion as an absolute obstacle to the solution of the problem, the Russian Government did not exclude the possibility that there might be a change in the prevailing public opinion. The report proposed that it was indispensable to make known the real essence of the territorial issue, based in an objective and unbiased interpretation, to the people's deputies and the Russian people.

On October 8, the Japanese Government announced an aid package to the Soviet Union of 2.5 billion dollars. Japan was keen to sustaining the momentum with both the Soviet Union and the Russian Federation that was building since the failed coup. On October 14, Foreign Minister Pankin of the Soviet Union in his talk with Foreign Minister Nakayama in Moscow proposed that the Soviet and Japanese Foreign Ministries should work together to edit a collection of historical documents on the territorial issue, which should help enlighten the public opinion. At this meeting an agreement on mutual visits without a visa for Russian islanders and Japanese citizens was signed.

On November 16, President Yeltsin's letter to Russian nationals was made public. It contained the following passage: "From the viewpoint of Russian national interests, I firmly believe that it is impermissible to continue to be indulgent with a situation where, because of the absence of a peace treaty with Japan, our bilateral relations remain in fact frozen."

In short, this period in 1991 is characterized by positive and friendly rhetoric, particularly on the part of the Russian Federation. The Japanese side reciprocated with equally forthcoming statements.

Period from the Dissolution of the Soviet Union to the Supreme Soviet Hearing

On December 27, 1991, immediately after the dissolution of the Soviet Union, the Japanese ambassador called on Foreign Minister Kozyrev to deliver Prime Minister Miyazawa's formal letter addressed to President Yeltsin. The letter recognized Russia as a state with the continued and identical statehood as the Soviet Union, and confirmed the Japanese understanding that all treaties and other international agreements that had existed between Japan and the Soviet Union including the Japan–Soviet Union Joint Declaration of 1956 remained valid between Japan and Russia. Kozyrev thanked Japan for its recognition and verbally agreed to the Japanese understanding.

Foreign Minister Watanabe Michio attended the ministerial-level conference held on January 22, 1992, in Washington to coordinate international efforts to assist the countries of the former Soviet Union. The Japanese delegation was active at the conference, promising a grant in aid of $50 million in addition to the already announced aid package. In his speech, the foreign minister referred to three criteria—political, economic and international—in determining future Japanese assistance. These criteria were identical to those announced at the time of the London Summit the previous summer, during the era of the Soviet Union. This appears to have aroused a certain amount of disillusionment in some quarters in Moscow.

Prime Minister Miyazawa and President Yeltsin first met on January 31 in New York on the occasion of the summit-level meeting of the UN Security Council. Foreign Minister Watanabe visited Moscow at the end of January 1992 to attend a conference on the Middle East, but was not received by Yeltsin. On February 27, Liudvig Chizhov, the Russian ambassador in Tokyo, delivered to the Japanese Government President Yeltsin's personal letter to Prime Minister Miyazawa. This letter contained the following passages (the translation is unofficial):

> Russia as a sovereign state now regards Japan as a partner and potential ally bound by common permanent human values.
>
> Respecting consistently law and justice, we are determined to continue to search together for a solution to the problem of the conclusion of a peace treaty, including the aspect of the demarcation of the frontier.

The next day Kato Koichi, cabinet secretary, issued a statement welcoming the positive contents of the presidential letter.

On February 10 and 11 the first session of the Japan-Russia Working Group on a Peace Treaty was held in Moscow (the Japan-Soviet Working Group had met eight times). From March 19 through March 22, Foreign Minister Kozyrev visited Japan for the first Japan-Russia regular foreign ministers' meeting. Even though what was truly discussed at these meetings has still been kept ambiguous, it would be natural to assume that, in accordance with the letter and spirit of the presidential letter, serious explorations had been made on these occasions in search of a breakthrough on the territorial issue. As Russian recognition of the 1956 Joint Declaration had already been taken for granted, additional concessions must have been sought. Although the Japanese traditional position had been a comprehensive solution with the simultaneous transfer of all four islands, the possibility of departure from this traditional position may have been explored.

Apart from the debate on the territorial issue, it is known that the Russian side demanded repeal of the principle of no separation between politics and economics for the success of the president's visit to Japan. There was a shared expectation that the presidential visit would take place probably in September 1992. On April 18, Foreign Minister Watanabe made a speech to his constituency in Tochigi Prefecture, in which he mentioned that if Russia recognized Japanese sovereignty over the four islands, the continuation of Kunashiri and Etorofu under Russian administration for a limited period might be acceptable.

The exchange of visits without visas between the islanders and Japanese citizens started around this time. The first visit by islanders to Hokkaido took place in April, and Japanese people visited the islands in May. Both visits were carried out successfully in a friendly atmosphere.

By this time Oleg Rumyantsev, a deputy of the Supreme Soviet and the secretary of the Commission on the Constitution, started to write articles in the Russian press opposing the "cession of Russian territories." He voiced openly his suspicion that the Ministry of Foreign Affairs was engaged in a secret deal with the Japanese government to sell out the four islands. In response, the Russian Ministry of Foreign Affairs reacted also through the press, sometimes under the pseudonym of "Sergei Smolensky," refuting point by point Rumyantsev's mainly legal arguments against the solution of the territorial problem. The April 25 issue of *Nezavisimaia gazeta* carried another article by "Sergei Smolensky" with the headline "Progress in Russo-Japanese Relations Now Depends on the Russian Leadership—Diplomatic steps for the solution of the Kurile problem have already been exhausted." The article took the guise of clearing away the suspicion of a secret deal voiced by Rumyantsev, on the grounds that in the absence of a clear directive by the Russian leadership the Ministry was unable to strike any deal. The true purpose of the article, however, appeared to be to urge the president to make a political decision for an early solution of the territorial issue.

Foreign Minister Watanabe visited Moscow and was received by President Yeltsin on May 4. The meeting was cordial, and the president indicated the concrete dates of his planned official visit to Japan. He would arrive in Tokyo on September 13 and would spend the 14th and 15th in meetings with Japanese leaders. But when Watanabe inquired about the president's thinking on the territorial issue, Yeltsin evaded a direct answer, stating that he had not yet discussed it even with his own foreign minister. He mentioned that there was some progress on the problem in accordance with his "five-stage proposal," referring to the planned reduction of armed forces stationed on the islands. (The third stage of the proposal stipulated the demilitarization of the islands.) He stressed at the same time the difficulty of the issue owing to the delicate public opinion at a time when Russia was experiencing hardships.

The first public sign of the president's irritation toward Japan was observed on June 30 at the time of his televised telephone interview with readers of *Komsomolskaia pravda.* He criticized Japan for linking economic cooperation to the solution of the Kurile problem, and attacked Japan for having "invested" not one cent in Russia, using the phrase "Zero from Japan."

On July 8, President Yeltsin was invited to a session with G-7 leaders on the occasion of the Munich Summit. The political declaration issued by the G-7 leaders contained the following paragraph:

> We welcome Russia's commitment to a foreign policy based on the principle of law and justice. We believe that this represents a basis for full normalization of the Russo-Japanese relationship through resolving the territorial issue.

Yeltsin and his close circle criticized Japan for having internationalized the bilateral issue. This was echoed by nationalistic deputies in the Supreme Soviet, who attacked the Russian Ministry of Foreign Affairs for failing to block the internationalization of the problem. Tension surrounding the problem reached a peak on July 28, when Rumyantsev convened a closed-door hearing at the Supreme Soviet. It was rumored that he had two aims in mind when he convened the hearing. One was to block the announced presidential visit to Japan. The other was to force Kunadze and other members of the "pro-Japan lobby" in the Ministry of Foreign Affairs to resign.

Papers submitted at this hearing included those from Rumyantsev himself, Kunadze, a separate one on behalf of the Ministry of Foreign Affairs, the Institute of World Economy and International Relations, the Fisheries Commission, and the General Staff of the Russian Armed Forces, among others. Kunadze's paper included the following points: (a) by handling the territorial issue in accordance with the principle of law and justice, Russia will be able to secure support for its position from Western countries; (b) the 1956 Joint Declaration is valid for Russia as a state succeeding the Soviet Union, with the obligation for Russia to hand over eventually Habomai and Shikotan to Japan: (c) no legally recognized frontier existed between Russia and Japan, and international law obliges the two countries to resolve their conflicting claims on the four islands through negotiations. The Foreign Ministry's paper contained the following points: (a) the Russian official position is still identical with the Soviet one, which clearly could not be a basis for negotiations with Japan for the conclusion of a peace treaty; (b) the approach to the territorial issue should be based on President Yeltsin's letter of November 1991. The positions of other government agencies generally opposed territorial concessions to Japan. A split within the Russian government surfaced clearly at this time.

Reviewing this half-year period, we see that Foreign Minister Kozyrev's reaction to Prime Minister Miyazawa's letter of December 1991, as well as President Yeltsin's message to Miyazawa of February 1992, were encouraging for the Japanese side. They were interpreted as clear signals that the now full-fledged sovereign Russia would seriously tackle the territorial issue for its final resolution in accordance with the principles of law and justice. They must have been equally encouraging for Russian negotiators within the Ministry of Foreign Affairs. In this favorable mood the Japanese and Russian negotiators apparently achieved through their contacts in February and March a considerable degree of meeting of minds for further progress.

The problem for the Russian negotiators was their failure to obtain a clear directive from the president beyond those nice and forthcoming words contained in presidential messages. "Smolensky's" open appeal to the president showed how desperately they needed such a directive. Indeed, the lack of communication between the Presidency and the Ministry of Foreign Affairs was a perennial problem throughout my tenure as ambassador.

In the meantime, the territorial dispute became a subject of open controversy in Russia, with the risk of rekindling nationalistic sentiment. The problem clearly acquired a national dimension. Some Russians question whether it was wise for the Russian negotiators to engage in an open and public debate with people like Rumyantsev because it might have had the effect of unnecessarily antagonizing the Supreme Soviet against the Ministry of Foreign Affairs. Sometimes it was alleged that certain steps taken by the Japanese side helped exacerbate the situation. The reference to the three criteria for Japanese aid at the Washington conference, Foreign Minister Watanabe's Tochigi speech, which deepened the suspicion of a secret deal, and the publicity given to the Japanese efforts to solicit other G-7 members' consent to the inclusion of a passage on the territorial issue in the political declaration at the Munich Summit were cited as examples.

The President's statement "Zero from Japan" was, of course, a product of misunderstanding. Shokhin, the Deputy Prime Minister for Economics, apparently had submitted to the President a list of foreign credits on a disbursement basis. No disbursement of Japanese Exim Bank credits had been effected by that date, owing to Russian bureaucratic tardiness, while Japanese grant aids were being disbursed. The first batch of Japanese credits started to be disbursed in the fall of 1992 right after the postponement of the presidential visit to Japan. The public show of Presidential ire toward Japan must have been a tremendous encouragement for those opposed to conciliation with Japan, particularly in the circle close to the President.

The closed-door hearing produced neither of the feared consequences. No recommendation for cancellation of the presidential visit prevailed. Demand for the dismissal of officials of the Foreign Ministry was not raised or not heeded. Nonetheless, it proved that even within the government there was considerable resistance to the accommodation with Japan. Widespread reporting on the hearing may have further aroused nationalistic sentiment against a territorial concession.

The Russian Ministry of Foreign Affairs, supported by such people as researchers at the Institute of World Economy and International Relations, upheld its basic stance in favor of an early solution of the issue on the basis of relevant international agreements. This was encouraging, of course, but it was clearly not yet the prevailing opinion in the government. Neither was it clear whether it enjoyed the support of the President.

Period around the Postponement of President Yeltsin's Visit

In August two Russian high officials considered to be close to the President visited Japan: Deputy Prime Minister Poltranin in charge of press and information, and Petrov, Secretary General of the Presidential Office. They were both received in Tokyo by the Prime Minister and Foreign Minister. They brought totally conflicting messages. Poltranin was very understanding of the Japanese position. He even went to Okinawa with the avowed aim of studying in situ possible problems pertaining to the territorial transfer. In his memoir *Transformation,* Kozyrev criticizes Poltranin's behavior during his stay in Japan for inciting Russian public opinion. Petrov, in contrast, took an extremely harsh attitude, denying the possibility that the President, during his forthcoming visit, would go so far as to recognize the validity of the territorial clauses in the 1956 Joint Declaration.

No disposition was visible on the part of Russian economic ministries to make the necessary arrangements for early disbursement of committed Japanese assistance, in spite of repeated urgings by the Japanese Embassy at various levels. No viable initiative for widening the scope of economic cooperation was forthcoming from the Russian side. In short, no enthusiasm was noticeable in the Russian economic ministries to make their own President's visit a success.

At the end of August Foreign Minister Watanabe arrived in Moscow for final preparations for the presidential visit. He met Foreign Minister Kozyrev on September 1. Kozyrev appreciated the flexibility shown by Watanabe as to the handling of the territorial issue at the time of the President's visit. The next day Burbulis, State Secretary and Chairman of the Commission for the Preparation of the Presidential Visit, even more enthusiastically received Watanabe's expose. He said "I support your approach whole-heartedly as an approach both constructive and flexible for the solution of the territorial problem." But Yeltsin's reception of Watanabe was less than cordial at the meeting that took place only one hour after the meeting with Burbulis. Yeltsin complained of Japan's negative attitude regarding assistance to Russia, and dismissed Watanabe's proposal on the territorial issue as nothing new. In response to Watanabe's inquiry, Yeltsin said that he would make known his position on the problem only after he had arrived in Japan. Later on September 6, in an interview with a Japanese audience by television transmission, Yeltsin said that he had in hand 14 proposals regarding the territorial issue, but had not yet decided which to choose.

Around this time some visible signs were noticed that disinformation regarding the stability of Miyazawa's cabinet and the Japanese political situation in general was being circulated within the Russian government, including the circle close to the President. On September 3, the Security Office of the Presidential Office issued a public statement that Japanese security authorities did not sufficiently guarantee the President's personal security, so that cancellation of the planned visit might have to be recommended. On September 9, only three days prior to the planned date of his arrival, Yeltsin telephoned Prime Minister Miyazawa to propose the postponement of his visit. He cited both the Russian situation and the Japanese situation as reasons for his decision. Miyazawa rejected the reference to the Japanese situation as a reason for this decision. Yeltsin acknowledged that he had no "pretenziya" against Japan, repeatedly assuring Miyazawa that it was only a postponement and not a cancellation.

On the basis of these assurances the Japanese government decided to handle the matter with restraint, and not change its policy toward Russia, including aid to that country. But within the Japanese political circle there was a demand for harsher measures in light of this shameful discourtesy. On September 12, the Japanese Ambassador called on Foreign Minister Kozyrev in Moscow, and Kozyrev proposed that both governments should refrain from recriminations against each other over this incident. The Japanese Ambassador replied that the Japanese Government was already acting with restraint and agreed to Kozyrev's proposal. He called the Foreign Minister's attention to the fact that the Russian President, contrary to his personal assurances to the Japanese Prime Minister, had made accusatory statements, holding "Japanese stubborn attitudes" responsible for the postponement.

In clear breach of the above agreement, Russian efforts to accuse Japan openly persisted, spearheaded by Kostikov, the President's Press Secretary. Papers with distorted information were circulated to Japanese correspondents stationed in Moscow. One such paper was reprinted in part as a reliable document in a prestigious weekly on international affairs and was published by a Japanese news agency. The original version of the paper contained such calumnies as "Watanabe was not a wise diplomat" or "Miyazawa was drunk when Yeltsin tried to telephone him." As seen in this example, the Japanese press was not sufficiently alerted to the danger of a disinformation campaign.

Ambassador Bob Strauss of the United States was quoted by Kostikov as having told Yeltsin that the U.S. government understood the reasons behind the decision to postpone the visit and that it was a wise decision. To my inquiry Ambassador Strauss evaded a direct answer, but admitted at least that he had used the word "understand" in his conversation with Yeltsin. A similar attribution was made to Prime Minister Kohl of Germany, with whom Yeltsin had a telephone conversation. In this case the German spokesman quickly denied the accuracy of the attribution.

On October 29 and 30, the third round of the international conference to coordinate aid to CIS countries was held in Tokyo, as a follow-up of those held in Washington and Lisbon. Shokhin, the chief Russian delegate, when received by Prime Minister Miyazawa, asked whether President Yeltsin would be invited to the G-7 Tokyo Summit scheduled for the next summer. Miyazawa replied flatly that he understood, as Yeltsin had indicated, that for now he did not wish to come to Japan.

In this period, the confusion seen in the attitudes of high officials regarding the territorial issue was due to their different interpretations of the President's thinking on it. For instance, it was clear from my own conversation with Poltranin at Sheremetevo Airport that he went to Tokyo convinced that the President would take bold action in support of the solution of the problem. Kozyrev, referring to such confusion, admits in his memoirs that there were no proper preparations, on the Russian part, to make the presidential visit a success.

The confusion seen in the Russian Government, together with the absence of a clear reaction from the President himself, had led the Japanese government to believe that the Russian Ministry of Foreign Affairs did not control the situation, and that the attempt to work out a viable scenario, as pursued with the Russian negotiators from February and March of that year, would not prevail. The mounting sensitivity seen in the Russian mass media also advised caution rather than boldness. By the end of August, therefore, it was decided that the Japanese government should take a flexible attitude regarding the territorial issue, not expecting too much of the coming presidential visit. This flexibility, shown by Watanabe during his visit to Moscow in September 1991, was properly understood and appreciated by both Kozyrev and Burbulis, but rejected as nothing new by Yeltsin. There is some evidence that the President and his close circle were already affected by the disinformation campaign by this time.

Probably motives of the disinformation campaign were twofold. One was political, based on the conviction that it was in the Russian national interest to obstruct the presidential visit, and prevent possible concessions on the territorial issue. The other was sychophantic. Many people by that time must have come to realize that Yeltsin was more and more irritated with the state of relations with Japan and had started to regard his planned visit to Japan as an onerous burden. It should please Yeltsin if justifiable causes were produced to rid him of this unpleasant burden. In his memoir, *Romance with the President,* Kostikov describes quite vividly President Yeltsin's agony trapped between his desire to show a progressive posture in foreign policy and his fear of possible adverse reaction any concession to Japan could trigger.

Who were responsible for this disinformation campaign is not clear, but it is obvious that, at least at that time in Russia, there were institutions with the capacity inherited from the KGB to carry it out effectively. Those institutions must have been able to execute the operation unobstructed by any branch of the government, including the President. Alexandr Yakovlev writes in his memoirs that Gorbachev as well as Yeltsin were preferred targets of disinformation.

The Japanese Government reacted to this disinformation with remarkable restraint. In particular, it was admirable that Foreign Minister Watanabe, toward whom much of the defamation was directed, maintained his composure and utterly ignored the cowardly calumnies.

With all the restraint, however, it was clearly embarrassing for the Japanese government, as seen in Miyazawa's reaction to Shokhin's inquiry, to invite Yeltsin to the G-7 Tokyo Summit when there were no visible Russian efforts to repair the bilateral relations badly damaged by the sudden cancellation of the state visit. It was assumed on the other hand that Yeltsin, ever so sensitive to any pressure, would not tolerate that his participation in the Summit be made conditional to a reconciliatory move on the bilateral issue. Thus, a mood of stagnation prevailed in the fall and winter of 1992–1993.

Period Leading to the Tokyo Summit

Starting in early 1993, however, frequent contacts were held between the Japanese and Russian Ministries of Foreign Affairs to find a way out of this entanglement. In the middle of January the Foreign Ministers exchanged views while attending the international conference for the signing of the treaty banning chemical weapons. In February Matsunaga Nobuo, former Ambassador to the United States and a Government Representative with quasi-ministerial rank, visited Moscow unofficially. Through these contacts there emerged a kind of understanding between the two Foreign Ministries that each party would take a seemingly spontaneous step to break the impasse. The Japanese Prime Minister would make a statement to the effect that Japan would invite Yeltsin, regardless of the state of affairs in bilateral relations. President Yeltsin would state that he would promptly dispatch his Foreign Minister to Tokyo to start anew the preparations for the presidential visit.

By the end of February Japanese officials quickly obtained the Prime Minister's authorization for this operation and tried to coordinate the timing of the execution with the Russian side. Time passed without a clear reaction from the Russian side. It was not clear whether Kozyrev really talked to Yeltsin on this understanding. But the schedule of preparations for the Summit warranted no more delay; so the Japanese Government decided to proceed unilaterally.

On March 27, Mr. Matsunaga, who visited Moscow this time officially as Government Representative, was received by President Yeltsin, and delivered the Prime Minister's letter inviting Yeltsin to the 7+1 session at the time of the Tokyo Summit. Yeltsin accepted the invitation with thanks, and stated that he wished to realize the postponed state visit at the earliest possible opportunity. On April 1, furthermore, Prime Minister Miyazawa stated at a press conference that the invitation to President Yeltsin to the Tokyo Summit would be extended without linking it to any aspect of bilateral relations. Kozyrev visited Japan with Boris Fyodorov to attend the joint conference of G-7 Foreign and Finance Ministers in the middle of April. On this occasion a bilateral talk between the Foreign Ministers was held, and preparations for the President's state visit were resumed.

On July 8, Yeltsin arrived at Tokyo's Haneda Airport to take part in the Summit. In his statement on arrival, he mentioned, after offering thanks for Japanese support for Russian reform, the following, which was meant to be an apology for the sudden postponement of the previous year's planned state visit. "It was regrettable that the visit planned for September last year could not be implemented. I would like to thank the Government and people of Japan for their understanding of the situation which prevented the visit being carried out as scheduled. This postponed visit shall be realized without fail."

At the meeting held on July 8 between Miyazawa and Yeltsin it was provisionally agreed that the postponed state visit would take place from October 12 to 14. At this summit meeting in Tokyo no attempt was made to include reference in the political declaration to the Northern Territorial question, but an alternative arrangement was reached at the beginning of the 7+1 session when President Clinton reviewed the international situation. In this statement he requested Russia to overcome difficult problems inherited from the past through the execution of foreign policy based on international law and justice. He added that the full normalization of Japanese-Russian relations would be an important step in that direction.

President Yeltsin appeared to be content with all of the arrangements for his participation in the Summit meeting, including the handling of bilateral relations with Japan. He confided to former Prime Minister Nakasone that he was pleasantly surprised to see no sign of anti-Yeltsin calls during his stay in Tokyo.

As seen above, coordination of the timing of the spontaneous statements did not work well, again because of the lack of communication between the President and the Foreign Ministry. The President, for instance, did not understand properly the purport of Miyazawa's April 1 statement, which meant no linkage between the invitation to the Summit and the bilateral issues. He apparently understood it as a declaration to abandon the policy of linking politics and economics, and, at a banquet held in the Kremlin on April

9, he openly reproved the new Japanese Foreign Minister Muto Kabun for having made remarks contravening Miyazawa's statement. It was appropriately refuted by the Japanese Ambassador on the spot.

Before going to Tokyo for the Summit meeting, President Yeltsin approved the inclusion of an apology in his arrival statement at Haneda. The idea of an apology on arrival had been discussed through diplomatic channels, and some Japanese, including former Prime Minister Nakasone, had personally advised Yeltsin to do so.

The Japanese Government, as the host of the Summit meeting, of course, carried on the necessary coordination with the other G-7 partners, especially with the United States, regarding Russian participation, including the handling of the Northern Territorial issue. The U.S. government showed a readiness to help Japan's efforts to maintain its basic position without embarrassing Yeltsin publicly. President Clinton's statement in the 7+1 session reflected this readiness to help. In the process, Ambassadors Talbott and Pickering were particularly helpful.

Yeltsin's admission to Nakasone that he had expected an openly hostile reception in Japan shows that Yeltsin had still been under the effect of disinformation at that time. "Seeing is believing." It is probable that with this visit to Tokyo on the occasion of the Summit, Yeltsin's feeling toward Japan became more reasonable.

Period Surrounding Yeltsin's State Visit to Japan

Despite the domestic political tension caused by the open confrontation between the President and the Parliament, preparations for the state visit planned for October continued between the Foreign Ministries of the two countries. Eighteen documents were readied to be signed at the time of the visit. Complying with the Russian request, an economic declaration was to be issued separately from the main political declaration. Japanese aid, including humanitarian aid and aid related to nuclear problems, had started to be disbursed.

On the morning of October 5, immediately following the surrender of the rebel forces on the 4th, the President's office made an announcement that the visit to Japan would take place as planned from October 11 through 13. The reaction in Tokyo to this announcement was generally cool. Some influential newspapers argued in their editorials that the visit should be deferred until the political situation in Russia became calmer. The Liberal Democratic Party, which had become an opposition party after the defeat in the general elections in July, but still held the largest number of seats in the parliament, issued a, on the whole, rational statement concerning the visit. But within the party there were voices that were very critical of Yeltsin's handling of the disturbances in Moscow, especially the shelling of the parliamentary building. Even within the coalition government, headed by Hosokawa Morihiro, there was an uncomfortable feeling to have to welcome Yeltsin so soon after the "bloodshed." The dominant view in Tokyo was that the visit was being utilized to serve Yeltsin's political purpose, namely to demonstrate the stability of his administration, despite the gravity of the recent disturbances.

The visit, however, proceeded smoothly without any visible show of hostility. At his meeting with the Emperor, Yeltsin unexpectedly apologized for the illegal and inhuman detention of Japanese soldiers in Siberia. At the luncheon with economic and financial circles Yeltsin again interrupted his speech to lower his head for 30 seconds to apologize for the inhuman act. At the state dinner hosted by the Emperor Yeltsin changed the prepared text to strengthen the words of apology for the same incident.

At the end of the visit the "Tokyo Declaration" was issued. The second paragraph of the Declaration, which deals with the territorial issue, reads as follows:

2. The Prime Minister of Japan and the President of the Russian Federation, sharing the recognition that the difficult legacies of the past in the relations between the two countries must be overcome, have undertaken serious negotiations on the issue of where Etorofu, Kunashiri, Shikotan and Habomai Islands belong. They agree that the negotiations towards an early conclusion of the peace treaty through the solution of this issue on the basis of historical and legal facts and based on the documents produced with the two countries' agreement as well as on the principles of law and justice should continue, and that the relations between the two countries should thus be normalized. In this regard, the Government of Japan and the Government of the Russian Federation confirm that the Russian Federation is the state retaining continued identity with the Soviet

Union and that all treaties and other international agreements between Japan and the Soviet Union continue to be applicable between Japan and the Russian Federation.

At the press conference after the signing ceremony, when a question was asked as to whether the phrase "all treaties and other international agreements . . . continue to be applicable" included the Japan-Soviet Joint Declaration of 1956, Yeltsin answered affirmatively. On October 13 at noon Moscow time on the day of Yeltsin's departure, Ostankino TV broadcast these words by him. "This was the first substantial summit-level meeting held between Russia and Japan. We discussed all the problems existing between our two countries as well as international problems of our mutual concern. I am personally satisfied, and I believe that this visit has been a great success."

Given the overwhelming importance of the "Tokyo Declaration," it is worth focusing on the analysis of paragraph 2, which deals with the territorial issue. It sets forth three criteria on which the solution of the territorial issue should be based: "historical and legal facts," "the documents produced with the two countries' agreement," and "the principles of law and justice."

What is meant by "historical and legal facts"? In this connection it is significant that later in the same paragraph there is a specific reference to the Joint Compendium jointly published by the Japanese and Russian Ministries of Foreign Affairs in September 1992. The Compendium comprises the following instructions of Nicholas I to Admiral Putyatin in 1853: "The southernmost end of the Kurile Islands which belong to Russia is Uruppu, . . . for Japan the northern tip of Etorofu Island shall be their frontier." It also comprises Article 2 of the Japan-Russian Treaty of Commerce and Amity, which reads "Hereinafter, the frontier between Japan and Russia shall lie between Etorofu Island and Uruppu Island." The second paragraph of the preface of the Joint Compendium, supposedly based on these historical and legal facts, records the view shared by the Japanese and Russian Foreign Ministries that the frontier between Etorofu and Uruppu was peacefully demarcated.

As to "the documents produced with the two countries' agreement," it is confirmed that "the Russian Federation is the state retaining continuing identity with the Soviet Union and that all treaties and other international agreements between Japan and the Soviet Union continue to be applied between Japan and the Russian

Federation." Furthermore, as mentioned above, President Yeltsin confirmed at a press conference that the Joint Declaration of 1956 was included in "all treaties and other international agreements" which continue to be applied between Japan and Russia. "The principles of law and justice" require no elaboration, but they carry special weight because they have often been mentioned by President Yeltsin as a guiding concept for Japanese-Russian relations.

As seen above, the "Tokyo Declaration" laid down quite a positive foundation for solving the territorial issue, but its significance has not been fully appreciated by the mass media and opinion leaders of Japan. There are even some who mistakenly assume that the Japanese side was rejected in pressing for recognition of the 1956 Declaration at the time of Yeltsin's visit. This misunderstanding may result from the negative feeling with which Yeltsin's visit, in the midst of the highly unstable political situation in Russia in October 1993, was received in Japan. This feeling was perpetuated by the results of the parliamentary elections held not long after the visit. The large number of votes garnered by communists and rightists was interpreted as a sign of continued political instability in Russia, which would not allow Yeltsin to take positive steps in relations with Japan. In reality, Yeltsin at the time of his visit was at the peak of his power, following the liquidation of the undemocratic and reactionary forces. He was in a position to be able to carry out foreign policy based on the principles of law and justice in relations with Japan. Even after the parliamentary election reverses, he maintained wide freedom of action in foreign policy thanks to the strong and almost exclusive powers granted to the presidency by the new Constitution.

Epilogue

I may be wrong, but I have the feeling that a kind of fatigue prevailed after the sudden postponement of Yeltsin's visit in 1992 among those Russian negotiators and opinion leaders who had worked hard with the aim of bringing about an early resolution of the territorial issue. In spite of this fatigue, they had continued to work courageously to bring about the successful visit in 1993. In their mind, however, the memory of the frustration in 1992 appears to dominate over the pride in what they achieved in 1993. Some of them even confided that they had been too naive and romantic at the start of the Yeltsin administration.

This disillusionment in Russia and the lack of understanding in Japan, coupled with the volatile political situation in both Russia and Japan, induced relations to fall into a state of "dormancy" for the following two or three years. Recently, however, there have been a number of encouraging signs that the Japanese and Russian governments have started a serious attempt to advance relations on the basis of the "Tokyo Declaration." The participation of Russia as a full member in annual summit meetings makes it appear almost grotesque that two partners in the highest forum of world democracies are incapable of liquidating the unlawful state of affairs existing between them. Apparently a chance has come again for a successful breakthrough in Japanese and Russian relations, with a solution of the territorial issue based on the principles of law and justice.

In my view the overwhelming determinant in Japanese-Russian relations in the period under review was President Yeltsin's personality. He is endowed with all the necessary qualifications to be a powerful leader of a great nation, but there is no denying also that his behavior on occasion created an impression that he is authoritarian and unpredictable. In relations with Japan, also, it often appeared that there was little that Russian negotiators could do to influence Yeltsin's decisions, and the formation of those decisions was often left to chance. Japan's ability to influence the president's determination was at best indirect and limited. Nevertheless, I have always believed that President Yeltsin's basic orientation is democratic and internationalist and he has a genuine desire to improve relations with Japan via a resolution of the territorial problem. We have seen this basic orientation surface whenever he felt that he had good control of the situation in Russia.

Lest the chance that has come around again be missed, I would stress the following seven steps that past lessons advise us to take in order to achieve a final resolution of the territorial issue through a conclusion of a peace treaty based on the "Tokyo Declaration:" (1) development of trust between the leaders of the two countries through frequent contacts and careful checking of each other's true intentions before reacting to press reports; (2) better coordination within the government, in the Russian case especially between the Presidency and the Ministry of Foreign Affairs; (3) conscious efforts to eliminate adverse feeling in the public toward the other country, through leaders refraining from careless remarks, and promoting mutual understanding of the need to establish bilateral relations firmly based on the "Tokyo Declaration;" (4) better control in Russia of state institutions capable of disseminating disinformation; (5) enhanced assistance by Japan for Russia's own efforts to establish strong democratic institutions and to achieve prosperity under a market economy in order to reduce the risk of obstruction by undemocratic forces of an improvement in bilateral relations, including a final resolution of the territorial problem; (6) intensified intercourse with the current residents on the four islands, with active Japanese participation in projects designed to improve their well-being and reduce their anxiety over the future; and (7) understanding and encouragement on the part of the other G-8 partners for an early elimination of this ugly and unlawful legacy of the unfortunate past between their two partners. In particular, the United States could play a role, whenever appropriate, to smooth dialogue between Russia and Japan, while respecting always the essentially bilateral nature of the issues they are addressing.

Note: The text of this chapter was written in the Summer of 1997.

CHAPTER 9

A Russian View of Russo-Japanese Relations, 1991–1993

Deputy Foreign Minister
Georgi Kunadze*

IN THE DEVELOPMENT OF RELATIONS BETWEEN RUSSIA and Japan many vague perceptions still persist. For several decades, starting from the mid-1950s, scholars, politicians, and journalists have continued to discuss ways of improving relations between the USSR (to become Russia in 1992) and Japan. While many proposals were put forward, none of them succeeded. On the surface, the reason for this lack of progress can be explained by the territorial dispute that remained unresolved through all these years. But this is only a partial explanation. After all, Japan used to have or still has territorial disputes with other neighbors and partners (the United States, South Korea, China), and has never let them get out of control to become serious stumbling blocks in its bilateral relations. We have to look more closely at the real nature of the dispute between Russia and Japan in order to appreciate why the clash over four disputed islands has gained such prominence.

Well-recognized limits have always existed in Soviet-Japanese relations. To a very great extent, these limits derived from the cold war and the bipolar structure of international affairs. To be sure, the territorial dispute has been a plus alpha element in the strained bilateral relationship, but the dispute has more reflected and flavored the enmity than actually shaped it. Indeed, the territorial issue or rather the desire to settle it has encouraged Japan to seek a certain accommodation with the USSR, if only on a limited scale. Ironic as it may appear, the territorial issue has, in this way, played a positive role in the relationship.

The most interesting question is whether settlement of the territorial issue would have led to genuine improvement in relations. By definition, issues between governments are of a political nature. They are negotiated and settled not on the merit of legal arguments alone; political considerations of both sides are always involved and normally prevail. The settlement of any territorial issue brings politics directly into play, requiring both sides to make concessions and thus retreat from their opening positions in order to reach a compromise, or necessitating that one side alone totally surrender its position. In the former case each government would have to explain to its own people the reasons for such a retreat, the motives behind the compromise. Not everyone would be persuaded. Some would be tempted to exploit the compromise to attack the government. The settlement of the territorial dispute would become an issue in domestic politics, hampering implementation of the agreed formula and, not infrequently, triggering a hostile public reaction toward the other negotiating party.

In the latter case, the government that surrendered its position would be engulfed by a full-scale crisis and would ultimately face an almost impossible task of demonstrating to its people the benefits commensurate with the loss brought about by the surrender. Naturally, these benefits would have to be furnished mainly by the other party. As in the former scenario, the sequence could well become: explanation of the results of negotiations, exploitation of the results for political ends, problems in implementation, and mutual bitterness. Therefore, speaking hypothetically, settlement of a territorial dispute either by compromise or by the surrender of one side does not necessarily lead to an improvement in relations. What is more, in the absence of other important ingredients such a settlement may turn out to be a dead end, and may even result in worse rather than better relations. The type of political regime matters. Territorial disputes between democratic countries have very little chance of settlement unless widespread understanding and support by the general public are secured in advance. On the contrary, totalitarian regimes are inherently better equipped to settle such disputes since they are virtually free from public control and therefore capable of both agreeing to just about any settlement and implementing it.

Ironically, Japan had its best chance to settle the territorial dispute with the USSR under Stalin, Khrushchev, or Brezhnev. All of them would have certainly demanded a huge compensation. So, in plain language, it may be suggested that Japan failed to settle the territorial dispute with the USSR because it was not prepared to pay the envisaged price of strategic, political, and economic compensation.

In the early years of the Gorbachev administration with totalitarian controls still readily available and communist authority unchallenged, a settlement was, perhaps, not entirely beyond reach, albeit in some unorthodox form provided that Japan was ready to pay a really large compensation or the USSR was desperate enough to settle for a much smaller one. As it turned out, neither was the case, and nothing substantial happened. (But even this failure was not without consequences for the future.)

Gorbachev's Failure

In the late 1980s Gorbachev's perestroika, caught between the deterioration of the old economic system and the absence of a new one, started to run out of money. On the contrary, Japan seemed to have all the money in the world. Viewed from Moscow, the principal motive for a rapprochement was to secure Japanese financial assistance. However, when viewed from Tokyo, the motive for a rapprochement looked different: to secure the return of the "Northern Territories" in exchange for financial assistance. In the contest that followed between two simplistic concepts, the Japanese government was somewhat successful in making the Soviet government believe that the money would really be forthcoming provided that a settlement of the territorial issue be brought about. This is not, of course, to say that the Japanese government proved itself to be smarter than its Soviet counterpart. The simple truth was that since Tokyo had been consistently raising this issue both officially and informally for a long time, in the kind of poker game that followed it found itself much better equipped than Moscow, which had been equally consistent in suppressing any discussion of the territorial issue. Another simple truth was that the Gorbachev administration, rooted in a totalitarian political system, still fancied itself to be free from public control and able to pursue any policy. Apparently some officials in the Japanese government steeped in old ways of thinking shared this belief in the omnipotence of the leaders in Moscow.

Basically, any communist government in the USSR was always inherently ready and cynical enough to consider any deal when real money was promised. After all, the communists had a record of selling priceless masterpieces of Russian art. Once, before World War II, they had even seriously considered selling the northern part of Sakhalin to Japan. But this time it did not work. Perhaps Gorbachev was not communist enough to consider such a deal. Perhaps he was too much of a politician not to think about the consequences. As for the Japanese, perhaps they were too vague by implying a lot, yet never promising anything firmly. In any case, both sides hesitated and thus lost time and momentum to consider seriously the territorial issue in its complexity. In the meantime, glasnost was gathering strength. Views long suppressed were coming into the open in the USSR in the fashion of "let one hundred flowers bloom." Tokyo was unprepared to grasp the phenomenon of glasnost and kept tracking the outpouring of views as if they were indications of shifts in the official Soviet position.

President Gorbachev finally went to Tokyo well versed on the issues, but poorly prepared to make a deal, with neither genuine conviction nor a pragmatic goal. His hosts were even less prepared for genuine progress, let alone a breakthrough. Unless carefully prepared in advance, summit meetings rarely lead to the settlement of any issue. Needless to say, no settlement was negotiated in advance. Apparently, the only idea considered in Tokyo was the idea of "residual sovereignty" of Japan over all four islands, to be acknowledged by the USSR at the summit. The idea was neither legally correct nor politically sound. In a nutshell, it stipulated a total Soviet surrender in a legal contest over the islands in exchange for a vague Japanese promise not to insist on the transfer of the islands in the immediate future. The whole scheme was seen as preposterous and unacceptable for the USSR. The summit meeting was thus reduced to a last-minute search for a face-saving formula, which was duly found, only to be disavowed by Gorbachev shortly thereafter. Anyway, it did not matter much: by the time of Gorbachev's visit his reputation back home was damaged, his political base eroded, and his freedom of maneuver and moral authority virtually gone. A totally new government under Russian President Yeltsin was emerging in Moscow, and public politics absent since 1917 were rapidly gaining momentum.

A contest between two governments claiming authority over virtually the same country developed in full conformity with the logic of politics. By the early spring of 1991, after bloody suppression of the Baltic republics, to support Yeltsin and oppose Gorbachev was already a matter of liberal conviction, a political fashion in Moscow, and a public passion prevailing in the provinces too. It was only natural that were Gorbachev to have made some progress in Tokyo the general public back home would have opposed it. In the black-and-white world of the newly born Soviet domestic politics it was that simple. This author's personal experience is testimony to this point. Having been involved initially in the preparations for Gorbachev's visit from June to December 1990, I left the Communist party in January 1991 in protest against the Baltic oppression. By the spring of 1991 I had already joined Yeltsin's camp and had mixed feelings about the visit, hoping for a breakthrough but fearing that it would enhance Gorbachev's position and thus hamper the prospects for Yeltsin. Ironic as it may sound, the mediocre results of Gorbachev's visit provided an additional positive impetus for the Yeltsin camp, which was still getting itself organized.

Opening Moves in Russo-Japanese Relations

Initially the Russian government did not have much ambition in foreign policy. It strongly demanded an equal say with the USSR government on domestic reforms in order to accelerate them, while making them more consistent and purposeful. In contrast, foreign policy was generally recognized as sound and, moreover, beyond the reach of the governments of the republics. Also, in the plain language of politics, it did not provide the Russian government with enough substance to attack Gorbachev from a democratic standpoint. To attack Gorbachev from a conservative position was, of course, out of the question.

The main task of the Russian Ministry of Foreign Affairs, as I saw it, was to provide the Russian government with expertise, to educate it about the outside world, and gradually to involve it in the foreign policy decision making of the USSR government. Naturally, some foreign policy issues, relations with Japan in particular, needed clarification, which was duly sought but to no practical effect. In the immediate aftermath of Gorbachev's visit to Japan, the Soviet foreign policy establishment was apparently content with the results and reluctant to consider serious follow-up steps. As one says in the world of soccer, "The game is over, forget about it." We were placated by assurances to the effect that since relations with Japan primarily concern Russia, no step could be considered without prior consent from the Russian government, which would immediately be consulted when something came up. When, in exasperation, we tried to introduce some ideas of our own and even suggested that Russia might take the initiative and deal with Japan on behalf of the USSR, we were bluntly advised that everything would ultimately have to be approved by Gorbachev, who for the time being was not to be bothered with proposals about Japan. Thus the USSR government could not move without the consent of the Russian government, which could not move without the approval of the USSR government. In this perfect catch–22 situation, there was nothing to do but wait.

At the same time, the Japanese government was reluctant to deal with Russia directly. Preparations for the visit to Japan by Russian Prime Minister Ivan Silaev proceeded at a leisurely pace without much interest on the part of the Japanese. Obviously, Russia was suspected of desiring to get exclusive economic benefits from Japan by utilizing the positive atmosphere that existed after Gorbachev's visit while delivering nothing in the way of political concessions in return. Also the Japanese government was definitely concerned with not offending the Gorbachev administration by giving an impression of leaning toward Yeltsin. And on top of everything else, the Japanese government was understandably confused by the emergence of the Russian government, which claimed sovereign status, including jurisdiction over the islands that Japan was demanding.

Then came the coup of August 1991. Although the Japanese government was typically slow in determining its stance, the Russian government was not offended. Most Russians, politicians included, simply noticed nothing. As for the professional Japan watchers, in any case a tiny minority, no one in this group has ever expected Japan to stop being Japan, to stand tall for some abstract principles and to rush forward with moral support for Russia without carefully considering its own pragmatic interests first and foremost. The coup was presumed to be successful; so Japan had to secure relations with the new "Soviet leadership." When the coup failed, Japan moved quickly to establish contact with the Russian government, which was duly appreciated.

A couple of days after the coup had failed, a high ranking diplomat from the Japanese embassy in Moscow came to see me. Seemingly speaking in a private capacity, he suggested that in order to make a fresh start in bilateral relations, the Russian government should simply denounce Stalin's policy toward Japan, pronouncing it predatory and illegal. He insisted that such a symbolic act of justice would dramatically improve the image of Russia in Japan. He also implied that if only the Russian government made such a declaration, the Japanese government would be prepared to let the territorial issue rest and not push it forward until the time was ripe for both sides.

Indeed, what would have been more natural for the democratic government of the new Russia, which was at the moment riding high on the nationwide anticommunist emotions, than to denounce an old policy of a communist dictator? Yet, the proposal was a trap, the same "residual sovereignty" in disguise. Its acceptance would have rendered the Russian legal position irrelevant, opening a Pandora's box. By the time this proposal was made it was already clear that sooner or later Russia would become a successor state to the USSR. In this capacity Russia did not have to share responsibility for the Soviet policy of the past, but could not of course afford the luxury of indiscriminately surrendering its international positions brought about by this policy. Besides, personally I was sure that the legal status of the South Kuriles was very complicated and controversial. It did not provide Japan with a clear-cut mandate to claim the islands as its legitimate possession, although the Japanese government has always operated on this presumption. Since the Soviet government operated on the opposite premise, the legal status of the South Kuriles has never been seriously discussed by diplomats of the two governments. To break the deadlock we had to start sorting things out from the very beginning, to compare the arguments of both sides without prejudice. In short, we could anticipate an open contest. To enter it with the outcome predetermined was absolutely out of the question. After careful consideration, the proposal of my Japanese friend, whether official or informal, was left unanswered.

The Russian government emerged from the coup politically and morally predominant over the USSR government; therefore, it aspired to an important, if not the overall leading, role in foreign policy decision making and moved rapidly to seize the initiative. The prevailing mood in Moscow was that of pride, exultation, and absolute conviction that the era of cooperation and shared values with the outside world had finally arrived. In this spirit it was considered of primary importance to get beyond the foreign policy issues that might stand in the way of a general opening to the world. Needless to say, relations with Japan figured high on the list of issues to be tackled without delay. The task at hand appeared to be simple: to bring the problems into the open, to let all of the people know and understand them, and thus to push the USSR government toward their settlement.

A visit to Japan by Ruslan Khasbulatov, the acting speaker of the Russian parliament who carried a letter from President Yeltsin, presented an opportunity to assert the newly acquired influence of Russia in the foreign policy of the USSR. During his stay in Tokyo Khasbulatov met top political and business leaders. Inevitably, his hosts focused attention on the territorial issue, which of course might have been expected. They were consistent in presenting the official view, but never tried to venture anything new. Apparently, the grand design behind this tactic was to dazzle the newcomers in the Russian leadership with the flawless logic of the Japanese position. In contrast, the Russian side introduced some new ideas that could have been instrumental in breaking the deadlock: the idea of "law and justice" as a basis for the territorial settlement; the idea of dropping the distinction between "the victor" and "the vanquished," etc. Neither Yeltsin in his letter nor Khasbulatov in his discussions made specific reference to the joint Soviet-Japanese Declaration of 1956, but Khasbulatov did not hesitate to indicate that all legally binding international treaties and agreements into which the USSR had entered were to be honored by Russia. It was, of course, a common sense approach, not an indication of any specific political decision made by Moscow.

Almost immediately after the trip to Tokyo I decided to go to the South Kuriles. With the approval of Foreign Minister Kozyrev, I invited to accompany me two members of the Russian parliament: O. Kalugin (a retired KGB general well known for his denunciation of the KGB) and S. Sirotkin (a human rights expert). In those days of bureaucratic innocence no one bothered with detailed instructions for the trip. The operational idea was simple: to see the islands, to talk with the residents, and of course to tell them the controversial story of the issue in which they had inadvertently become involved.

Upon arrival at the only operational airfield on the South Kuriles (a former kamikaze airbase) the three of us became absolutely fascinated with the natural beauty and wilderness of the islands, but gradually we became depressed and finally shocked by the picture of neglect and misery we saw everywhere we went. To all practical purposes the local residents had become hostages of the old economic system and bankrupt policy. Understandably all of them were angry with the authorities. As virtually the first officials from Moscow to visit the islands for several days, not just several hours, we had to listen to outbursts of human anger that had accumulated over many years. We also encountered protests, some of them reflecting the spontaneous reaction of misguided people, others clearly instigated and organized by Valentin Fedorov, the nationalist governor of Sakhalin oblast. Yet, wherever we went we were privileged to meet reasonable and thoughtful people. We did not have to humiliate them with lies; we showed them respect by telling the truth.

Later, in light of the nationalist mass media's denunciation of the Foreign Ministry and myself personally, a lot of people asked me whether it had been worthwhile going to the South Kuriles in the first place. My answer was always in the affirmative. I have firmly believed that the only way to settle the territorial dispute is to do so not as a backroom deal but with the wide acknowledgment of the general public. It was not only the moral side of diplomacy that was involved. One has to think not only about the formula of a settlement but also of the means of implementing it. It is worth remembering that the border agreement with China concluded in the last months of the Gorbachev administration encountered bitter domestic opposition because nobody apparently thought of explaining it and, in fact, promoting it to the public in advance. Having visited the South Kuriles, we managed to bring the territorial issue into the open, which in itself was vitally important.

Among other results of the trip was a much better understanding of the role of the token military force deployed on the islands since 1978. The initial purpose of the deployment was to irritate or "punish" Japan for the peace and friendship treaty it had signed with China despite Soviet protests. The whole scheme was rather simple if not entirely silly, but the Japanese government in its response to the deployment displayed about the same level of sophistication, duly getting irritated and continuing to demand a withdrawal ever since. During the Gorbachev administration when the goal of getting friendly with Japan rose to the forefront, the idea of withdrawing the troops from the South Kuriles became somewhat popular. When Russia succeeded the USSR this idea was still on the agenda.

Personally, I was not very enthusiastic about the withdrawal. The Russian troops on the islands presented no military threat to Hokkaido. There were no serious motives behind the Japanese demands for their withdrawal except for the purpose of getting Russia circumstantially to admit some kind of special legal status for the islands. Therefore, in my view, whatever had been the original purpose of the troop deployment, to have withdrawn them as a concession to Japan might have complicated our negotiating position by giving Japan some legal and political advantage before we had even started serious negotiations.

While visiting the South Kuriles I discovered another, human or grassroots, side of the withdrawal issue. As a matter of fact, the civilian population on the islands heavily relied on the military for emergency transportation, communications, supplies, and many other things vital for their survival. By withdrawing the troops we would have made life on the islands even more difficult. After the trip to the South Kuriles I made it a point not to push the troop withdrawal issue very hard. Needless to say, military officers, ever reluctant to withdraw, did not push the scheme either, limiting it to some modest rotation of personnel and equipment.

The Game in Progress: Hope, Frustration, Hope

From September 1991 the Russian government, while still without operational control of foreign policy, found itself fully burdened with foreign policy issues. This unique and irrational situation deserves special study. It caused both Russia and its partners a lot of confusion and brought no benefits. By December it was over.

The new government did not have a free choice: the international community expected and in fact insisted that Russia play strictly by the established rules, i.e., be a genuine successor state. In the case of relations with Japan, this left in place an unbalanced and rigid system deadlocked by the territorial issue and fueled mainly by Japanese hopes of reaching a settlement. Obviously, at that moment Japanese hopes were at their highest level yet, which was not exactly helpful due to the special aberration of the Japanese mentality. Traditionally, Japanese are inclined to divide foreigners into two principal groups: those who like, know, and understand Japan, and those who do not. Those in the first group are normally expected to share Japanese views and support Japan's positions without reservation. Those in the second group are to be educated about Japan. In this particular case, a number of newcomers to the Russian government, including the Foreign Ministry, had the dubious "privilege" of having been "associated" with the first group.

Hence, in my personal encounters with the Japanese I had a strange feeling that, whatever I said or did, they simply could not believe that by starting negotiations with them we meant business, not surrender. Whatever concessions might have been considered by Russia were invariably questioned and, in fact, rejected by Japan for not being far-reaching enough. In a grim irony, after the establishment of the Russian Federation, the gap between what was expected by Japan and what was actually possible widened, hampering the whole negotiating process.

Another problem was soon added. On the one hand, on the territorial issue the Japanese government professed to have the full support of the people. Personally, I doubted this notion, suspecting that the majority of the Japanese public simply did not care enough either about Russia or the territorial issue. On the other hand, the attitudes of the Russian people had not yet been tested at all. In the case of the South Kuriles we needed time to explore these attitudes and, if necessary, to educate people about some new facts. Alas, we were not given the time we needed. The Japanese government appeared to be in a terrible hurry, anxious to settle the issue on its own terms as soon as possible. In a very fluid political situation with prime ministers and foreign ministers coming and going, one set after another of Japanese government leaders apparently were anxious to get the credit for a breakthrough, before it was too late for them personally. So, efforts by the Russian side to introduce new knowledge about the territorial issue to the Russian people, which normally should have preceded the talks, had to be conducted simultaneously with them. As a result, even to the present day, the attitudes of the Russian public as of the Japanese public have not been fully explored, even as they were being exploited for political ends.

Naturally, such haste backfired. By the spring of 1992 whoever in Russia spoke in favor of a settlement became an easy target of accusations of selling out to the Japanese. Public opinion exploded with all kinds of extremist views neither accurate nor fair. The majority, of course, voiced absolute opposition to any settlement. While claiming Russian sovereign rights over the South Kuriles, some of the advocates of these views eagerly acknowledged that the islands had been acquired by force only to point out that in the not-so-distant past the United States, for example, had used the same methods while expanding its territory westward and southward. They also ridiculed moral or political obligations as a basis of foreign policy. (Incidentally, now that the eastward expansion of NATO has become a fact despite all the solemn promises to the contrary given to the USSR, this particular view is rapidly gaining strength in Russia.) Only a tiny minority of the Russian public cautiously spoke in favor of a territorial settlement along the lines demanded by Japan, i.e., in favor of instant and unconditional surrender of the islands. Almost no one in the general public took an interest in the details or was prepared to listen to arguments and reason.

Frankly speaking, I was not fully prepared for the defamatory campaign that we encountered. It was 1992; Russian democracy was still an infant and not a very healthy one as we were soon to find out. The struggle between the democratic camp and die-hard conservatives was in full swing, resulting in a black-and-white approach to domestic politics. The democrats appeared united and basked in the image of good guys. In this context, opposition to the territorial settlement with Japan from the conservatives and nationalists had been fully anticipated. What had not been expected was that some of the self-appointed democrats would try to exploit the territorial issue to enhance their political standing. One of the most distressing episodes happened as early as October 1991, when Kozyrev asked me to meet with Oleg Rumyantsev, a well-known democratic member of parliament and an executive secretary of the constitutional committee. Apparently, Rumyantsev wanted some candid information about the Russian policy toward Japan. I visited his office and briefed him and one of his legal advisers as candidly as I possibly could. In the course of our encounter he never voiced disagreement. When the session was over Rumyantsev suggested that we meet again in a couple of days to continue the briefing. In the meantime, we specifically agreed to keep our discussion confidential and not to rush to any conclusions prematurely. To my total surprise, the very next day Rumyantsev on behalf of his personal "party" issued a long statement squarely condemning the Foreign Ministry for usurping the powers of the parliament while conducting negotiations with Japan. This was an act of petty yet damaging betrayal on the part of a person who was considered an ally.

As far as public opinion was concerned, we found ourselves in a no-win situation. Obviously, we could not afford to draw a lot of public attention to the negotiations. At the same time, we had the standing responsibility to educate the public. Owing to many reasons, among them intentional leaks by some people in important positions, we failed to reconcile these two inherently contradictory tasks.

Russia also became the successor to one more major problem of a special nature. While handling the territorial issue, it was imperative that Russia and Japan avoid the impression of any linkage of a territorial settlement with Japanese financial assistance. This was difficult to do; after all, the principle of "expanded equilibrium" that had been put forward by Japan during the Gorbachev administration was never discarded. And in all fairness, it would have been next to impossible to avoid the impression that a deal of "islands for money" was considered unless financial assistance from Japan arrived in a volume that really mattered before any territorial settlement was envisaged. In my informal contacts with the Japanese I suggested that in order to really break the ice of mistrust accumulated over a century, Japan consider launching some kind of Marshall Plan for Russia, and that by not doing so Japan was missing a historic chance not only to help Russia when the help was most needed, but also to emerge as a great power prepared to take upon itself responsibility for the global transformation. It was all in vain, and suspicions of a deal kept greatly hampering our efforts.

Against all of these odds, the Russian government introduced the concept of "law and justice," developed from the idea that had appeared in Yeltsin's letter to the Japanese prime minister in September 1991 as a basis for the settlement. Its original meaning was simple: whatever was stipulated by international law, i.e., by legally valid agreements between the two countries, was to be implemented; whatever was not could be discussed and perhaps negotiated in the future; whatever settlement was finally to be determined, the well-being and dignity of both the Russian and Japanese people who were subject to its implementation must be ensured. For close to nine months from late 1991 we tried to explain this concept to our Japanese counterparts as well as to the Russians. It proved to be extremely frustrating, if not pointless.

In Tokyo we received a very cautious and, in fact, cool reception. Apparently, our Japanese counterparts were prepared to discuss nothing but the conditions and timetable of the transfer of all four islands, which in their view (which we found simply not true) was fully stipulated by international law. Amazingly, they were sticking to the same "residual sovereignty" position that had already been proven to be a patent nonstarter. To this day I wonder what might have been their fallback position. Perhaps, there was none at all. The whole affair grew even more complicated when the Japanese government initiated a number of contacts with Russian politicians and opinion leaders, knocking at every door of importance in Moscow with the same message. As a result, rumors mushroomed in Moscow and the Foreign Ministry spent considerable time denying them. In the meantime, we were facing our own share of misperceptions and blunders. Some of them resulted from inexperience and lack of coordination, others from the polarization of political forces and Russian society.

One of the worst mistakes on our part was to allow the Japanese government to draw us into committing to a specific date for Yeltsin's visit to Japan. Initially, I insisted that no timetable for the visit should be set before we arrive at a definite political decision of our own and work out with the Japanese at least some of the principal guidelines for an agreement to emerge as a result of the summit. Unfortunately, it did not work out that way, and we ended up fighting a deadline, which was of course a favorite Japanese tactic and something at which we have never excelled.

By mid-summer 1992 it was already clear that we were approaching a deadlock not just on the territorial issue. In fact, the whole relationship was becoming stalled. No new agreements were forthcoming; nothing substantial was being discussed. Unfortunately, both Moscow and Tokyo were late to recognize this troubling reality. I am not going to comment on the immediate circumstances that led to the postponement of President Yeltsin's visit to Tokyo. Suffice it to say, it was perhaps one of the most difficult foreign policy decisions taken by the president in the first years of his administration. When after a year the visit finally took place both sides were wise enough to be content with its results, which represented the biggest progress possible under the circumstances.

Conclusions

Looking back on the first years of the Yeltsin administration, I cannot help feeling that never before or after have we been so close to a settlement of the territorial issue in terms of standard conditions for a diplomatic formula, yet so far from it in terms of limitations brought about by the domestic politics of the two countries and the mentality of both societies. Given these circumstances, it is perhaps as well that the settlement of the territorial issue has not yet been reached by the diplomats and leaders of the two countries, while our relations have finally been steadied on an even keel along a course leading toward evolutionary improvement. In due time the collapse of communism as the state ideology of a superpower is certain to bring about an entirely new (or perhaps renewed) system of international relations that will be much more complicated and dynamic than ever before, with zero-sum games no longer the rule. In the long run Russia and Japan will need each other in order not just to settle the territorial issue but also to ensure each other's strategic stability in one or another meaning of these words. In the final analysis, this is why Russia and Japan need a fundamental improvement in their relations.

I believe that Russia and Japan may find quite a bit of encouragement from the new rapprochement that has developed between them. Hopefully, they will proceed to build a strong and stable relationship of interdependence, trust, and cooperation. Then the two countries might be ready to settle the territorial issue as a minor problem, or perhaps to drop it altogether as a relic of the past.

NOTES

* No part of this chapter should be construed as reflecting the opinions or policies of the Ministry of Foreign Affairs of Russia.

CHAPTER 10

Why Did Russia and Japan Fail to Achieve Rapprochement in 1991–1996?

Tsuyoshi Hasegawa

THIS CHAPTER DEALS WITH RUSSO-JAPANESE RELATIONS between the failed August coup in 1991, and March 1996, when bilateral relations began to change drastically in a positive direction. During this period the collapse of the Soviet Union and the emergence of a new Russian state under Boris Yeltsin brought about drastic changes in international relations. Nevertheless, Russo-Japanese relations alone remained in a state of stalemate.

How can we explain this anomaly? A facile answer is to blame the intractability of the territorial question. But then why was it impossible for both countries to resolve the territorial question in view of the new situation created by the collapse of the Soviet Union?

There are two fundamental problems that prevented Russia and Japan from finding common ground for the resolution of the territorial question during this period. The first, the most important cause, was Japan's intransigent position on what the Japanese call the "Northern Territories problem." Throughout the period, the Japanese government and its Ministry of Foreign Affairs (Gaimusho) continued to adhere to the demand that Russia's recognition of sovereignty over all the disputed islands was the precondition not only for a peace treaty, but also for Japan's economic assistance to Russia. This demand proved to be unrealistic, unacceptable to the Russian side, throwing the most serious roadblocks in the way for rapprochement.

The second important cause, if not as important as the first, was of Russian political development since the August coup. The Russian domestic situation made the resolution of the territorial question exceedingly difficult, since Yeltsin and the Russian Ministry of Foreign Affairs (MID) had to face nationalistic opposition within Russia to any territorial concessions.

Although these two factors constituted the deeper causes for the failure of Russia and Japan to achieve rapprochement during this period, however, the failure was by no mean inevitable. Such accidental factors as miscalculations, bad timing, lack of leadership, and clumsy diplomatic skills all contributed to the failure.

This chapter examines how these two fundamental causes were combined with these accidental factors, leading ultimately to the inability of both countries to overcome the past legacies of hostility and construct the new relationship of friendship and cooperation.

Contradictions of Japan's Policy of Balanced Expansion

Until August 1991, Japan sought the return of all disputed islands, which the Japanese call the Northern Territories, as the most important goal of its policy toward the Soviet Union. Although there was a change in Japan's policy from the inseparability of politics and economics (*seikei fukabun*) to balanced expansion or expanded equilibrium (*kakudai kinko),* the territorial question continued to be Japan's top priority to which all other issues were subordinated.[1] It was only after the August coup in 1991 that Japan attempted to reassess its policy toward Russia. At the end of September, Foreign Minister Nakayama Taro enunciated five new principles, in which he stressed Japan's willingness to expand the realm of cooperation. More importantly, the demand for the resolution of the territorial issue was conspicuously relegated to the last place of these principles.[2] Following these new principles, Japan announced in October that it would grant aid to the Soviet Union amounting to $2.5 billion. Chief Cabinet Secretary Sakamoto Misoji took pains to explain that this aid would be granted without a resolution to the territorial issue.[3] This initiative was a new departure of Japan's policy toward the Soviet Union, virtually decoupling economic aid from the territorial issue. This would have meant not only the rejection of the inseparability of politics and economics but also a departure from the politics of balanced expansion, since economic aid would not have to be "balanced" with the territorial question.

Had this trajectory been followed, the next logical step would have been to break the linkage between economic aid and territorial demand. Japan had two opportunities to make this break clear: first, when the Miyazawa government was formed in November, and second, when the Soviet Union ended its existence in December. In neither case was Japan able to exploit the opportunity, and the linkage between economic aid and the territorial question continued to be maintained, virtually nullifying whatever positive steps Japan was prepared to take in the area of economic cooperation.

Ironically, the Miyazawa government came to power with good intentions to improve relations with the Soviet Union. In his first speech after his assumption of the premiership, Miyazawa expressed his interest in concluding a peace treaty with the Soviet Union. While emphasizing the need to resolve the Northern Territories question, the prime minister stressed that a resolution should not create fear and displeasure among those who lived on the disputed islands.[4] With this the Japanese government began studying concrete legal and financial measures for the transfer of the islands to Japanese jurisdiction. The Gaimusho also made a major policy change in its approach to the Northern Territories question. Previously, its official position was to demand the "simultaneous return" (*ikkatsu henkan*) of all four islands. Now it dropped "simultaneous" from its demand, and took the position that as long as Japan's sovereignty over the islands was recognized, Japan would be flexible about the timing and modality of their return.

Despite its desire to improve relations, however, the Miyazawa government could not resolve two fundamental questions that lay at the core of Japan's Russian/Soviet policy: the relationship between economic aid and the territorial demand, and the specific islands to which "residual sovereignty" should be applied. The first question was whether or not Japan should attach a precondition to large-scale economic aid to Russia. It is important to note that a subtle difference occurred in the emphasis that Japan attached to the linkage. Previously, the territorial issue had stood ahead of economic aid, which was used as bait to induce concessions on the territory from the Soviet side. After the August coup, there was a reversal of order between the two: Japan began to take the position that economic aid would have to be implemented for Japan's national interests, and for this purpose, the territorial dispute had to be settled. Despite this important shift, however, the linkage remained. The Gaimusho was not prepared to cut this umbilical cord, despite the obvious fact that the decision to extend $2.5 billion in aid had already violated the policy of balanced expansion.

The second question can be formulated as a choice between two or four islands. If the simultaneous return could not be gained, the territorial question had to be resolved in two stages: the return of Habomai and Shikotan on the basis of the 1956 Joint Declaration, and the resolution of sovereignty of Kunashiri and Etorofu. The Gaimusho appears to have taken it for granted that the Soviet/Russian government had already committed itself to honoring the 1956 Joint Declaration. Since the return of Habomai and Shikotan could be assumed to be guaranteed, Japan's major task would be to have the Russians accept residual sovereignty over Kunashiri and Etorofu.

"Law and Justice" and "Five-Stage Proposal"

Russia's initial approach to Japan after the August coup reinforced the Gaimusho's conviction that Russia might be prepared to resolve the territorial question once and for all. However, Russia's policy toward Japan was filled with contradictions. The Russian government had committed itself to two variants with regard to the territorial issue. The first variant was Yeltsin's five-stage proposal that he had revealed in January 1990, when he visited Japan as the leader of the radical reformers' opposition to Gorbachev. This proposal consisted of the following stages: (1) recognizing the existence of the territorial dispute; (2) declaring the islands as a free economic zone; (3) demilitarizing the islands; (4) concluding a peace treaty; and (5) leaving the territorial dispute to be resolved within 15 to 20 years. By proposing the first three stages, he had set himself apart from Gorbachev, who at that time had not acknowledged the existence of the territorial question. When Yeltsin had initially made this proposal, therefore, it had represented a radical departure from the intransigent position held by the Soviet government.[5] But by 1991 the Soviet government had already recognized the existence of the territorial dispute, and the initial step of demilitarization had been promised by Gorbachev at the summit. After the Gorbachev-Kaifu summit in April 1991 the crucial issue of the territorial dispute had shifted to three questions: (1) would the Joint Declaration of 1956 be honored; (2) would the Russian government agree to negotiate on the status of Kunashiri and Etorofu; and (3) would the Russians acknowledge Japan's sovereignty over Etorofu and Kunashiri? Yeltsin's five-stage proposal, which gave negative answers to all these questions, was therefore a step backward from the Gorbachev-Kaifu Joint Statement and could not serve as a basis for a realistic solution to the territorial dispute.[6]

The notion of "law and justice" represented a completely different approach to the territorial question from those expressed in the five-stage proposal. In September 1991 Yeltsin sent his personal letter to Kaifu, in which he expressed his desire to resolve the territorial issue "based on law and justice," and to restore the relationship between Russia and Japan as equal partners without making any distinctions between the "victor" and the "vanquished" in World War II.[7] It is widely believed that "law and justice" was Georgi Kunadze's formulation.[8] Despite the Japanese government's official claim, "law" does not necessarily vindicate Japan's claims. A careful examination of the legal complexities with regard to the Northern Territories dispute inevitably leads one to the conclusion that the only legal document both sides signed and ratified is the 1956 Joint Declaration, which promised the return of Habomai and Shikotan to Japan after the conclusion of a peace treaty.[9] Therefore, specifically, "law" means the acceptance of the 1956 Joint Declaration. From strictly legal grounds, it is impossible to determine the sovereignty issue of Kunashiri and Etorofu; it must be resolved by political compromises. But when the concept of "justice" is introduced, Japan's claims to Kunashiri and Etorofu are justified. Since 1855 until the Soviet occupation at the last stage of the Soviet-Japanese War, these islands legally and politically belonged to Japan, and the Soviet occupation and subsequent annexation of these islands represented nothing but Stalin's expansionist ambitions. And this understanding was in line with Kunadze's own interpretation of the territorial issue.[10]

No matter how admirable his scholarly integrity was, however, Kunadze's interpretation had no possibility of being accepted as Russia's official policy. Kunadze might have been motivated by his sincere and moral desire to make a clean break with the past Soviet policy, and begin a new era of Russian foreign policy founded on "law and justice" by righting the wrongs of the communist regime. And this desire corresponded with the first idealistic, euphoric stage of Russian foreign policy pursued under the stewardship of Foreign Minister Andrei Kozyrev after the demise of the August coup. Nevertheless, this formulation turned out to be an oversell, bringing negative consequences. It gave the Japanese false hope that the territorial dispute would be resolved once and for all in terms that the Japanese had consistently claimed. If it were only "law and *compromise*" rather than "law and *justice,*" this would have meant the affirmation of the 1956 Joint Declaration as the first step—law—and continuing negotiations on Kunashiri and Etorofu—compromise. But law and justice gave Japan the unrealistic hope of recovering all four islands without going through the first step. In fact, since the introduction of this formulation, "law and justice" became, to the Japanese, shorthand for returning all four islands.

Moreover, this formula immediately clashed with the Russian domestic political reality. Kunadze's trip to the disputed islands in September 1991 provoked a storm of protests, not merely from islanders on the disputed islands and the patriotic-communist conservatives, but also from reformists as well. It was impossible for a newly created Russian state to begin its existence by surrendering its territory, especially when the dissolution of the Soviet Union wounded the national pride of the Russians.[11] It soon became clear that the maximum concessions that the Russian government could possibly make would be the reaffirmation of the 1956 Joint Declaration—and this itself became a difficult task. Kunadze and the Russian MID had to struggle against all foes, some of whom resided within Yeltsin's closest inner circle. In other words, the Russian domestic reality dictated that all Kunadze could deliver was law, but not justice. Thus, the difference between two islands or four islands remained unresolved between the two governments, and a part of the blame was perhaps placed on the introduction of "justice" into the territorial question.

In addition, the formulation of law and justice was in contradiction with Yeltsin's five-stage proposal. Kunadze attempted to reconcile this contradiction. He explained that the first stage had been already resolved. As for demilitarization (third stage), he indicated that a 30 percent troop reduction was being planned. But with regard to the second stage—the joint economic development—Kunadze pointed out the difficulty associated with Japan's position in that for any full economic cooperation on these islands, the resolution of the territorial problem would be a prerequisite. "The legal questions that are raised by the Japanese position," Kunadze argued, "must be determined in the complex of the other remaining questions."[12] In other words, although he did not directly touch upon Yeltsin's last stage, he was obviously raising his objections to postponing the territorial settlement to the last stage. Despite Kunadze's efforts, however, Yeltsin's five-stage proposal was never repudiated.

The End of the Soviet Union and the Lack of its Impact on Japan

The dissolution of the Soviet Union in December 1991 marked a fundamental change in the geopolitical equation in international relations in Northeast Asia, forcing each major power to reassess its relations with Russia.[13] This would have been a good occasion for Japan to reexamine its policy toward Russia by cutting the umbilical cord between economic aid and the territorial issue, and presenting a compromise on the territorial issue, acceptable to the young emerging Russia. This did not happen. In fact, the end of the Soviet Union did not have much impact on Japan's Russian policy. Unlike in Western Europe, the Middle East, Central Asia, and China, where the geopolitical equation drastically changed with new borders, such change did not take place in the Far East. The borders between Russia and Japan remained the same, and as far as Japan was concerned, the Soviet Union had merely been replaced by the Russian Federation.[14]

The end of the Soviet Union and the creation of 15 independent states, however, had a profound impact on domestic politics within the Russian Federation. The Russians saw the fruit of past imperial expansion since Peter the Great violently snatched from them overnight and a 25 million diaspora scattered around in the lands that became foreign countries. This changed the dynamics of Russian public opinion with regard to the Kurile question. All these factors, however, did not prompt Japan to change its policy toward Russia. On the contrary, Japan saw in the dissolution of the Soviet Union an opportune moment to resolve the territorial question in its own terms.

This conclusion was not merely based on its wishful thinking; rather the initial reaction of the Russian government misled Japan to hold on to such an illusion. On December 27, 1991, the day after Gorbachev dissolved the Soviet Union, Kozyrev reaffirmed Russia's commitment to all the international treaties and agreements, publicly declaring that the Soviet government's unilateral abrogation of the 1956 Joint Declaration was unjustified.[15] It was evident that the Russians were sending the signal that they were prepared to accept the two-island solution on the basis of the 1956 Joint Declaration. Japan, however, never considered this to be sufficient: it wanted Russia's acceptance of Japan's sovereignty over all four islands. In other words, Russia was prepared to accept "law," but not "justice," while Japan appears to have concluded that since "law" had been already taken care of, the most urgent task in negotiations with Russia would be to gain "justice." This difference did not narrow, but, on the contrary, further widened.

In January 1992, Foreign Minister Watanabe attended a coordinating conference, called by the United States, on aid to the Commonwealth of Independent States (CIS). In his first public speech to announce Japan's policy toward Russia after the end of the Soviet Union, Watanabe clearly linked economic aid with implementation of foreign policy based on law and justice.[16] As Russian observers noted, the territory and economic aid became more closely linked than Nakayama's five principles. Later in the month, at the first foreign ministerial conference, Watanabe officially revealed Japan's new position that once Russia agreed to return all four islands, Japan would be flexible with regard to the timing and the modality. To Watanabe and the Gaimusho this proposal was meant to be a major concession, but in the wake of the New York conference this did not register as a radical departure. On the contrary, this proposal struck the Russians as Japan's renewed intransigence.

At the first working group meeting held in Moscow on February 10–11, Kunadze and Saito Kunihiko (the Gaimusho's new deputy foreign minister) clashed over the difference between two or four islands. Kunadze reaffirmed the Russian government's intention of honoring all treaties and agreements concluded by the Soviet government and said that Moscow "must overcome a 1960 government memorandum that negated the Soviet-Japanese Joint Declaration." Saito replied that "if Moscow can accept in principle the return of the islands to Japan, the details can be worked out later."

While Saito insisted on the need to resolve the dispute on the basis of law and justice, Kunadze reminded him of Russia's domestic opposition and counseled a policy of realism.[17]

In the meantime, met with domestic opposition to any concessions to Japan's territorial claims, Kozyrev had to retreat from his previous commitment to the 1956 Joint Declaration. At the second foreign ministerial conference in March, the foreign minister reaffirmed Russia's commitment to honoring all the international obligations, but he stopped short of committing himself to the return of the two islands after the conclusion of a peace treaty, citing the vociferous opposition from reactionary quarters. Russia's commitment to "law" itself, not to speak of "justice," had become shaky. Watanabe pointed out that because of the pending territorial question, Japan would not be able to go beyond certain limits in extending aid to Russia.[18] As Russia was retreating from its commitment to "law," Japan all the more insistently emphasized the linkage and "justice."

According to an inside source close to the Russian MID, at this time the Russian negotiators were frustrated by Yeltsin's commitment to the compromise position based on the two-island formula that the MID was advocating. At one of the working group sessions, possibly in February or in March, the Russian side proposed to the Japanese side that Japan make a proposal to accept a two-island formula, leaving the sovereignty of Kunashiri and Etorofu undecided so that the Russian negotiators would be able to force Yeltsin to commit to this solution. In other words, the Russian side was interested in forcing the proposal it preferred, pretending that it came from the Japanese side. This proposal, however, was rejected by the Japanese negotiators right out of hand. The Japanese remained uninterested in the two-island solution.[19] This episode is important for at least two reasons. First, it reveals the inner working of Russian decision making. The MID was anxious to commit Yeltsin to a compromise solution, while Yeltsin remained hopelessly elusive on this issue. Second, the interpretation often repeated by the Japanese side, that the Russians did not take any initiative to break the logjam of the territorial dispute, is false. The Russians did make a move, and the Japanese rejected it.

In April, Watanabe clarified Japan's official position on the territorial question: Japan would accept Russia's right of administration (*shiseiken*) over the Northern Territories as long as Russia accepted Japan's "residual sovereignty" over the islands.[20] Cabinet

Secretary Kato Koichi confirmed the foreign minister's statement by saying that Japan had consistently held the view that as long as Russia recognized that the four islands were an inalienable part of Japanese territory, Japan would respond flexibly in the timing, modality, and conditions of return. However, Kato added a major clarification: Japan's recognition of Russia's administration would not be extended to Habomai and Shikotan.[21] This position not only sharpened the difference between Russia's two-island approach and Japan's four-island demand, but also appeared to the Russians as though Japan had upped the ante in its position. Immediately after Kato's clarification, the Russian MID flatly rejected it as unacceptable, considering it tantamount to imposing a precondition for negotiations.[22]

Had Japan adopted two specific policy positions, the situation might have turned out differently. The first, an easier step, would have been to repudiate the inseparability of politics and economics, and conveyed this change of policy unambiguously to the Russian side. Japan could have expanded the realm of economic cooperation with Russia without any linkage with the territorial question—a policy that had partially been implemented with its $2.5 billion aid, and subsequently adopted under the rubric of the "multilayered approach." In fact, Ambassador Sumio Edamura advocated exactly such a policy already.[23] The second step, to accept the 1956 Joint Declaration as the basis of concluding a peace treaty, would have been more difficult, but would not have been totally impossible. Already, the Gorbachev-Kaifu Joint Declaration had accepted the four islands as the subject of negotiations. If Japan had made concessions to accept a two-stage return, it would have been logical to commit both sides to the first stage, leaving sovereignty over Kunashiri and Etorofu undecided and for further negotiations, without compromising Japan's principle and without fearing that Russia would renege on further negotiations on the two islands.

Why was the Gaimusho unable to adopt such policies? It appears that the Gaimusho was not unanimous about the policy it followed. Although Edamura in his otherwise informative memoirs was careful not to reveal any internal conflict within the Gaimusho, his line of thinking was clearly at variance with the line pursued by the high echelon policymakers in the Gaimusho main office in Kasumigaseki, led by Owada Hisashi (later Saito Kunihiko) and Hyodo Nagao (which I call here the Hyodo line). Two important motivations lay behind this policy. The first was their deep-seated suspicion that once Japan made a concession on the territorial issue, either by detaching the linkage between economics and the territorial issue or concluding a peace treaty on the basis of the 1956 Joint Declaration, the Russians would lose incentive to return the two other islands. This was the fear that "Russians might eat and run" (*kuinige suru*). To them, the territorial issue thus took precedence over the need to achieve rapprochement with Russia. Concealed under this assumption was also the second important factor, the judgement that Japan could well afford to postpone rapprochement with Russia indefinitely without risking its national interests.

What I might call the Edamura line—Edamura must have been supported by many other diplomats both at the embassy and the home ministry—placed the achievement of rapprochement with Russia at the center of Japan's Russian policy, which should be pursued in itself for Japan's national interests in the post–cold war geopolitical reality.[24] As for Japan's economic aid, Edamura took the position that Japan's economic aid would help stabilize Russia, which in turn would serve Japan's national interests in the long run. Needless to say, the Japanese ambassador had to defend Japan's territorial demand, but here too, Edamura attempted to persuade the Russian public that "to the extent that the resolution of the territorial question is the task Russia cannot avoid in order to be accepted as a member of the international community, its settlement should also serve Russia's national interests." Herein one can see the genesis of the policy later to be developed into the "multilayered approach."

Perhaps it is not correct to characterize Japan's Russian policy from August 1991 to September 1992 as the complete domination of the Owada-Hyodo line. More accurately, it proceeded with the dynamic interplay of these two lines, but always with the Owada-Hyodo line occupying a predominant position, only occasionally allowing for aspects of the Edamura line to surface. For that reason, the inseparability of politics and economics was never repudiated; Japan's economic assistance had to be balanced with the territorial question; and despite Russia's mounting opposition to any territorial concessions to Japan, the major goal for the forthcoming summit between Yeltsin and Miyazawa was unrealistically set to have Yeltsin accept "residual sovereignty" over all four islands. The Owada-Hyodo line was also responsible for the fiasco at the Munich G-7 summit, where Japan sought to mobilize the other G-7 governments to accept Japan's territorial claims in its political statement—an incident that hopelessly soured relations between Russia and Japan on the eve of Yeltsin's scheduled trip to Tokyo.[25]

In the end, the cancellation of Yeltsin's trip revealed the unmitigated failure of the Owada-Hyodo line. Setting an unattainable goal—four islands—it failed to gain any of the islands back, although two islands, if not a guaranteed success, might have been achievable. The high echelon of the Gaimusho was slow to react to the new and quickly changing geostrategic reality after the collapse of the Soviet Union, and it also read the Russian domestic situation totally wrong.

Yeltsin's Decision-Making Style and Russian Domestic Politics

Yet, Japan was not the sole culprit of the September 1992 fiasco. By the summer of 1992 the Kurile issue was entangled with Russian domestic politics, becoming the hottest political issue against which the Russians vented their frustrations and anger caused by the wounded national pride that was stung by the dissolution of the Soviet Union. The Kurile issue was also a focal point of a power struggle between the president and the parliament. Furthermore, this issue was exploited by another serious power struggle within Yeltsin's inner circle. Yeltsin's erratic and impulsive character did not lend itself to a more streamlined, normal channel of decision-making process. He tended to be swayed by those who happened to be closest at any given time. And under domestic pressure, he increasingly preferred to talk more about his five-stage proposal and less about law and justice.[26]

As Yeltsin began to distance himself from law and justice, the Gaimusho still maintained good relations with the Russian MID and the Burbulis Commission that was preparing Yeltsin's visit. The problem was that neither the MID nor the Burbulis Commission had decisive influence over Yeltsin. The parliamentary hearings masterminded by the ambitious but unprincipled Oleg Rumyantsev in July galvanized opposition to Yeltsin, succeeding in isolating Kunadze and the Russian MID, who were fighting a lone battle for a compromise settlement on the territorial issue.[27] At this critical juncture, Vice Minister in Charge of Information Mikhail Poltoranin came to Japan in the beginning of August, and trumpeted his sympathy for Japan's position on the territorial issue, but his grandstanding, apparently without any mandate from Yeltsin, made the situation worse, helping anti-Japanese sentiments to grow further while raising Japanese hope that the four-island solution would be within reach. Immediately after Poltoranin, Iurii Petrov, who was involved in the personal fight against Burbulis, flew to Japan, telling exactly the opposite of what Poltoranin had said—Russia would be in no position to make any territorial concessions. It appears that the Kurile issue was deeply embroiled in the Byzantine intrigues of the Kremlin inner politics, in which Petrov, Iurii Skokov, and Aleksandr Korzhakov exploited the issue to enhance their personal influence upon Yeltsin. All were united in opposition to Kunadze, Kozyrev, and Burbulis.

And yet, the final decision was obviously Yeltsin's alone. Yeltsin had a press conference on August 21. He bitterly complained, patently falsely, that Japan's aid was the lowest of all advanced nations, and he in no uncertain terms accused Japan of making territorial concessions the prerequisite for economic aid. Asked about the territorial question, he stated: "I have at my disposal twelve different proposals for the solution to this question. I will reveal my option only on the second day of the summit in Tokyo."[28] Two things are clear from his statement. First, at this point he did not entertain any thoughts of canceling his trip. Second, he intended to adopt one of the 12 options at his disposal, depending on what Japan offered at the negotiating table. According to a Yeltsin adviser, Lev Sukhanov, and his press secretary, Viacheslav Kostikov, it was important that Yeltsin had stated that he would reveal his final decision on the second day of the summit. Sukhanov and Kostikov fault Japan for not paying attention to this. In their view, Yeltsin was waiting for a signal of Japan's softening position.[29]

It appears that the Gaimusho was divided on how to react to the worsening domestic situation in Russia. Judging from press releases, the Gaimusho's main strategy was the continued adherence to the Owada-Hyodo line: to maintain that the minimum condition was Yeltsin's acceptance of Japan's sovereignty over all four islands. To various suggestions coming from Moscow along the lines of the Kunadze option, the Gaimusho generally reacted with suspicion, believing that they were intended to shortchange Japan's principled territorial demand. It wrongly concluded that Yeltsin was already committed to the Kunadze option, which would accept the return of the two islands, but leave the question of sovereignty of Etorofu and Kunashiri unresolved. This was precisely the main purpose of the Kunadze option, and it should be rejected.[30] Saito categorically stated: "Japan would not be satisfied unless the Russian side clearly expressed that the four islands would fall under Japan's sovereignty, and acknowledged that they would be returned to Japan in the near future."[31] Nevertheless, the Gaimusho does not seem to have been unanimous on this. Sometime in August Edamura sent a dispatch to Tokyo recommending that Japan lower the expectations from the forthcoming summit and consider it merely the first step toward the eventual rapprochement in a longer perspective.[32] The precise contents of this recommendation are not known, but it would not be surprising if he had suggested something along the line of suspending the inseparability of politics and economics, or even the acceptance of the 1956 Joint Declaration as the interim solution to the territorial question.[33]

Edamura's recommendation must have been overruled by the Gaimusho high echelon. In the end the Owada-Hyodo line prevailed. The only hope to break this stalemate now rested with Watanabe's talk with Yeltsin, whose only interest was to detect any change in Japan's policy. Watanabe flew to Moscow on August 29 and met with Yeltsin on September 2. This was the crucial meeting that eventually led to the cancellation of Yeltsin's trip. Watanabe's opening remarks greatly infuriated Yeltsin. The Japanese foreign minister made the major faux pas of comparing Yeltsin's forthcoming visit with that of his archenemy Gorbachev. This angered Yeltsin, who sat throughout the rest of the meeting in sullen indignation.[34] Watanabe and Yeltsin then debated about Japan's economic aid to Russia. Watanabe explained that Japan was prepared to grant aid, but what it had previously pledged had turned out to be impossible to implement due to the domestic conditions in Russia. Yeltsin retorted sarcastically that the same domestic constraints did not prevent other nations from extending aid, and repeated the false accusation that Japan was the stingiest among the G-7 nations in terms of aid to Russia. Watanabe pointed out that at the end of October Tokyo would host a conference on aid to the former Soviet states, and this would be followed by the Tokyo G-7 summit, where Japan's policy on aid to Russia would be more clearly developed.

But for that reason, it would be necessary to achieve a breakthrough in the territorial question. As long as Russia accepted Japan's sovereignty over the disputed islands, Japan would be flexible on conditions, modality, and timing. But Japan would not support Yeltsin's five-stage proposal: "It is a matter of course that we make the 1956 Joint Declaration our starting point," Watanabe stated, "but the big question is the problem of Kunashiri and Etorofu." He hoped that Yeltsin would make a courageous decision (*daieidan*). Yeltsin coldly responded that he was aware of Japan's position on the territorial question. "His basic approach is that neither side should impose any preconditions for negotiations," but he would not make his own ideas known until he met with Miyazawa.[35]

There is a consensus among those who observed the Watanabe-Yeltsin meeting. It was chilly and brief: it lasted only 20 minutes. Beyond that, two contradictory views have been presented. The first view blames Watanabe for being overly intransigent on the territorial question. But others take the view that there was nothing wrong with Watanabe's performance; they attribute the cancellation of Yeltsin's trip entirely to the Russian domestic situation.[36] The truth seems to lie somewhere in between. Hyodo's briefing and Kostikov's notes concur that Watanabe was extremely conciliatory, stressing Japan's willingness to extend aid to Russia. Not a word was mentioned about the inseparability of economics and politics. But it is also true that Watanabe did not reject this principle, either. In fact, he presented the possibility of large-scale economic assistance as closely connected with the resolution of the territorial question. Furthermore, he repeated the position demanding Russia's acceptance of Japan's "residual sovereignty" of all four islands—the position that had absolutely nothing new. Yeltsin also saw no signs of softening of Japan's position on either the territorial issue or the linkage between the territory and economic aid. Whoever was at fault, the Yeltsin-Watanabe meeting sealed the fate of Yeltsin's trip to Tokyo.[37]

Watanabe's lack of diplomatic skill certainly contributed to this fiasco. Gorbachev's name should have been taboo in front of Yeltsin, but he carelessly mentioned his name, thereby unnecessarily provoking Yeltsin's anger. Nevertheless, the fiasco cannot be attributed merely to a diplomatic error: it was the failure of Japan's foreign policy, and the failure of the Owada-Hyodo line.

On the night of September 6, Yeltsin appeared on a satellite program between Moscow and Japan. His reference to the territorial question was unusually blunt. He stated that he had at his disposal 14 proposals (thus obtaining 2 more than he had revealed a week before). However, he issued a belligerent warning: whatever proposal he chose at the summit, the Japanese should not expect any part of the islands to be handed over to Japan during the visit. Why did he make such a statement that was sure to provoke resentment among the Japanese? According to Sukhanov, Yeltsin expressed displeasure with the atmosphere of this television program: he felt that he was sitting on the dock in the Japanese kangaroo court to be interrogated endlessly on the territorial question. During the program he grew visibly irritated and angered, but his anger was not sufficiently translated for the Japanese audience.[38] Or was this statement a calculated propaganda move for Russian domestic consumption? Or, perhaps, he had already made up his mind not to go to Tokyo, and the whole television interview was intended to provoke Japan's reaction so that he could exploit it as an excuse for the cancellation of the trip.

Three days later, he stunned the world by announcing that he had decided not to go to Tokyo.

Aftermath of the Cancellation

After the September fiasco, the Russian government unabashedly attempted to shift the blame for its actions entirely on the Japanese. Yeltsin and Kostikov claimed that the cancellation had resulted from Japan's political calculations. Moreover, clearly to punish the Japanese, Yeltsin courted South Korea and China. Prior to his trip to Seoul, he handed to the South Korean and U.S. families of the victims of the KAL plane shot down by the Soviet pilots in 1983 a transcribed record from the black box, but refused to give it to the Japanese.[39] He traveled to Beijing in December, and hailed Russian-Chinese relations as "a new partnership." The Japanese government was visibly shaken by the September fiasco. One might have expected that anger and humiliation from this gross violation of diplomatic protocol might have provoked an emotional backlash against Russia, destroying all the positive gains that Japan had accumulated piecemeal in the framework of balanced expansion. Nevertheless, in sharp contrast to the crass Russian behavior after the cancellation of the summit, Japan's reaction was markedly measured and restrained. Some voices did exist within the Gaimusho and the LDP supporting strong retaliatory measures against Russia, but they were confined to private airings of anger and frustrations, and never gained influence in policy.

On September 10, immediately after Yeltsin's telephone conversation with Miyazawa, the Gaimusho held an emergency meeting, attended by Owada, Hyodo, Edamura, and others. They unanimously decided to continue the previous policy of balanced expansion and to exert utmost effort not to let Yeltsin's decision damage the basic framework of the relationship. This recommendation was accepted by an emergency cabinet meeting presided over by Miyazawa, and attended by Watanabe and Owada. The government issued a statement that the Japanese government did not consider Yeltsin's decision to be a cancellation, but rather a postponement of his trip. Moreover, the Gaimusho announced that Japan had decided to extend an additional $100 million in grant-in-aid in food and medical supplies to Russia beyond what it had pledged at the coordinating conference in New York in January.[40] This virtually marked the end of the Owada-Hyodo line, and the belated vindication of the Edamura line.

After the September fiasco, the Edamura line became the dominant color, replacing the Owada-Hyodo line. In February 1993 Watanabe officially announced that Japan would invite Yeltsin to the G-7 summit in Tokyo. Japan hosted a G-7 foreign and finance ministers' conference in April 1993, where it unveiled its own aid package of $1.82 billion in addition to what it had already pledged. In April, presumably for domestic reasons, Yeltsin announced that he was prepared to visit Japan in May, but as soon as he temporarily avoided the domestic political crisis by having overwhelming support in the national referendum, he canceled his trip for the second time. Despite these repeated humiliations, Japan's response remained conciliatory. Japan's patience and restraint paid off. Yeltsin attended the G-7 summit in July. As soon as he stepped off the airplane, he issued a statement to the Japanese people, apologizing for the past cancellations, and referring to the need to "remove the problems left over from World War II based on law and justice."[41] Miyazawa and Japanese officials in turn behaved themselves by refraining from uttering a word about the territorial question during Yeltsin's stay in Tokyo during the summit. Miyazawa, in the role of the gracious host, enthusiastically supported the G-7 aid policy toward Russia. A Miyazawa-Yeltsin meeting was conducted amicably, serving as a stepping stone for a summit in October.

After the G-7 Tokyo summit, the domestic situation in both countries changed drastically. In Japan the LDP fell from its position as the ruling party, and the Hosokawa coalition government took over in July. In Russia, the conflict between the president and the parliament led to bloodshed in October. The first and foremost task of the Hosokawa government was domestic political reform. Neither Hosokawa nor Foreign Minister Hata Tsutomu had any new ideas about Japan's policy toward Russia, and all the preparations for the forthcoming summit were made by the Gaimusho with little input from the government. Divided, and still unable to recover from the shock inflicted by the September fiasco, the Gaimusho judged that the major purpose of Yeltsin's visit should be to put bilateral relations back on the right track. Thus it did not even insist upon the Russian reaffirmation of the 1956 Joint Declaration.[42]

Yeltsin's Visit to Japan, October 1993

Unlike the Gorbachev-Kaifu summit, the Yeltsin-Hosokawa summit was conducted smoothly only because the territorial question was not the subject of discussion. At the first general meeting on October 12, Hosokawa emphasized Japan's unflinching support for Russia's democratization, and expressed his hope that Yeltsin's visit would mark the beginning of a new era of Russo-Japanese relations. Yeltsin responded by saying that Russia desired to develop Russo-Japanese relations on the basis of law and justice. It is important to note that he chose to refer to law and justice, not to his five-stage proposal. Furthermore, he stressed that Russia as the successor state of the Soviet Union is committed to observe all the treaties and agreements concluded by the Soviet government, and will fulfill its responsibility and obligations.[43] He asked his interpreter to make sure that this part of his statement was accurately translated. Yeltsin was determined to avoid any reference to the 1956 Joint Declaration, and this statement was Yeltsin's signal to the Japanese that this was as far as he was prepared to go on the territorial issue.[44] Hosokawa did not press further, and stressed that Japan's contribution of $4.5 billion in aid to Russia was third to only those made by the United States and Germany.

Only at the Yeltsin-Hosokawa summit did Hosokawa bring up the territorial issue. He praised Yeltsin's letter to Kaifu as the most positive signal, unthinkable under the Soviet period, and pointed out that the occupation of the Northern Territories represented the remnants of the totalitarian system. Japan was prepared to resolve this thorny question in a democratic, humanitarian way, but the Japanese government did not consider it possible to resolve this matter at the time. Yeltsin expressed gratitude for Japan not presenting this question in terms of either "yes" or "no," or either "islands" or "the visit." In Yeltsin's view, the Russians clearly understood that sooner or later this question would have to be resolved, and Russia would go on record to honor all agreements that the Soviet government had concluded and fulfill its obligations. The resolution of this question should be based on law and justice. But the timing of the resolution would depend on the development of further bilateral relations and the psychological conditions of both peoples.[45] The exchange on the territorial issue was limited to these conversations, and both sides agreed on the wording of the Tokyo Declaration, which had been already worked out in advance.

The most important part of the Tokyo Declaration was devoted to the territorial issue. It stated: "Sharing the common view that the remnants of the difficult past in bilateral relations must be overcome, the Japanese prime minister and the Russian president conducted serious negotiations on the question of final possession of Etorofu, Kunashiri, Shikotan, and the Habomai group." It further pledged that both sides should strive for the conclusion of a peace treaty by resolving the territorial question on the basis of law and justice. Further, the Tokyo Declaration clearly stated that the Russian government, as a successor state of the Soviet Union, would honor all the agreements and treaties concluded by the Soviet Union.

Yeltsin's Tokyo visit succeeded in erasing the negative consequences he had inflicted with his previous cancellations of the trip, and bringing Russo-Japanese relations back on the right track. Furthermore, Yeltsin committed himself to the resolution of the territorial dispute on the basis of law and justice, not on the basis of his five-stage proposal. But beyond this, little progress was made. The Tokyo Declaration acknowledged that the four islands would be the subject of further negotiations, but this did not differ much from the joint statement signed by Gorbachev and Kaifu. Although Yeltsin pledged to honor all the earlier agreements, he refused to make any specific reference to the 1956 Joint Declaration. Together with the Tokyo Declaration, the summit adopted a separate economic declaration, in which the Japanese government pledged economic assistance to Russia in the framework of the policy of balanced expansion.

The Pendulum Swings Back Again: A New Stalemate

Perhaps, the Tokyo Declaration was a necessary step for further improvement in Russo-Japanese relations, and for this purpose the Edamura line that had been pursued by the Gaimusho since September 1992 should be credited in repairing the damage inflicted by the cancellation of Yeltsin's trip. Japan purposely did not push the territorial issue at the summit, and this was the major reason for enticing Yeltsin to visit Tokyo. On Yeltsin's part, in the wake of his bruising struggle with the parliament, he could not afford to make any specific territorial concessions at this time. He may have concluded that a resolution could come only after he had consolidated his power after the new elections in the Duma.

If both sides envisioned such a scenario, they were betrayed by an unexpected political development in Russia. Contrary to Yeltsin's expectations, the popular verdict in the December 1993 election overwhelming favored Vladimir Zhirinovsky, significantly undercutting Yeltsin's political power. The Zhirinovsky phenomenon forced Yeltsin to make a sharp right turn in all policies. Under this circumstance, it became impossible for Japan even to raise the territorial issue in its negotiations with Russia.

When Foreign Minister Hata visited Moscow in March 1994, his major goal was to reaffirm the Tokyo Declaration, but he found it difficult to extract the pledge to the Tokyo Declaration from Russian officials. Although Kozyrev reluctantly acknowledged Russia's commitment to it, Yeltsin refused to meet Hata. Yeltsin was obviously making the point of not allowing the territorial dispute with Japan to resurface to the forefront of political debate. Clearly, by relegating Russia's relations with Japan to a lower priority, Yeltsin began backtracking from the Tokyo Declaration. Suddenly, Tokyo's major concern became to prevent relations from deteriorating. For this purpose, Tokyo found it necessary to remind Moscow of the existence of the Tokyo Declaration; anything beyond this appeared an impossible task in the face of the right-wing swing of Russia's domestic politics.

The political situation in Japan also drastically changed. Hosokawa abruptly resigned from his post in April, and Hata briefly became the new prime minister. The coalition against the LDP collapsed. Two former archenemies, the LDP and the Socialists, coalesced to form a new coalition government, headed by Socialist Murayama Tomiichi. The LDP's head, Kono Yohei, occupied the foreign minister's post. Little could be expected in foreign policy from such a weak government. Lacking unity, ideas, and energy, the Murayama government never took new foreign policy initiatives. The task of steering Japan's foreign policy on an even keel fell exclusively to the Gaimusho. But the Gaimusho itself continued its schizophrenic approach to Russia.

After Yeltsin's cancellation of the trip, Japan gradually shifted its policy toward Russia, constructing it on two pillars: the resolution of the territorial dispute, and active support of Russia's transition to a market economy with economic aid. Nevertheless, the ambiguity remained about the relationship between these two pillars. On crucial issues where economic cooperation and the territorial question intersected, the territorial issue served as a brake slowing down economic cooperation. Furthermore, after Zhirinovsky's victory in the 1993 election, it became virtually impossible to even negotiate with the Russian government on the territorial question.

Russia's domestic politics narrowed the window of opportunity that could be exploited for the improvement of relations. There did exist, however, two such opportunities, but Japan failed to take advantage of them. The first was the proposal initiated by Nikolai Pogidin, mayor of the South Kurile District, to allow Japanese fishermen to operate in what the Russians considered to be their territorial waters around the Northern Territories in return for fishing fees from the Japanese fishing cooperatives. The two governments began official negotiations alternately in Tokyo and Moscow, but the sovereignty issue became the major obstacle to producing any concrete agreement.

The second chance came with the October 1994 earthquake that devastated the Northern Territories in 1994. The Japanese government reacted to this tragedy quickly, offering humanitarian aid to the island. First Deputy Prime Minister Oleg Soskovets expressed the hope that Japanese aid would be effectively utilized not only for the reconstruction of the devastated islands, but also for construction of a modern infrastructure.[46] Despite its initial attitude that the rescue operation should be handled without raising the territorial issue, Japan was forced to announce that its aid to the victims of the earthquake would be limited to humanitarian emergency aid, and no aid would be extended to any long-term project intended to reconstruct the infrastructure.[47] Japan thus lost a good opportunity to extend economic assistance involving development in the Northern Territories. In both cases the territorial issue became the major obstacle for Japan to extend economic cooperation directly affecting the residents on the disputed islands.

Meanwhile, faced with the unstable domestic situations both in Japan and Russia, the best that the Gaimusho could hope for was to keep bilateral relations from further deterioration rather than to work on improving them. Reaffirming the Tokyo Declaration itself proved to be an uphill fight. Soskovets visited Tokyo immediately after the October earthquake in 1994. Soskovets and Kono agreed to begin formal negotiations on fishing rights around the disputed islands and to establish an intergovernmental conference on Russo-Japanese economic and trade relations. Kono also promised Japan's support for Russia's application to become a member of GATT and the World Trade Organization (WTO). But other than these agreements, little was accomplished at Soskovets' visit. Although both sides reaffirmed the validity of the Tokyo Declaration, that was as far as Russia could go. No progress on the territorial question took place.[48]

Kozyrev's enthusiasm to improve relations with Japan had waned considerably, as he became the favorite target of attack from the right wing. In fact, he found it convenient to engage in Japan bashing on his own to prop up his sagging popularity. The beleaguered foreign minister, who was supposed to visit Tokyo by the end of 1994, continued to put off his visit to Japan, citing Japan's "political instability" as being unsuitable for his visit. When he finally did come to Tokyo in March 1995, he did not show as much enthusiasm at the negotiation table as at the tennis court in the hotel. The foreign ministerial conference was marked by a rancorous atmosphere. Both foreign ministers exchanged sharp words on the Chechen situation. Kono then expressed his disappointment that no progress had been made on the territorial question since Yeltsin's Tokyo visit, and pressed Kozyrev to move forward on this issue as spelled out in the Tokyo Declaration. Kozyrev reaffirmed the Tokyo Declaration, but citing domestic difficulty, suggested that both sides move slowly. Kono suggested two specific measures to break the stalemate: expansion of the nonvisa visits between the Northern Territories and Hokkaido, and the complete demilitarization of the Northern Territories. Kozyrev agreed on the first, but as for the demilitarization, he avoided any commitment. Regarding the fishing negotiations around the disputed islands, both agreed to begin talks in the middle of March. Kozyrev further requested that Japan support Russia's membership in the APEC, but Kono, citing the long waiting list and the decision to freeze the membership, refused to commit Japan's support.[49]

After the March foreign ministerial conference, Russo-Japanese relations remained in a frozen state for about a year. Fishing negotiations were conducted five times in Moscow and Tokyo from March 1995 to February 1996 without any results.[50] Fewer articles and books were published in the press about the Kuriles after Yeltsin's Tokyo visit, compared with the previous year, and if such publications appeared, they were written in a predominantly nationalistic-chauvinistic vein not conducive to the resolution of the territorial question.[51]

In the meantime, the political situation in both countries had developed in a direction that made it virtually impossible to resolve the territorial question. In Japan, Murayama resigned in January 1996, and the LDP's new head, Hashimoto Ryutaro assumed a new premiership. In Russia, the December 1995 election for the Duma ushered Gennadii Zyuganov's Communist Party of the Russian Federation into the largest party in the Duma, capturing 157 of the 450 seats. Viktor Chernomyrdin's "Our Home Russia," considered to be Yeltsin's party, suffered a setback, with only 54 members. The Communists, combined with Zhirinovsky's LDP (51 seats) and other conservative groups, clearly dominated the parliament.

During the election campaign, *Hokkaido shimbun* surveyed the views of the various parties on the Northern Territories question. As anticipated, the conservative and patriotic parties categorically rejected the idea of making any concessions to Japan's territorial claims. The Communist Party, citing the San Francisco Peace Treaty, rejected Japan's claims as groundless, while Zhirinovsky replied that his party would not tolerate territorial concessions to any foreign country. The Agrarian Party repeated the old Soviet thesis that there existed no territorial question between Russia and Japan. The KOR (the Congress of Russian Communities), led by General Lebed and Skokov, sent an ingenious tongue-in-cheek answer: it suggested that the sovereignty of the Kuriles should be transferred to Ukraine in return for the transfer of the Crimea to Russia, and further, that if Russia were to gain all the territories lost as a result of the collapse of the Soviet Union, it would consider the possibility of returning the Kuriles to Japan. Even Grigorii Yavlinsky of Yabloko, who had previously advocated the return of all four islands to Japan, retreated to the position that the territorial question should not be debated at this time. Aleksandr Yakovlev's Social Democratic Party took the position that it would be suicidal to raise the territorial issue during the election campaign. Chernomyrdin's party, and the small party centered around Duma Chairman Ivan Rybkin, made no comment, perhaps in deference to Yeltsin.

Zyuganov's victory in the Duma election marked another right-wing turn in the Yeltsin government. Kozyrev was finally dismissed, and replaced by Primakov as foreign minister. Primakov's first press conference augured ill for Japan, since he resurfaced the notion of shelving the territorial question. The Gaimusho protested, reminding the new foreign minister of the pledge that the Russian government had made in the Tokyo Declaration.

As the Russian domestic political situation changed from bad to worse, it became clear to the Gaimusho that the repeated insistence upon the pledge to the Tokyo Declaration would not be sufficient. Something had to be done to move bilateral relations in a positive direction.

Factors that Led to the New Policy

Since Konstantin Sarkisov and Shigeki Hakamada have written chapters on the current stage of Russo-Japanese relations, I will not analyze in detail what factors influenced both sides to adopt a new policy seeking improvement of bilateral relations. It suffices to list here some of the important factors.

On the Japanese side, it was ironically the pessimistic outlook on the resolution of the territorial question under a severe domestic political situation in Russia that led to the reassessment of its policy. It became clear to the Gaimusho that the insistence on the adherence to the Tokyo Declaration itself would not be sufficient to prevent the downward slide of relations. More importantly, it finally dawned on the Japanese that keeping Russo-Japanese relations in stalemate would not be in Japan's best interests. The quick pace with which Russia and China were forging a new "strategic partnership" alarmed Japan, particularly at a time that the U.S.-Japanese security alliance was undergoing careful scrutiny with the Okinawa base issue catching the headlines of newspapers. Furthermore, the economic and ecological deterioration of the Russian Far East, vividly illustrated by a catastrophic oil spill on Japan's coast, dumping of nuclear waste in the Japan Sea, and depletion of natural and ocean resources, caused a great concern. Under the fluid post–cold war geostrategic situation, it became no longer possible to take the view that Japan could endure a stalemate in Russo-Japanese relations without affecting its vital national interests.

On the Russian side as well, the NATO expansion forced Russia to seek a counterweight to balance the aggressive U.S. and West European policy. This led the Russian government to seek closer cooperation with China. And yet, for a variety of reasons the Russians could not rely on China alone to avoid its diplomatic isolation. Hence, the need to improve relations with Japan was keenly felt on the Russian side as well.

These factors explain why the new stage of bilateral relations began with Foreign Minister Ikeda's visit to Moscow in March 1996.

Conclusion

In my view, what happened for five years between August 1991 and March 1996 was not necessarily an inevitable and unavoidable process. Both countries were going through the pains of political transition, which admittedly gave policymakers little leverage to maneuver. Nevertheless, opportunities to radically improve relations were present during this period. In the final analysis, the failure to reach rapprochement during these five crucial years was above all the failure of decision makers, who did not exploit these opportunities.

Throughout the period, accidental factors such as miscalculations and misperceptions, bad diplomacy, bad timing, and weak leadership plagued the process of negotiations. If Japan brought the territorial problem to the G-7 summit in Munich, believing that international pressure would persuade Yeltsin to accept Japan's demand on the territorial issue, Yeltsin needlessly alienated the Japanese with his unprecedented cancellation of his scheduled trip to Tokyo only four days before the scheduled departure and his carelessly made rude remarks about Japan. Kunadze's formula of law and justice gave the Japanese false expectations that their demand would be fulfilled by the Yeltsin government. Watanabe made a major gaffe by mentioning Gorbachev's name during the crucial meeting with Yeltsin. No leaders on either side were willing to take the political risk to seek a compromise solution on the territorial problem.

If one were to seek the most important cause for the failure, however, one must point a finger at the intransigence of the Owada-Hyodo line that the Gaimusho persistently and undeviatingly pursued. Had the Edamura line been adopted earlier by decoupling the economic aid from the territorial question, as it became the official policy after the rude shock of the cancellation of Yeltsin's trip, or had the multilayered approach or Hashimoto's three principles enunciated in his Keizai Doyukai (Association of Corporate Executives) speech, Russo-Japanese relations might have taken a completely different turn.

There are several lessons that we can learn from the failure of both countries to achieve rapprochement during this period. Skillful diplomacy, backed up by strong leadership and a good sense of timing, is crucial. There must be a shared recognition that rapprochement serves the best interests of both countries. And this recognition must be also accompanied by mutual respect and trust for each other. Perhaps, these unfruitful five years provided a necessary learning experience for further negotiations.

Above all, however, the most important stumbling block continues to be the territorial question. In the final analysis, the resolution of the territorial question hinged on Japan's willingness to part with its rigid stand demanding the return of all disputed islands. This was the root cause of the failure of rapprochement during the period between 1991 and 1996. As long as Japan is not prepared to change this intransigent position, and willing to entertain an interim solution based on the two-island formula, it is unlikely that, despite the recent positive development of bilateral relations, rapprochement between the two countries will be achieved.

NOTES

1. For the background of Soviet-Japanese relations, see Tsuyoshi Hasegawa, *The Northern Territories Dispute and Russo-Japanese Relations,* vol. 1. *Between War and Peace, 1697–1985,* and vol. 2, *Neither War Nor Peace, 1985–1998* (Berkeley: University of California at Berkeley, International and Area Studies Publications, 1998), Part 2.
2. Togo Kazuhiko, *Nichiro shinjidai e no joso* (Tokyo: Simul Press, 1993), pp. 214–15; *SUPAR Report,* No. 12 (January 1992), p. 51; TASS, Seriia "AK" 3, September 26, 1991; Edamura Sumio, "Teikoku kaitai zengo: moto chu Mosukuwa taishi no kaiso," *Gaiko foramu,* No. 3, 1997, pp. 81–82.
3. Togo Kazuhiko, *Nichiro shinjidai,* pp. 216–17; *Asahi shimbun,* October 9, 1991.
4. *Hoppo ryodo,* no. 264 (November 20, 1991); TASS, November 6, 1991.
5. The conservative nature of this proposal was pointed out by Kimura Hiroshi already in 1990. At the public forum held in Sapporo, Kimura noted that postponing the resolution of the territorial question after the conclusion of a peace treaty would not be a realistic proposal. In fact, it would make it impossible for Japan to implement joint economic development on the islands. Yeltsin refused to engage in a debate, and walked out of the lecture hall in anger. See Kimura Hiroshi, *Borisu Eritsin: Ichi Roshia seijika no kiseki* (Tokyo: Maruzen raiburari, 1997), pp. iv-vii.
6. Wada Haruki, "Hoppo ryodo mondai o saiko suru: Sorenpo no shuen o mukaete," *Sekai,* No. 2 (1992), p. 221.
7. *Asahi shimbun,* September 10, 1991; *Komsomol'skaia pravda,* September 14, 1991; *Pravda,* September 19, 1991; I. Latyshev, *Kto i kak prodaet Rossiu: khronika rossiisko-iaponskikh territorial'nykh torgov (1991–1994 gody)* (Moscow: Poleia, 1994), pp. 24–26.
8. In the keynote speech he delivered at the seminar on Soviet-Japanese relations at the State Institute of International Relations (MGIMO) in March 1991, Kunadze made this formulation of law and order. I was also present at the seminar as an outside observer.
9. For more detailed examination of the legal aspects of the Northern Territories question, see *Neither War Nor Peace,* Chapter 14.

Kostikov, pp. 104–5. This part of the meeting was omitted from the Gaimusho briefing. See "Dai 3-kai Nichiro gaiso kan teiki kyogi, 92.9.2, Hyodo Oakyokucho burifu," unpublished Gaimusho document (handwritten).

35. "Dai 3-kai Nichiro gaiso kan teiki kyogi, 92.9.2, Hyodo Oakyokucho burifu," Unpublished Gaimusho document (handwritten). This recounting of the meeting basically corresponds to Kostikov's description of the meeting. Kostikov, pp. 104–6.
36. Two of the participants at the meeting, ambassadors Edamura and Soloviev, told me that Watanabe had performed well. They both blamed the failure of the meeting entirely on Russian domestic politics. See Edamura's unpublished address, "Address to the Moscow International Press Club, January 27, 1993," pp. 6–7; also Edamura, *Gaiko foramu,* No. 5 (1997), p. 118. For the contrary version, see Sukhanov, p. 260; my interview with Vladlen Martynov.
37. Kostikov believes that this meeting was decisive for Yeltsin's final decision to cancel his trip to Japan. Kostikov, p. 106.
38. Sukhanov, p. 263.
39. Edamura Sumio, *Gaiko foramu,* No. 6 (1997), p. 91.
40. *Yomiuri shimbun,* 10, 10 (evening), 14, September 17, 1992; *Asahi shimbun,* September 10, 1992; "Off-the-Record Background Briefing by Hyodo, 10 September," from the notes of a diplomatic correspondent.
41. *Yomiuri shimbun,* July 9, 1993.
42. *Asahi shimbun,* October 28, 1993; *Yomiuri shimbun,* October 2, 1993.
43. *Neither War Nor Peace,* p. 483.
44. "Eritsin daitoryo honichi (zentai kaigi no burifu) (93.10.12), Nomura Oakyokucho burifu," unpublished Gaimusho document.
45. "Eritsin daitoryo honichi, (dai 1-kai shunokaidan)," unpublished Gaimusho document.
46. *Asahi shimbun,* October 6–7, 1994; *Hokkaido shimbun,* October 7, 1994.
47. Asahi shimbum, October 11, 1994; *Nihon keizai shumbum,* October 11, 1994.
48. See, "Kono fukusori ken gaimudaijin to Sasukobettsu-roshia daiichi fukushusho no kaidan ni kansuru kisha burifu gaiyo (zentaikaigo) (94.11.17)"; "Kono fukusori ken gaimudaijin to Sasukobettsu-Roshia daiichi fukushusho no kaidan ni kansuru kisha burifu gaiyo (94.11.17) (Harada Roshia kacho burifu)"; "Murayama sori to Sasukobettsu Roshia renpo daiichi fukushusho no kaidan ni kansuru Harada Roshia kacho ni yoru kisha burifu (94.11.28)";"Sasukobettsu Roshia renpo daiichi fukushushono kishakaiken"; "O. Enu.

Sasukobettsu Roshia renpo daiichi fukushusho no honichi ni kansuru Nichiro kyodo shimbun happyo," unpublished Gaimusho documents. Iurii Nikolaev, *Rossiiskie vesti,* November 29, 1996; Agafonov, *Izvestiia,* November 29, 30, 1994; Pavel Potapov, *Komsomol skaia pravda,* November 29, 1994.

49. "Kozuirefu gaiso honichi (dai 5-kai Nichiro gaisokan teiki kyogi)," unpublished Gaimusho document.
50. *Hokkado shimbum*, February 24, 1996.
51. See, for instance, Viacheslav Zilanov, *Nezavisimaia gazeta,* May 12, 1994; I. Latyshev, *Kto i kak prodaet Rossiiu.*

CHAPTER 11

Cross-Border Relations and Russo-Japanese Bilateral Ties in the 1990s

Gilbert Rozman

ALTHOUGH THE BORDERS BETWEEN RUSSIA AND JAPAN have long been a source of dispute, at times they have also offered a glimmer of hope for cooperation. Two symbols highlight these conflicting images: (1) the Northern Territories, representing Japan's lingering grievances and the mutual suspicions that block a peace treaty; and (2) the Japan Sea rim economic sphere, a concept that embodies the dreams of an emerging era of close economic integration across national boundaries. In the 1990s preoccupation with one or another of these symbols conspired to hide the real forces of change in cross-border relations such as a changing balance of power, a shift in economic complementarities, and criminalization of bilateral trade. Beginning with visa-free exchanges of visitors between Russians on the disputed islands and Japanese in northern Hokkaido and continuing with Japanese humanitarian aid to relieve the consumer shortages of the early post-Soviet transition, new ties across the border were targeted to pave the way for good neighborly relations. Instead, they reinforced strategic, economic, and civilizational suspicions.

In the long countdowns preceding Mikhail Gorbachev's and then Boris Yeltsin's visit to Tokyo, observers wondered if the abrupt expansion of contacts between the Russian Far East and the Japan Sea coastal areas of Japan might jump-start relations between Moscow and Tokyo that continued to unfold very slowly. Would the diversity and flexibility offered by such local contacts speed the normalization of relations between the two countries while bringing bilateral cooperation in the formation of regionalism in Northeast Asia? Despite much evidence to the contrary, such hope lingered through the mid-1990s. The "no necktie summit" in Krasnoyarsk in November 1997 between Boris Yeltsin and Hashimoto Ryutaro shifted attention from the formal barriers immobilizing relations in the capitals to informal means to uplift public opinion and to dramatize the prospects of economic and political partnership. It added momentum to the search for a regional breakthrough centered on Russian areas from Krasnoyarsk to the Sea of Japan and potential partners in Japan, both local and national. Yet, while both sides heralded the results, the contrasting interpretations of what was accomplished underscored the contradictory place cross-border relations had already assumed in Tokyo's ties to Moscow. In Russia hopes focused on Japan's apparent readiness to set aside the territorial issue while accelerating the push for a peace treaty by the year 2000, and investments, especially in the Far East. In Japan reference in the official communiqué to the signing of a peace treaty on the basis of the Tokyo Declaration of 1993 fueled hopes for a territorial agreement, while few expected that Russia would establish law and order domestically capable of enticing investors and thus increasing trade beyond some obligatory projects to smooth the territorial deal. Instead of providing a shortcut to trust and integration, such ambivalent agreements could add to cynicism at the same time as local ties were actually exacerbating problems separating the two countries.

Since the 1960s, circles in both Japan and Russia have shown an interest in forging a link between the two economies and polities through the development of energy and natural resources in the Russian Far East.[1] For some political circles, such cooperation would act as a wedge for a geopolitical adjustment after decades of Japan leaning to the West and depending on the United States, and Russia neglecting the Asia-Pacific region. For some business interests, it promised a geoeconomic transformation as the rise of East Asia shifted the locus of development from the Pacific Ocean coast to areas that had languished as Japan's "backdoor" (*ura Nippon*) and from European Russia to its Far East borders with Japan, Korea, and China long treated as military outposts rather than economic zones open to dynamic neighbors. By the early 1990s academic voices on both sides also foresaw geocivilizational potential for regionalism in Northeast Asia as Japan reentered Asia and Russia balanced East and West, changing the very character of national identity, and Russia rejected a solely European identity for some version of Eurasianism as its "national idea." But all such proposals have confronted both the ugly reality of the power brokers in the Russian Far East, who have not trusted foreign encroachments and have not found a common language with Japanese authorities or business leaders, and the idealism or cynicism of Japanese administrators along the Japan and Okhotsk seas, who have been prepared to brush aside the true barriers to trust. The treasure house of the Far East at the end of the decade still has the potential to become the cornerstone of a new partnership between Japan and Russia, but so far it most vividly symbolizes the frustration of all hopes for a breakthrough.

This chapter reviews cross-border relations between Japan and Russia. On the Russian side attention focuses on Primorskii krai, Khabarovskii krai, and Sakhalinskaia oblast as well as Moscow. On the Japanese side attention concentrates on Niigata prefecture and Hokkaido as well as Tokyo. In each case, the interplay between local and central attitudes and initiatives stands in the forefront. Three aspects of relations are highlighted: (1) efforts to establish cultural and political ties across the narrow Sea of Japan creating a basis for trust, mutual understanding, and networks that could lead to economic cooperation; (2) demagoguery and lawlessness taking advantage of lessened central control, capable of damaging mutual perceptions and allowing criminal groups to dominate in economic networks; and (3) government, media, and scholarly efforts to identify the problems of cooperation and to take countermeasures to alleviate them.

From Sister-Localities to Strategies for Economic Cooperation

Encouraged by national campaigns for decentralization, prefectures from Toyama to Hokkaido and krai and oblasts of the Russian Far East pressed for greater authority to advance relations between Japan and Russia in the early 1990s. Memories of what might have been in the 1970s when Japanese investments in the Russian Far East had been expected to rise sharply prompted fresh hopes of success. On both sides of the border there was eagerness for the center to relax barriers to relations with a natural partner close at hand. The Japanese took the initiative. Prefectural and even city administrations sent delegations to Russia to establish administrative networks with formal sister-city or sister-state ties that would lead to exchanges of cultural groups. They envisioned a multistep process: local administrations would forge ties; cultural, sports, and educational groups would involve the public and influence public opinion; new air routes and other transportation would favor their locations; national offices would bless these developments with infrastructural investments and preferential policies; a favorable climate would spread to business; and finally, economic regionalism would regularize relations for the long run.[2] Although this sequence did not advance as predicted, local administrations in Japan kept their hopes for several years. Simplifying the above scenario, advocates argued that investing in infrastructure would remove the major barrier to economic exchange, which in turn would improve the political climate.[3] Intense competition continued in order to engage the most promising regional partners and to register the most activity and secure the newest air routes.

Dreams of partnership on the Japanese side were symbolized by the spell cast by the concept of the Sea of Japan rim economic zone. Although granting a place in this zone to South Korea, North Korea, and Northeast China, advocates in local administrations, universities, think tanks, and the media zeroed in on the Russian Far East as the key to success. Two facts about Russia mesmerized these proponents: its proximity to their prefectures in Japan and its abundance of natural resources including energy. It followed that the future regional division of labor would be sharp with Russia primarily in the role of resource supplier; it would be based on macroprojects with Japan in the role of investor or supplier of know-how through multinational corporations; and it would be directed to seaports facing the Sea of Japan. Conferences explored many facets of cooperation without questioning these assumptions or looking carefully at emerging problems. The Society for Japan Sea Rim Studies at Niigata University began this process in 1988, which before long yielded a national association dedicated to promoting the Japan Sea rim and to international conferences in many countries.[4] Contrary to the many conference papers, Russian authorities balked at developing natural resources in the manner intended,[5] Japanese and other foreign corporations failed to make inroads in the Russian Far East, and what trade did develop apart from marine products and used cars largely bypassed the expected beneficiaries for destinations in the large ports on the Pacific coast. Widespread public consciousness of the "Sea of Japan rim" proved to be no substitute for interest groups with a stake in advancing relations.[6]

A succession of projects occupied the spotlight of local economic relations from 1991 to 1997. Several were blatant failures, prominent among which was Japanese investment in rebuilding the Khabarovsk air terminal, leaving some Japanese feeling that they had been criminally stripped of their assets.[7] A free economic zone in the port of Nakhodka was slow to materialize, although even in late 1997 the Russian government was making plans to allow South Korea to set up a large industrial complex with more than 100 firms oriented to exports.[8]

The early strategies failed for many reasons. The Japanese initiators were too idealistic and uninformed about their Russian partners. Initial Russian counterparts included reform intellectuals, and Japanese were slow to recognize or draw lessons from the switchover to the second-generation of governors and their associates with less market-oriented leanings. Deepening poverty in the Russian Far East left the entire financial burden on Japanese shoulders with little or nothing to show for these efforts. But most importantly, while insider privatization gave control over natural resources to those more interested in making a quick killing rather than in long-term development, a resurgent great power national identity stirred resentment against Russia's place in a presumed colonial-type division of labor.[9]

To bring order and a higher degree of professionalism to the stampede for partners across the Sea of Japan, Niigata prefecture with the assistance of MITI and others established in the fall of 1993 ERINA, the Economic Research Institute of Northeast Asia. Its annual conferences and regular journal (Vol. 31 appeared in December 1999) explore prospects for regionalism with a decided shift toward short-term economics and infrastructure in comparison to the early literature. Yet, ERINA could not escape from the shadow of boosterism, never becoming a center for research on Russia or an academic environment for criticism of the real barriers to cooperation. Even when leading scholars were gathered by ERINA, the prescribed task focused on building a framework for cooperation, not explaining how barriers could be overcome. For instance, although the goal of the July 1997 ERINA conference was to discuss political issues that can bring Japan and Russia closer, there was no mention of what could be done about corruption or nationalist limitations on laws and taxes essential to Japanese investment. It sufficed to mention that the Russian government needs to minimize and remove impediments to economic interaction, while balancing this vague criticism with an appeal for the Japanese side to do more since Russia deserves its support.[10]

On the Japanese side strategies lacked realism. Academics approached regionalism idealistically without research on potential partners across the sea and with the odd attitude that open discussion of problems is best avoided in order to build trust and enthusiasm. Local administrations funded exchanges without any analysis of how cultural ties in the context of Russia's problems could forge networks of value for economic relations and capable of overcoming differences between political systems.[11] They also counted on local small- and medium-sized businesses to outperform multinational corporations in Tokyo and to steer imports more efficiently to ports along the Japan Sea, again without careful economic analysis especially of the Russian side. As long as Japanese and other organizations were willing to fund conferences, authors originating in border cities of several countries were happy to oblige with papers extolling the merits of cooperation, but this did not mean that the strategies of their countries or local administrations were compatible.[12]

On the Russian side, there was never any excitement about the Japan Sea rim. The only strategies for development were programs demanded of Moscow with vague promises and little or no follow-through. The Russian Federation failed despite repeated consideration to make Nakhodka a genuine free economic zone. The State Duma did not pass a production sharing agreement that unambiguously allowed projects apart from Sakhalin–1 and Sakhalin–2 offshore oil and gas development to advance. Prohibitive taxation threatened registered economic transactions. Even when President Yeltsin declared that he was firmly behind a plan, as in the 1996 Presidential Program for the Development of the Russian Far East and TransBaikal with a big role for foreign investment, of which First Deputy Premier Boris Nemtsov took charge in the spring of 1997 leading to travel to Japan to stimulate interest, the program remained vague and its implementation in Russia doubtful. Japan could do little when Russia failed to put its own house in order.

Hope was not lost despite the many early setbacks to cross-border relations. On the Russian side the image remained of a punitive Japan holding economic assistance and investment back because of linkage to the territorial dispute. When Japan worked hard to overcome that image, especially at the November 1997 summit, Russian expectations rose that at last money to which their economy is deserving would flow in. Ironically, the symbol of the "Northern Territories" had begun to blind Russians to the true nature of economic problems in the Far East. On the Japanese side the image of a future booming "Japan Sea economic rim" added to wishful thinking that Russia was serious about addressing the economic problems leaving its Far East in crisis. When Yeltsin came to Krasnoyarsk in November with an economic wish list and with Nemtsov rather than a Foreign Ministry aid, the Japanese mass media took this as a sign of seriousness that Moscow was keen on doing all that it could to resolve the problems of this century by the year 2000. Neither side brought before the public the real barriers to cooperation that had to be overcome.

From Demagoguery to Criminality on the Sea of Japan

For several years it was an open secret that most local trade between Japan and Russia was of a criminal nature. The two most conspicuous products were fish and crabs exported from the Russian side and used automobiles exported from the Japanese side. The Russian side was riddled with the most far-reaching criminality—tax evasion, resulting in only a small fraction of total exports officially recorded at home; Mafia extortion and threats insuring monopoly practices and eliminating market competition from freelancers in the profitable export-import business; bribes to officials, enlisting local administrations and law enforcement agencies firmly on the side of criminal organizations and meaning that there would be no challenge to falsified documents offering proof in Japanese ports that trade was properly authorized. But the Japanese side could not avoid complicity, whether simply turning its eyes away from the true nature of this commerce or actually joining through the yakuza to expand the scale of criminality and to keep it out of sight of the authorities. As scandals unfolded of how financial institutions in Japan maintained cozy relations with criminal elements at the expense of fair and proper business practices, ties to Russian gangs did not require much explanation.

At last in the second half of 1997 muckrakers on the Russian side, taking advantage of a struggle for control between Moscow officials desperate to increase tax revenues and local authorities in the Far East relying on criminal practices, began to expose the dimensions of the marine contraband. This followed by a year a virtually unfunded and unsuccessful project of the Russian government to establish a state system of observation and control over a 200-kilometer economic zone and finally a decree by President Yeltsin on preserving marine resources and state control, transferring to the Federal Border Service, whose patrol boats and resources make some enforcement possible, control over policing Russia's territorial waters. In the interest of revenue collection in the Russian Federation and preservation of resources rapidly being depleted, the central government had at last challenged highly profitable local arrangements for disposing of the rich marine resources in the Sea of Okhotsk. Crabs and shellfish alone accounted for a hefty chunk in the illicit trade. According to Russian statistics, in 1994 exports of crabs and shellfish brought in $90.4 million, while Japanese statistics indicated imports of these products from Russia of $510.9 million. Moreover, in the next two years the Japanese numbers kept rising; the gap in records grew to about 9:1.[13]

While some interests alleged that the new law and aggressiveness in dealing with marine contraband were predicated on exaggerated estimates of $4 billion in lost revenue[14] and leaders of the fish industry in the Far East published a letter to President Yeltsin in which they warned him to defend the fishermen and not break up the unified fish complex of Russia,[15] a three-part expose in *Izvestiia* in October 1997 revealed a scandal of stunning proportions. On the basis of an extensive eight-month investigation in both the Russian Far East and Hokkaido, reporters found an annual illegal outflow in one region alone of billions of dollars, predatory destruction of the bioresources in the Far Eastern seas, and an uncounted armada of conspirators defrauding a region in crisis of the financial wherewithal to normalize living conditions and begin the process of development.[16]

Although Japanese consumers benefited from the dumping of crabs and other marine products at reduced prices, some authorities and public groups recognized that the consequences could be disastrous for Japan as well as Russia. Indeed, Japanese who had become alarmed over the past five years about the destruction of the seas separating their country from Russia by the dumping of radioactive waste and large-scale oil spills now were worried about economic chaos leading to the barbaric extermination of much valued bioresources. In the city of Kushiro on Hokkaido local authorities had begun an investigation into violations of foreign trade laws. They uncovered Japanese firms with joint ventures in Russia that were cooperating in concealing funds and laundering them for use by Russians in Japan. *Hokkaido shimbun* published a chart of the ties between the Japanese and Russian fish Mafias, naming names and pointing to the paths by which money moves to pay off officials.[17] But exposés of organized crime remain the exception rather than the rule; Japanese and Russian media skirt over the realities of regional ties without leaving a complete or even reasonably accurate impression of what is transpiring.

A Russian correspondent who considers such illegal trade to have been the most effective achievement in economic relations between Japan and Russia asks of what value it is to Russia where workers can find no labor processing sea products and the Southern Kuriles remain forsaken islands instead of benefiting from money that have could have turned them into "heaven on earth."[18] In doubt too is the long-term value to Japan, whose shoppers are indifferent as to who caught and how their country purchased the newly cheap crabs and whose less developed north, including the town of Nemuro, would be likely before long to feel a sharp blow from the collapse of a cozy arrangement.

The export of used cars had launched the pattern of criminality. Russian sailors in the first months of foreign trade decentralization found that they could bring back from Japan automobiles beginning to rust in used car lots since Japanese consumers had little interest in them even if they were valued at only a few hundred dollars, while at home they could fetch thousands of dollars and—even if they were four to six years old—were seen as superior to brand-new Russian produced machines. Before long the lone sailor returning with a vehicle for personal use or resale gave way to organized gangs attacking returning vessels on pirate ships, customs agents working to channel imports into criminal hands, and a massive trade that brought at least 200,000 cars through Russia's eastern ports. If eventually Moscow tried to clamp down on imports of cars with their steering wheels on the right side supposedly for the purpose of improving safety and on individual imports for the purpose of raising tax revenues, many assumed that this was little more than a turf battle won by Mafia groups importing cars from Western Europe eager to thwart their competition. Since city dwellers in the Russian Far East managed to purchase Japanese cars in large numbers, the criminality was not enough to blind them to the benefits of regionalism. Japanese crab eaters also could appreciate these benefits. In effect, the division of labor had become cars for crabs.

Despite some efforts, automobile and marine products did not become the basis for broader cooperation. Japanese car firms took an interest in servicing centers and the training of mechanics—a centerpiece in programs to offer technical assistance to small businesses and management. But such initiatives did not reach far, producing neither a plan for assembly plants in the Russian Far East nor a large distribution system regulated from Japan. After all, criminalization of the traffic in used cars ruled out such channels. Negotiations over fishing did preoccupy both countries, but at the center of attention were quotas for Japanese fishermen operating in Russian "territorial" waters. As in the past 40 years, such negotiations were often tense. In the post-Soviet era this atmosphere was worsened by the intermittent gun battle between Japanese fishing boats allegedly darting close to the Russian-controlled islands to poach and Russian patrol boats chasing and firing at them. Seizures, shootings, arrests, and fines left a residue of ill feeling on both sides.

While Japanese local governors exercised caution in discussing Russia in the hope of winning some economic benefit, Russian governors were less restrained. Valentin Fedorov in Sakhalinskaia oblast led in the outcry against Japanese territorial designs and then attempted to sign agreements on joint development of resources in disputed territories with South Korea that would teach Japan a lesson. Although his successor Igor Farkhutdinov was less outspoken, he too argued strongly against signs of Russian weakness before Japan's designs. More progress was made in developing relations, including establishing a consular office in Iuzhno-Sakhalinsk, under Farkhutdinov, but economic integration proceeded slowly as conditions on the Russian side continued to deteriorate. Evgenii Nazdratenko in Primorskii krai reserved his most fiery rhetoric for China, gradually silencing his criticisms of Japan. Yet, his demagogic and xenophobic manner left in doubt plans for cooperative projects such as the Tumen river area development project on the border of China and North Korea or even the scaled down Zarubino transit corridor from Northeast China to the Sea of Japan. Tensions between local governors and Moscow, especially the ongoing struggle with Nazdratenko that saw Yeltsin unsuccessfully try to fire him in 1997, complicated any strategy by Japanese officials to develop long-term relations with a reliable partner.

Prospects for Establishing Stable, Long-Term Cross-Border Relations

A decade has passed since the Sea of Japan rim became a focus of Japanese attention, but administrative linkages remain unsettled. First hopes settled on reform administrators in the Russian Far East—newly appointed governors Vladimir Kuznetsov in Primorskii krai and Valentin Fedorov in Sakhalinskaia oblast and Vice-Governor Pavel Minakir in Khabarovskii krai. All of these leaders were ousted, however, as Russian politics turned toward nationalism and *nomenklatura* monopoly capitalism. Later aspirations turned toward Viktor Ishaev, governor of Khabarovskii krai, working in concert with high officials in Moscow. When Boris Nemtsov was named in the spring of 1997 as chair of the commission in charge of implementing the Presidential Program and also to take charge of economic relations with Japan, the line of authority clarified. If Nazdratenko was a problem, perhaps Nemtsov working with Ishaev could at last bring a coordinated and responsible Russian position to the bargaining table. After years of dashed hopes, expectations were not high.

Whatever the long-term prospects, the summer of 1997 brought much disconcerting news to local proponents of the Presidential Program as the lynchpin of renewal in the Far East and cooperation with Japan. Aleksandr Granberg, the Moscow economist designated to guide and represent what he referred to as Russia's lone "super-program," acknowledged that no mechanism existed to combine local programs. He pointed to the program as an example of how much we cannot do in comparison to more scientific regional programming in the Soviet Union 15 to 20 years earlier, and appealed for more quality in future programs.[19] Apart from the State Duma's unwillingness to pass supportive legislation and fiscal belt-tightening under Anatoly Chubais, allowing only driblets of central funding, the program itself was deeply flawed and far from adequate as a basis for regionalism. While praising Japanese assistance for an oil refinery and an infant food enterprise in Khabarovskii krai, Viktor Ishaev warned that the disintegration processes were continuing and put a price tag of $75 billion on the structural perestroika needed for the region.[20] Even the most supportive local governor could find little sign of a turnaround. And Igor Farkhutdinov warned that conditions on the Kuriles are two or three times tougher than in the rest of Russia; people lack confidence in the future, and they are abandoning this area.[21] Separately, he warned that those in the State Duma interfering with the implementation of Sakhalin–1 and Sakhalin–2 oil and gas projects because they regard such deals as "robbery of the motherland" were leaving the local population with no recourse.[22] Meanwhile, the most severe crisis of authority persisted in Primorskii krai, where Governor Evgenii Nazdratenko, after being fired in May by Boris Yeltsin, received unanimous support from the Federation Council, extricated himself from this impasse when he reached an agreement with Boris Nemtsov in June on payment of wage arrears through consolidation in the energy sector, and then failed to fulfill the agreement while his krai plunged deeper into crisis.[23] The disarray in Russia was not lifting.

Japan faced a difficult challenge, complicated by the spreading Asian economic flu in the last months of 1997 and then the Russian financial crisis a year later. A commission to promote decentralization (*chiho bunken suishin iinkai)* as part of Prime Minister Hashimoto Ryutaro's "big bang" approach to reform was stumbling before resistance to consolidating prefectural and local administrative units. The very governments in Niigata, Hokkaido, and elsewhere pressing for decentralization to advance prospects for the Sea of Japan economic rim had been searching for increased infrastructure investments to add to their economic strength. Instead, they were threatened with increased autonomy, perhaps in unfamiliar boundaries, accompanied by greater fiscal responsibility made worse by national retrenchment. Economic uncertainties spreading through Asia diminished prospects for large long-term investments in a risky market such as Russia.

Multilateralism is not favorable to the Russian Far East either. Sino-Russian border trade and joint ventures fell into a tailspin in 1994 from which they have yet to recover fully. South Korea incurred large economic losses from its "northern strategy" of loans and investments in Russia in return for political recognition, and after its financial battering and presidential change at the end of 1997 cannot be expected to provide much sustenance to Russia. North Korea's economy remains in desperate straits marked by famine and negligible foreign trade. In place of the earlier mood of a region poised on all sides for an economic takeoff, Japan and Russia face a region in despair with a record of false starts and unrealized expectations.

Perhaps adversity would add a necessary ingredient to the recipe for regionalism that overconfidence and bluster before potential foreign partners had not provided. Realism could become a springboard for regionalism as each side tallied the cost of inaction. The key continued to be the Russian Far East, mired in crisis. Moscow is in no position to save it. But Moscow could cooperate with local leaders and elites to launch a multilateral solution, building on the Presidential Program of 1996. And Japan could become the prime source of investments and know-how in a multilateral approach to regionalism focused on energy but not neglecting industry. Since the total population along the Sea of Japan and Sea of Okhotsk in Russia is less than 5 million, the costs to Japan of this kind of regional economic leadership need not be prohibitively high. But the danger of becoming embroiled in a criminalized region and an intense internal struggle between forces in Moscow and local administrations must make Japan wary. If Japan had concluded a deal in 1991 with Gorbachev involving huge commitments of loans and investments, there is every reason to think that the result would have been enormous financial losses and a loss of hope that relations could be set back on the right track. Similarly, it would be worse to bank on inflated expectations and waste an opportunity that may only come once to build a firm cross-border foundation for bilateral relations and regionalism. Russia must provide favorable conditions not only through the right laws and tax policies, but also through reliable and trustworthy networks for long-term projects. The criminal nature of cross-border ties is not just a nuisance to be swept aside through a high-level agreement; it is a cancer threatening the very health of Russo-Japanese relations.

NOTES

1. Shibuya Tadashi, *Kannihonkaiiki ni okeru kokusai kankyo no keisei to henryo ni kansuru yobiteki kenkyu* (Niigata: Niigata Univeristy report to the Mombusho 1990), pp. 39–43.
2. "Niigata: kannihonkai keizaiken no chusu toshi o mezasu," *Forbes,* October 1992, pp. 166–70; *Kannihonkai keizai koryu ni kansuru chosa, kenkyu* (Toyama: Toyama University Nihonkai keizai kenkyujo, 1993);
3. Nobuo Arai, Takeshi Miyamoto, and Makoto Uryu, *Economic Reform of the Russian Far East* (Tokyo: MITI Research Institute of International Trade and Industry, 1994), p. 20.
4. *Kannihonkai tsushin,* Niigata University Kannihonkai kenkyukai; *Kannihonkai kokusaigaku koryu shimpojiumu: kannihonkaigaku setsuritsu daikai* (Niigata: November 26–27, 1994).
5. Viktor Larin and Evgenii Plaksen, "Primor'e: perspektivy razvitiia cherez prizmu obshchestvennogo mneniia," *Rossiia i ATR,* No. 1, 1993, pp. 5–21.
6. "Kyakko abiru kannihonkai keizai ken to Niigata ken no yakuwari," *Senta geppo,* November 1992, pp. 1–2.
7. Gilbert Rozman, "Troubled Choices for the Russian Far East: Decentralization, Open Regionalism, and Internationalism," *The Journal of East Asian Affairs,* Vol. 9, No. 2, Summer/Fall 1997, pp. 554–55.
8. "Breaking News," *Russian Regional Report,* Vol. 2, No. 33, October 2, 1997, p. 8,
9. My review of the press in Vladivostok from 1993 shows an abundance of distrustful articles not only on China but also on other potential foreign partners, including Japan. "Russian Populist Reactions in 1993–94 to the Coming of the Chinese," unpublished manuscript.
10. "Japan and Russia in Northeast Asia: Building a Framework for Cooperation in the Twenty-First Century," Report of the Workshop in Tainai, Niigata, 29–30 July, 1997, Economic Research Institute for Northeast Asia, pp. iv and 14.
11. Ikuo Hirayama, "'Kannihonkai ken' no kanban orosazu genjitsu rosen e: Niigata ken no kokusai koryu," *Toyo keizai,* July 13, 1994, p. 129.
12. Gilbert Rozman, "Flawed Regionalism," *Pacific Review,* Vol. 11, No. 1, 1998, pp. 1–27.
13. *Izvestiia,* September 12, 1997.
14. *Segodnia,* September 9, 1997.
15. *Izvestiia,* October 4, 1997.

16. *Izvestiia,* October 21, 1997.
17. *Izvestiia,* October 23, 1997.
18. Ibid.
19. Alexandr Granberg, "Regional'nye programmy: pravo na sushchestovanie," *Rossiiskie regiony,* No. 30, August 1997, pp. 5–6.
20. Viktor Ishaev, *Rossiiskie regiony,* No. 25, June 1997, pp. 4–6.
21. Igor' Farkhutdinov, "Osnovlenie Sakhalina," *Rossiiskie regiony,* No. 37, October 1997, pp. 10–11.
22. *Rossiiskaia gazeta,* August 6, 1997, p. 3
23. Gilbert Rozman, "The Crisis of the Russian Far East: Who Is To Blame?" *Problems of Post- Communism,* Vol. 44, No. 5 September-October 1997, pp. 3–12.

CHAPTER 12

Russo-Japanese Relations after Yeltsin's Reelection in 1996

Konstantin Sarkisov

RUSSIAN POLITICS IN THE 1990S HAVE BEEN OF GREAT consequence not only for Russia itself but also for the evolution of international relations. Boris Yeltsin's reelection in mid-summer 1996 preserved, at least for the time being, Russia's fledgling democracy. It prevented the communists from returning to power and gave hope to the international community by conveying an image of Russia as a democratic country. As for ties to most of the great powers, the election served to keep relations on course. But in the case of Russo-Japanese relations, the aftermath of the elections, particularly following Yeltsin's recovery from severe health problems, brought a sudden acceleration of contacts. Did the election alter the dynamics of relations between Moscow and Tokyo and, if so, why? Two years after the election, when the spreading Asian financial crisis caused a loss of confidence in Russia and led to an economic and political crisis, did a new dynamic emerge? This chapter reviews first the time of Yeltsin's ascendancy to mid-1998 and then the early signs of change in the wake of the crisis.

In 1996 the only real alternative to Yeltsin was Gennadii Zyuganov, leader of the communists and a figure capable of rallying many self-proclaimed nationalists. Although Zyuganov had visited Japan several times at the invitation not of the Communist Party of Japan but of a political group that was striving to get back the four disputed islands and had helped publish his book in Japanese, his election would have threatened to damage Russian-Japanese relations. Bilateral ties remained at an impasse, but quietly diplomats in the two countries had been working, notably since 1994, to build a foundation for negotiations. The spirit of cooperation was rather positive. Moreover, Japan was feeling the pressure of the United States and other Western countries to do more to assist Russia's precarious transition. Zyuganov's election would have called such support into question. Yeltsin's election stabilized an improving situation, and it allowed forces already at work to begin to shape the course of Russo-Japanese relations.

Election Preparations

At the beginning of 1996 Yeltsin decided to defy his low popularity ratings and try to continue as president of Russia for another five-year term. To this end, he made sharp changes in his policies inside Russia. Accepting the reality of a bitter defeat in Chechnya, he shifted his sympathy from hardliners to democrats and reformers. In the foreign policy realm his new inclination was to favor professionalism and those who could meet new challenges, including cooler relations with the West as a result of the imminent expansion of NATO. While the stress on democratic values in foreign policy remained intact, the romantic flavor of the democratic "alliance" with the West was replaced by a foreign policy focused on defending national interests.

In the first days of 1996 Yeltsin dropped his loyal lieutenant Andrei Kozyrev and appointed Yevgeny Primakov as the new foreign minister. This was received in the West as a signal of a hardening of Russian foreign policy. Media speculation of a pro-Asian and anti-Western slant in Russian policy based on Primakov's prominence as a specialist on Arab countries or on his background as head of the Russian External Intelligence Service is beside the point. Those who happened to work with him in one or another research institute of the Soviet Academy of Sciences knew him as a person partial to hard analytical analysis without any particular ideological slant. As to his personal views, he always sided with the reformists in the Brezhnev era, and after Gorbachev came to power he ceased working as an academician and joined the presidential and governmental institutions. He was known to be close to Alexandr Yakovlev, one of the architects of Gorbachev's perestroika. It was surprising that Yeltsin still chose Primakov despite his reputation as a person close to Gorbachev.[1]

At the outset, Primakov refrained from any sensational declaration or any kind of criticism of his predecessor. He avoided populism and excessive media attention, while paying close attention to working out the new priorities of Russian foreign policy. Three stand out: (1) to develop relations with the countries of the Commonwealth of Independent States (CIS) that would eliminate the tense issues plaguing ties with Ukraine and the Baltic states and advance the process of economic and political integration within the fragile CIS framework; (2) to construct a new relationship with Western countries on the premise of a more precise balance between Russia's new democratic values and its enduring national interests, including the interest of preserving the Yeltsin regime despite severe pressure from opposition forces and decreasing popularity and that of sustaining economic reforms (in part by obtaining all conceivable concessions from the West in exchange for final compliance with NATO's expansion eastward); and (3) to undertake a more active and professional foreign policy in the East, striving to balance the western and eastern directions in Russian policy.

Russian diplomacy toward Japan became part of this new strategy. One other factor was at play—the fact that throughout Yeltsin's tenure in office Japan has been a matter of particular interest to him. His prior experience, including abortive attempts to push bilateral relations ahead and work out a formula for a territorial solution (the five-stage solution plan) as well as his clumsy postponement of the planned official visit to Japan in September 1992, created a special background for policy to Japan. Although Yeltsin over the course of time had become too cautious and required strong efforts from the Ministry of Foreign Affairs to prod him into a more active stance, the appointment of Primakov, who was experienced in dealing with Japan, set the stage for renewed activity. As director of the Institute of Oriental Studies and then of the Institute of World Economy and International Relations, Primakov had done his best to bolster ties with Japan from the lean years of the late 1970s and first half of the 1980s and to find a formula for working out a mutually acceptable scheme to free the two countries from the territorial stalemate. He had a longstanding interest in Japan.

Diplomatic personnel including the new vice-minister responsible for Japan under Primakov proceeded quickly to develop a conceptual framework for bilateral relations. At the outset it was decided to avoid the extremes of two previous concepts: the longstanding Soviet approach insisting that no territorial dispute exists between the two countries; and the approach of the post-Soviet "romantic period" seeking to solve this problem at one stroke. Both had proven counterproductive. In their place the Foreign Ministry decided to move ahead by slow and steady steps that produce positive results, enhancing relations and building a favorable environment for an eventual territorial solution. This policy had at least five aims: (1) to remove the traditional imbalance in Russian foreign policy in East Asia, the weakest point of which was relations with Japan stalemated by the territorial dispute; (2) to create a new configuration of powers in the region, facilitating cooperation among the major powers including the United States; (3) to avoid a unilateral slant in relations with China by counterbalancing these with relations with Japan, thus forestalling a situation in which China's power may become overwhelmingly strong; (4) to secure Japanese support for Russia's entry into regional structures, especially APEC; and (5) to attract Japanese direct investment and technology into the Russian Far East and Siberia.

Primakov's diplomacy toward Japan did not start off well. Reflecting the wariness of Russia's president, the foreign minister proposed an old formula used in territorial negotiations with China to postpone a territorial solution to the next generation and rely upon the wisdom of the future. This apparently contradicted the 1993 Tokyo Declaration signed by Yeltsin and confirmed by him many times from 1993 through 1995 both in oral and written form. It declared (paragraph 2) that "both sides agreed to proceed with negotiations in order to sign the Peace Treaty as soon as possible by solving the territorial issue on the basis of historical and juridical facts and documents worked out through agreements between the two countries, as well as the principles of law and justice and by this fully normalize bilateral relations." Primakov should have known this agreement and the importance of it for bilateral relations beginning in October 1993. What was his real intention? Perhaps, he was trying to warn the Japanese side that matters could get worse and to persuade them that priority should be given to the idea of expanding bilateral relations. At the time of Yeltsin's election the controversial statements by the new foreign minister had left some uneasiness in Japan, but there was also some hope that once the election battle was over a fresh start could be made.

Primakov's Visit to Japan in November 1996 and Follow-up

The visit by Primakov to Japan signaled the formulation of a new Russian agenda for Japan. It did not reject the preceding approach, but added concrete ideas and a greater sense of urgency. Primakov confirmed the 1993 Tokyo Declaration and made it clear that Russia would abide by all previous agreements. He made it crystal clear that Moscow regards its relations with Tokyo as of the highest priority, adding that the president and the Ministry of Foreign Affairs would do their utmost to enhance bilateral relations. At that time Yeltsin's health was poor and the political situation in Russia was uncertain. By his visit, Primakov underscored that Russia regarded bilateral relations as a matter of great long-term importance.

The main idea put forward by Primakov was his proposal for joint development of the disputed islands. This idea was, in fact, not a new one. Actually, it had been proposed during Gorbachev's visit to Japan in April 1991. Nevertheless, the Japanese government also was eager to invigorate relations and accepted it as a new central point of Russian diplomacy without directly committing itself. A second indication by Primakov of Russia's renewed commitment to improve relations was his mention of Yeltsin's adherence to his old promise to withdraw Russian forces from the islands except the border-defense units.[2]

Primakov's diplomacy was marked by an emphasis on symbolic gestures that are taken seriously in countries such as Japan. In Tokyo he convened a ceremony for conferring Russian decorations on Japanese who had played a distinguished role in bilateral relations. Among those decorated, to the surprise of many, was Suetsugu Ichiro, the leader of the movement for returning the disputed islands to Japan. For many years Suetsugu had arranged unofficial contacts between Soviet and Japanese experts on the territorial issue and deserved acclaim not only as the main Japanese proponent of territorial claims but also as the principal supporter of dialogue on the issue. Though Suetsugu joked that he would prefer to get the territories from Primakov rather than a decoration, the symbolism demonstrated that Russia does not regard him or others who are striving for the return of the islands as political foes.

The visit of Japanese Foreign Minister Ikeda Yukihiko in March 1997 built on the momentum achieved from Primakov's visit. An agreement was reached to open a branch of Japan's General Consulate in Yuzhno-Sakhalinsk, the main city on the island that had once belonged to Japan. This was a dramatic achievement because it meant a change in Tokyo's previous position that the sovereignty over the southern part of Sakhalin had not been legally resolved and, therefore, although Japan was not making territorial claims for it, it did not belong to Russia in the strictest sense of international law. A compromise could be achieved within Japan's Ministry of Foreign Affairs on the premise that this is not a consulate but an outlet of the consulate located elsewhere. In response to Primakov's encouraging tone the previous fall, the Japanese side had shown its own flexibility on the territorial dispute. A new pragmatic atmosphere held promise for the future.

Defense Minister Rodionov's Visit to Japan and the Strategic Dimension

The first ever visit to Japan of a defense minister from Moscow, in May 1997, yielded surprising results that indicated that strategic factors could help the process of rapprochement. A new geostrategic paradigm presented by the high ranking military leader conveyed a strong message to the Japanese government, which had been slow to cease issuing warnings about the Soviet and later Russian threat. Rodionov's most important points were: (1) Russia does not regard Japan as a potential military threat; (2) Russia does not regard the U.S.-Japan defense treaty as a military agreement injurious to its security; moreover it sees the treaty as a factor of stability in the Asia-Pacific region; (3) Russia does not oppose the new security guidelines enhancing the defense capability of Japan and the United States in case of an emergency.

Indirect approval of the U.S.-Japan Security Treaty had been expressed several times by officials of the Foreign Ministry of Russia but never by a top military official. The military in Russia was considered to be more cautious and even suspicious in its assessment of the military pact between Tokyo and Washington. Traditionally it was inclined to overestimate the threat of military pacts, especially of the U.S.-Japan Security Treaty, justifying its own claims for more defense spending. A positive attitude toward the new defense guidelines came as a complete surprise.

Just before Rodionov's visit to Japan in April 1997 a Russian-Chinese Declaration was signed by Yeltsin and Jiang Zemin in

Moscow declaring their common outlook on a multipolar world and reinforcing the strategic partnership between their countries proclaimed in April 1996. A bilateral posture against the hegemony of any country in the region and any steps toward enhancing military blocs was also spelled out in this declaration. Chinese leaders had unequivocally backed Russia's negative reaction to NATO's eastward expansion and assumed that Russia correspondingly backed China's position toward the U.S.-Japan security guidelines, a matter made more urgent because of suggestions that they now approved of joint actions in the area of the Taiwan Straits in case of a clash between China and Taiwan. Rodionov's comments in Tokyo defied the logic of the month-old agreement. They impressed the Japanese media, if not as a clear-cut approval, at least as a statement of understanding for the U.S.-Japanese defense guidelines.

Rodionov's statement fit into Russia's emerging strategic paradigm during the spring of 1997. The compromise achieved in Primakov's hard and exhaustive negotiations with Secretary of State Madeleine Albright on the NATO issue changed the whole geostrategic picture in the world. Russia's agreement to comply with the expansion was compensated by a solid agreement with NATO giving Moscow not a veto but an instrument to influence NATO's decisions. At the same time Russia became a full member of what many regard as the world's highest political body, now renamed the Group of Eight. This fundamental shift in the global situation greatly influenced Moscow's strategy. Instead of drawing close to Beijing and working with it to create a kind of political counterbalance to NATO, Russia chose a different approach—a balanced and omnidirectional policy of cooperation with the major powers. To some extent, strategic apprehension toward China's growing power among the Russian military was reflected in Rodionov's statement and even in the first inklings of three-way cooperation on security among Japan, Russia, and the United States.

Deputy Prime Minister Boris Nemtsov's Visit to Japan and Economic Cooperation

The appointment of Boris Nemtsov, who with much fanfare became first deputy prime minister in March 1997, as chairman of the Russian side of the Russian-Japanese Joint Commission on trade and economic cooperation, was another sign of a new commitment to bilateral relations. Since Nemtsov was rumored at the time to be the most promising candidate to succeed Yeltsin in 2000, his appointment was assessed in Japan as an upgrading of relations by Moscow and as a sign of seriousness about involving Japan in the Russian market. Among other issues, Nemtsov had to tackle proposals for joint development of the disputed islands. Seen as close to Grigorii Yavlinsky, the most outspoken Russian politician in favor of handing all four islands over to Japan, Nemtsov was particularly welcomed by the Japanese.

Nemtsov's visit to Japan in June 1997 fell short of expectations. He avoided any discussion of the territorial issue, referring to the fact that this question was under the sole competence of Yeltsin. Nemtsov insisted that his expertise allows him to push forward the economic agenda with Japan, including joint development of the four islands. The most promising topic on this agenda was investment in energy development projects in Siberia and the Russian Far East. This attracted extensive attention from the Japanese side. Yet, Nemtsov's limited contacts in Tokyo demonstrated the insignificance of existing economic ties between the two countries. It became clear that any efforts to break out of the impasse in relations would have to include a vigorous set of initiatives to broaden economic ties.

The Denver Summit and the New Hashimoto Principles

The G-8 summit in Denver on June 20–22, 1997 was a turning point in Russian-Japanese relations. Meetings between Yeltsin and Hashimoto persuaded the Japanese prime minister to pursue a fundamentally new policy highlighted by flexibility and building a constructive atmosphere. A month later Hashimoto enunciated three principles for bilateral relations. The high tide of anticipation of a breakthrough had begun.

After some visible reluctance about accepting Russia as a full member of the G-7 club of industrial powers, Tokyo agreed to this arrangement recognizing that it would serve as a psychological breakthrough. American support for Russia's membership had pushed the matter forward, and during his meeting with Hashimoto, President Bill Clinton hinted that a Japanese-Russian reconciliation and the signing of a peace treaty would be consistent with American national interests. There were even rumors that Clinton had proposed to Hashimoto that he would be willing to serve as a fair broker between him and the Russian president. No doubt, the momentum gained by the U.S.-Russian agreement on NATO expansion facilitated Washington's more positive posture toward an eventual Russian-Japanese compromise.

The U.S. position was vital for a decisive improvement in Japanese-Russian relations for several reasons. Not only has American influence on Japanese diplomacy continued to be great even more than four decades after the end of the American occupation, but memories remain fresh of Washington's capacity in the cold war to block a bilateral compromise on the territorial issue, including through legal means. Clause 26 of the San Francisco Peace Treaty of September 1951 empowered the United States and other signatories to use legal means to defy any concessions made by Japan to a third party inconsistent with the provisions of the treaty. The San Francisco Treaty does not specify that Russia will receive title over the Kurile islands and the southern part of Sakhalin, opening the possibility for outside involvement.

In Denver, Yeltsin made a positive impression on Hashimoto and Japanese officials. He confirmed the Tokyo Declaration, endorsed the Japanese move to become a permanent member of the United Nations Security Council, a matter of considerable importance considering Russia's right to veto any decision, and proposed a "strategic partnership" between the two countries. However unrealistic such a partnership might have seemed, its mere proposal had a positive impact in demonstrating that Russia seeks closer relations with Japan. The Russian president also proposed a process of regular summits as a mechanism to sustain progress in relations.

Barely a month later, on July 24, Hashimoto responded to the opportunity created in Denver with an unprecedented speech in the history of bilateral relations with Russia. Although the central point of the speech was Japan's relations with Russia, Hashimoto went further in raising regional and global issues to the point that some considered it a starting point for a new Japanese strategy for facing the upcoming century. For the first time close ties with Russia had gained a prominent place in planning for Japan's future.

The new course toward Russia, which was interlocked with broader perspectives on the balance of power, incorporated Japanese recognition of the following seven features.

1. International relations are undergoing dramatic and fundamental changes not only because of the collapse of the cold war system but also due to the growing economic globalization.
2. A new system of international relations will be characterized by increased interdependence of the interests of European and Asian countries and by the emergence of a Eurasian system of relations, or, in terms of an old metaphor, "silk road" relations.
3. While pursuing its national interests and its new global role by giving priority to its relations with the United States, Japan should strive for a partnership with other centers of power, particularly with Russia and China.
4. Relations with Russia must be considered as the highest priority since in the emerging quadrangle—the United States, Japan, China, and Russia—the Russian-Japanese side has been the weakest, taking into account the lingering territorial question and the absence of a peace treaty.
5. Japan is going to build its relations with Russia upon three principles: trust, mutual benefit, and long-term perspective. Regaining the four islands remains a national strategic goal, but the policy of achieving this objective should be changed and based on the development of bilateral cooperation and the creation of an appropriate atmosphere.
6. In carrying out the new constructive diplomacy toward Russia, Japan will pay particular attention to economic cooperation and, specifically, the development of energy resources in Siberia and the Russian Far East.
7. In diplomatic activity toward Russia Japan will emphasize personal relations between the leaders of the two countries provided that during the next two years they will be Yeltsin and Hashimoto.

In comparison to the earlier policy concepts advocated by Japanese leaders for relations with Russia, Hashimoto's three principles noted in point five marked a significant step forward. Through 1988 Japanese policy was characterized as the "entrance approach" or the inseparability of politics and economics, requiring Soviet agreement on the four islands before other relations could develop. From 1989 it shifted to the "balanced expansion" approach, allowing for parallel progress in politics and economics but still making the latter dependent on advances in resolving the territorial question. At the start of 1997, Hashimoto replaced this notion with the concept of a "multilayered approach." To promote diverse negotiations the Japanese side widened the range of areas of cooperation to be discussed and agreed that progress on them did not need to be balanced with progress on the Northern Territories question.[3] This separation was reinforced by the new principles, which no longer linked the solution to the territorial question to progress in economic and other relations.

The Hashimoto address had a conspicuous impact on the Russian side. It was perceived as a positive signal presenting a new Japanese philosophy toward a territorial solution. The speech also led to a misinterpretation, as some Russian analysts interpreted it as a declaration of "tanaage" (shelving the territorial issue) and that view filtered into the Russian media. This produced some tension in Japan. Officials of the Japanese Ministry of Foreign Affairs who had prepared the blueprint of the speech including the three principles were allegedly criticized for making a serious mistake by using the wording "long-term perspective," which critics believed might have been perceived by Moscow as Japan's readiness to shelve the territorial issue.

The Krasnoyarsk Summit and Its Aftermath

With Japanese upbeat about the new seriousness in the Yeltsin administration to address bilateral relations and Russians excited by the promise of Hashimoto's three principles, anticipation mounted for the first "no-necktie" summit between leaders of the two countries. Could a formula be found in Krasnoyarsk to launch high intensity efforts to achieve a breakthrough in a situation still regarded as at an impasse? Both sides were determined to find a positive answer to this question.

Only one person from each side accompanied the leaders during the talks. On the Russian side it was First Deputy Prime Minister Boris Nemtsov, and on the Japanese side it was Tamba Minoru, councilor or second vice minister of foreign affairs. Moreover, most essential talks occurred aboard a riverboat on the Yenisei River in the presence only of interpreters. If the absence of neckties had been meant to suggest not only a relaxed mood but also low expectations for the outcome of the summit, the results far exceeded the public's expectations. The most surprising agreement was to "take all efforts in order to sign a peace treaty between the two countries by the year 2000 based on the 1993 Tokyo Declaration." Not long before the summit, Yeltsin himself and his press secretary, Sergei Yastrezembsky, had asserted several times that it would not be appropriate to put a time limit on the solution of the territorial issue. What changed Yeltsin's mind, causing him to take the initiative in proposing this limit to the Japanese side, which eagerly concurred? Putting aside the customary unpredictability and even erratic nature of the Russian president, Yeltsin may have been seriously considering combining a possible solution on the territorial issue with a dramatic expansion of economic cooperation, particularly huge Japanese investments in Siberia and the Russian Far East.

The agreements at Krasnoyarsk can be divided into two parts. On the Russian side most attention centered on the "Yeltsin-Hashimoto plan" consisting of 43 items of bilateral cooperation. These ranged from trade and investments to promotion of small enterprises to cooperation between the navies of both countries in rescue operations. On the Japanese side there was surprise and optimism with the accelerated process to sign a peace treaty. The two parts were, of course, interdependent. After the meeting Russian officials made it absolutely clear that the signing of a peace treaty implying a solution of the territorial dispute depends on implementation of the Yeltsin-Hashimoto plan. And before long Japanese officials were calling for more progress toward a peace treaty as a factor that would boost confidence in addressing economic issues.

Even if Yeltsin and Hashimoto had arrived at their agreements with the best intentions and expectations of success, there were forces operating against their plans. Huge Japanese investments depend not only on the will of politicians, but also on the behavior of investors responding to real incentives and objective economic conditions. On the one hand, the Russian parliament continued to delay in passing laws that would provide the necessary conditions and Russian regional leaders failed to provide a secure environment. On the other hand, the traditional caution of Japanese investors was reinforced by the spreading Asian financial crisis, Japan's own banking crisis, and the sharp fall in oil and commodity prices that warned investors of an oversupply.

It was also unclear what would constitute a mutually acceptable solution of the territorial dispute. The Krasnoyarsk agreement refers to the 1993 Tokyo Declaration that affirms only the necessity of a territorial solution on the basis of law, justice, and historical facts. If Japanese see this as unambiguously signifying that Russia must return all four islands, this view is not shared by many Russians. The most obvious compromise is for Russia to hand over the two islands of Habomai and Shikotan on the basis of law, that is the 1956 Joint Declaration that, having been ratified by both parliaments, is obligatory for both sides. But that leaves the meaning of "justice" and "historical facts" unclear, and could suggest a two-stage solution whereby they continue to be the subject of negotiations.

Even before the political crisis in Russia of late summer 1998, the fact that general elections to the State Duma were scheduled for 1999 and presidential elections for 2000 seemed to make it very difficult for Yeltsin to make territorial concessions even of two islands that would arouse a nationalistic outcry. Already 40 years ago, the Japanese government rejected a two island transfer and over the past decade they have more than once indicated that this would not be acceptable. Why would Japan accept this formula now as the basis for a peace treaty? No doubt such a compromise would arouse a nationalistic reaction in Japan, too.

NOTES

1. Aleksandr Korzhakov, the bodyguard of Boris Yeltsin who became his close associate, recalled that when Primakov was appointed as chief of Russia's foreign intelligence service he had been surprised and asked his boss what was the reason for this. Yeltsin replied that Primakov never said a single bad word about him. Aleksandr Korzhakov, *Boris El'tsin: Ot rassveta do zakata* (Moscow: 1997), p. 118.
2. According to data given by Primakov to the Japanese Minister of Foreign Affairs Ikeda in March 1997 on the islands of Kunashir and Iturup were stationed 3,500 Russian soldiers and on Shikotan and Habomai none.
3. Tsuyoshi Hasegawa, *The Northern Territories Dispute and Russo-Japanese Relations*, Volume 2, *Neither War Nor Peace, 1985–1998* (Berkeley: University of California, International and Area Studies, 1998), p. 504.

CHAPTER 13

Japanese-Russian Relations in 1997–1999: The Struggle against Illusions

Shigeki Hakamada

FROM 1996 THROUGH 1998 JAPANESE-RUSSIAN RELATIONS showed signs of qualitative change. On the surface, relations between the two countries improved to an unprecedented degree. However, to no small extent, these improvements were forged on the basis of illusions in both countries. In other words, expectations with little basis in reality were driving the advance in relations. The challenge in 1999–2000 is to prevent a groundswell of disillusionment that began at the end of 1998 from setting relations back again.

The illusion on the Japanese side was the thought that the basic agreement in the Tokyo Declaration of 1993, in other words the agreement signed when Boris Yeltsin visited Japan to resolve the territorial question and conclude a peace treaty, would be realized in the near future. On the Russian side the illusion was the expectation that the territorial problem could be pigeon-holed while bilateral economic relations and other ties would develop. The positive posture of the administration of Hashimoto Ryutaro appeared at first glance to exhibit a softer stance than previously toward the territorial issue. Nonetheless, the Japanese government had not actually softened its basic attitude concerning the problem, and despite the upbeat stance adopted toward Russia, its fundamental aim remained to do its utmost to resolve the territorial question. The Russian side, however, did not necessarily correctly understand this reality.

In Japan already following the November 1998 Moscow summit, disillusionment was spreading rapidly. In the background was the presentment that a strong possibility existed that from 1999 bilateral ties would cool. In Russia the initial hope after the summit that Japan would take seriously a new offer by Boris Yeltsin did not last long. Russians also became concerned that relations may have reached an impasse.

This chapter centers on the delicate state in 1996–99 of bilateral relations, principally those focused on concluding a peace treaty. As background, the first section expands on preceding chapters by presenting an overview of Japanese-Russian relations over the preceding quarter century, pointing to reasons for and against improving relations in the periods of Brezhnev, perestroika, and Yeltsin's first term. The second section concentrates on bilateral ties from the end of 1996 to the start of 1999.

Three Opportunities

A Lost Opportunity

In the Brezhnev era, as described above by Berton and Kimura, the cold war structure strongly prescribed Japanese-Russian relations. Nonetheless, relations in the early 1970s saw a slight advance. The Japanese side did not necessarily stick tightly to the position of the inseparability of politics and economics. Appeals arose inside Japan to separate politics and economics by striving for bilateral cooperation in the development of Siberia separate from the Northern Territories question. At the same time, the Soviet side began to examine carefully the possibility of improving relations with Japan. The Soviet leadership resolved to propose to Japan negotiations to conclude a peace treaty. It is said that preparations were underway to specify the return to Japan of Habomai and Shikotan, starting from the position approved in the 1956 Joint Declaration for a peace treaty. During the January 1972 visit of Andrei Gromyko to Japan it was hinted that Moscow was ready to resolve the territorial problem on the basis of the 1956 declaration. Foreign Minister Ohira and others on the Japanese side understood that the Soviet Union was trying to settle this problem through the return of two islands.

We should, as a result, take note that if Japan at that moment had had the intention of compromising on the two islands of the Habomai group and Shikotan, the two countries had the possibility of an agreement over territory, a peace treaty, and a boost to bilateral relations in general. However, already the argument for returning two islands that in 1956 had drawn support from a tiny group in the leadership had been completely rejected. Moreover, we should keep in mind that although the wording "two islands return" and "four islands return" was used, the two islands of Habomai and Shikotan do not exceed about 7 percent of the land in the northern four islands. In October 1973, Prime Minister Tanaka Kakuei visited the Soviet Union and met with General Secretary Brezhnev. He made clear that the Japanese side had no intention of compromising on the return of just two islands. Before long, although there was work toward drawing Japan and Russia closer together, negotiations for a peace treaty ended unsuccessfully.

One more thing we should note is that at the beginning of the 1970s Japan was actually on the verge of a position of "separation of politics and economics" toward the Soviet Union. In March 1973, Tanaka sent a personal letter to Brezhnev in which he proposed advancing Japanese-Soviet cooperation through the development of Siberia, separating this from the Northern Territories problem. Although there was a misconception in the late 1980s, before Japan's adoption of a policy of "expanded equilibrium," that Japan had consistently maintained an attitude of the "inseparability of politics and economics" toward the Soviet Union, this is refuted by the facts.

Let's try to draw conclusions about the causes and the background that favored in the early 1970s a Japanese-Soviet rapprochement or, on the contrary, blocked compromise on the territorial question. We can divide the causes for rapprochement into three: the international situation, Japan's domestic situation, and the Russian side. Internationally, the atmosphere of general East-West détente was born, and the sharp U.S.-Soviet confrontation had ameliorated to a degree. A cooperative Japanese-Soviet plan for the development of Siberia was impossible without the spirit of détente. At that time rapprochements also occurred between the United States and China, and Japan and China in circumstances of a continuing Sino-Soviet split. As for the Japanese side, despite the friendship and good-neighborly policy to China, it was necessary to improve Japanese-Soviet relations for a degree of balance. They had implications for broadening the field of diplomatic choice in a multipolar era. As a resource-poor country, Japan also had an economic interest in the rich natural resources of Siberia.

As for the reasons why the Russian side pursued rapprochement at the beginning of the 1970s, first there were the Sino-American and Japanese-Chinese rapprochements. These two events dealt a deep blow to the Soviet Union, even more so at a time when the Sino-Soviet split was extremely serious. Moscow had a strong apprehension of becoming isolated. In addition, it had become impossible to overlook the rise in Japan's economic and political status. In the 1970s it was not only Japan's economic power, there was also a certain interest in developments on the technological side.

In spite of movement in this way toward a Japanese-Soviet rapprochement in the 1970s, the peace treaty negotiations ended in failure. There were also various reasons for this in the international situation, Japanese domestic events, and internal conditions on the Soviet side. First, internationally even if an atmosphere of détente had been born, the cold war structure still formed the basis for ties between the United States and the Soviet Union, and a Japanese-Soviet rapprochement through resolution of the territorial question would have alarmed the United States. In this situation, we cannot overlook that the existence of the Northern Territories problem had special political implications. In other words, the thought existed that if this problem were solved and Japanese-Soviet relations grew closer it would create a complication on both the Japanese and American sides among those in political circles and concerned with the military. Thus, the U.S. factor was in one sense a cause for rapprochement, but from another side it was an inhibiting force.

On the Japanese side, still under the influence of the cold war, in domestic politics the territorial question was used politically. In postwar Japan, with the public critical of strengthening national defense, the existence of the Soviet Union as a hypothetical enemy was necessary for maintaining the Self Defense Forces and purchasing the arms necessary to equip them. For that purpose the existence of the Northern Territories question played a special political role. Also Japan was already at this time strongly emphasizing the return of four islands in one batch, and the possibility that existed in 1956 of returning two islands plus continuing negotiations had been excluded. Moreover, in the 1970s distrust for the Soviet Union in Japanese political circles was intense. Communications and relations of trust among leaders had not been developed at all. Trust between the heads of state was totally lacking, and when Brezhnev in the course of the talks ended up getting angry as a negotiating device, matters were further set back. Japanese public opinion also was negative, and the movement to return the Northern Territories had little interest in concluding a peace treaty. At the time, this movement was at a high pitch, mainly drawing on anticommunist groups and right wing forces, and it could not necessarily be said to have been a broad national movement. Thus, on the Japanese side reasons existed that interfered with an advance in Japanese-Russian relations.

As for reasons on the Russian side, we must put at the top the atmosphere of looking down on Japan. At first glance it may seem to be a contradiction to point out that the reason for the rapprochement with Japan was the upgrading of Japan's political and economic power, but basically after the war the Soviet Union persistently perceived Japan as a U.S. dependency. Even if we can say that in the 1970s among a portion of the Soviet leadership there arose an argument to reassess Japan, this was still a minority opinion. The top leaders of the Communist Party of the Soviet Union in general belittled Japan as a country without independent military power and having almost no resources. Moreover, among Soviet leaders there was distrust of Japanese politicians. In the Central Committee of the Communist Party we cannot ignore the influence of Ivan Kovalenko and others of the anti-Japan faction who continued to exert a strong impact on policies toward Japan. In addition, after making concessions to Japan on the territorial question in 1956, the military, now led by Defense Minister Grechko, had hardened its position. To the end the Soviet side expected to achieve a final resolution through the return of the two islands of Habomai and Shikotan as a compromise with Japan. Concessions beyond that never became an issue. Here we can see the limits of bilateral rapprochement.

The Time of Perestroika

After General Secretary Gorbachev came to power in 1985, Russian relations with the West changed qualitatively. Leaders of the Gorbachev reform faction abandoned the traditional antagonist attitude toward the Western world, and they advocated "universal human values" and "new thinking diplomacy." The idea was advanced that the Euro-American world and Russia could join into one, while U.S.-Soviet relations are fundamentally changed. The Western world, beginning with the G-7 advanced nations, tried to assist socialist Russia's reform and democratization. This qualitative change in the international situation transformed the strategic significance of Japan. In other words, Japan lost its value as the frontline of the free world camp facing the Soviet Union and then Russia, while the Kurile Islands and Northern Territories were not necessarily any longer life-and-death matters for security. In the government and the public an atmosphere was born for honest dialogue without getting embroiled in ideology. But how did this kind of new situation change bilateral relations?

Under the impact of changes in the international situation, the reality in both Japan and the Soviet Union was that some changes occurred. However, in the end, in comparison to the great transformations in relations between Euro-American countries and Russia, Japanese-Russian relations continued to stagnate. To understand this, we first must review the changes that did occur.

First, on the Japanese side, reacting to the path of perestroika, the mass media in Japan heightened its interest in the Soviet Union. Also, the image of the Soviet Union among the Japanese people, while not to the extent of the countries of Europe and North America, changed in a somewhat positive direction. Among Japanese politicians too there appeared persons such as Abe Shintaro, Nakayama Taro, Nakasone Yasuhiro, and Ozawa Ichiro, with a strong interest in the Soviet Union. At this time the interest of Japanese citizens in the Northern Territories question rose, and all political parties came to demand their return. Even in the Japanese Foreign Ministry a move appeared to try to change policy toward the Soviet Union. Ambassador Sumio Edamura, who was posted in Moscow in June 1990, and Togo Kazuhiko, head of the Soviet desk, were among those who positively trusted the Gorbachev reform path and sought to support it while striving to advance Japan's diplomacy toward the Soviet Union in a forward- looking direction.

As for reasons on the Russian side, along with changes in consciousness toward the West among the reform faction, there were continuing reevaluations of the Japanese-U.S. Security Treaty. In January 1986, Foreign Minister Eduard Shevardnadze visited Japan.

Gorbachev, in his Vladivostok speech later that year and in the Krasnoyarsk speech of 1988, expressed an outlook in favor of improving relations with the countries of Asia, including Japan. The memoirs of Gorbachev, Aleksandr Yakovlev, Shevardnadze, and others tell us that this outlook was genuine. In December 1988 Shevardnadze came to Japan again, and a working group was established at the deputy minister level in order to conclude a peace treaty.

Within the Russian reform faction the view of Japan changed greatly from the second half of the 1980s to the first half of the 1990s. Instead of being seen as a small power that did not possess any resources, Japan became an economic and technological great power battling for hegemony with the United States. This was a great shock to the Russians. A "Japan myth" of a country that could become the model of the twenty-first century gathered strength beyond that seen in Europe and America. In all likelihood, for Russians the sense of Japan's existence reached its postwar peak at this time.

Furthermore, through glasnost the political consciousness and historical worldview of Russians was changing. Revelations to correct the excesses of the Stalin era and the socialist era as a whole appeared one after another. Among these were new insights into Japan, including many positive assertions for improving Japanese-Russian relations from Moscow reform intellectuals at IMEMO (the Institute of World Economy and International Relations). Views also appeared in the mass media and elsewhere that it is incorrect to call the disputed territories Soviet land and that two or even four islands should be returned to Japan. Exchanges at the Japanese-Soviet Specialists' Conference that had started in 1973 played a certain role in changing the consciousness of the Soviets.

In spite of these changes in the perestroika era, bilateral relations did not experience a qualitative change. If we look at the international situation, compared to changes between the European-American countries and the Soviet Union, changes in Asia were small, and the cold war structure lasted longer. First, to 1990 the Japanese government largely doubted the fundamental nature of Soviet change through perestroika and new thinking diplomacy. Although disarmament between the Euro-American countries and the Soviet Union was advancing, in the Soviet Far East there was no reduction in military preparedness. To 1990 the Japanese government maintained its policy of the inseparability of politics and economics, which gave absolute preference to the resolution of the Northern Territories question, and Japan's Soviet policy could not shed its hard line. Even if a group of politicians who displayed an interest in Russia began to play an individual role in policies toward the Soviet Union, ultimately they exerted little influence on bilateral relations.

Japan's Soviet policy in the perestroika era was caught in a basic dilemma. As a member of the G-7, Japan alone could not reject reform assistance. Because in the 1980s Japan's economy was the most dynamic among the developed countries, this was even more the case. However, the Japanese government could not pigeonhole the Northern Territories question and positively promote assistance to Russia. Caught in the horns of this dilemma, the Japanese government could not hammer out a clear-cut strategy toward the Soviet Union.

On the Russian side too during the perestroika period there were reasons limiting the advance of bilateral relations. First, Gorbachev and other Russian leaders concentrated their interest on Europe and the United States with disarmament centered there, and they did not devote sufficient interest to Asia. The Asian security frameworks proposed in Gorbachev's Vladivostok and Krasnoyarsk speeches reinforced this inclination toward the great powers and did not sufficiently consider the realities of the Asia-Pacific region. The Japanese government opposed attempts to realize in Asia a security framework along the lines of the Helsinki Accords, which had stabilized the European postwar balance.

The struggle between President Gorbachev and the conservative faction that comprised a majority in the newly active parliament was also a negative influence on Japanese-Russian relations. In April 1991, when a Soviet president visited Japan for the first time, there was a possibility that Gorbachev would make concessions on the Northern Territories question, at least by reacknowledging the 1956 Japanese-Russian joint communiqué. However, in fact, inside Russia since the fall of 1990 conservatives in the Supreme Soviet and the Communist Party and the military were exerting a strong influence on Gorbachev opposing the reform line. In April 1991 when Gorbachev had just managed at last to revive the reform group's position, he could not resolutely settle the territorial question.

The policy of glasnost had a dual influence on bilateral relations. On the one hand, it gave rise to public opinion that Soviet economic policies should be reexamined, while on the other hand, it made it more difficult for the president freely to decide on the territorial question disregarding the conservative faction, nationalist public opinion, the military, the parliament, etc. It became clear too that the opinion that Japan and Russia are economically mutually complementary and will develop increasingly close economic relations was an illusion.

The Yeltsin Era (to 1996)

Although the Soviet Union had collapsed and the Yeltsin era had begun before the end of 1991, there was almost no advance in bilateral relations until 1996. Unfortunately the territorial question and policy toward Japan became weapons in a domestic political struggle in which reform and conservative factions clashed. President Yeltsin's visit in September 1992 was suddenly cancelled, and this too was linked to domestic political struggle. It was possible that if Yeltsin had made the trip and returned without coming to an agreement, the outcome would have been found unacceptable at home. If, on the contrary, he had made some concessions to Japan, they would have become an object of attack at home. Finally, Yeltsin cancelled his visit, and as a result hardened Japanese opinion toward Russia. In 1993 in Russia the extreme right led by Zhirinovsky rose to the forefront, joining the democrats and the Communist Party, shocking not only Russian politics but also world opinion. Under the influence of this strengthening nationalism at the beginning of 1994 Yeltsin turned away from the path of leaning to the West toward the path of national interests.

In October 1993 right after his bombardment of the parliament, President Yeltsin finally visited Japan. In the "Tokyo Declaration" of this time, it was agreed to conclude a peace treaty by determining ownership for the four islands on the basis of: (1) historical and legal facts; (2) documents of agreement between the two countries; and (3) the principles of law and justice. For a Russian president at this time, these were the maximum possible concessions to Japan. The Japanese government viewed the Tokyo Declaration as a big achievement in bilateral relations. However, in a Russia leaning more and more to nationalism, this was the limit. In 1998 the Russian side retreated from the Tokyo Declaration agreement.

Japan had shifted by 1990 from a policy of "the inseparability of politics and economics" to one of "expanded equilibrium." The delay resulted from the fact that while the developed countries had been hammering out a program of support for the reform line, Japan alone could not promote cooperation with Russia due to the Northern Territories. However, despite shifting to the path of "expanded equilibrium," the Japanese government did not change the fact that it put the Northern Territories at the center of its Russian policy. This attitude drew criticism from the other G-7 countries.

Also after the collapse of the Soviet Union, the images of Russia and President Yeltsin were more negative in Japan than in Europe and America. The Japanese mass media generally reported in a negative tone on Russia. When in October 1993 the parliament was shelled by Yeltsin, Europe and America were largely sympathetic to Yeltsin, who was battling with the Communist Party, while in contrast both Japanese mass media and public opinion took a very critical attitude toward him. The Japanese government as a member of the G-7, nonetheless, worked out an overall posture of support for assistance to Russian reforms. Accordingly, the Japanese Foreign Ministry basically supported Yeltsin's position. However, the position of the Japanese government toward Russia and Yeltsin was subject to harsh domestic public opinion. Lots of citizens could not understand how despite the fact the Russian government took an unrelenting position toward Japan on the territorial question the Japanese government had to assist Russia. The Japanese government was caught in a scissors between domestic and international opinion.

In contrast to the spirit of enthusiastic support for Yeltsin's reform policies and democratic path that existed in Europe and America, there was little of this atmosphere inside Japan. One reason is that as opposed to a tradition of absolute values verging on religion in support of the concepts of democracy, freedom, and human rights in European and American culture, Japan lacked this kind of cultural and political heritage. As a result, we can say that Japanese perceived even Russian democratization with a more detached eye than Europeans and Americans. Another reason, of course, is that distrust toward Russia continued due to the fact that Japanese continued to take a hard-line attitude on the Northern Territories question.

When we view Japan's posture from the cold war to the present, we can detect a kind of "reverse phenomenon" between the government and public opinion. In the cold war the Japanese government, especially the Foreign Ministry, took a hard-line stance toward the Soviet Union, while public opinion had more goodwill. In contrast to the Japanese government, which was jointly coordinating its response with the United States, the influence on public opinion was strong from the so-called progressive intelligentsia, the Communist Party, the Japan Socialist Party, the Soho Labor Union, the Nikkyoso Teachers' Union, and other left-wing forces. It was because the socialist Soviet Union was seen as a "force for peace." In contrast, with the collapse of the Soviet Union there was no atmosphere at all of public opinion beautifying Russia. Rather, latent distrust toward Russia rose strongly to the fore. Even as Russian reform policies used democratization and marketization as slogans, in Japan these did not give rise to illusions. Only confusion appeared close-up. Thus, on the one hand, for the general public in the Yeltsin era the Russian image was darker than in the Soviet era. On the other hand, the Japanese government and Foreign Ministry in order to extend a posture of assisting Russian reform turned more positive. This gave rise to a reversal from the cold war in the attitudes of public opinion and the Japanese Foreign Ministry.

Japanese-Russian Relations Built on Illusions

The Time of Illusions

It was in the spring of 1996 that new activity commenced in Japanese-Russian relations. Then, after Prime Minister Hashimoto's July 1997 speech announcing "Three Principles Toward Russia," until the Kawana talks of April 1998, occurred the best period in the history of bilateral relations. However, the November 1998 Moscow summit between Prime Minister Obuchi and President Yeltsin foretold the impending return of a difficult period. In Japan for a time expectations for the resolution of the territorial problem had intensified, but because at the November 1998 summit the Russian side had revealed a tough position these had changed into disappointment and disillusionment. Expectations for improved bilateral relations swiftly cooled. To understand this, let us start with an overview of the high tide of relations from 1996 to November 1998.

In March 1996 Foreign Minister Ikeda visited Russia, and the first meeting was convened of the Japanese-Russian government-level committee on trade and the economy. Ikeda wanted to bring about a visit to Russia of Prime Minister Hashimoto and a summit with President Yeltsin. Yeltsin knew that Hashimoto, from his days as minister of MITI, had shown a positive stance toward economic cooperation with Russia. Unlike lots of Japanese, Hashimoto, in principle, felt personal goodwill toward Russia, and, in April, he sent the director of the Self Defense Forces to Russia for the first time. Then in July the Japanese naval ship *Kurama* paid a goodwill visit to Vladivostok for the 300th anniversary of the Russian navy. This was followed in May 1997 by a visit to Japan from the Russian defense minister, and then in June a goodwill trip of the Russian ship *Admiral Vinogradov.* Thus, between the two countries it was in the security sphere that exchanges and cooperation to build trust began to take an actual form.

The forerunner of these changes was the Japanese-American-Russian Trilateral Forum on Northeast Asian Security, which began in February 1994 with a meeting in Tokyo. This was a forum for unofficial exchanges by government, military, and academic specialists on relations among the three countries, centering on Asian security questions. Here efforts began, involving military officials, to understand each other better. The forum was created at the Japanese side's initiative, and the fundamental consciousness was to draw on the cooperation of the United States to deepen Japanese-Russian communications. Of the bilateral ties among the four major countries in the Asia-Pacific Region—Japan, the United States, Russia, and China—it was Japanese-Russian relations that faced the weakest level of understanding. Because this was not good for the stability of the region, the United States was ready to cooperate to improve communications between the two sides. One aim of this forum was to resolve the territorial question, but rather than concentrating narrowly on this issue, a new consciousness was born of the structure of a Japanese-Russian relationship with a broad field of vision. In December 1998 the sixth Trilateral Forum met in Tokyo and reflected the rapid development of relations since the first meeting. The Trilateral Forum had played a role in changing bilateral relations.

In September 1996 the Japanese government established a Japan Center in Iuzhno-Sakhalinsk. Other Japan Centers are in Moscow, Khabarovsk, and Vladivostok, but the new location had special meaning. Previously, the Japanese government took the position that Japan had renounced Southern Sakhalin at the San Francisco Treaty, but by international law its ownership was still not settled, and Japan officially refused to have relations with Southern Sakhalin on Russian territory. This was the reason why regular airplane service could not be established between Japan and Southern Sakhalin. The establishment of a Japan Center meant that the Japanese government in fact recognized Southern Sakhalin as Russian territory. The Russian Foreign Ministry highly evaluated this concession of the Japanese government. In things like this, the Japanese government showed that it was really changing its attitude toward Russia.

From about August 1996 Japanese government officials were searching to construct new concepts for bilateral relations that would be more forward-looking than "expanded equilibrium." They sought an approach to broaden relations into a multidimensional form embracing not only political and economic ties but also security, international politics, environmental issues from a global viewpoint, culture, science and technology, human exchanges, etc. At the beginning of 1997 this positive attitude crystallized under the label a "multilayered approach."

At the June 1997 Denver summit, President Yeltsin showed a different face to Japan than in previous contacts. It was clear that in Yeltsin's heart a big change had occurred toward Japan. Previously he felt that Japanese politicians were always thrusting the territorial question under the Russians' noses, causing unpleasant feelings. However, at this summit he paid greatest attention to his talks with the Japanese prime minister and clearly showed his goodwill toward Japan. Yeltsin proposed a "strategic partnership," "regular summit meetings," a "Moscow-Tokyo hotline," "support for Japan's entry as a permanent member in the United Nations Security Council," etc. These were positive attitudes toward Japan never before seen from Yeltsin. Clearly, this was the Russian side's response to the earlier signals from the Japanese side.

The Japanese side, under the initiative of Prime Minister Hashimoto and the chief secretary of the cabinet, hammered out a policy to depend on President Yeltsin for resolving the Northern Territories problem and concluding a peace treaty. The reason for this approach was that experience between the two countries over a long time had shown that the territorial problem was not something that could be resolved automatically by the two countries simply by piling up historical arguments and arguments based on international law. It was clearly understood that a political decision between the top leaders of the two countries would be required. There were two essential conditions for that. First, the leaders needed to establish personal relations of trust. Second, the leaders also had to have established at home a stable power base. Hashimoto strove to develop the first condition and then planned to avail himself of closer relations with the Russian president as a lever for solidifying a power base that could meet the second condition.

In July 1997 the Japanese prime minister worked out what became known as "Hashimoto's Three Principles Toward Russia," policies based on "trust," "mutual interest," and "long-term perspective" as one link in his "Eurasian policy as seen from the Pacific." This document prepared by the prime minister and his cabinet secretary formed the basis of Japan's approach. Because the Foreign Ministry played a broad role on the Japanese side, it was pretty much in step with the prime minister. Russia responded right away, evaluating very highly the positive posture of Hashimoto. Especially welcome were the policies of mutual interest and long-term perspective, which were seen as a concession that changed Japan's former hard-line attitude concerning the Northern Territories question.

Relations of trust between Yeltsin and Hashimoto became decisive as a result of this new policy toward Russia initiated by Hashimoto. Amid these currents, an informal summit in November 1997 was realized in Krasnoyarsk. We can say that this was the first case of building personal relations of trust between the leaders of the two countries. At this meeting, on the political side the leaders agreed to do their utmost to conclude a peace treaty by the year 2000 on the basis of the Tokyo Declaration, and on the economic side they agreed to cooperate in the form of the Hashimoto-Yeltsin plan.

According to the testimony of the participants, it was Yeltsin's own idea to specify a time limit by the year 2000. Meanwhile, the wording "on the basis of the Tokyo Declaration" was included at the strong insistence of the Japanese side. This meant that resolving the problem of the return of four islands was recognized as a precondition for a peace treaty. In the Krasnoyarsk agreement there was no direct wording on resolving the territorial problem, in order not to provoke opposition parties inside Russia and Russian public opinion. This caution succeeded. Inside Russia in general the Krasnoyarsk agreement was favorably received. The Communist Party and the nationalist factions did not strongly attack Yeltsin on the territorial issue. The reason was that there was hardly anyone in Russia who knew the contents of the Tokyo Declaration. In fact, many people in Russia felt good about the November 1997 agreement, perceiving that Japan finally is relaxing its insistence on the territorial issue and is plunging ahead to conclude a peace treaty.

Representatives of the Japanese Foreign Ministry presented this agreement as "megaton news," and the Japanese government hailed this as the biggest achievement of recent times in Japanese-Russian relations. The Japanese mass media played up the Krasnoyarsk agreement on a large scale, highlighting it as a diplomatic success for the Hashimoto regime. In November 1997, with Japan's positive backing, Russia was recognized as an official member of APEC. Russia highly appreciated Japan's influence on this.

But already at the outset of this upturn in relations a huge gap had arisen in the consciousness of the two sides. On the one hand, the Japanese side, while hammering out a multilayered approach to Russia, had not changed its fundamental reasoning that the biggest point is to resolve the territorial question and conclude a peace treaty. On the other hand, the Russian side stressed economic cooperation through the Hashimoto-Yeltsin plan, while doubting that it would be possible in the near future to resolve the territorial question. Thus, on the Russian side there were widespread expectations that even if the territorial issue were postponed, economic cooperation and even the conclusion of a peace treaty were possible. While Russia held that at present it was difficult to resolve the territorial question, Japan had the opposite design to emphasize exclusively the importance of building an environment for concluding a peace treaty.

In the Krasnoyarsk agreement President Yeltsin, First Deputy Prime Minister Nemtsov, and close associates took the initiative, while most of the Russian government including the Foreign Ministry beginning with Primakov had almost no involvement. The Russian Foreign Ministry was extremely cautious and conservative on the territorial question, and it had a strong apprehension about Yeltsin and the presidential office doing something rash to stand out. In the presidential office too, the presidential spokesmen and others displayed a cautious attitude, anxious to forestall attacks from domestic conservatives. Nonetheless, Foreign Minister Primakov visited Japan right after the informal summit, and he and

Japanese Foreign Minister Obuchi recognized the Krasnoyarsk agreement as an accord between the two governments.

At the end of 1997 there were many indications that Yeltsin's initiative in November had given a big impetus to bilateral relations. For instance, negotiations over a framework for the operation of Japanese fishing boats in the waters around the four northern islands had continued for 12 meetings from March 1995 to October 1997, but they had been stalled on the question of sovereignty, that is, which country's laws would apply to illegal operations. However, after Yeltsin at Krasnoyarsk invited negotiators to find a solution by the end of the year, a compromise was reached at the thirteenth meeting in December that left the sovereignty issue vague. At this point in time on the Japanese side there were expectations in the near future that even a difficult matter such as the territorial question might be settled through this kind of personal initiative by Yeltsin. In January 1998 in vice-ministerial talks between Tamba and Karasin there was an agreement to shelve the vice-ministerial peace treaty working group that had been meeting for some time and to create a Japanese-Russian Joint Committee on the Problem of Concluding a Peace Treaty. In February Obuchi went to Russia and the committee met for the first time.

After the Krasnoyarsk talks, in both Japan and Russia, together with expectations about rapid improvements in bilateral relations, there were some people, including this author, who posited their concern about illusions. They warned that excessive predictions of a breakthrough existed in each country, and as the year 2000 approached these illusions about bilateral relations could turn into disillusionment. In March 1998 in Russia when this author met with Vladimir Lukin, chair of the Foreign Relations Committee of the State Duma, entirely the same concerns were discussed.

The second Japanese-Russian unofficial summit occurred at Kawana on the Izu peninsula in April 1998. At this meeting Hashimoto made a concrete proposal for demarcating an international border in order to conclude a peace treaty. Although the contents were not made public, if one were to judge from various official reports, the Russian side would recognize Japanese sovereignty over the four islands, and the Japanese side would concede to the future the return of actual administrative authority. Then if this agreement were possible, Japan would act positively on joint economic assistance on the four islands, as Russia had proposed.

Seen objectively, this proposal was very realistic. For the Russian side, at the present time some of the conditions for recognizing Japanese sovereignty over the four islands are not present. The Japanese mass media loudly reported this proposal by the Japanese side (the proposal for border demarcation to the north of Etorofu island), and the Russian side showed its unhappiness at this coverage. Inside Japan through this kind of reporting, expectations and misunderstandings were born that perhaps in the near future a border demarcation line would be drawn.

Here, I would like to generalize about the reasons that propelled an improvement in bilateral relations and also the problems in both countries' policies. As for the Japanese side's reasons, there was realism that in previous approaches limits had been reached in making a breakthrough in bilateral relations. Prime Minister Hashimoto had the ambition to resolve the territorial question and make a historical achievement that would completely normalize Japanese-Russian relations. In order to do this, it became recognized that a new approach was necessary surpassing the old approach of "expanded equilibrium." The business world too hoped for a positive attitude toward Russia, where the investment environment was poor, seeking trade insurance by the Japanese government and assistance in energy and other development projects. Also in the Foreign Ministry, in response to criticisms from international public opinion that Japan was fixated on the territorial problem and remained negative toward assistance to Russian reforms, there was a feeling that only through real actions could refutations become convincing and could Japan win the support of the international community. In addition, through intensifying relations with Russia, there was a plan to broaden the options for Japanese diplomacy and to strengthen Japan's bargaining position in international politics. Especially at a time when relations between Japan and China had become more complicated, improved Japanese-Russian relations had implications for using the "Russian card" versus China.

What were the reasons for the Russian side to advance bilateral relations? First, illusions had been dispelled about assistance to Russia from Europe and America, for which the expansion of NATO was especially decisive. Through the shift from Andrei Kozyrev to Evgenii Primakov as foreign minister, attention turned more strongly to China, Japan, India, and other Asian countries. In the midst of a financial crisis and also in order to push ahead with economic reform, Russia could expect that drawing in capital from Japan had an important meaning. Moreover, it was necessary to change the situation in which Russia's strategic presence in the Asia-Pacific region was too small, especially in a region where Russia and North Korea were practically alone in being left behind by economic development. In order for Russia to join in the region's economic growth, improved economic relations with Japan and intensified introduction of capital from Japan were indispensable. Russia, too had an interest in using the "Japan card" against China. In other words, in the Asian region, as China's influence was strengthening excessively, inside Russia there was a certain unease. Through improving relations with Japan, the thought even existed among Russian leaders that they could try to control China's influence.

As discussed above, from 1996 bilateral relations improved to an unprecedented degree; however, in the manner of an adventure story, they were built on illusions in each country. Japan's illusion was that lots of Japanese citizens were filled with expectations that in the near future the northern four islands stood a good chance of being returned to their country. At Krasnoyarsk these expectations were raised by the agreement for a "peace treaty by the year 2000." Moreover, the atmosphere created by Japan's mass media at the time of the Kawana talks further strengthened this illusion. Then media reports carried big headlines such as "Demarcation North of the Four Islands," "Plan for Demarcating International Border, Spells Out Return of Four Islands," "Proposal to Russia Ensures Recognition of Japan's Sovereignty," "The President, A Forward-Looking Examination." Moreover, part of the illusion was to overestimate the leadership of President Yeltsin. Finally, the Japanese side exaggerated the prospects for changing the consciousness of the Russian people through "visa-free exchanges," etc.

First among the illusions on the Russian side was the temporary misunderstanding that Japan had agreed to "shelve the territorial question." Another misunderstanding was that what was drawing Japan nearer to Russia was the worsening of the Japanese economy. Also, there was the idea that Japan was becoming more and more isolated internationally; thus Russia had now become necessary to it. Even if Russia did not make concessions on the territorial question, the perception spread that Japan would continue its cooperation with Russia. In addition, there was the misunderstanding that the reason for Japan to desire the islands was the natural resources on the northern territories or those in the seas close to the four islands.

The illusions in the two countries did not wait to the year 2000. By early 1999 they were turning into disappointment and disillusionment.

From Illusion to Disillusionment

In July 1998 the IMF, Europe, America, and Japan promised a sum of $22.6 billion to Russia in order to assist in Russia's financial crisis. Japan's share was $1.5 billion, but at that time only Japan decided bilaterally on this kind of financing for Russia. The fact that among these countries Japan displayed the most positive attitude in supporting Russia was proof that Japan's posture toward Russia had changed. In order to deepen bilateral exchanges and to create a structure for new relations, the Russian side formed the "Twenty-First Century Committee," and then in September the Japanese side formed the "Japanese-Russian Friendship Forum 21." These were founded at the suggestion of Foreign Minister Obuchi, who had visited President Yeltsin in Moscow in June 1998, and Yuri Luzhkov, the mayor of Moscow, who became the chairman on the Russian side. It was thought that his motive in accepting this chairmanship was concern for the impending presidential election and an attempt to strengthen his relations internationally. As for Japan's intent, the main interest was to construct an environment aimed at concluding a peace treaty. However, in the fall of 1998 bilateral relations began a downslide. Afterwards, illusions were rapidly changing into disillusionment.

In November 1998 in Moscow, Prime Minister Obuchi and President Yeltsin held an official summit. At these talks the Russian side delivered to the Japanese side a response to the Hashimoto plan proposed at the Kawana talks in the form of the Russian side's opposing plan. Although this was not formally made public, because Foreign Ministry authorities on the Russian side intentionally leaked the news, its contents have become pretty much clear. Its points are: (1) for both countries to establish a special legal system for joint economic assistance on the four islands, and (2) to do this in a form that will not damage the national interests of the two countries, for the two to carry out the delineation of a borderline, but this border demarcation should be accomplished through a separate treaty from the peace treaty. In essence, the peace treaty was to become a separate short-term goal, while the border dispute would be set aside as joint economic development on the islands proceeded and the two countries continued to be mired in conflicting interpretations of historical and legal realities and the various principles of international law and justice.

In contrast to this, the Japanese side proposed establishing within the existing framework of the Joint Committee on the Question of Concluding a Peace Treaty two new committees, a Border Demarcation Committee and a Joint Economic Activities Committee. The Russian side accepted this. As for the Japanese side, it sought the establishment of the Border Demarcation Committee to try to block a dilution of the peace treaty process. The Joint Economic Activities Committee was a concession in order to get the demarcation committee recognized.

Joint economic activity on the four islands was first suggested when Foreign Minister Primakov visited Japan in November 1996, but Japan reacted negatively to this proposal. The first reason is that even if it is called joint economic activity, because Russia lacks capital, in fact, the economic assistance is from Japan, and this has no merit for the Japanese side. Second, because the economic activity would occur under Russian law on the four islands that Russia effectively controls, this would mean recognizing Russian sovereignty. The Japanese government has consistently taken a negative attitude toward this proposal, responding only within the limits of expanding three established policies: humanistic assistance, visa-free exchanges, and fishing zones. If the Russian side's proposal means to realize joint economic activity by establishing a free economic zone or special economic zone through a special legal system simply under the Russian legal system, the Japanese side could not accept it. If it means not only Russian sovereignty but also recognition of Japanese sovereignty, then Japan could accept it. But there is no possibility of Russia, as it has responded to date, of making this concession.

Especially problematic in the Russian side's response is the proposal to settle border demarcation and a peace treaty through separate treaties. Because this is clearly contrary to the Tokyo Declaration agreement to resolve the ownership of the four islands and conclude a peace treaty, the Japanese side strongly resisted. The fact that the Russian side made this kind of proposal originated probably from the following kind of thinking. A response that would not return the four islands completely to Japan, in other words a plan to set the borderline between Habomai, Shikotan, and Hokkaido, was presumably the Russian side's intent; however, until such a proposal would in fact be issued, it would be necessary to avoid, in one quick step, a cooling of bilateral relations. Also even if there were a prospect of the return of the islands of Habomai and Shikotan, in today's situation Russian domestic forces would not accept it. Of course, it is completely impossible to accept the Japanese side's proposal to recognize Japan's sovereignty over the four islands. Accordingly, in order to postpone matters, leaving the question in a gray area for some time, it was decided to separate a peace treaty and border demarcation. For the Russian side it is in the national interest to advance only economic and other cooperative relations, while on border demarcation letting the current situation continue.

The summary of the Russian proposal was reported in Japan without delay, and domestically a strong sense of disappointment arose. It was because the Russian response rejected even the Tokyo Declaration agreement of 1993, thus causing a retreat in bilateral relations back to that time. In one fell swoop, it cooled off the uplifting atmosphere in bilateral relations that had extended from the Krasnoyarsk agreement to the Kawana talks. Inside Japan the positive policy toward Russia that had advanced since the Hashimoto administration fell into doubt. Even within the Japanese Foreign Ministry, the faction positive to Russia, centered on Tamba Minoru, lost influence.

There are various reasons why Russia gave this kind of response. First, because Yeltsin had lost influence on Japan policy. Especially in November 1998, when the summit occurred, Yeltsin's health was quite unclear, and he was hardly involved in the contents of the response to Japan. Also at the time of the summit meeting in Moscow the Russian side responded by document, and that was something prepared at the initiative of the Russian Foreign Ministry and Prime Minister Primakov. According to those involved in the November talks, Yeltsin himself scarcely uttered a word. In this respect, the November 1998 summit was fundamentally different from the Krasnoyarsk and Kawana summits in which the president had taken the initiative and the Foreign Ministry was absent. The

Russian Foreign Ministry and Prime Minister Primakov feared criticism from the military, the border police, the Fisheries Bureau, the Duma, Sakhalin oblast, and others of the seven ministries and offices that took a tough position on the territorial issue as well as from the Communist Party and nationalist factions. As for Primakov, he would have done all he could to avoid provoking the parliament through concessions to Japan on the territorial problem at a time when Russia had been losing its identity as a nation, and he needed, at whatever the cost, parliamentary support on the budget and other issues. Thus, in the November 1998 summit at which Yeltsin's influence had greatly declined, the negative stance toward the territorial issue of the Russian government and Foreign Ministry was reflected straight out to the Japanese government.

In the disappointment of the Japanese side, Japan itself also bears responsibility. In spite of the fact that, considering the situation inside Russia realistically, it was impossible to resolve the territorial problem by the year 2000 in a form that Japan desired, inside Japan matters kept being reported as if this were possible. The problem was that Japanese politicians and the mass media fueled these kinds of unrealistic expectations.

In fact, inside Russia hardly anyone correctly understood both the Tokyo Declaration and the Krasnoyarsk agreement. Politicians seriously thinking about addressing the territorial dispute with Japan were virtually absent in Russia. The demerits of Russian politicians in handling this issue far outweigh their merits. However, in Japan, especially after the Krasnoyarsk agreement, many were led astray by misperceptions of Russian government policies regarding the territorial problem with Japan and the conclusion of a peace treaty.

On January 21, 1999, when Tamba visited Moscow and cochaired with Deputy Foreign Minister Karasin the subministerial talks of the Joint Committee on the Question of Concluding a Peace Treaty, the first meetings were held of the Border Demarcation Committee and the Joint Economic Activities Committee. At that time the Japanese side stressed that the Russian side's proposal contradicted the Tokyo Declaration, and it also sought to determine the meaning of the Russian side's proposal for a special legal system for the purpose of joint economic activity. On February 21 in Tokyo, at talks between Foreign Minister Ivanov and Foreign Minister Komura, the Russian side stuck to a tough position on the sovereignty of the four islands, and the Japanese side too made clear its continued principled position that resolution of the territorial question is a condition for concluding a peace treaty. It can be said that Japanese-Russian relations directed at a peace treaty, in some sense, now have to make a fresh start, going back to the situation before the Tokyo Declaration.

Both governments have not changed their basic posture of wanting to expand cooperation and to develop forward-looking relations hereafter as well. That is because for both countries this has merit. Nevertheless, it will be difficult for Japan's leaders in the future to embrace the desire of a positive Russian policy in the manner of the Hashimoto period.

In this way, Japanese-Russian relations targeted at a peace treaty have rapidly cooled down from their temporary season of high tide. In the summer of 1998 Russia was beset with a severe economic and financial crisis, and this destabilized Russian policies. The worsening of Yeltsin's health also compounded the problem and led to further weakening of his power. It is an indisputable fact that this negatively influenced the resolution of the peace treaty question. Furthermore, Russia's economic crisis has led to the retreat of Boris Nemtsov and other influential figures who had a strong interest in improving relations with Japan, while on the contrary boosting the power of the nationalists and communists.

A problem for Japan is that "goodwill" does not necessarily work. There was naive thinking that Japan, by showing its "goodwill," would induce the Russian side to make concessions. This kind of optimistic policy has now run into a brick wall. Meanwhile, an essential problem remains: there is no strategy toward Russia that transcends the territorial and peace treaty questions and that is based on a globalized, long-term field of vision. One can say that this is the fundamental reason for today's disillusionment and what makes Japanese-Russian relations go this way and that.

Part III

Mutual Influences and Comparisons

Chapter 14

Factors Shaping the Formation of Views on Japan in the USSR in the Postwar Period

Semyon Verbitsky

In the postwar period, historic changes in the USSR led to the breakup of a totalitarian state, to acute weakening in Marxist ideology and censorship, and to the emergence of a more pluralistic society and genuine public opinion. Naturally, these changes had to be reflected in the understanding in the USSR and later in Russia of the outside world, including Japan. This chapter examines the factors that exerted the most significant influence on the formation of views of Japan during the cold war, the Gorbachev era, and finally the Yeltsin administration. As background, we briefly consider also historical images that formed during the course of almost 300 years of prior contact between Russians and Japanese.

Many factors connected to the extremely sharp differences between the two countries in their history, culture, traditions, territory, climate, and demography were reflected in Russian views of Japan. More than exotic, Japan loomed as a contrast. But interest in Japan on the part of a large part of Russian society, apart from periods of military activity, was generally inconsequential. Japan was located far from the administrative, industrial, and especially the cultural centers of Russia. Also, apart from sporadic reports of brief contacts, Russians became acquainted with Japan relatively late, long after firm ties had formed with European nations. This led to Asian countries being seen by "enlightened Russians" as backward and uncivilized, worthy only of sympathy. A significant shift occurred as a result of the Meiji reforms. In the eyes of an increasingly critical Russian society, these reforms testified to Japan joining the civilized world, and, simultaneously, to Russia's unpreparedness for a rapid transformation.

As Russia and Japan hurried as latecomers onto the path of industrial development and battled with each other for spheres of influence in the Far East, especially in their war of 1904–1905, an image formed of Japan as the "yellow peril" and a historical opponent of Russia in the Far East. War left an impression of cruelty and perfidy, as well as bravery and patriotism.

After the October Revolution, an image of Japan as the principal threat to the USSR became dominant in the consciousness of the Soviet people. The intervention of the Japanese army in the Russian Far East and China contributed to a Soviet propaganda campaign that left firm stereotypes of Japanese as "samurai," militaristic in their conduct.

It should be noted that in Russia as in the USSR there existed substantial differences in views of Japan among diverse groups in the population. In Russia these differences were conditioned mainly by educational levels. In the USSR they were tied, above all, to conditions of an ideological press and strict censorship, to different possibilities of obtaining objective information on Japan. This factor led to three main levels of interpretation of Japan: the leadership of the country, the ideological *nomenklatura,* and the broad public. As for the last group, there were also distinct levels linked to education and place of residence since almost all contacts in the cultural, economic, and other spheres occurred in the capital cities. In the postcommunist period, after the weakening of ideology and censorship, differentiation in views of Japan began to narrow and the political and ideological priorities of various political forces in Russian society rose to the forefront.

The Cold War: Japan in the Eyes of the Kremlin and Public Opinion

The most important tendency in the understanding of Japan in the period of the cold war was the increasing difference in views between the Soviet leadership and population. The leadership reacted to Japan, above all, from the position of victor in World War II and nuclear superpower. It is not surprising that relations with this "defeated country" were never seen in the Kremlin as one of the priority foreign policy interests of the USSR. Correspondingly, the territorial demands of Japan were regarded as an attempt by the Japanese to deprive the USSR of the fruits of its victory, to lower this great socialist power.

Soviet authorities looked at Japan through the prism of its military alliance with the United States, which clearly represented the principal threat to the USSR and blocked the extension of Soviet influence in the Far East. Total rejection of the Japanese-U.S. Security Treaty determined their response to Japanese leaders, political parties, and the possible scope of Soviet-Japanese cooperation. In his memoirs, A. Gromyko spoke most frankly about this, "The historical challenge of Japan is not to allow the security treaty to tie a noose around its neck to deprive it of independence. In the name of the Soviet leadership, I as Minister of Foreign Affairs of the USSR constantly repeated this point of view to all officials of Japan at all levels."[1]

As for the Soviet leadership's understanding of the political situation in Japan, this was formed above all under the influence of ideological dogma and political presuppositions. Over the entire postwar period Moscow offered support, including financial assistance, to the "democratic forces" of Japan, in the hope that they would come to power and weaken or annul the Japan-U.S. military alliance. It is not surprising that Moscow, in contrast to Beijing, did not have its own lobby in the ruling camp of Japan.

A significant, but mixed, impact on the Soviet leadership's understanding was exerted by the rise of Japan into a strong world power. The USSR was not prepared to understand either the causes of the postwar successes of Japan nor the lack of interest of Japanese businessmen in cooperation with the USSR. Not surprisingly, Moscow could not achieve any success in the development of economic ties with Japan.

Changes in the Soviet leadership—from the totalitarian rule of Stalin to the thaw of Khrushchev and then the bureaucratic and cynical regime of the Brezhnev epoch—can be seen as landmarks in the understanding of Japan in the USSR. Stalin's attitude to Japan was marked by a feeling of revenge for the defeat of Russia in the war of 1904–1905, interest in expanding the Russian empire, and hatred of Americans who blocked his plans. The refusal of Truman to allow the landing of Soviet troops on Hokkaido to no small degree foreordained the start of the cold war and Stalin's decision not to sign the San Francisco Peace Treaty with Japan.[2]

Of special interest are the factors driving Khrushchev to enter into negotiations with Japan in 1955–1956 and his decision to return to Japan part of the Kurile Islands. Above all, he considered that an improvement in relations with Japan would weaken the Japan-U.S. military alliance. With his characteristic emotionalism Khrushchev wrote in his memoirs, "The biggest gift which we could give to the Americans would be obstinately to refuse contacts with Japan. This would allow the Americans to achieve absolute power in that country, which to an even greater extent would strengthen the anti-Soviet disposition there."[3] Second was the revolutionary romanticism of Khrushchev—his belief in the victory of the proletarian revolution in Japan. He was certain that just the appearance of a Soviet embassy in Tokyo would lead to the consolidation of all of the democratic forces and their coming to power. Third, a product of Khrushchev's common sense, was his interest in expanding economic cooperation with a new industrial power. Not surprisingly, Khrushchev interpreted the extension of the security treaty in 1960 extremely emotionally, as a personal humiliation and the dashing of his revolutionary illusions.

In the late Brezhnev period and its uncertain aftermath the foremost influence on the formation of the Kremlin's views of Japan was the cooperation of Tokyo with Washington in the development of the newest technology for star wars and in joint sanctions against the entry of Soviet forces into Afghanistan. No one any longer was under any illusions about the possibility that the democratic parties would come to power, but as before they continued to orient policies to the communists and socialists and their radical programs and slogans, which exerted no influence on Japanese policies.

Since Kremlin leaders sought a smattering of knowledge about Asian countries, this allowed for a significant role for that part of the party, diplomatic, and academic *nomenklatura* that served as the main suppliers of information and recommendations for the leadership in relations with Japan.[4] Among them one could find dogmatic believers who would not be persuaded to change their minds by any Japanese miracle as well as people driven by cold war logic to strive, in any way possible, to maintain the anti-Japanese direction in Soviet policies. However, we should recognize that the main features of the Soviet *nomenklatura* were conformism, attachment to party discipline, and—in the Brezhnev epoch at the top of the list—cynicism. Precisely these features determined their activity in preparing party documents on Japan and various bilateral proposals that, as they very well knew, had no chance of being adopted.[5] They were largely concerned that their recommendation on Japan did not contradict the prevailing inclinations in the Politburo.

The role of Soviet-Japanese studies in the formation of views on Japan during the cold war was two-sided. On the one hand, they to no small degree were responsible for "theoretical elaboration" and propaganda for the official ideological stereotypes on Japan and also justification of the foreign policy course of the Soviet leadership in relation to that country. On the other, in the late Brezhnev era there were also a variety of economic and cultural studies in which authors presented on the whole an objective analysis of the postwar development of Japan. Such studies tempered or even contradicted the message in official propaganda and, for those alert to academic writings, provided a framework for interpreting unofficial information filtering into Russia.

The broader public could not avoid the official propaganda, but also gained increasing knowledge of Japan through unofficial sources. The ideological apparatus, using its powerful means of information, academic institutes, the "Knowledge" society, and other mass organs, strove to inculcate into the consciousness of the Soviet people stereotypes of Japan as the "main military springboard of the U.S. in the Far East" and a country "going on the path of militarization." In the period of the cold war, on no other problem related to Japan were published such a quantity of articles and popular brochures and "studies" as on "Japanese militarism."[6] They continued a hypertrophy of images on the scale and significance of the armed forces of Japan.

The ideological apparatus paid a lot of attention to propaganda presenting various stereotypes of Japan as a country of irreconcilable class contradictions, of sharp struggle between the democratic and reactionary forces. Pictures of demonstrations by Japanese workers did not leave the television screens. This propaganda brought certain results. For example, during the first joint Soviet-Japanese survey of public opinion conducted at the beginning of 1988, already in the period of perestroika, 30 percent of those questioned declared that they did not consider Japan either a peace-loving or a democratic country.[7]

At the same time a variety of factors appeared that contributed to the erosion of stereotypes and the formation of positive impressions of Japan and the Japanese people. Most important were the loss of faith and the cynical reaction to official propaganda, also the softening of censorship after Stalin's death, and the appearance of informal sources of information.

After the reestablishment of diplomatic relations with Japan in 1956, economic and cultural cooperation between the two countries expanded. In various cities of the USSR exhibits of Japanese art were held, Japanese drama companies made guest performances, translations of contemporary Japanese writers began to be published, and vivid popular works of Soviet writers and journalists on Japanese culture and national character drew a wide following.[8] Interest in Japanese culture facilitated the growth in popularity among various strata of Japanese traditional and martial arts. However, undoubtedly postwar economic successes, which were associated with images of the "Japanese miracle," exerted the principal influence on the formation of a positive image of Japan among the Soviet people. During lectures on Japan in the most diverse auditoriums the question always was raised, "Why can the Japanese do it, and we cannot?"

As for the territorial problem, the Soviet people were little interested in small islands located at the end of the world, about which they were reminded only in news about typhoons and tsunami inundating them. They considered it completely natural that the Kurile Islands after the victory over Japan were annexed to the USSR, more than half of the territory of which had similarly been conquered and incorporated into the Russian empire and the USSR. The overwhelming majority of the Soviet people supported the official stereotype on the "resolved problem." The means of mass information presented only the Soviet point of view on this problem and always linked Japan's pretenses to the Kurile Islands with the growth of revanchionist and nationalistic forces in Japan.

At the same time, nobody would have protested had Khrushchev or another Soviet leader returned these islands to Japan as had occurred with the transfer of small islands in the Baltic Sea to Finland and Port Arthur to China.

In the first half of the 1980s quite a paradoxical situation took shape. At this time the attitude of officials and the mass media to Japan, in connection with its participation in so-called anti-Soviet actions, was the most negative in the entire postwar period, while among the public at large Japan had become one of the most popular foreign countries. Thus, at the time of the first joint study of public opinion of Japanese and Soviet students conducted in 1979 by the *Sankei shimbun* and the Institute of Sociology of the Academy of Sciences of the USSR, more than 70 percent of Soviet young people questioned asserted they had good or satisfactory attitudes toward Japan. (The results were published in Japan, but not in the USSR.)[9] Awareness at the end of the cold war by a part of the Soviet leadership and *nomenklatura* of the important role of Japan as one of the leading economic centers of the contemporary world helped prepare public opinion to be receptive in the period of perestroika of "new thinking" toward Japan.

The Period of Perestroika: The Japan Boom in the USSR

Three factors in the period of perestroika led to great changes in views of Japan: democratization of public life, the end of the cold war, and interest on the part of the new leadership and the broad public in economic cooperation with Japan. The declaration of glasnost, the weakening of censorship, the gradual de-ideologization of the mass media, and scientific research led to more objective information on Japan reaching the Soviet people.

In this period there began to be conducted and, more importantly, published, studies of public opinion showing the views of diverse groups on various aspects of the political life of Japan and Soviet-Japanese relations. Already the first surveys conducted in May 1988 by the Institute of Sociology and the *Yomiuri shimbun* offered an opportunity to better understand the role of various sources of information and the problems that most interested Soviet opinion. The majority questioned counted among these problems culture, art, and history (44 percent), science and technology (43 percent), politics and diplomacy (34 percent), and nature and the state of the environment (17 percent).[10] At the start of perestroika the territorial problem, as before, little interested the Soviet people.

The creation of more objective images of Japan facilitated new tendencies in Japanese studies. Above all, a new generation of specialists played a large role in reexamining imperial and ideological stereotypes of Japan and acquainting the broad public with historical, legal, and political aspects of the territorial problem. As censorship weakened, people were disabused of Marxist stereotypes of Japan as a country of sharp class struggle. Toward the end of perestroika the majority of Soviets saw Japan as a democratic country.[11] From the end of the 1980s, meetings on a high level between "fraternal parties" to all intents and purposes stopped and at the same time contacts broadened with leaders of the ruling LDP. The end of the cold war and the appearance of objective information on the military policies of Japan diminished imperial stereotypes of Japan as a military threat to the USSR and the aggressive character of the Japan-U.S. military alliance. Studies of public opinion conducted in 1990 demonstrated that more than 60 percent of Soviets were convinced of the peace-loving attitudes of the Japanese.[12] The Japan-U.S. Security Treaty also began to be seen by a significant part of the public as an important factor in stability in the Far East. At the same time changes in strategic thinking were far from smooth. At the end of the 1980s a popular point of view, especially among the military, was that after a whole series of "concessions" to the United States and Western Europe it was necessary to draw a line and that line should be in the Far East.

Especially important changes in understanding Japan in the period of perestroika were linked with awareness of the role of this Asian country as a world economic power. The first joint Soviet-Japanese survey of public opinion conducted in 1988 showed that 97.9 percent of respondents considered Japan to be an "economically developed country."[13] In his speech in Vladivostok in 1986 Gorbachev first declared that Japan had turned into a power of first-order significance. In Moscow people began to be aware that without the support of Japan it would not be possible to achieve the participation of the USSR in international economic and regional structures on which depended the possibility of obtaining Western assistance and credits essential for carrying out economic reforms in the USSR.

Among a broad public the preceding image of the "Japanese miracle" was transformed into an impression of the "Japanese model" of economic development. Quite popular at this time was the point of view that precisely the Japanese experience in modernization best of all corresponds to the mentality of the Soviet people: collectivism, planning, and administrative guidance of the economy. Academic Leonid Abalkin, in the article "Will the Japanese Experience Help Russia?," published in *Izvestiia,* which was the most popular paper at that time, wrote, "Now we have noticed changes in thinking about the foreign economic, socio-cultural makeup of the Japanese model, among which are the presence of a society with a great and united national idea, the use of informal relations among people, a high level of education, an innate diligence and responsibility."[14]

Preparation for the visit of Gorbachev drew wide attention from the Soviet public. Every newspaper and weekly magazine published diverse material on Japan. Every day television programs were shown on the achievements of the Japanese in the newest technologies, and on Japan's culture and traditions. Moscow-Tokyo "telebridge" broadcasts enjoyed wide popularity. At this time Japanese became positive personages in Soviet films and even in anecdotes. Never before in the history of the USSR was there such a high rating of Japan as before the visit of Gorbachev to Tokyo.

Perceptions of Japan as the richest economic power in the world played the principal role in the change in attitude of both the new Soviet leadership and the broad public toward the territorial problem. The point of view grew ever more widespread that resolution of the territorial problem would lead to receiving significant financial and technological assistance from this rich country and would facilitate the rebirth of Siberia and the Far East. "Japan today," wrote the economic commentator of *Izvestiia,* M. Berger, "is the greatest holder of free capital, the scale of which more than twice exceeds the possibilities of all international financial organizations."[15]

In perceptions of the territorial problem during preparations for the visit of Gorbachev to Japan, the following tendencies were characteristic. First, the broad public in the USSR gained the opportunity to express its attitudes toward a foreign policy question. Some newspapers and journals began regularly to publish letters to the editor that set forth readers' viewpoints regarding Soviet-Japanese relations. Surveys of public opinion testified to certain changes in the perceptions of the Soviet people on the territorial question. In the first joint study of public opinion that included a question on the territorial problem, conducted by TASS and Kyodo tsushin in February 1988, in response to the question "Do you consider the borders between Japan and the USSR established after the Second World War just?," 72 percent of Japanese answered in the negative and only 2.5 percent of Soviets.[16] But curiously, *Pravda,* which published the results of the survey, decided not to convey even these figures; the "taboo" on the territorial problem still was sacred for the party press.

Another survey in February 1991 in the Russian Republic before the visit of Gorbachev to Japan already demonstrated a wider spectrum of views among the Soviet public. Responding to a question about the sequence of stages in resolving the territorial question, 13 percent answered that it is necessary to resolve this question first, 37 percent considered that things should begin with an improvement in bilateral relations, and as many adhered to the opinion that both problems should be decided simultaneously.[17] One can conclude that on the whole the political climate for the Gorbachev visit was quite favorable. Why then did the visit not lead to normalization of Soviet-Japanese relations?

Preparation for the visit occurred during the disintegration of the USSR, a sharp decline in the authority of the president, and pluralization of the Soviet political system. This forced Gorbachev to consider the points of view of various institutes and political forces that exerted an ever larger influence on the decision-making process—the military, the leadership of the Supreme Soviet, the leaderships of the Far Eastern regions. A principal barrier on the Russian side to achieving a compromise in Tokyo was the position of the president of the Russian Federation, Boris Yeltsin. On the one hand, Yeltsin and his democratic supporters spoke out in ways that seemed amenable to the return to Japan of the South Kurile Islands illegally occupied by Stalin. On the other, they feared that success by Gorbachev in negotiations in Tokyo could strengthen his position both inside the country and abroad. The results of the negotiations of Gorbachev in Tokyo were on the whole favorably assessed in the press and by public opinion and did not lead to any real change in perceptions of Japan in the USSR.

Perceptions of Japan in Russia: The Shattering of Illusions

After the collapse of the USSR it was widely expected among diverse social strata that the new Russian leadership would succeed in reaching a compromise with Japan and attracting this great economic power into the process of modernization of the Russian economy. Yeltsin had earlier announced his own plan for a multistage resolution of the territorial problem. The influence of advisors and diplomats with a democratic orientation on the formation of foreign policy toward Japan had visibly risen. The broad public continued to see Japan as a democratic state and an important factor in stability in the Far East, and Japanese economic assistance and the Japanese model of development as important for Russia's transition to a market economy. Reflecting views popular at this time, the observer for *Nezavisimaia gazeta* wrote that "Only Japan, possessing the greatest bank capital in the world, is capable now of giving us the decisive investment and technological assistance, to pull us out of a deep hole, to offer credit of tens of billions of dollars without which we cannot escape the economic collapse. . . ."[18] However, these expectations were unwarranted. Perceptions of Japan in Russia at this time were influenced above all by political and psychological factors linked to the fall of the USSR and the failure of democratic and economic reforms in the period of perestroika.

Discussions of the territorial problem in preparation for Yeltsin's visit to Japan were the object of a fierce domestic political struggle, including inside the presidential apparatus and the Supreme Soviet. This struggle found broad reflection in the mass media and led to politicization of public opinion in Russia. Discussion of a territorial problem that would be sensitive for any society occurred in a period of establishment of a new political system, with a new elite, and a new mechanism of decision making, and a search for a new geopolitical role in the world and the Asian-Pacific region. Politicians of various orientations tried, and not without success, to use this discussion to raise their own role in the process of formulating new domestic and foreign policy priorities for Russia. Precisely during discussion of the territorial problem in the Supreme Soviet the group known as *derzhavniki* was formed and proclaimed the basic postulates of Russian policy to be: a strong state, a strong army, and a strong foreign policy.

The collapse of the USSR and the transformation of Russia into a second-rate power gave rise to a sense of loss and, in connection with that, activation of nationalist and patriotic attitudes among various social strata and the political elite. At the same time as supporters of compromise with Japan turned to reason, accentuating the need to adhere to a civilized approach to resolving international problems, "patriots" turned above all to emotion, playing on the feelings of people who suffered from the decline of their state. Not surprisingly the slogans of "patriots" about "selling Russian territory," and that "Japan is using Russia's weakness" to gain the return of "purely Russian" territory and "to enslave the Far East" met a warm response not only among nationalists and communists but also among others, especially in the provinces. The survey conducted in the provincial city of Penza not long before the proposed visit of Yeltsin to Japan showed that almost 60 percent of those questioned favored the South Kuriles remaining under Russian sovereignty, only 8 percent declared themselves in favor of transferring them to Japan, and just 2 percent responded that they had no interest in this problem.[19]

In this period the process of regionalization intensified, and the influence of the center weakened especially in the Far East. Sakhalin and the Kurile Islands became a kind of proving ground for Russian ultrapatriotic forces for playing out scenarios in opposition to any forces of central authority to achieve a compromise with Japan over the territorial problem. As an important card in its game with Moscow, local leadership used the threat of conducting a partisan war and establishing a Far Eastern Republic in the event of the transfer of the islands.

Positive images of Japan that had formed in the period of perestroika to a significant degree were marked by a distinctive Russian mentality of expectation of a "miracle" from the Japanese side: assistance, credit, the creation of joint economic zones, etc. Postponement of the visit of Yeltsin to Japan was a kind of indicator of this mood. When the miracle did not occur and illusions dissipated, a new stage in perceptions of Japan began. Failure in carrying out economic reforms and a sharp worsening in the social position of the nation led to a loss of interest in various foreign models of economic development and loss of faith in the possibility of Russia's modernization. At this time a series of negative stereotypes of Japan appeared. Among the "new Russians" the point of view became popular that it is "impossible to do business" with Japanese businessmen, or that "Japan's experience is not applicable to Russia."

The postponement of Yeltsin's visit had an especially significant influence on changes in the views of the Russian leadership on Far East foreign policy priorities. In the opinion of Academician A. Arbatov, after the postponement, the anti-American, anti-Western direction in the sentiments of the Russian political elite became more pronounced.[20] This led to a certain reorientation of Russia's Far Eastern policies, from Japan to other Asian countries. To more than a little extent, Japanese policies had an input in changing the perceptions of Russians of Japan, too. The course of tightly linking the territorial problem with economic cooperation and constant stress on Russia's inability to modernize its country played into the hands of nationalists, the power-holding forces in Russia.

The main tendency in Russian views of Japan after September 1992 was the absence of any expectations of rapid improvement in relations between the two countries in the political and economic spheres and, in connection with this, a significant loss of interest in that country on the part of the mass media, politicians, and the public at large. Thus in Russia as in Japan people became aware that no realistic possibilities existed in the near future to achieve a breakthrough in bilateral relations on the basis of resolving the territorial problem.

From Stereotypes to a Real Understanding of Japan

The visit of Yeltsin to Japan in October 1993 demonstrated a more realistic perception of leaders of both countries of the problems standing in the way of improvement in Russian-Japanese relations. After the signing of the concluding Tokyo Declaration, a correspondent of *Izvestiia* wrote that "Both countries were able to depart from years of inculcation of unfriendliness and the custom of listening only to themselves and the tendency to use any means to 'provoke' their opponent."[21]

In the middle of the 1990s the following tendencies were most characteristic of views of Japan in Russia. In connection with the aggravation of the political situation in the country the problem of

Russian-Japanese relations stopped being an important factor in domestic political life. Surveys of public opinion on Japan stopped being conducted. In newspapers and journals primary attention in this period was given to "Japanese perestroika" and the crisis situation in the Japanese economy. In the mid-1990s a process of depoliticization of the territorial problem occurred. Although nationalist publications continued from time to time to spend some time on this theme, it stopped being an important factor in the internal political life of Russia. It is revealing that two candidates for the post of president of Russia—Yavlinsky and Lebed—officially declared that the Kurile Islands should be returned to Japan.[22] Attitudes of the leadership and population in the Russian Far East to this problem began to change as they began to regard as the principal threat not Japan but China. In the perceptions of this problem by Russian official circles a significant influence was exerted by the point of view that the global community was losing interest. An official of the Far Eastern department of the Foreign Ministry, Iurii Kuznetsov, declared in an interview with an observer of *Novoe vremia,* "The world would have been prepared to support a weak Japan, offended by a superpower. Now the world is irritated by a 'high-handed Japan.'"[23] Substantial attention in Soviet mass media was given to the change in the hardline position of Japanese politicians and public opinion in relation to the territorial problem.

The severe earthquake on the Kurile Islands in October 1994 was a kind of psychological shock both for Russians and for Japanese politicians. They came to recognize that further games over this problem did not bring any gain to either of these countries. As an important sign of change in official Japanese policies Russian observers watched the quiet response of the Japanese Foreign Ministry to the 1996 proposal of Foreign Minister Primakov to discuss the possibility of establishing joint projects on the Kurile Islands.[24] In the mid-1990s new tendencies became evident in the coverage of the mass media of the possibility of Russian-Japanese economic cooperation. In the article "The unfinished duel of the knight and the samurai," published in the weekly *Novoe vremia,* V. Golovnin wrote that "Japanese judging by everything are beginning to believe that capitalism in Russia, although rather wild, is strengthening over the long run. . . ."[25]

Japan continued to be seen by the Russian leadership as an important factor in the entrance of Russia into global and regional political, economic, and financial structures. Special attention in Moscow was given to the favorable position of Japan with regard to Russia's participation in the G-7 and its incorporation into APEC. A new factor in the perceptions of the Russian leadership of Japan were contacts in the military arena. In the spring of 1996 the leader of the Self Defense Forces first visited Moscow. A Japanese destroyer, which conducted a study with ships of the Pacific Fleet, sailed into Vladivostok for the first time. In Tokyo talk was beginning of interest in Russian military technology.[26] In November 1996 the commander of the Pacific Fleet visited Japan, as did in the middle of May 1997 Minister of Defense Rodionov. He made it clear that Russia did not view Japan as its strategic opponent and considered the Japan-U.S. Security Treaty as a factor in the stability of the Asia Pacific region. Moreover, he proposed discussing the question of developing triangular defense cooperation among Russia, Japan, and the United States.

New tendencies in understanding Japan as a potential partner in the military arena reflect, above all, the search by Russia for a geopolitical role in the Asia Pacific region. If in the period of the cold war the Soviet leadership looked on Japan through the prism of its military alliance with the United States, then Russian politicians all the more often are interpreting Japan from the point of view of Russia's relations with the PRC.

The new tendencies in Russian perceptions of Japan during the mid-1990s were preconditions for the meeting of Yeltsin and Hashimoto in Krasnoyarsk. In the Russian media this was widely covered and brought what was called a "mini-boom" in relations. Russian observers evaluated Hashimoto's statements as a sign that Japanese politicians had rejected linking the return of the South Kurile Islands with improving relations. They assumed that the most important factor causing Japan to change course was Russia's rising role in global and regional policies. "The aggravation of the situation on the Korean peninsula and the prospect of a unified Korea forming whose ideological basis could be nationalism with clear anti-Japanese coloring worries the Japanese greatly. . . . Japanese tremble at each news item about the delivery to China of Russian fighter planes and ships."[27] Therefore, the establishment of a friendly dialogue with Russia, which has good relations with China, South Korea, and North Korea can give Tokyo an additional and very real influence on the complex situation in this region. An important stimulus for

Hashimoto, in the opinion of Russian observers, is pressure from business circles, which are interested in oil and gas from deposits in Siberia and Sakhalin.[28]

It is worth noting that the mass media paid special attention to the informal nature of the meeting, including statements that both leaders switched to using the personal "you" and began to call each other by their nicknames "Boris" and "Ryu." It is entirely possible that this side of the meeting will have no less significance for improving bilateral relations than the political and economic declarations of the leaders. It facilitates the erosion of the most vivid stereotypes in Japan about Russian politicians as dogmatic Mr. "Nyet" and impressions in Russia about Japanese leaders as "cunning" and hooked only on the territorial problem.

Conclusions

The postwar period of Russian history offers a rare opportunity for researchers to understand those factors that exerted the principal influence on the formation of perceptions in the USSR (and, later, Russia) on Japan. Why were some stereotypes stable and withstood the test of time, while others quite quickly eroded or changed sharply? Among the latter were factors that were rooted in the history of relations, above all the impression of Japan both as a potential opponent and as a potential trading partner and a country with a unique culture. These were fixed in the historical memory of the nation, in literature, and in art. Precisely these perceptions exerted the most impact, and continue to the present. In contrast, stereotypes formed under the influence of ideological propaganda were of little effect, receding with the lessening of censorship and the collapse of the communist system.

The absence of an ideological factor is no guarantee of a positive view of Japan in Russia. Influencing this process are the psychological consequences of the collapse of the socialist empire, the internal political and economic processes in Russia, and the search by Russia for a geopolitical role in the Far East. Japan itself is not first in determining these views. The psychological factor to a degree is linked to the competition in historical development between the two countries. Despite strong leanings toward the West in Russian society, Russians have since the Meiji reforms reacted with a degree of envy and admiration to the successes of Japan on the path of modernization and its capacity to maintain its national values. Precisely here we can trace the interest in the Japanese miracle, Japanese culture, and Japanese national character.

In the post-communist period perceptions of Japan as a great economic power began to exert a decisive influence on the process of normalization of relations between the two countries. At the same time the absence of interest by Japan in economic cooperation with Russia and the stress on Russia's inability to modernize contributed to the loss of interest in the Japanese model of development and the appearance among Russians of feelings of inferiority that in turn led to more nationalist attitudes.

In the West and Japan, writings on the territorial question often use the expression "misperception" to refer to differences in views between Russian and Japanese of each other, above all in connection with the territorial problem. In fact, the territorial problem has not exerted any significant influence on Russian views of Japan. Only a small number of Russian specialists and diplomats were familiar with the specifics, and they were largely engaged in finding counterarguments in discussions with Japanese representatives during official and unofficial discussions of this problem. Many who took part in preparing diplomatic or propagandistic presentations on the territorial problem did not doubt that the South Kurile Islands rightfully belonged to Japan. Their public position was defined not by objective factors, but above all by taking into account beliefs. As for the broad public, its attitudes to the territorial problem were indifferent and exerted little influence on perceptions of Japan. Even in the period of widespread discussion of this problem in preparation for the visits of Gorbachev and Yeltsin to Japan, they reflected above all the complex and critical domestic political problems of those periods and left behind no serious anti-Japanese inclinations.

A quite lively discussion of the territorial problem testifies to the fact that in Russia the process of formation of public opinion has begun, and is starting to influence foreign policy decision making. As in other countries with a pluralistic regime, foreign policy problems are becoming an important factor in internal political life. Unlike in the USSR, where foreign policy decisions were made by a small circle of people, in Russia the territorial problem can be resolved only with the consensus of the domestic political elite and support of the majority of the population of the country.

Broad interest in Japanese culture and traditional values is explained above all by the significance given to culture in Russian society. The increase in attention to traditional forms of Japanese art was a kind of reaction to the spiritual emptiness of socialist culture. In surveys of public opinion about the principal characteristics of Japanese conducted in the period of perestroika, respondents accentuated above all qualities linked to attitudes toward work and a unique culture.

Increasingly Russians see the world through the lens of its impact on Russia's economy. This means that if no sharp political shift occurs in Russia, Japan will be perceived at the beginning of the next century by the majority as an important economic partner as well as a factor for stability. This bodes well for public support for a breakthrough in relations.

NOTES

1. A. Gromyko, *Memoirs* (New York: 1990), p. 224.
2. Nikita Khrushchev, *Khrushchev Remembers* (Boston: Little, Brown, 1970), p. 84.
3. Nikita Khrushchev, *Khrushchev Remembers,* p. 84.
4. Gilbert Rozman, "Moscow's Japan Watchers in the First Years of the Gorbachev Era: The Struggle for Realism and Respect in Foreign Affairs," *The Pacific Review,* Vol. 1, No. 4, 1988, pp. 257–75.
5. Among such projects were the "Treaty on Friendship and Cooperation," "On Measures for Trust in the Military Arena," and the widely heralded concept "On Collective Security in Asia."
6. I. Sergienko, *Rebirth of Militarism in Japan* (Moscow: 1968); A. Markov, *Japan—the Course of Rearmament* (Moscow: 1970); S. Mazhorov, *The Military-Economic Potential of Contemporary Japan* (Moscow: 1979); I. Ivkov, *Japan—Again on the Path of Militarization* (Moscow: 1980); E. Zaitsev and I. Tamginskii, *Japan: Again the Path of Militarism* (Moscow: 1985).
7. *Pravda,* November 3, 1983.
8. In 1975, publication of the book *Branch of the Cherry Tree* by *Pravda* correspondent V. Ovchinnikov proved to be a major event in the cultural life of Russia and contributed to the rapid growth in interest of the Soviet people in the traditional values of Japan and the national character of the Japanese people.
9. *Sankei shimbun,* August 25, 1979.
10. *Yomiuri shimbun,* May 15, 1988.

11. *Izvestiia,* April 25, 1990.
12. *Izvestiia,* April 25, 1990.
13. *Pravda,* November 3, 1988.
14. *Nezavisimaia gazeta,* June 20, 1992.
15. *Izvestiia,* July 22, 1991.
16. *Yomiuri shimbun,* May 15, 1988.
17. *Rossiiskaia gazeta,* September 17, 1991.
18. *Nezavisimaia gazeta,* July 23, 1991.
19. *Nezavisimaia gazeta,* June 14, 1992.
20. *Mirovaia ekonomika i mezhdunarodnye otnosheniia,* No. 7. 1994, p. 94.
21. *Izvestiia,* October 10, 1993.
22. During a visit to Japan, A. Lebed declared that he did not see the basis for considering the South Kuriles "age-old Russian territories." *Novoe Russkoe slovo,* October 19, 1997.
23. *Novoe vremia,* No. 23, 1993, p. 25.
24. Ibid., p. 35.
25. Ibid., p. 34.
26. Ibid.
27. *Izvestiia,* August 27, 1997.
28. Ibid.

CHAPTER 15

Japanese Perceptions of the Soviet Union and Russia in the Postwar Period

Tsuyoshi Hasegawa

GORBACHEV'S PERESTROIKA, THE END OF THE COLD WAR, and the collapse of the Soviet Union have fundamentally changed international relations. The superpower competition and the East-West conflict that once appeared to be the solid bedrock of international relations have receded into the past. The collapse of Soviet communism also dissolved Sino-Soviet conflict that had provided an important framework of international relations in Asia for more than a quarter of a century. The world is in a state of flux in search for a new international system. Freed from the cold war paradigm that provided the stable framework of the international system for half a century after the end of World War II, states are exploring the new rules of the game.

In the reconfiguration of international relations in the post–cold war world, there is one factor that has not been changed from the cold war period: the continuing stalemate of Russo-Japanese relations. Japan was the only major power that failed to achieve rapprochement with the Soviet Union during Gorbachev's perestroika period. Even after the collapse of the Soviet Union, Russia and Japan have been unable to overcome legacies of not only the cold war but also of World War II.[1] In a world where the Berlin Wall is no more and divided Germany has been reunited, and where Russian and Chinese leaders embrace each other as "strategic partners," the continuing stalemate of Russo-Japanese relations is puzzling.

This anomaly is not derived from divergence of national interests, since clearly both sides' national interests are better served by rapprochement. Then, what prevents both countries from achieving reconciliation? The short answer is, obviously, the Northern Territories dispute. But it appears strange for both countries to let this seemingly minor question stand in the way of rapprochement. And it is precisely this oddity that characterized the basic nature of Russo-Japanese relations. It is the perceptions and misperceptions that have played a larger role in Russo-Japanese relations than overriding national interests. Without taking into account mutual perceptions and psychological factors that underlay decisions and actions of both countries, the singularly undistinguished Russo-Japanese relations in the postwar period cannot be understood. Since Semyon Verbitsky has written of Soviet perceptions of Japan, I will examine in this chapter specific features of Japanese perceptions of the Soviet Union/Russia in the postwar period.

Public Opinion Polls and Popular Perceptions of the Soviet Union/Russia

Jiji Tsushinsha has been taking interesting public opinion surveys since 1960.[2] The survey is conducted in the first four days of each month, taking a random sample of approximately 2,000 adults. Among the questions asked, two are relevant to Japanese perceptions of the Soviet Union: "Name three countries you like most from the following list," and "Name three countries you dislike most from the following list."[3]

The Jiji surveys are an important source of information describing the changing perceptions of the Japanese about other countries. First, the same questions have been asked every month for almost 40 years. This gives us a fairly accurate picture of the general trend of popular preference of foreign countries. Second, because of its regularity, the Jiji surveys are different from other irregularly conducted surveys by various newspapers and broadcasting companies. Third, the Jiji surveys are useful precisely because of the simplicity of the questions. The countries named by respondents are those countries they chose as important for either positive or negative reasons. Thus, the result of the surveys can serve as a relatively accurate reflection of the respondents' image of foreign countries.

Fourth, since the Jiji surveys are taken every month, the annual mean average has the effect of minimizing the margin of errors and monthly fluctuations. Furthermore, it is useful to be able to see how important events influenced popular perceptions by looking at the monthly results.

Figure 15.1 shows the changes from 1960 through 1999 in percentages of the Soviet Union/CIS/Russia, the United States, and the People's Republic of China selected by the respondents as the countries they like [*suki na kuni*]. Figure 15.2 shows the changes in percentages of the Soviet Union, the United States, and the PRC from 1960 through 1999 selected by the respondents as the countries they dislike most [*kirai na kuni*].

The first and foremost characteristic of the positive image of the Soviet Union is its lowness. In the 1960s the popularity of the Soviet Union was around 4 percent, but after 1977 it dropped to between 1 and 2 percent, and in 1980, in the wake of the Afghanistan invasion, it dropped to 0.8 percent, the lowest since 1960. During the perestroika period, the positive rating gradually improved above 1 percent, but never came near the highest point in the 1960s. In 1990, it reached 2.0 percent, and 2.1 percent in 1991. The collapse of the Soviet Union did not result in a positive image of Russia. On the contrary, it negatively affected a positive image, which fell to below 1 percent. In 1993, after Yeltsin canceled his trip to Tokyo, it dropped to an all-time low of 0.6 percent, which is 0.2 percent lower than the lowest point during the cold war. If one compares the positive image of the Soviet Union/Russia with the positive image of the United States and the PRC, the unpopularity of the Soviet Union/Russia is evident. The United States experienced the lowest point in 1972 and 1973 (18 percent), but reached close to 50 percent in the middle of 1960 and in the most recent years. The PRC started out at a comparable low point during the 1960s, but around the normalization of relations in 1973, it rose to above 10 percent, and peaked at above 20 percent in the second half of the 1980s. The Tiananmen Incident contributed to a sharp decline (to 10 percent). In the first half of the 1990s, the popularity of China was somewhat restored, but not much. Despite this decline, the PRC's popularity has far outstripped that of the Soviet Union/Russia.

Lowness of the positive image alone does not translate as unpopularity in itself. It may simply mean that most Japanese could care less about the Soviet Union, as they could care less about, say,

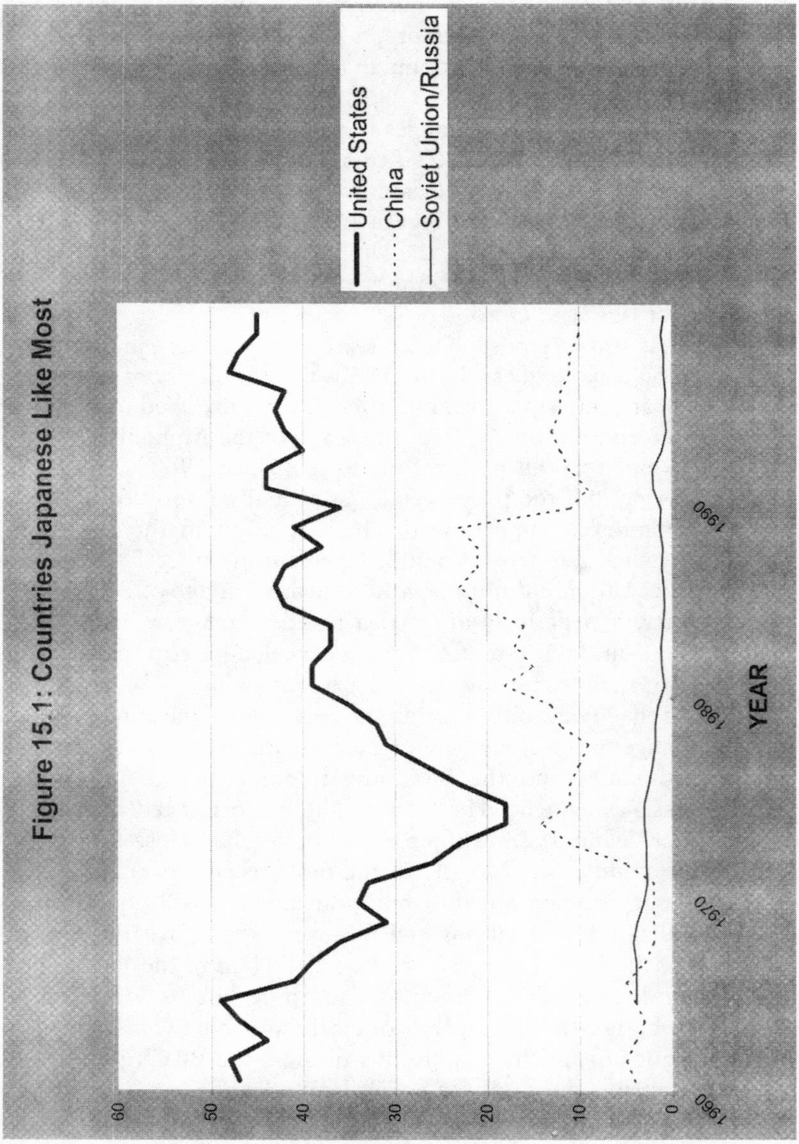

Figure 15.1: Countries Japanese Like Most

Figure 15.2: Countries Japanese Dislike Most

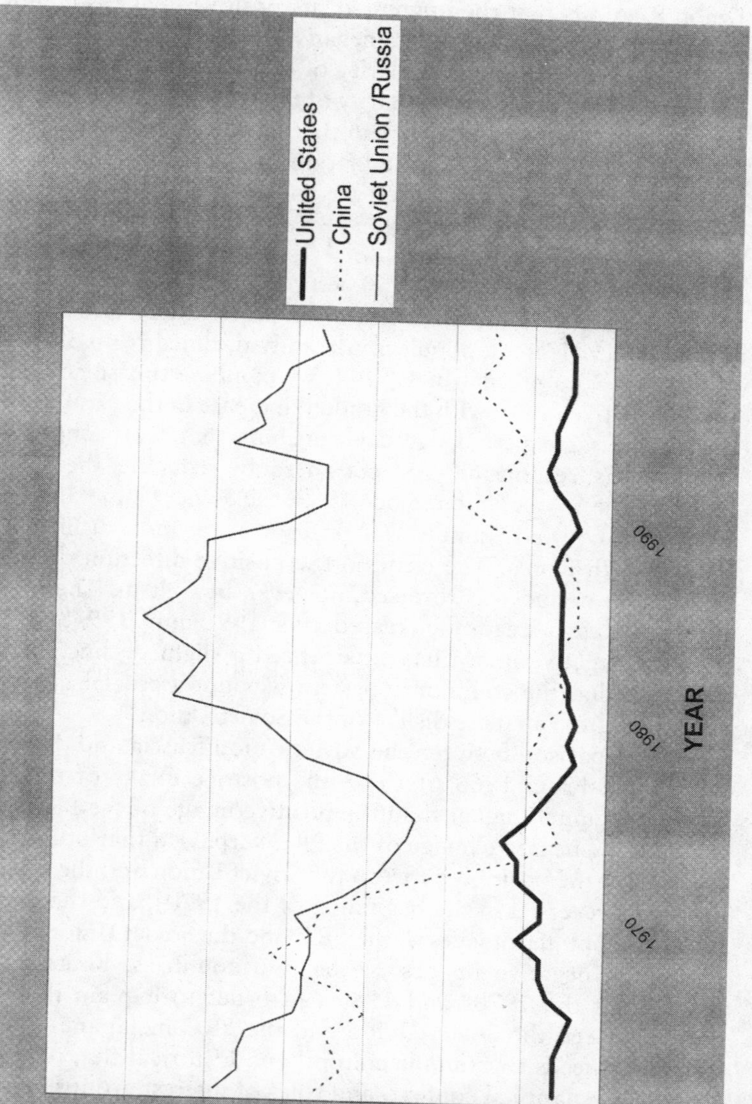

Zimbabwe or Costa Rica. But the important fact about the Soviet Union/Russia is that the lowness of its positive image is combined with the high percentage of its negative image. Figure 15.2 shows, first, that until 1985, unpopularity of the USSR was—with the exception of 1967 when unpopularity of the PRC surpassed that of the Soviet Union—always higher than that of the United States and the PRC and after 1970 by a wide margin. It also shows that between 1974 and 1985 the gap between the Soviet Union, on the one hand, and the United States and the PRC, on the other, was greatly widened. Especially after the Soviet invasion of Afghanistan, the negative image reached above 50 percent: in 1984, it even registered an astounding 59 percent. During the perestroika period between 1985 and 1991, its unpopularity steadily declined from 55 percent in 1985 to 35.6 percent in 1991. If we combine this steady decline in the negative image with the gradual increase in the positive image during the same period, we can conclude that Gorbachev's perestroika was responsible for considerably reducing the negative image of the Soviet Union. Since 1989, the Soviet Union and Russia yielded the coveted Number One position as the most disliked country to North Korea. The trend in the positive direction during the perestroika period was reversed, however, by Yeltsin. The negative image of Russia steadily increased after 1991 until 1995, but since then the negative image has experienced a slight decline. This underscores that the communist system was not a crucial factor that contributed to Japanese dislike of the Soviet Union.

A comparison between the Soviet Union/Russia and the PRC is interesting. From 1966 to 1970, the positive image of the Soviet Union was much higher than the positive image of the PRC, while in 1967, the negative image of the PRC surpassed that of the Soviet Union. But the position between the Soviet Union and the PRC was decisively reversed in the beginning of the 1970s, and the gaps between the popular images of the PRC and the Soviet Union, and between the negative images of the two countries, became wider throughout the 1970s and 1980s. In order to explain the differences between the Soviet Union and the PRC in Japanese perceptions, one needs to examine cultural and historical ties, contingent events, international context, and roles of interest groups in the Japanese political process. But one thing is clear: the communist system and ideology played little part in Japan's perceptions of these countries.

Unfortunately, we have little data showing Japanese perceptions of foreign countries before 1960. I have found only two such surveys. The first is the *Yomiuri shimbun* public opinion survey conducted in August 1950. To the question: Which of the following countries do you like most, 65.7 percent chose the United States, but only 1.6 percent chose the Soviet Union. As for the country they disliked most, 67.9 percent picked the Soviet Union, 3.9 percent the PRC, and 1.6 percent the United States.[4] Interestingly, during the Occupation period, U.S. popularity and Soviet unpopularity were much higher than any time after 1960.

The second was a 1957 Chuo Chosasha national survey. In this survey, the percentages of the most favored countries are as follows: the United States (27 percent), the PRC (2 percent), and the Soviet Union (1 percent). The percentages of the most disliked countries are: the Soviet Union (31 percent), the PRC (4 percent), and the United States (4 percent).[5] This survey is interesting, since it shows the unpopular image of the Soviet Union one year after Japan and the Soviet Union normalized relations.

In addition to countries they like most and dislike most, the Jiji survey also asks the question: to which political camp should Japan belong? Figure 15.3 shows the trend of the political affiliation the Japanese felt about where Japan should belong. It indicates, first, that Japanese sympathy for the communist camp is negligibly low. There could be only two possibilities for Japan's political alignment: either to remain in the pro-Western, procapitalist camp or to choose neutrality. Japanese sympathy for neutrality experienced two peaks, first, in 1959, during the political upheaval revolving around the revision of the U.S.-Japanese Security Treaty, and second, in 1973, at the last stage of the war in Vietnam and the aftermath of the Nixon shocks. But their sympathy for neutrality in both cases proved to be temporary, with public opinion quickly swinging back to a pro-Western stand. The pro-Western stand, which peaked in the year of the Tokyo Olympics in 1964, did not decline markedly throughout the 1960s despite the unpopularity of the war in Vietnam. Only in 1973 did the neutralist stand become slightly more popular than the pro-Western stand. But the change after 1974 is striking. Since 1974 the gap between neutrality and the pro-Western stand sharply and steadily widened, with the pro-Western stand surpassing 60 percent before the collapse of the Soviet Union in 1991. Nevertheless, it should be noted that despite a sharp rise in the pro-Western stand,

Figure 15.3: Which Bloc Should Japan Join?

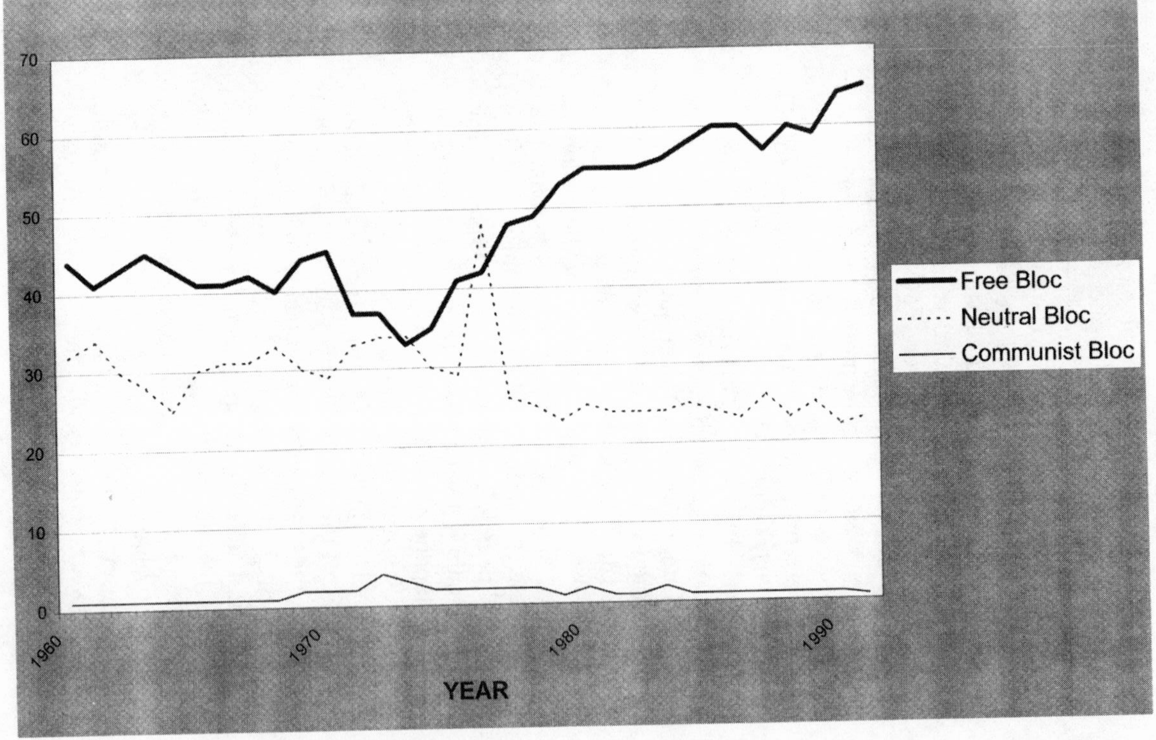

the neutralist sentiment did not decline markedly, registering somewhere between 20 to 25 percent support among the Japanese.[6] This shift in the pro-Western stand also coincided with the results of various public opinion surveys indicating the growing approval of the U.S.-Japanese Security Pact (54 percent approval in 1980) and the Self Defense Forces (78 percent approval in 1980).[7]

How is the trend of Soviet unpopularity related to the trend of U.S. popularity and that of political affiliations? Figure 15.4 shows the relations among these three trends. It indicates that until 1985 these three trends followed a similar pattern: namely, the Soviet unpopularity dropped as the U.S. popularity and pro-Western stand dropped, and vice versa. Second, with the exception of the periods between 1963 and 1967 and between 1989 and 1992, Soviet unpopularity always surpassed U.S. popularity, which is to say that the Japanese tend to dislike the Russians more than they like the Americans. At first glance Figure 15.4 seems to show that the rate by which the Japanese favored the pro-Western stand was much higher than U.S. popularity and Soviet unpopularity. But since the interviewees are asked to choose one out of three on the political camp question, and the two other questions allow multiple choices, the political camp graph cannot be compared with the like or dislike graphs. Another interesting feature of this graph is that the trends after Gorbachev's assumption of power indicated a distinct pattern that did not exist before. As Soviet unpopularity moved downward, U.S. popularity and the pro-Western stand moved upward until 1991. This could be understood in two ways. First, Gorbachev's perestroika contributed more to the relevancy of the pro-Western capitalist order. Second, Gorbachev reduced Soviet unpopularity among those who support the pro-Western camp. This trend was reversed, however, after Yeltsin took over.

Causes for Soviet/Russian Unpopularity

One opinion poll after another conducted in postwar Japan consistently and convincingly proves the decisive unpopularity of the Soviet Union and Russia among the Japanese. In fact, the Soviet Union and Russia consistently maintained the status of the most disliked country until 1988. Since 1988, North Korea has replaced it as the most disliked country. This fact, however, was not necessarily good

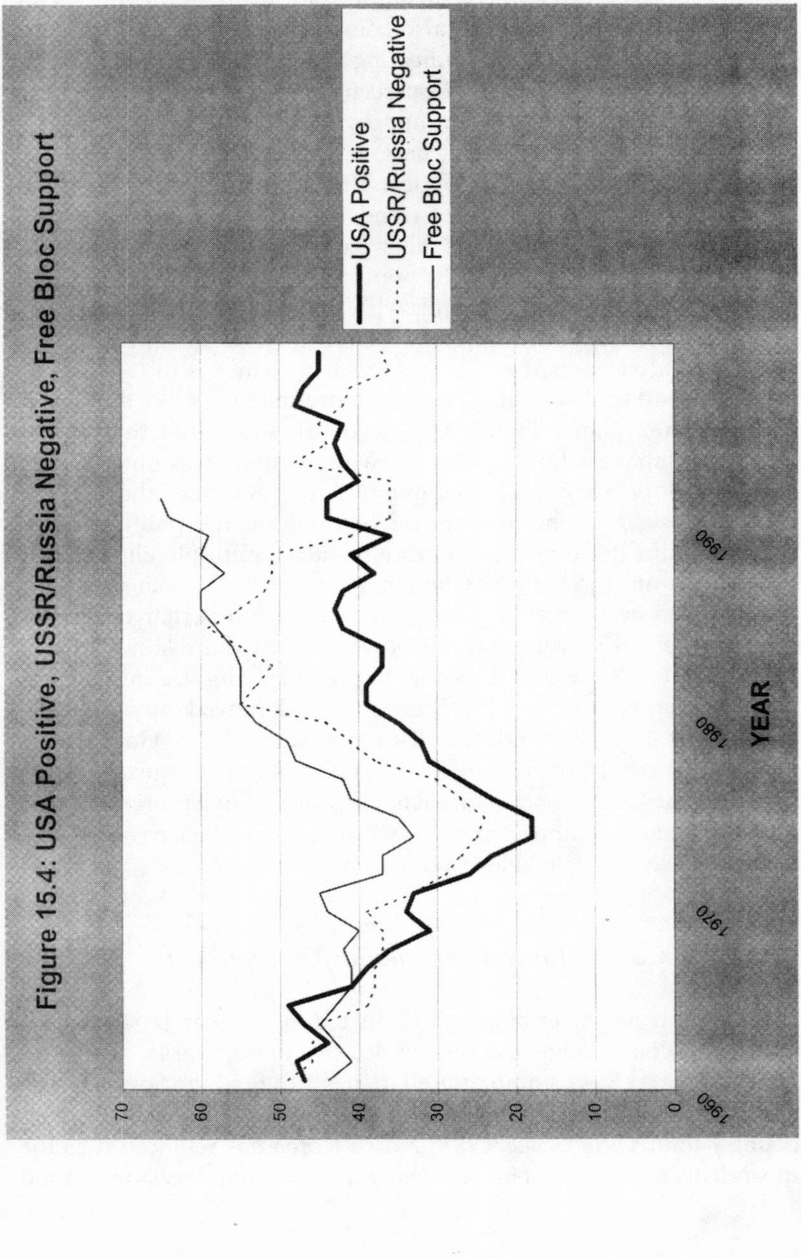

Figure 15.4: USA Positive, USSR/Russia Negative, Free Bloc Support

news. The Soviet Union and Russia have nonetheless occupied second place. Also, vacating the dubious distinction of being the most disliked country meant that the Japanese did not take the Soviet Union/Russia as seriously as previously.

The most decisive factor explaining this unpopularity is the collective memory of the Soviet-Japanese war in the summer of 1945. The Japanese are divided on responsibility and guilt in their conduct in the Pacific War. According to the opinion poll conducted by Hosoyoron Chosashitsu in 1983, 51.4 percent of respondents agreed with the statement that 50 years' history of Japan, to the end of the Pacific War, was a history of aggression against Asian neighbors, although 44.4 percent believed that the military expansion was a necessary means for Japan's survival.[8] Despite this division, it is important to note that more than half of those polled are willing to accept Japan's responsibility for the war. To the question of how Japan is regarded by Asian neighbors, 42 percent answered that the Japanese lack a sufficient sense of self-criticism about their past aggression in Asia.[9]

With regard to the Soviet Union and Russia, however, the Japanese do not feel such a sense of guilt. On the contrary, the Soviet Union/Russia is perceived as a *kajiba dorobo,* a thief who steals when somebody else's house is on fire—the party who took advantage of Japan's weakness at the end of the Pacific War. There are four specific charges Japanese would level against the Russians. First, the Soviet Union violated the Neutrality Pact, and launched an attack against Japan precisely at the crucial moment when Japan was desperately attempting to terminate the war through the mediation of the Soviet government. Second, the Soviet troops attacked the Japanese in Manchuria, Sakhalin, and the Kuriles, committing plunders, rapes, and murders against Japanese civilians. Third, 640,000 Japanese were seized as prisoners of war, and detained for many years in the forced labor camps in the Russian Far East, Siberia, and Central Asia. More than 60,000 died in the Soviet Union. Fourth, Soviet troops occupied and annexed the Kuriles that had never before belonged to Russia.

A peculiar factor of Japan's perception of the Soviet-Japanese war is that most of the Japanese treat the Soviet-Japanese war that began on August 9 totally separate from the Pacific War, despite the unassailable facts that Soviet participation was requested by the United States, that the violation of the Neutrality Pact by the Soviet

Union did not concern the United States at that time, and that the Kurile occupation by the Soviet troops had the blessing of the Truman administration at the time of operation. The psychological factor plays a paramount role in this separation. It is difficult for the Japanese to accept that the Soviet Union was a part of the larger war for which they were responsible. To many Japanese the Soviet-Japanese war served as a psychological means by which to acquire a sense of victimization. It is remarkable that many serious people in Japan who show sensitivity to the pain and tragedy that Japan's militarism and colonialism inflicted upon its Asian neighbors rarely reflect on how it also cast a shadow over the Soviet Union during the 1930s. When the Japanese talk about the history of Soviet-Japanese relations, they begin only from August 9, 1945, and rarely go back further to the Russo-Japanese War, the Japanese intervention in Siberia, and the Japanese military threat to the Soviet Far East.

For the Japanese it has become almost an obsession to pinpoint the origins of postwar Soviet-Japanese relations as the Soviet violation of the Neutrality Pact. This argument is advanced strictly on legal and moral grounds. The historical record demonstrates, however, that the Japanese government had seriously contemplated the possibility of discarding the Neutrality Pact, when Nazi Germany invaded the Soviet Union in June 1941. Japan elected not to attack the Soviet Union, not because it felt bound by the Neutrality Pact, but because it found the circumstances were not ripe enough to wage war against the Soviet Union. Maintenance of the Neutrality Pact during the Pacific War was necessitated by the deteriorating military situation, not by its legal commitment. In the end Japan was pushed into a corner where the only way to terminate the war short of unconditional surrender was to seek the mediation of the Soviet government. Stalin took advantage of Japan's peace overtures to prolong the war long enough to enter it. This was admittedly a cold-blooded Machiavellian manipulation on Stalin's part, but it also represented the colossal failure of Japanese diplomacy.

This, of course, does not mean that the Japanese must accept whatever happened at the end of the Pacific War. What was once the official Soviet explanation for the war—that Soviet participation in the war in the Far East was an act of self-sacrifice intended to keep a wartime commitment to its allies, liberate the Asian people from Japanese militarism, and put an end to the miseries of war—is a historical distortion. Stalin's motivation was primarily geostrategic. He sought to restore Soviet influence in Manchuria, regain southern Sakhalin, and place all of the Kurile Islands under Soviet occupation. Stalin's Kurile operation began only after Japan had accepted the Potsdam Declaration, and this operation was totally unnecessary if the objective was to terminate the war. The occupation of Habomai was not completed until September 5, three days after Japan had formally signed the surrender document. The Soviet occupation of the Kuriles—as distinguished from its operations in Manchuria, Korea, and Sakhalin—was a clear violation of the Cairo Declaration.

The war also caused the suffering of the Japanese at Soviet hands. There were approximately 2.7 million Japanese in the Soviet occupied territories at the end of the war. Brutalities were committed by Soviet soldiers against civilian Japanese in Manchuria and Korea. Millions were driven from their homes, forced to trek through difficult terrain, and evacuate to Japan. The more unfortunate committed mass suicide or were killed or captured by the Soviets. Approximately 150,000 disappeared during the war. Many children were separated from relatives rushing to escape Soviet soldiers and have remained in China. Brutalities were less pronounced in Sakhalin and the Kurile Islands, although 426,000 Japanese on these islands were ordered to evacuate to Japan.[10] In clear violation of the Geneva convention, Japanese POWs were sent to gulags scattered all over the Soviet Union. Some could not return to Japan for 12 years. More than 60,000 of the 640,000 Japanese interned in the Soviet Union perished without being able to see their homeland.[11]

A great difficulty for the Japanese is to navigate the treacherous moral channels between their culpability in the Pacific War and their justifiable grievances against Stalinist expansionism. There is no question that many Japanese were victimized by the Soviet-Japanese War. Strangely, however, the most important cause for this tragedy—the Japanese government's delay in terminating the war—has not been seriously debated in Japan. After all, had the Japanese government accepted the Potsdam Declaration on July 26, 1945, there would not have been either a Soviet-Japanese War nor the atomic bombings of Hiroshima/Nagasaki.

But how could the collective memory of a war that happened half a century ago serve as a decisive factor determining the unpopularity of the Soviet Union? The lack of contact between these distant neighbors can partially explain the persistence of the wartime memory. But the more decisive factor is the Northern Territories issue.

The Northern Territories Problem

The Northern Territories problem is not merely a territorial problem, but a symbolic expression of national pride and prestige. To the Soviet Union and Russia, it was the symbol of its self-sacrifice to winning the war in the East, and hence of its legitimacy and territorial integrity. Moreover, for the Soviet leadership, adherence to the World War II settlements was the foundation on which Soviet domestic and international stability rested. The Soviets had good reason to believe that any territorial concessions would start a floodgate of irredentist demands from other countries and from nationality minorities within its own empire. To Japan, the Northern Territories question is a constant reminder that the humiliation of the Pacific War and the Occupation have not been completely eradicated In fact, the return of the Northern Territories represents the only remaining legacy of the Pacific War and the Occupation to be removed before Japan will finally become a normal, independent state.

Table 15.1 shows the results of the Sorifu (Prime Minister's Office) surveys on whether the Japanese think that Soviet-Japanese relations are good or bad at the height of the cold war between 1979 and 1983. Those who answered that the relations are not good or not so good were further asked what reasons were contributing to bad relations. Table 15.2 shows the distribution of percentages given to various reasons. It indicates that for these five years, which were the height of what the Japanese media called "the Soviet military threat," the largest percentage of respondents regarded the Soviet refusal to make concessions on the Northern Territories question as the most important reason for bad relations, far outstripping the Soviet military buildup. Nor was the communist system itself perceived by the Japanese as an important factor for bad relations as the Northern Territories question.

It has been taken for granted both in and outside of Japan that the demand for the return of all four islands that the Japanese call the Northern Territories is a solid consensus among the Japanese. It is on this assumption after all that the Japanese government and the

Table 15.1: Do You Think Japan-USSR Relations Are Good?

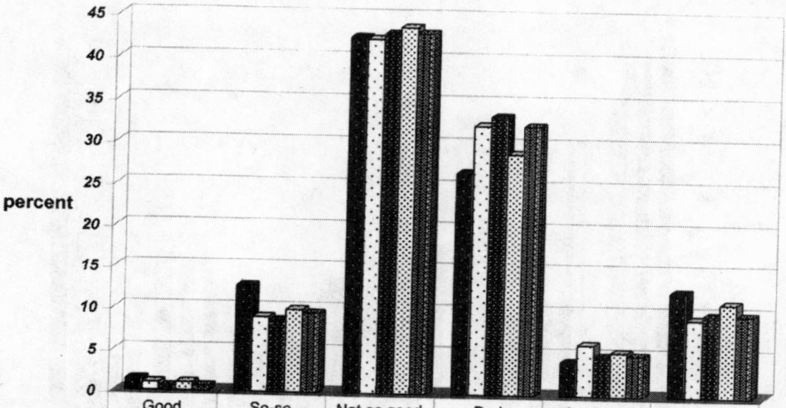

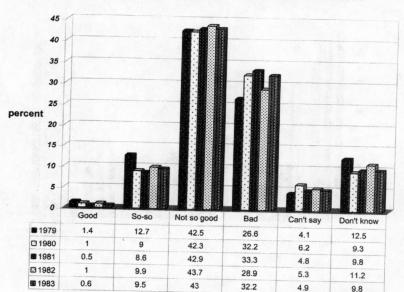

	Good	So-so	Not so good	Bad	Can't say	Don't know
1979	1.4	12.7	42.5	26.6	4.1	12.5
1980	1	9	42.3	32.2	6.2	9.3
1981	0.5	8.6	42.9	33.3	4.8	9.8
1982	1	9.9	43.7	28.9	5.3	11.2
1983	0.6	9.5	43	32.2	4.9	9.8

Source: Naikaku Soridaijin Kanbo Kohoshitsu, ed., Zenkoku Yoronchosha no Genkyo, 1980, p.136; ibid., 1981, p.115; ibid., 1982, p.121; ibid., 1983, p.106; ibid., 1984, p.105.

Gaimusho have adamantly adhered to the intransigent position that the return of all four islands should be the precondition for rapprochement with the Soviet Union and Russia. Let us take a look at the *Hokkaido shimbun* surveys taken of the citizens in Hokkaido in 1981 and 1985.

Examining these surveys, Wada Haruki came up with the following results:

This survey seems to indicate that as far as Hokkaido residents are concerned, an overwhelming number of people support the return of four islands. It is interesting to note that from one third to one fifth of those surveyed insisted that they should demand the return of the entire Kuriles. Nevertheless, more than one third supported the return of four islands. Those who advocated the two-island solution were a minority. Another interesting fact about the *Hokkaido shimbun* surveys is that more than ten percent of the residents supported the position that as long as the Soviet Union

Table 15.2: Reasons for Bad Relations between Japan and the USSR

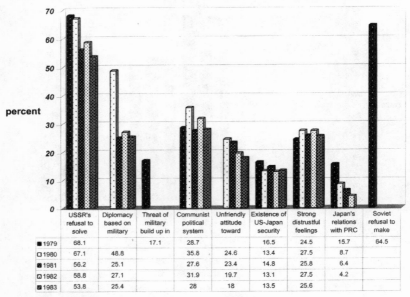

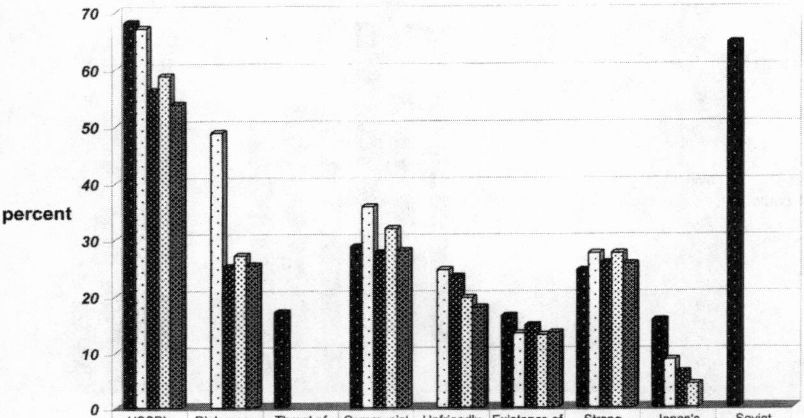

	USSR's refusal to solve	Diplomacy based on military	Threat of military build up in	Communist political system	Unfriendly attitude toward	Existence of US-Japan security	Strong distrustful feelings	Japan's relations with PRC	Soviet refusal to make
■ 1979	68.1		17.1	28.7		16.5	24.5	15.7	64.5
□ 1980	67.1	48.8		35.8	24.6	13.4	27.5	8.7	
1981	56.2	25.1		27.6	23.4	14.8	25.8	6.4	
1982	58.8	27.1		31.9	19.7	13.1	27.5	4.2	
1983	53.8	25.4		28	18	13.5	25.6		

Source: Same as table 1.

gave concessions in fishing negotiations, the territorial demand should not be advanced.

The *Hokkaido shimbun* survey in 1985 included a question: "Do you think the Soviet Union will change its position and begin negotiations on the territorial question?" Only 27.5 percent answered yes, but 66.2 percent answered negatively. Strangely, those who believe that Japan should demand either the entire Kuriles or all four islands did not actually believe that these demands could realistically be achievable. To the question: "What do you think about the return of the Northern Territories?" in the 1985 survey, 30.3 percent answered that the government should take a stronger stand to demand the return of the Northern Territories; 56.4 percent were for promoting friendly cooperative relations while continuing to insist on the return of the islands; and 10.4 percent believed that Japan should give up the islands by recognizing the

Table 15.3: Demands on Northern Territories

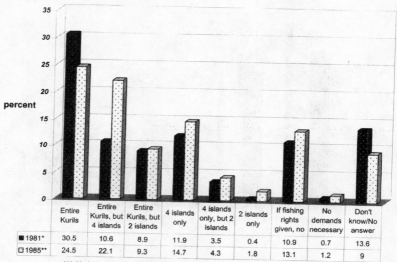

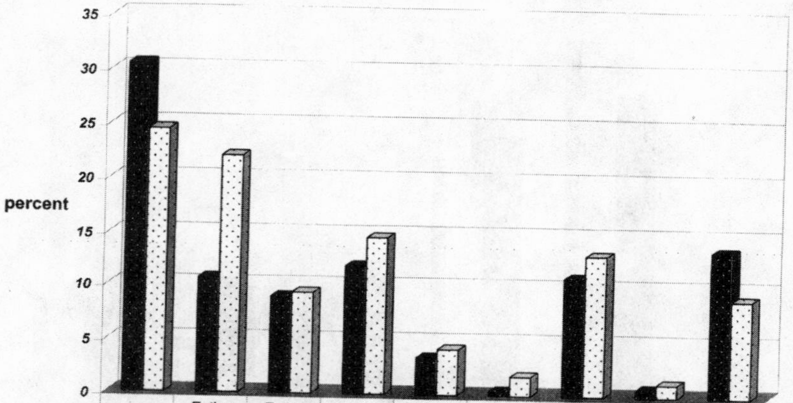

	Entire Kurils	Entire Kurils, but 4 islands	Entire Kurils, but 2 islands	4 islands only	4 islands only, but 2 islands	2 islands only	If fishing rights given, no	No demands necessary	Don't know/No answer
■ 1981*	30.5	10.6	8.9	11.9	3.5	0.4	10.9	0.7	13.6
□ 1985**	24.5	22.1	9.3	14.7	4.3	1.8	13.1	1.2	9

**Hokkaido shimbun* poll, 22, 23, July 1981, *Hokkaido shimbun,* 12 August, 1981. ***Hokkaido shimbun* poll, 1, 2 December 1985, *Hokkaido shimbun,* 3 January 1986.

World War II settlements. To the question: "How should Soviet-Japanese relations be developed in the future?" 61.0 percent answered that Japan should promote friendly relations with the Soviet Union regardless of the status of the Northern Territories question, while 26.1 percent insisted that Japan should insist on the return of the Northern Territories. The results of the 1985 survey indicate two contradictory tendencies among the Hokkaido residents. A large majority supported either the return of the entire Kuriles or all four islands, but they believed that such maximum demands were out of the realm of possibility. In the meantime, more Hokkaido residents supported the promotion of friendly, cooperative relations rather than insisting on the intransigent demand for the return of the Northern Territories at the detriment of the deterioration of relations.

Hokkaido shimbun conducted another survey in 1988. In this survey, 30.9 percent supported the return of the entire Kuriles; 50.6 percent were for all four islands; and 10.5 percent for two islands.

Table 15.4: Demands on Northern Territories: Another Variation*

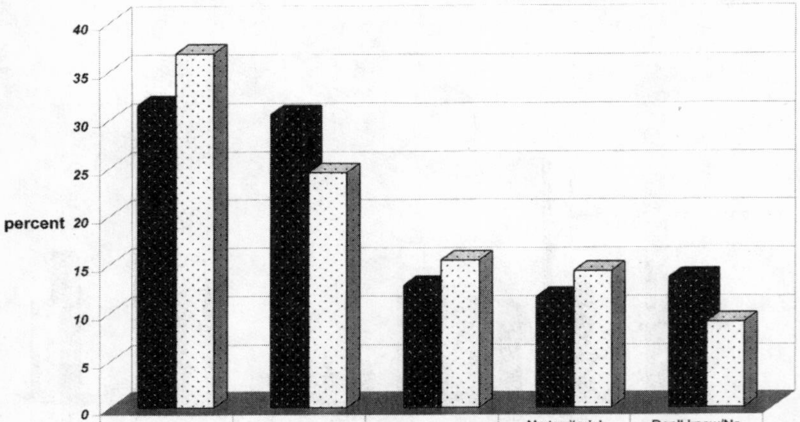

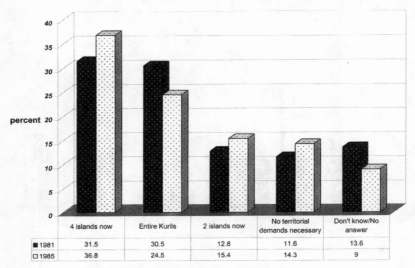

	4 islands now	Entire Kurils	2 islands now	No territorial demands necessary	Don't know/No answer
■ 1981	31.5	30.5	12.8	11.6	13.6
□ 1985	36.8	24.5	15.4	14.3	9

*Wada Haruki, Hopporyodo mondai o kangaeru, pp. 314-15.

And yet, there was another question in the survey: "The Japanese government insists on the simultaneous return of all four islands; how do you react if the Soviet government proposed the return of two islands?" To this question, 26.3 percent answered that Japan should not accept the two-island proposal; 48.0 percent took the position that Japan should accept the proposal while leaving the possibility for the return of the other two; 10.1 percent advocated giving up two of the islands and settling for the return of the other two; and 6.4 percent insisted that Japan should insist on the return of the entire Kuriles, and should not accept such a proposal.[12] This answer is quite interesting, indicating that Hokkaido residents were well disposed to a two-island solution as an interim method to resolve the territorial dispute.

Hokkaido residents are known to be more interested in the Northern Territories question. How about the rest of the population? According to a national survey conducted by *Asahi shimbun* in 1990, 53 percent favored the return of all four islands; 20

percent supported the return of two islands; 17 percent favored joint ownership, and only 2 percent believed that Japan should give up any territorial claims. It is possible to argue, therefore, that nationally, the return of all four islands had wide support among the Japanese. Nevertheless, there was another interesting question in this survey: "The Japanese government takes the position that as long as the Northern Territories problem is unresolved, Japan will not extend economic cooperation to the Soviet Union. Do you support this position?" To this question, 33 percent answered that they supported this position, while 55 percent took the position that the Japanese government should adopt a more flexible policy.[13]

It is clear from these surveys that when asked if they support the return of the Northern Territories, a majority answered that they favored this position. It is difficult to conclude from this, however, that most Japanese supported the government's intransigent position that unless the Northern Territories problem is resolved, no fundamental improvement in Soviet-Japanese relations should take place. A majority favored promotion of friendly relations, especially economic cooperation, regardless of the status of the territorial question. Moreover, although the two-island proposal did not command the support of the majority, it had a distinct possibility of being accepted as an interim solution. It is important to note that the government's intransigent position did not have solid support among the Japanese.

Finally, there is the question of how solid the Japanese consensus is on the Northern Territories demand. The Sorifu presumably conducts a public opinion survey on the Northern Territories, but the results of these surveys have never been published. I have obtained the unpublished results of these surveys from 1983 to 1986. These surveys are extremely interesting, indicating the degree of Japanese interest in and knowledge about the Northern Territories question. These surveys indicate that only 17.1 percent knew the names of all four islands, 8.6 percent knew the names of three islands, 17.2 percent knew the names of two islands, 9.0 percent knew the names of only one island, and 36.8 percent did not know the names of any islands. Those who knew the historical background on the Northern Territories dispute were overwhelming outnumbered by those who had no knowledge.

Table 15.5: Are You Interested in the Northern Territories Problem?*

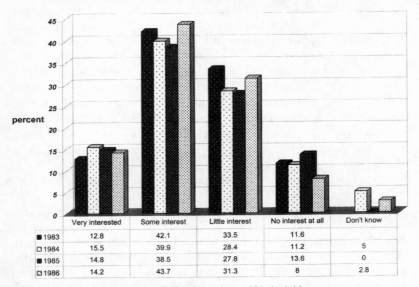

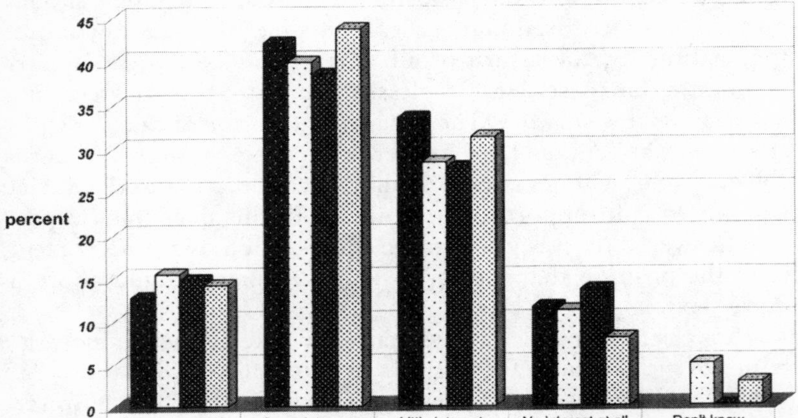

	Very interested	Some interest	Little interest	No interest at all	Don't know
1983	12.8	42.1	33.5	11.6	
1984	15.5	39.9	28.4	11.2	5
1985	14.8	38.5	27.8	13.6	0
1986	14.2	43.7	31.3	8	2.8

*Sorihu, Hopporyodo mondai ni kansuru yoronsha, unpublished material.

As Table 15.5 shows, slightly more than 50 percent showed interest in the Northern Territories question, and somewhere between 40 percent and 45 percent indicated that they had either little interest or no interest whatever in the problem. To the question as to why they were not interested in the question, 54 to 60 percent responded that this question had no direct relations to them personally, and 19 to 24 percent responded that the Soviet Union would never return the islands. As Table 15.6 shows, those who expressed interest in joining in the irredentist movement were in a distinct minority. These surveys show that the Northern Territories irredentist movement has been mostly a government sponsored movement that never took popular roots among the Japanese. If asked whether they support the demand for the return of the Northern Territories, a majority would answer that they would, but by and large the Japanese are not enthusiastically involved in the irredentist movement, displaying more or less indifference to this question.

Table 15.6: Will You Actively Participate in the Northern Territories Movement?*

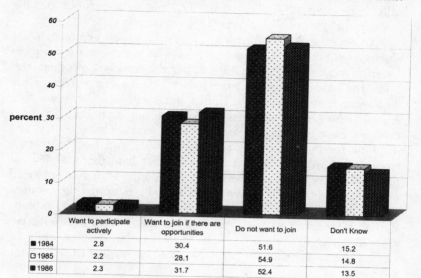

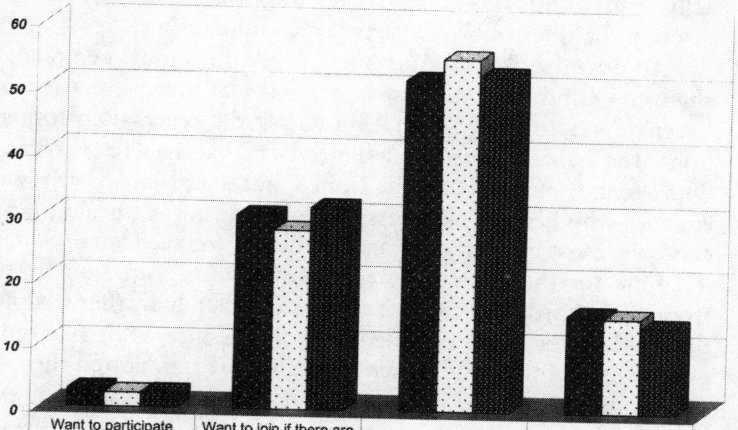

	Want to participate actively	Want to join if there are opportunities	Do not want to join	Don't Know
■ 1984	2.8	30.4	51.6	15.2
□ 1985	2.2	28.1	54.9	14.8
■ 1986	2.3	31.7	52.4	13.5

*Sorifu, Hopporyodo mondai ni kansuru yoronsha, unpublished material.

The above surveys seem to indicate that the assumptions that the return of the Northern Territories enjoy solid consensus among the Japanese, and that the government's intransigent position demanding the return of all islands have the solid backing of the Japanese people, must be seriously questioned.

The Cold War and Japanese Perceptions of the Soviet Union

Another important factor that determined Japanese perceptions of the Soviet Union was the cold war.[14] The cold war confrontation began before problems created by the war in Asia were settled, and it helped define the relationship that has prevailed between Moscow and Tokyo in the ensuing decades. The view of the Soviet Union that the great majority of Japanese formed on the basis of Soviet-Japanese conflict was placed on a continuum that linked it—both psychologically and politically—directly to the cold war without passing through the filter of World War II reexamination.

An obvious reversal of triangular relations must be noted. What changed with the advent of the cold war was not the relationship between Japan and the Soviet Union, but the reversals of other relations: the United States and the Soviet Union were wartime allies who became enemies, and the United States and Japan were wartime enemies who became allies. As the cold war in Asia began, Japan became the most important strategic outpost for the United States. The dilemma for the United States was that an occupation by foreign troops can hardly be expected to be popular with the occupied nation. Even after Japan regained its independence, Okinawa remained under U.S. control, and American military bases dotted the country. The United States had to avoid letting Japanese resentment explode into anti-American nationalism. The Northern Territories issue enabled America to build Japan into its own global strategy while diverting the antagonism of Japanese nationalism from itself to the Soviet Union.

The Northern Territories problem was largely a creation of the United States; more specifically, a masterpiece created by John Foster Dulles. He single-handedly wrote the San Francisco Peace Treaty, by which he sought to exacerbate the territorial conflict between the Soviet Union and Japan by forcing Japan to give up any claim to sovereignty over the Kurile Islands, while refusing to give a precise definition of the Kurile Islands that Japan had renounced and making it ambiguous as to which country the Kuriles should be handed over. To gain independence, the Japanese government had to swallow this condition. The Soviet government, on its part, refused to sign the treaty. When the Soviet Union and Japan began negotiations for a peace treaty in 1955–56, Dulles forcefully intervened again to wreck the nearly agreed-upon territorial settlement with a threat: Had the Japanese government accepted the Soviet offer to conclude a peace treaty on the basis of the return of two islands, the United States would hold on to Okinawa indefinitely. By 1957 the United States government made a 180 degree turnaround about its position on the Northern Territories question. In February 1945, in the Yalta Agreement, Roosevelt agreed to grant the Soviet Union the right to claim the Kuriles. In 1957, the U.S. government fully supported the Japanese arguments that the lands that Japan had renounced in the San Francisco Peace Treaty did not include the Northern Territories, and that the Yalta Agreement could not be the basis of the territorial settlement between the Soviet Union and Japan. This has become the official position taken by the U.S. government ever since. Clearly, this position was designed to prevent Japan from achieving rapprochement with the Soviet Union, thereby keeping Japan within the orbit of U.S. global strategy. This master stroke by Dulles worked well as long as the cold war lasted. For a variety of reasons—ideological, national prestige, fear of irredentism from other countries, fear of nationality movements within its own empire—the Soviet government clung to the fiction that there existed no territorial problem, and justified this fiction on the basis of the Yalta Agreement. The more tenaciously the Soviets clung to this fiction, the more irritated the Japanese became with what the Japanese considered—justifiably so in my view—to be the flimsy legal basis of their claim. And the United States, which was actually the initiator of this dispute, could wash its hands, conveniently ignoring the commitment it once had made to Stalin, and recede into the background while egging both countries on to continue the dispute.

This strategy was also convenient for Japan's conservative government. Japan needed an enemy to facilitate its efforts to recover from its defeat, win back its independence, rebuild its economy, and reinstate itself into the international community while relying on American military power to assure its security. The memory of the humiliation suffered at Soviet hands, combined with the threat of postwar communism, helped it take advantage of the cold war situation. When it later became necessary and desirable for an economically mature Japan to bolster its military strength to a level commensurate with its status as an economic superpower, the "Soviet threat" provided a convenient excuse for doing so without splitting public opinion and running the risks that would have been incurred if any substantial discussion of national security had taken place.

One factor that prompted the Japanese conservatives to exploit the Northern Territories problem to advance their pro-American cause was the threat of internal subversion by the Japanese Communist Party (JCP) directed by Moscow. The JCP commanded considerable influence in the political process during the Occupation period. Although its internal division and the reckless adventurist position that it took from the Cominform decisively undermined its influence, the Soviet Union as a champion of the socialist camp in opposition to "American imperialism" had evoked a responding chord among "progressive" segments of society unhappy with the American occupation. Marxism-Leninism had far wider appeal than the voting for the Communist Party indicated, especially among the intellectuals. Social sciences and humanities in universities were dominated by Marxist-oriented professors, while Marxists and their fellow travelers enjoyed great influence in popular journals and newspapers. It was this fear of communist subversion that drove the conservatives to sabotage Prime Minister Hatoyama Ichiro's attempt to achieve rapprochement with the Soviet Union during the negotiations for normalization of diplomatic relations in 1955–56. This policy was by and large successful. As the *Asahi shimbun* opinion poll conducted three days after the signing of the San Francisco Peace Treaty indicated, 69 percent of respondents thought that the United States had conducted itself in a friendly manner toward Japan, while 56 percent felt displeasure and resentment toward the Soviet Union.[15] Also during the normalization negotiations in 1955–56, major newspapers supported Japan's demand for the recovery of the Northern Territories.[16]

The de-Stalinization and the Sino-Soviet split had serious consequences for the Japanese Communist Party. Since 1964 the JCP has taken a critical stand toward the Soviet Union, eagerly distancing itself from Moscow in order to eschew the public image that it worked on behalf of Soviet interests. When the JCP defected from Moscow, the Japan-Soviet Friendship Association, supported by the JCP, with generous financial help from Moscow, was also split, seriously damaging the propaganda activities on behalf of the Soviet Union. The Japanese Socialist Party (JSP) was divided into two factions. The right wing socialists, like the communists, distanced themselves from Moscow, while the left wing was eager to court Soviet favor as well as Soviet money.[17] For a long time, this tiny minority of Marxists with the JSP was the only group on which the Soviets could pin their hope for influencing Japanese public opinion. The Democratic Socialist Party took a more anti-Soviet stance than some of the more liberal members of the conservative LDP, while the Komeito was basically uninterested in the Soviet Union until the Gorbachev period. There was never a powerful Soviet lobby within the LDP comparable to the China lobby. Those who did have some contact with the Soviet Union, such as Ishida Hakuei, lost influence after the Levchenko incident, wherein the celebrated Soviet KGB agent exposed a number of Japanese public figures who had received Soviet payments in exchange for information. All political parties were united in a demand for the return of the Northern Territories. Disagreements among the parties centered on how many of the Kuriles Japan should demand. Ironically, the LDP was the most moderate, limiting itself to the retrocession of the Northern Territories, namely the four southernmost islands. Both the JSP and JCP demanded the return of all the Kurile Islands in return for the abrogation of the U.S.-Japanese Security Treaty, until only the JSP finally dropped this demand during the Gorbachev period. The Komeito and the Democratic Socialist Party also demanded the return of all the Kuriles, but unlike the JCP and JSP, they did not set the abrogation of the U.S.-Japanese Security Treaty as a precondition of regaining the islands. Thus, there were no political groups in Japan that actively championed a normalization of relations with the Soviet Union. In Japan's domestic politics, improvement of relations with the Soviet Union has never become an important political issue. On the contrary, all political parties avoided any sympathy for improving relations with the Soviet Union, lest they should encounter displeasure from voters.

This does not imply, however, that the Soviet Union was not important in Japanese public opinion. It is true that, as Figure 15.3 shows, the communist camp commanded little respect among the Japanese. But it is important to note that there existed a strong neutralist sentiment among the Japanese, constantly commanding 20 to 30 percent throughout the postwar period. Especially, while the United States was engaged in the Vietnam War from 1964 to 1975, the neutralist sentiment steadily rose while the pro-Western sentiment sharply declined. In 1973, when Japan was hit by the double punches of the oil shock and the Nixon shocks, the neutralist sentiment registered higher than the pro-Western sentiment for the first (and the last) time. Although after 1974 the pro-Western sentiment grew quickly, the pro-neutralist sentiment did not experience a corresponding sharp decline, constantly maintaining a level of support above 20 percent. It is easy to see that this segment became the mainstay for the support of the JSP during the 1970s and the 1980s. Thus, although communist subversion was never a goal of the Soviet Union except for the period immediately after the war, the Soviets believed that they could sway the Japanese public opinion by cultivating the neutralist sentiment in order to undermine the U.S.-Japanese alliance. Throughout the 1960s, the Soviets thus concentrated on the efforts to decouple Japan from the United States. But these attempts were often too clumsy and high-handed to be effective, earning more enmity than sympathy among the Japanese. In 1960, Khrushchev unilaterally abrogated the provision of the 1956 Joint Declaration that promised the return of two islands, when the United States and Japan renewed the security pact. Sato Eisaku's overtures for resumption of negotiations for a peace treaty were never seriously entertained by the Soviets.

In the Shadow of the Strategic Triangle

During the 1970s and the first half of the 1980s the international environment changed considerably. First, because of the relentless Soviet military buildup, the Soviet Union attained strategic parity with the United States and global superpower status, giving the Soviet leadership a sense of pride and confidence. Second, a new danger that threatened Soviet security loomed in the East: the Sino-Soviet conflict intensified, no longer confined to an ideological feud but now extended to military confrontations. As Sino-Soviet relations worsened, China broke its diplomatic isolation by achieving Sino-American rapprochement, immediately followed by Sino-Japanese rapprochement. Third, as Japan was becoming a global economic power, world economic dynamics changed. The Asia-Pacific region under Japan's economic hegemony was transforming itself into the most dynamic economic region in the world. All these changes interjected a new element into Soviet-Japanese relations and Japanese perceptions of the Soviet Union.

The confidence that the Japanese acquired from their global economic status added a new dimension to their perceptions of the Soviet Union. The dislike that Japanese felt toward the Soviet Union was augmented by contempt. The Japanese discovered that this heavily armed neighbor was actually not far above the developing nations if measured by standard of living, economic performance, and technological level. They concluded that the Soviets offered nothing they needed to learn. This gave them the illusion that Japan had nothing to gain from rapprochement with the Soviet Union except the return of the Northern Territories, while rapprochement would benefit only the Soviet Union since it would gain economic and technological cooperation from Japan. In turn the arrogance and smugness with which Japanese officials dealt with the Soviets grated on the pride of the latter. This psychological factor explains much about the Gaimusho's lack of initiative in seeking rapprochement with Russia.

Nothing illustrates more vividly the conflicting images held by each country than the Tanaka-Brezhnev summit in 1973. Tanaka and the Gaimusho wanted to impress upon the Soviets that the Japan now negotiating was different from the weak Japan that had agreed to sign the Joint Declaration of 1956. Therefore it was more conscious of the need to go further than what Hatoyama had accomplished in 1956. Hence it clung to the demand for the return of the four islands. Tanaka's attitude irritated Brezhnev. Self-confident with the superpower status that the Soviet Union had achieved, the USSR could not tolerate an upstart politician from an upstart country that was militarily nothing but an appendage of the United States. Tanaka came to Moscow to demand the return of the territory without making any concessions on the China issue—a situation tantamount to presenting an ultimatum. In the minds of the Soviet leadership, no superpower worth its status would accept such an ultimatum. Japan's argument with regard to Moscow was the same as that of the United States. But such an argument itself stung the pride of the Soviet leaders, since as far as they were concerned, Japan was not a superpower and should not behave like one. This psychological factor was perhaps the most important in explaining the fiasco of the Tanaka-Brezhnev summit. It was the clash of two nouveaux riches who wanted to do everything to remind the other that the two were not in the same league.

Despite the Soviet need to entice Japan from China, the Soviets never wanted to achieve this goal by paying the right price: to meet Japan's demands for the return of the Northern Territories. In 1969, Brezhnev proposed an Asian collective security aimed to isolate China. In 1972, Gromyko offered to revive the two-island solution to the territorial dispute. In 1978, Brezhnev offered a treaty of good neighborliness in order to circumvent the impending Sino-Japanese peace treaty. In all these attempts, the Soviet government never took into consideration Japan's territorial demands, clinging to the fiction that there existed no territorial problem between the two countries. This further infuriated the Japanese. This also explains the sharp increase in the USSR's unpopularity rate in the late 1970s and the first half of the 1980s.

Ironically, the Japanese did not feel the Soviet military threat to be as menacing as the West Europeans did—perhaps because Japan was not contiguous with the Soviet Union, but more importantly, Japan's security was guaranteed by the United States. It was inconceivable that the Soviet Union would launch an attack on Japan alone, out of the blue. If Japan were to be attacked by the Soviet Union, it would only be as part of a wider global war, and such a contingency was remote from the consciousness of most Japanese. If the Europeans lived in real fear of nuclear war—and for this reason they had to achieve rapprochement with the Soviet Union—the Japanese lived blissfully in an unreal world far removed from the imminent danger of a nuclear holocaust, while in a perverted twist of nationalism, the progressive wing of the intellectuals, supported by the left-wing opposition parties, appropriated the fiction that by virtue of being the only victims of the atomic bombs, the Japanese were the only people who could speak of the horrors of nuclear weapons. In a way, as Gilbert Rozman aptly observed, postwar Japanese history is a history of competition between the Northern Territories syndrome and the Hiroshima syndrome, and during the 1970s and the first half of the 1980s, the Northern Territories syndrome was clearly winning this competition.[18]

Gorbachev's Perestroika and Change in Japanese Perceptions

Gorbachev's perestroika greatly contributed to changes in Japanese perceptions of the Soviet Union. As Figure 15.1 shows, those who like the Soviet Union in the Jiji public survey doubled during his tenure in office, from 1.1 percent in 1985 to 2.1 percent in 1991.

Monthly breakdowns are interesting. When Gorbachev took power in March 1985, the Soviet popularity rate was merely 0.9 percent. A significant change took place in 1989–90, with popularity climbing up to 3.6 percent in November 1990 and 3.0 percent in December 1990. More significant is the decline in the unpopularity rate in the Jiji surveys. As Figure 15.2 shows, the unpopularity rate constantly and sharply declined during Gorbachev's tenure: annually, 55.2 percent (1985), 52.4 (1986), 49.3 (1987), 46.1 (1988), 40.8 (1989), 36.1 (1990), and 35.6 (1991). When we examine the monthly breakdowns, the Soviet unpopularity registered highest with 59.4 percent in March 1985, when Gorbachev assumed power, but it began to drop below 50 percent in 1988. During 1989–90, the unpopularity rate even dropped below 40 percent in some months, and finally in November 1990, it registered the lowest point: 28.5 percent.

Rozman divides Japan's opinion leaders during the Gorbachev period into five groups: right, right of center, center, left of center, and left. As Rozman observes, in 1985–87, "the right of center and far right were beginning to lose their shared framework," and as the right of center moved toward the center, "a left of center or center position became prominent."[19] Indeed, Kimura Hiroshi, Ito Kenichi, and others in the right of center viewed Gorbachev's perestroika as a new, more imaginative strategy in dealing with Japan, and differed in their evaluation from the right, represented by Sono Akira and Hogen Shinsaku, who saw in Gorbachev nothing but the continuation of Soviet global expansion. Nevertheless, they shared the view that the fundamental goal of Soviet policy toward Japan was to decouple Japan from the security alliance with the United States. In addition, the right of center, especially Kimura, believed that facing desperate needs for economic reform, the Soviet Union found it necessary to mend fences in order to gain access to Japan's economic and technological assistance. The Soviet Union thus needed Japan more than Japan needed the Soviet Union, and therefore, Japan could negotiate with the Soviet Union from the position of strength in order to recover the Northern Territories.[20] Kimura's view and the views expressed by the right of center closely echoed the line pursued by the Gaimusho. During the same period, the left of center, represented by Haruki Wada and Nakajima Mineo, openly challenged the Gaimusho's policy. Viewing perestroika as a fundamental restructuring of the nature of the Soviet system, Nakajima and Wada called for Japan's creative approach to the Soviet Union to achieve rapprochement by offering a two-island solution to the Northern Territories problem. This proposal was denounced by right of center critiques as a betrayal of Japan's national interests.[21]

The debate between the left of center and the right of center is important for two reasons. First, this debate centered around the fundamental question: How to view Gorbachev's perestroika? The left of center (Haruki Wada, Nobuo Shimotomai, Sato Keimei, among others), and the center (Shigeki Hakamada and myself) argued that perestroika represented a radical change in the Soviet system. The right of center acknowledged that Gorbachev changed the strategy, but believed in the continuity of the goals of Soviet foreign policy as the attempt to undermine the U.S.-Japanese alliance. The Gaimusho basically accepted the view of the right of center, taking the view that perestroika was at best a cosmetic change. Second, this debate had serious political implications. Rejecting the left of center's view, the Gaimusho held on to the intransigent position that the nature of the Soviet Union had not changed, and hence that there was no need to alter Japan's approach to the Soviet Union. If anything, the Gaimusho concluded, since Gorbachev's policy became more sophisticated than Brezhnev's high-handed policy to attain the goal, Japan should become even tougher in presenting the territorial demand and insisting on the principle of the inseparability of politics and economics.

During 1988–89, when Gorbachev's new-thinking foreign policy began to change the international environment, the left of center and even the center began to note that there was an inherent connection between Gorbachev's Asian policy and domestic transformation. A subtle change took place during this period among the right of center intellectuals as well. Hiroshi Kimura, for instance, came to recognize the seriousness of Gorbachev's new-thinking foreign policy, seeing in it a good opportunity for resolving the Northern Territories question. In an important article published in May 1989, Kimura rejected Japan's passive wait-and-see policy and advocated a policy creating conditions that would make it easier for the Soviet leadership to resolve the territorial question.[22] One of the interesting aspects of Japanese public opinion at that time was that despite subtle differences, some of the center, notably Shigeki Hakamada, and the right of center, were beginning to coalesce, forming an influential group that buttressed the new policy of the Gaimusho, which enunciated a policy of balanced expansion by which Japan attempted to expand the realm of cooperation in accordance with progress on the territorial question.

Despite shifting positions in the public debate on the Soviet Union, however, it was not sufficient to change Japan's policy toward the Soviet Union. Initially, the Gaimusho took the position that Gorbachev's new-thinking foreign policy, which was beginning to drastically change the framework of East-West relations, was not applicable to Asia. When Gorbachev's policy achieved rapprochement with China and South Korea, and contributed to the ending of conflict in Cambodia, the Gaimusho presented the Northern Territories question as the litmus test for the seriousness of Gorbachev's new political thinking, clinging to the tautological argument that since Gorbachev did not offer any concessions to Japan's demand for the return of the Northern Territories, his new-thinking foreign policy did not extend to Japan. Nevertheless, the sea change in international environment was so obvious that the Gaimusho had to respond to the new situation. Hence, it adopted a policy of balanced expansion. Nevertheless, the previous policy of the inseparability of politics and economics was never repudiated. This ambiguity haunted Japan's policy toward the Soviet Union at the crucial time, when the East European revolutions toppled one communist regime after another, the Berlin Wall fell, and German reunification was accomplished. Japan missed the chance to resolve the Northern Territories question.

It was only after the colossal changes in Eastern Europe and Germany that Japanese public opinion finally and belatedly heated up in anticipation of Gorbachev's Tokyo visit in April 1991. Several points stand out in Japan's public debate before Gorbachev's visit. First, more commentators came to advocate the position of the left of center that questioned the intransigent Japanese position. The right of center, which continued to push the territorial issue to the forefront, clearly was on the defensive. In fact, more and more critics came to advocate abandoning the principle of the inseparability of politics and economics and proposed that Japan should instead take the initiative and extend massive economic aid to the Soviet Union.

As usual, Haruki Wada most forcefully presented the left of center's argument advocating the two-island plus alpha solution of the territorial dispute. Wada cited two public opinion surveys to buttress his argument. The first, conducted by Kyodo Tsushin in 1989 among 357 former Japanese islanders, indicated that 46.5 percent supported the return of the two islands, even if the resolution of Kunashiri and Etorofu were postponed. The second, a Kyodo Tsushin national opinion survey in October 1990, indicated that 46 percent supported the return of all the islands, while 26 percent favored the return of two islands first and Kunashiri and Etorofu later. From these polls Wada concluded that the majority of Japanese would support the first option.[23]

In the same month that Wada's article appeared in *Sekai,* the usually conservative *Bungei shunju* ran a debate among Nakajima Mineo, Morimoto Tadao, and Kamiya Fuji.[24] All three agreed that Soviet domestic constraints would tie Gorbachev's hands, leaving little room for concessions on the territorial issue. This led to a consensus of all three that it would be unrealistic to expect a resolution during Gorbachev's visit to Tokyo. But Nakajima and Morimoto, who belonged to the left of center, and Kamiya (right of center), differed on the implications of this prognosis. Nakajima argued that the Gaimusho was mistaken if it thought it could conduct "tough negotiations on the territory." Japan's unrealistic, intransigent presentation of territorial demands would be tantamount to slinging mud at Gorbachev. Instead, the most important task for Japan would be to utilize Gorbachev's visit as the first step toward an ultimate rapprochement with the Soviet Union. Both Nakajima and Morimoto assailed the principle of the inseparability of politics and economics, while Kamiya insisted on the need to maintain the inseparability principle, arguing that once economic aid was given to the Soviets, they would not return the Northern Territories. To Kamiya the most important task for Japan's Soviet policy was the resolution of the Northern Territories problem. If he had a pessimistic view on Gorbachev's forthcoming visit, it was because he did not think much of Gorbachev—nor for that matter of the Soviet Union. Kamiya's argument revealed the underlying assumptions of the right of center that any rapprochement with the Soviet Union would be of little significance to Japan's overall foreign policy.

If Wada and Nakajima were totally isolated in 1986 on the territorial question, they were now joined by many others, demanding a major change in Japan's Soviet policy. They called for the rejection of the policy of the inseparability of economics and politics and a compromise solution to the territorial dispute by accepting the 1956 Joint Declaration.[25] Compared with the avalanche of opinions representing the left of center position, the right of center position that backed the Gaimusho found itself considerably diminished.

It is possible to conclude that public opinion in Japan on the eve of Gorbachev's visit was basically split into two wings: one critical of the Gaimusho's intransigence and calling for a fundamental reorientation of Japan's Soviet policy, and the other clinging to the territorial question as the first and foremost issue of that policy. Possible linkage between economic aid and the territorial problem became the dividing line between the two camps. But behind these differences there existed a vast philosophical difference with regard to the role of the Soviet Union in Japan's overall foreign policy. While the first group considered it imperative to achieve rapprochement with the Soviet Union, the second believed that Japan could well afford to ignore it without damaging its international position.

An opinion poll conducted by the Japanese Public Opinion Survey Association on March 23 and 24, 1991, also indicated nationwide ambiguity. Clearly the majority of respondents favored the return of the four islands, but those who were willing to settle for the return of the two islands for the time being and those who insisted on the return of the four islands were evenly divided. Moreover, 46 percent responded that Japan should improve relations with the Soviets while trying to resolve the territorial question, whereas 37 percent insisted on the return of the islands as a precondition for the improvement of relations.[26]

What is interesting is the parallel development of public opinion in the Soviet Union and Japan.[27] While the conservative wing stubbornly clung to its old position, new political thinkers in the Soviet Union and the left of center intellectuals in Japan called for a major revision of their own government's policy toward the other. They counseled their countrymen and their government to be more tolerant of the other side. They insisted that only compromise could lead to a resolution and suggested that Gorbachev's visit would be only the first step toward compromise. The range of compromise suggested was remarkably similar. Indeed, there was an amazing degree of convergence of views.

Public opinion polls indicated at first glance that the views of the Soviets and the Japanese were diametrically opposed. While an overwhelming number of Soviet citizens opposed any return of the disputed islands to Japan, an equally overwhelming number of Japanese supported the return of all four islands. Nevertheless, a close examination of these polls indicated that despite the wide differences, a significant segment of the population in both countries favored some sort of compromise solution. Despite this shift in public opinion, however, the Gaimusho decided to push the territorial demand to the forefront at the summit between Gorbachev and Kaifu. Believing wrongly that it was taken for granted that Gorbachev would reaffirm the 1956 Joint Declaration, the Gaimusho judged that it was imperative for Japan to seek the return of all four islands. As it turned out, the battle was waged during the summit on whether the 1956 Joint Declaration should be reaffirmed. In the end, Gorbachev acknowledged that the four islands were the subject of territorial dispute between the two countries, but refused to reaffirm the Joint Declaration. In other words, Tokyo and Moscow failed to resolve the territorial dispute at this historic summit.[28]

Yeltsin and Japan's Perceptions of a New Russia

Immediately after the collapse of the Soviet Union, the unpopularity rate of Russia continued to decline: 33.4 percent (January 1992), 30.7 percent (February), 30.1 percent (March), and 28.6 percent (April). There was a euphoria about the new Russia shedding itself of communism. Yeltsin and his advisers consciously tried to cultivate the image of a new Russia as sharing common strategic values with the West. In this atmosphere, the Japanese expected that the time had finally come to settle the Northern Territories problem on Japan's terms. Yeltsin's promise to resolve the territorial question on the basis of "law and justice" reinforced this belief.

Nevertheless, Yeltsin's new policy invited a backlash. By July 1992, the "Kurile problem" became the lightening rod for the frustrations felt by the Russians about the ignominious shrinking of the empire. Yeltsin began to backpedal on his promise. After May 1992, Russia's unpopularity rate began to climb again. The great turning point came when Yeltsin canceled the scheduled trip to Japan in September: the unpopularity rate sharply went up: 44.2 percent in September, and 48.3 percent in October. From then on the negative rating for Russia climbed steadily to around 50 percent—about the same level it had been before Gorbachev's assumption of power. According to public opinion surveys conducted every year by the Prime Minister's Office, the feeling of friendliness toward the Soviet Union had increased from 13.2 percent in 1989 to 23.3 percent in 1990 to 25.4 percent in October 1991, but the figure suddenly dropped after Yeltsin's cancellation, to 15.2 percent. The category of those who did not feel friendliness increased from 69.5 percent in October 1991 to 79.6 percent in October 1992.[29] These public opinion surveys clearly indicated that with one single stroke Yeltsin had wiped out all the positive opinions that Gorbachev had carefully cultivated in Japan.

Russia's continuing unpopularity among the Japanese proves that the communist system had little to do with Japanese dislike of the Soviet Union. The dissolution of the Soviet Union in December 1991 had a greater impact on the geopolitical landscape of Western Europe, the Middle East, Central Asia, and China than on Japan. In the former regions the Russian borders had significantly altered, but in the Far East the borders between Russia and Japan remained the same. In the Japanese minds, the Soviet Union had merely been replaced by Russia, and there were no fundamental changes in the problems that existed between the two countries.

Nevertheless, a more serious danger for Russia's image in Japanese perceptions does not necessarily lie in its continuing unpopularity. It is in the tendency of Russia to being marginalized. Since 1997 the Jiji survey has asked a question: "Which countries and regions do you think will be important to Japan for the next five years?" Figure 15.5 shows that to the Japanese, China and the United States figure prominently as the most important countries. Southeast Asia ranks next, followed by Western Europe, and South Korea. To most Japanese, Russia comes only next to Western Europe in the order of priority, with only 8 to 14 percent of those surveyed considering Russia an important country, compared with around 50 to 60 percent who have chosen China and the United States. During the cold war, the Soviet Union was the country the Japanese most disliked, and yet its importance was acknowledged, though negatively. Ironically, as the Soviet military threat receded, the sense of importance of the country also dropped. The danger for Russia after the collapse of the Soviet Union is that it is being marginalized by the Japanese.

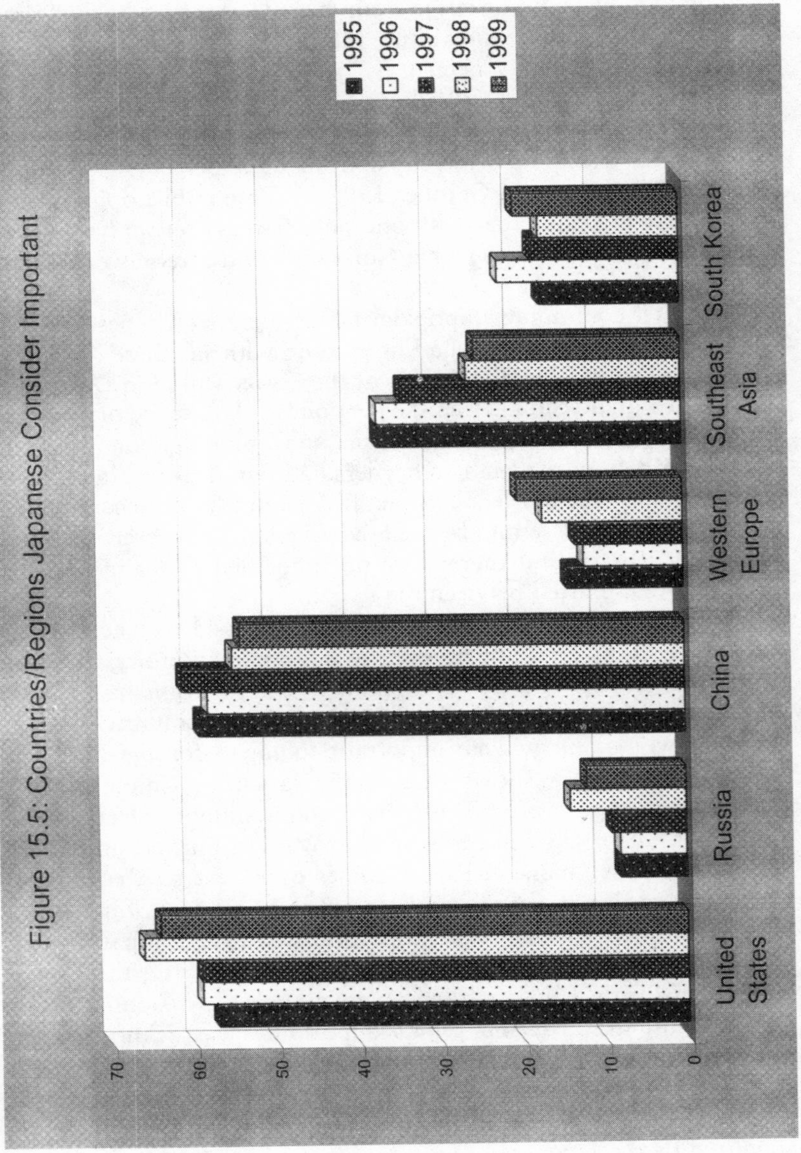

Figure 15.5: Countries/Regions Japanese Consider Important

Future Prospects

Developments since March 1996 have ushered Russo-Japanese relations to a new stage, resuming the dialogue in political, economic, and security areas. In July 1997 Prime Minister Hashimoto made a historic speech outlining three principles to govern Russo-Japanese relations; Hashimoto and Yeltsin held two "no-necktie" summits at Krasnoyarsk and Kawana. This momentum was halted, however, by the dual political crises that happened first in Japan and then in Russia in the summer of 1998, forcing the resignation of Hashimoto and weakening Yeltsin's power and prestige. Prime Minister Obuchi Keizo's visit to Moscow in November 1998 did not yield positive results. Despite the pious pledge made by Yeltsin and Hashimoto at Krasnoyarsk to conclude a peace treaty by the year 2000, bilateral negotiations have come to a grinding halt. The resolution of the territorial question and the conclusion of a peace treaty that have eluded Russia and Japan since the end of World War II have been postponed to the post-Yeltsin era.

Historical precedents demonstrate that Japan's intransigence with which it adhered to the territorial demand of the return of four islands has been a major hindrance to the ultimate settlement of this intractable question. The only solution to this question that can be acceptable to both is to reaffirm the 1956 Joint Declaration and to agree to continue negotiations on the ultimate sovereignty over Kunashiri and Etorofu. Even this variant will require political courage on the part of the Russian administration to accept, and will unavoidably encounter stiff opposition in and out of the Duma. And yet, Japanese reaction to the Krasnoyarsk summit indicates an unrealistic overexpectation that the territorial settlement on the terms that Japan has demanded is finally near at hand. Despite the promising shift in direction enunciated by the Gaimusho's "multilayered approach" and Hashimoto's three principles, the fact that the territorial question has been pushed to the foreground of negotiations indicates the continued domination of the Northern Territories in Japanese thinking. As long as Japan does not depart from the intransigence demanding Russia's acceptance of Japan's sovereignty over all the disputed islands, the prospect of rapprochement is dim. It appears at this point that the Japanese government is unlikely to bend on this crucial issue.

The Japanese government was enormously successful in creating a seeming consensus on Japan's irredentist demand, although, as indicated above, if examined closely, this consensus was never as solid as the government insisted and pretended to believe. But this putative consensus has created a simplified perception among the media and political commentators that the Northern Territories question was the most important agenda for Russo-Japanese relations.

The change in the government's policy toward Russia, presumably necessitated by its views on geostrategic change in Northeast Asia, is not effectively articulated to the public. As a consequence, public opinion is lagging behind the government's lead in seeking rapprochement with Russia. It looks as though the Japanese government, and the Gaimusho, in particular, are haunted by the ghost that they themselves have created. In my view, it will take the caliber of politician of a Nakasone Yasuhiro, Abe Shintaro, or Hashimoto, who combines a keen geostrategic vision with political leadership to overcome the legacy of the northern territories problem. Such a strategist is not visible on the Japanese political horizon at the moment.

NOTES

1. See Tsuyoshi Hasegawa, *The Northern Territories Dispute and Russo-Japanese Relations,* 2 vols (Berkeley: International and Area Studies Publications, University of California, 1998), vol. 2, *Neither War Nor Peace, 1985–1998.*
2. This part of the paper is an updated version of my previous article, "Japanese Perceptions of the Soviet Union: 1960–1985," *Acta Slavica Iaponika,* No. 5, 1987, pp. 37–70.
3. The Jiji survey used two-step random sampling, and selected 2,000 subjects from 34 places: 10 large cities, 88 middle-sized cities, and 36 smaller cities and villages. Respondents are both male and female adults over 20 years of age. The method of the survey is a personal interview by an investigator. The rate of return varies from month to month, but usually it is around 1,500.
4. *Yomiuri shimbun,* August 15, 1950.
5. D. H. Mendel, *Nihon yoron to gaiko,* tr. by Nakamura Kikuo, Horie Tan (Tokyo: Jiji Tsushinsha, 1963), p. 77.
6. Nakamura Kenichi, "Soren kyoiron kara no dakkyaku," *Sekai,* No. 4, 1985, p. 65.

7. NHK Hoso yoron chosashitsu, ed., polls. See *Zusetsu sengo yoronshi* (Tokyo: NHK, 1982), p. 162. Similar results are reported in *Asahi shimbun,* November 1, 1978; *Asahi shimbun,* March 5, 1979; *Yomiuri shimbun,* June 30, 1980; *Zenkoku yoronchosa no genkyo,* 1981, pp. 529–30.
8. Wakatani Michihiro, "Kokumin wa kako no rekishi o do mite iru ka," *Hoso kenkyu to chosa,* Vol. 33, No. 5, 1983, p. 55.
9. Ibid., p. 62.
10. Somewhat comparable is the Soviet treatment of the Germans in eastern Germany during the occupation. See Norman Naimark, *The Russians in Germany (*Cambridge, Mass.; Harvard University Press, 1995).
11. William F. Nimmo, *Behind a Curtain of Silence: Japanese in Soviet Custody, 1945–1956* (New York: Greenwood Press, 1988).
12. *Hokkaido shimbun,* January 1, 1989, quoted in Wada Haruki, *Hoppo ryodo mondai o kangaeru* (Tokyo: Iwanami shoten, 1990), p. 321.
13. *Asahi shimbun,* October 11, 1990.
14. This part is partially taken from chapter 15 of my book, *The Northern Territories Dispute and Russo-Japanese Relations,* vol. 2, *Neither War Nor Peace.*
15. Igarashi Takeshi, *Tainichi kowa to reisen: sengo Nichibei kankei no keisei* (Tokyo: Tokyo daigaku shuppankai, 1986), p. 267.
16. See Wada, *Hoppo ryodo mondai o kangaeru,* pp. 299–302.
17. Nagoshi Kenro, *Kuremurin himitsu bunsho* (Tokyo: Chuo koronsha, 1994), pp. 127–86.
18. Gilbert Rozman, *Japan's Response to the Gorbachev Era, 1985–1991: A Rising Superpower Views a Declining One* (Princeton: Princeton University Press, 1992), pp. 12–13.
19. Ibid., p. 106.
20. For a more detailed discussion on the debate, see *Neither War Nor Peace,* pp. 241–43.
21. See *Neither War Nor Peace,* pp. 252–54.
22. Kimura Hiroshi, "Ko sureba hoppo ryodo wa kaeru," *Voice,* May 1989, pp. 116–23.
23. Wada Haruki, "Hoppo ryodo: Futatsu no sentaku," *Sekai,* No. 2, 1992, pp. 150–58.
24. "Hoppo ryodo kosho: Ame ka muchi kano taiso senryaku," *Bungei shunju,* No. 2, 1991, pp. 112–26.
25. See a panel discussion in *Sekai;* Masuyama Eitaro in *Sekai shuho,* 15–22 (January 1991), pp. 14–17; and Tanaka Ryozo in *Jiyu,* No. 2, 1991, pp. 10–19.
26. *Hokkaido shimbun,* April 5, 1991.

27. As for Soviet public debate, see *Neither War Nor Peace,* pp. 313–19, 331–39.
28. As for the Kaifu-Gorbachev summit, see *Neither War Nor Peace,* pp. 389–401.
29. *Jiji yoron chosa tokuho,* August and September 1992; *Yomiuri shimbun,* March 28,1993.

CHAPTER 16

Overcoming the Legacy of History: Japanese Public Relations in Russia, 1990–1994

Akio Kawato

BETWEEN 1991 AND 1994, I WAS IN CHARGE OF PUBLIC RELATIONS and cultural exchange at the Embassy of Japan in Moscow. This was the most fascinating time in my life, being able to witness one of the most remarkable changes in modern history. Freedom created by glasnost and the Russian people's repentance of their government's past aggressive foreign policy provided us with a wonderful environment for public relations aimed at long-term confidence building and the improvement of understanding on the Northern Territories issue. I enjoyed extensive contact with Russians from all walks of life.

This paper provides basic information about public relations activity (PR) of the Embassy of Japan in the Soviet Union, later Russia, centering around the period between 1991 and 1992, and analyzes the perception gap between the peoples of Japan and Russia with a view to explore the ways to establish long-term friendship.

PR before President Gorbachev's Visit to Japan: Ideal Conditions for PR

When I arrived in Moscow in December 1990, Gorbachev's liberal policy had removed almost all obstacles for foreigners in approaching the Soviet people. Appointments were no longer controlled by the authorities: if you called someone in the morning, you might well see that person that afternoon. Our invitations to Soviet politicians, journalists, and other opinion leaders to visit Japan were no longer hindered by Party officials. Distribution of PR materials, even those concerning the territorial issue, was freely permitted. Contributions of articles to the Soviet press were welcomed, far from being controlled; interviews, movies, and video material were actively sought by the Soviet press and TV stations. Due to financial constraints, they relied upon foreign embassies for materials. Information about foreign countries was in great demand among the people, who had been newly freed from regulation.

The Embassy of Japan in Moscow (our Embassy) enjoyed extensive and intensive contacts with the Soviets, including President Gorbachev's entourage. The Soviet Ministry of Foreign Affairs' Japan Desk was staffed by younger diplomats who recognized the importance of Japan and were eager to solve the territorial issue. In preceding years, diplomats of both countries had gone through lengthy and tedious discussions on the territorial problem in the Peace Treaty Working Group. Through this process a general understanding had been reached that the Soviet people should be given more information regarding the historical facts surrounding the four islands at issue. The Soviet diplomats must have thought that this would facilitate an eventual solution of the problem. Our PR on the territorial question was thus condoned by the Soviet, and later the Russian, authorities.

Gorbachev's conservative tilt in the first half of 1991 did not substantially affect this picture. On the contrary, before Gorbachev's visit to Japan in April of that year, our Embassy undertook an unprecedented PR campaign. Ambassador Edamura, an excellent communicator, made four to five public speeches between December 1990 and March 1991. His interviews were printed in some seven papers, both liberal and conservative, and probably for the first time in history, in *Krasnaya zvezda*. In almost all public speeches and interviews, Ambassador Edamura spoke in a modest, nonaggressive manner, briefly introducing basic historical facts about the Northern Territory. His salient message was, however, that Japan sought an improvement in relations with the Soviet Union, and that the conclusion of a peace treaty is essential for mutual trust between the two nations.

In Sakhalin a small Japanese cultural week was held from February to March. In Moscow our Embassy sponsored two exhibitions: a photo exhibition of Japanese life, taken by Japanese and Soviet photographers, and an exhibition of Japanese dolls. Promising young journalists of 12 major newspapers, liberal and conservative, were invited to Japan in late March. These PR initiatives were "handmade" by the Embassy staff and, therefore, were limited in scale. Our Embassy had just embarked on serious PR and lacked personnel, funding, and infrastructure.

It is hard to measure the effect of this PR, as we did not conduct opinion polls. At any rate, the PR by our Embassy must have looked extraordinary and fresh to the Soviet people: many friends, even from the Soviet government, spoke positively about our PR work. The newspaper *Komsomol'skaya pravda* wrote after Gorbachev's visit that they were almost convinced by our PR.

We should not overestimate, however, the capacity of PR. Especially in today's Russia, major papers have lost their local distribution and TV is not always viewed by the people. Youngsters are increasingly skeptical, if not indifferent, to any story told by others. Therefore, I would limit myself to saying that all our PR efforts at that time had the effect of drawing Soviet opinion leaders' serious attention to the territorial issue and of changing the image of our Embassy, from cautious and inscrutable to frank and open. It is striking that opposition to a solution of the Northern Territory issue was not as explicit and widespread as in late 1992, when President Yeltsin's visit to Japan had to be postponed. This is probably because one opposition force at that time—liberals under Yeltsin—was committed to a solution of the territorial issue with Japan, and the other—conservatives—was within the government, able to exert negative pressure directly on Gorbachev.

Around the Postponement of Yeltsin's Visit to Japan

When President Gorbachev's visit to Japan ended without spectacular progress on the islands issue, both sides lost momentum for promoting relations in general. Fatigue after months of preparation took its toll, too. The ever-deteriorating situation in the Soviet Union augmented the despair of diplomats of both countries. We limited PR in the Soviet Union to small-scale cultural events at that time.

The situation after the failed coup d'etat in August 1991 created both favorable and negative conditions for our PR. At the end of August, Ruslan Khasbulatov, acting chairman of the Russian Supreme Soviet, made a sudden visit to Japan, bringing with him Russian President Yeltsin's personal letter to the Japanese Prime Minister, Kaifu Toshiki. In this letter, Yeltsin stated that Russia would no longer consider Russo-Japanese relations as relations between countries that had been victor and loser in World War II, and that Russia would strive for a solution of the territorial dispute on the basis of law and justice. This statement was more than welcomed by the Japanese side. In the widespread mood of repentance and negation of the Soviet past, Russian liberals who took power were active in promoting relations with Japan. The conservative forces had been pushed into the underground.[1]

In late September 1991, the Japanese Government published five principles in dealing with the newly born state of Russia, explicitly endorsing the support of democracy and economic reform in Russia and pledging $2.5 billion of financial support.

This was a clear departure from past policy, which had linked economic relations with the territorial issue.[2] These "principles," however, did not receive the expected welcome from the Russians because they failed to explicitly declare that Japan gave up the linkage. Many Russian journalists, governed by stereotypical views from the past, interpreted the principles as a continuation of the linkage, and considered the entire package not as a friendly gesture, but as a subtle pressure on the Russians. Our Embassy held a press conference a few days after the package was announced. However, it was too late, since the initial perception already had been formed by the first report from Tokyo.[3]

From October 1991 it became very clear that the Soviet government was about to collapse, tax revenue being usurped by the Russian government. Soviet diplomats left the Japanese desk one after another; some moving to the Russian Foreign Ministry, others being employed by the Japanese press and private companies (by now, though, almost all of the younger diplomats have been reinstated in the Russian Foreign Ministry). This was a transition period. Everyone sensed that the Soviet Union was doomed, but no one could predict exactly when it would collapse.

During this time, all we could do was establish contacts with Yeltsin's people and host cultural events. These events were almost always well attended, whether a traditional genre like the Noh Theater, or a contemporary event like a rock concert, or a symposium about current Japanese society. We usually advertised these events in the Soviet press; inquiries came even from the Far Eastern part of the Soviet Union. We promoted Japanese language-teaching and supported scholars who specialized in Japanese studies. One of the agreements reached during Gorbachev's visit to Japan was for the opening of the Center for the Study of Contemporary Japan, through which the Japan Foundation promoted Japanese studies in Russia. By that time a whole range of Japan Foundation programs had been introduced to the Soviet Union: Japanese speech competition; teaching materials provision; invitations to Russian teachers to visit Japan for training; publication of a Japanese study magazine, etc. Initially only a marginal recipient, in only two years the Soviet Union became a major—almost equal to France and Germany—recipient of Japan Foundation funding.

This was not achieved overnight nor by a single directive from Tokyo. Overall resources for cultural exchange and PR have limits, and competition for them is vigorous. The allocation of resources is in fact decided at the middle level of the bureaucracy. An annual lump sum is not allotted to each embassy: funding is given only to concrete projects. Therefore, the only way to obtain a budget is to repeatedly stress to one's colleagues in Tokyo the importance and opportunity of PR and cultural exchange in and with the Soviet Union. Moreover, the person in charge of the project should be regarded by his/her Tokyo colleagues as an able, responsible "producer." In other words, if you do not have this reputation, your projects may not be funded. In this system, a dynamic shift in funding is very rare.

After the eventual collapse of the Soviet Union in December 1991 and President Yeltsin's control of power, the Japanese government reinvigorated its efforts toward rapprochement with Russia. By the spring of 1992, the date for Yeltsin's visit to Japan had been fixed. In comparison with Gorbachev, who visited Japan only after six years in office, Yeltsin's early visit to Japan was considered proof of his enthusiasm to break the Japanese-Russian stalemate.

Preparations for the visit started around March 1992. Our Embassy revitalized its PR efforts. Interviews with Japanese Prime Minister Miyazawa Kiichi, were printed and aired in *Nezavisimaya gazeta* (March 14), *Komsomol'skaya pravda* (September 8) and on

Ostankino TV (today, ORT)(August 14). Interviews with the Japanese Foreign Minister, the late Watanabe Michio, were printed and broadcast in *Komsomol'skaya pravda* (April 29), *Izvestiia* (May 7), on Ostankino TV (May 10), and in *Izvestiia* again (September 7). Japanese Ambassador Sumio Edamura's interviews were published and aired on Ostankino TV (May 1), in *Pravda* (May 30), on Russian TV (June 13), in *Literaturnaya gazeta* (June 17), the weekly *Sobesednik* (June No. 24), *Moskovskii komsomolets* (June 25), *Sovetskii Sakhalin* in Yuzhno-Sakhalinsk (June 17), on Ostankino TV (July 8), *Argumenty i fakty* (July 24), *Zarya Vostoka* in Vladivostok (August 29), the magazine *Voprosy Dal'nevo Vostoka* (August), *Rossiya* (August 29) and on Russian TV (September 5).

Articles drafted by our Embassy staff were printed in *Krasnaya zvezda* (June 4), *Trud* (July 16), *Pravda* (July 25), *Ogonyok* (August No. 34), and *Kuranty* (September 9). Former Prime Minister Nakasone Yasuhiro's interview was aired on Russian TV (March 9). The Embassy of Japan in Moscow held press conferences with Russian journalists on April 23, June 16, and August 27. My own interviews were printed or aired by Moscow Radio (April 26), Radio Smena (May 20), Russian TV (May 31), Radio Yunost (July 9), the magazine *Stolitsa* (August, No. 34) and others.

In June 1992, the Japanese Foreign Ministry printed a pamphlet, "Japanese Northern Territory." Our Embassy sent copies to all members of the Supreme Soviet, and editors and reporters of major national and provincial mass media (the content of the brochure was almost entirely printed in the newspaper "Russia," August 29). The Ministry furthermore edited a videofilm, "Japanese Northern Territory." Our Embassy sent copies to national TV stations in Moscow and a part of it was aired on Russian TV on September 5.

Not all these interviews and articles referred to the territorial problem. Some were about current Japanese society or economic reforms in Japan just after World War II. All of them were presented in a friendly, modest tone. When the island issue was touched upon, the following points, which were not known by most Russian people at that time, were explained in nonpolemical manner: the four islands at issue never belonged to Russia or the Soviet Union after a formal relationship was established between the two countries in 1855; those four islands were occupied without the bloodshed of Soviet soldiers; the islands were annexed by the Soviet Union without a peace treaty; over ten thousand Japanese inhabitants on these islands were deported without any compensation, and yet the welfare of the current Russian inhabitants would be taken care of by the Japanese government even after a return of the islands to Japan; Japan will not demand an immediate return of all four islands, and is ready to discuss the formula of the return in a flexible manner, if the sovereignty of Japan over the four islands is recognized by the Russian government; Japan strives for the return of the islands not from a revanchist viewpoint but for the sake of law and justice, the common norms of the international community that the new Russia had just joined enable both nations to embark on frank, long-term cooperation; the Japanese government and people support democracy and free economy in Russia and will continue to render assistance.

Our Embassy tried hard to bring home to the Russians the existence of Japanese aid to Russia. In January 1992, the Japanese government had decided to send Russia $50 million worth of goods to mitigate the plight of the Russian people during the reforms. The arrivals of goods were frequently reported by Russian TV, and I was interviewed by Russian TV on February 9. In April our Embassy's bulletin informed 5,000 Russian opinion leaders and citizens of the entire range of Japanese aid and support to Russia. In July similar material was again distributed by the Embassy, this time followed by a press conference by the Minister-Councilor, Shigeta Hiroshi (August 27). Japanese companies in Moscow published a one-page advertisement in *Izvestiia* (September 8), explaining the extensive economic ties between the two countries.

The Japanese Government intensified its invitations to Russian parliamentarians and journalists to visit Japan. Between March and July, six deputies of the Supreme Soviet and six leading journalists were invited to Japan. The late Vladimir Tsvetov, political commentator on Russian TV at that time, had been invited to Japan in December 1991 to shoot a lengthy documentary on the Northern Territory issue (this theme was, to our surprise, proposed by Tsvetov himself). The result, "Ostrova razdora," was broadcast in three series (thirty minutes each) from February to March (rebroadcast in August). This was a full recounting of the history of the four islands. The Japanese position was explained to the Russian public in detail, and interviews with the previous Japanese inhabitants, noting that they do not desire revenge, were aired. Russian TV received protests against the program's "pro-Japan tone" from such people as Sakhalin's governor at that time, Valentin Fedorov. Russian TV under President Poptsov stood firmly against this criticism. Poptsov was not unaware of his government's intention to resolve this issue.

Other media also supported the desire to improve relations with Japan. Our Embassy's open and cordial attitude to the Russians was appreciated by many journalists of both liberal and conservative papers. Many articles and materials appeared in Russian newspapers, TV, and radio, describing the importance of Japan and the Asia-Pacific dimension. In addition to the liberal media, *Krasnaya zvezda, Pravda,* and Ostankino TV also printed or aired similar material. Ostankino TV broadcast an interview with a specialist of the Institute of Military History, who said that the official Soviet history about World War II, which depicts Japan as an aggressor toward the Soviet Union, was then under review (probably in April or May). From September on, Ostankino's most popular world travel program, "Club of Travelers," aired its most extensive and intensive features ever about Japanese life. It is striking that during this period malicious or critical articles on Japan almost never appeared.

Our Embassy's efforts in this PR endeavor were great, but one should not overestimate its role. Although the achievement appears enormous as indicated above, this was merely a drop in the ocean when compared with the immense quantity of other news presented daily. Moreover, in times of economic difficulty, the Russians read newspapers less. Circulation of national papers had dramatically decreased. The main source of information at this time (and today, too) was television. However, it is usually far more time consuming and difficult to arrange TV broadcasting than a newspaper article. Television broadcasts need pictures taken in Japan, and review and editing on machines that were in slim supply at Russian TV stations. Japanese feature films, documentary films, and animation films were broadcast from time to time: sometimes on the initiative of Russian TV stations themselves, sometimes by a joint effort of our Embassy and Russian TV stations. But, as a whole, the result was far less than was needed. Solving the issues surrounding the copyright jungle, translation of scenario, and sometimes fees for broadcast time, all inhibited a quick move. However, to the credit of the Russian media, all of the broadcasts noted above were achieved without any payment from the Japanese side (except for invitation to TV crews to Japan).

The Russian government condoned all of the PR initiatives undertaken by the Japanese side. Indeed, President Yeltsin's entourage and the Russian Foreign Ministry at that time were very aware of the necessity of PR. The true historical facts around the four islands were almost unknown to the Russian public. The communists had indoctrinated the people with the idea that the islands were Russian, distorting arguments to support this belief. Without changing this view, the political price for a solution of the territorial dispute would be immense. The Russian leadership was aware that without substantial progress on the islands issue, Yeltsin's visit to Japan, scheduled for the following September, would not be a success.

The Russian journalists, who are adept at following political tides, must have been aware of this in supporting the Japanese position (most papers survived on subsidies from the government). When the newspapers printed the Japanese position, they sometimes asked for comment by the Russian government. The comments were not negative and they were printed side by side with the Japanese position. (This in turn created an expectation in the Japanese press for a solution of the territorial quagmire.) Russian media's motives were manifold: not merely opportunism as indicated above. The Russian press had become totally free by this time and the personal convictions of journalists, and their friendly attitude toward the Japanese, could play a bigger role than in the past. Some journalists, however, were interested in this issue only from a commercial viewpoint: to increase circulation by reporting "sensational" news.

All this PR was done in a fair and not hysterical, sensational manner. I occasionally and informally informed the Russian Foreign Ministry about our plans and intentions. Although our PR efforts were minor, given the enormous amount of news, they could have contributed to a successful visit by President Yeltsin, had he ever visited as scheduled.

However, the political climate began to deteriorate in early July. Our Embassy received signals from the Russian side that our PR efforts regarding the territorial issue were becoming counterproductive, instigating negative repercussions from the conservative forces. This was not "pressure," but sincere advice. We listened to it and moderated the intensity of the PR, although some materials, which had been in the pipeline, were published occasionally.

After the postponement of Yeltsin's visit, the environment surrounding our PR dramatically changed. Some Russian officials attempted to shift the blame for the postponement to the Japanese side. The Western media created the perception that the Japanese were so hasty and overdemanding that they lost everything. Western countries tempered their support of the Japanese cause regarding the territory; some of them suggested that we shelve the territorial issue and embark upon unfettered economic assistance to Russia.

Looking back at this period, the following points would be noteworthy. Did we "overdo" the PR, thus providing the conservative forces with an opportunity to utilize the territorial issue in their fight against President Yeltsin? Some Russians told me "Yes," others, "No." One will never know the truth. Probably, even without our PR, the conservatives would have taken up the territorial issue with Japan. Our Embassy did not receive much direct response to our PR, and the Russian media did not disclose to us the whole spectrum of the readers' and viewers' reactions. Further, those reactions usually do not represent the entire spectrum of Russian social opinion. Pensioners have more time to write letters and make calls, responding to press or TV reports. Most of them are conservative. However, there was one occasion in which our Embassy did receive a direct response. When our Embassy distributed a brochure on the Northern Territory issue, one anonymous blackmail letter reached our Embassy, and this was reported in one Russian paper. Immediately, many Russians called us to get the pamphlet. Some of them even proposed to distribute this brochure as "part of their fight with the conservatives." This may be an indication that there was a fairly large number of Russians who support the Japanese position. But, usually they did not speak up.

The second point is that historical facts about the four islands, no matter how they seem to justify the Japanese position, do not necessarily convince the Russians to relinquish the islands. Intellectuals are afraid of an avalanche of other territorial claims if the problem with Japan is resolved. And some Russians suggest that we persevere, saying "Under Stalin all suffered, not only the Japanese but the Russians themselves."The third point is the difficulty involved in reaching "every" Russian citizen. Our Embassy published a variety of materials on Japan in major newspapers, but it was not clear how many readers actually read the material. During times of economic difficulty and political instability the Russians paid little attention to foreign news. Indeed, media space for foreign news was constantly reduced in favor of domestic news, entertainment, and advertisements. It was hard to bring home to the Russians the extent of Japanese economic assistance. The reasons were many: first, other Western countries, EU inter alia, were also active in helping the Russians; second, "good news" does not draw the media's attention in any country, reports about Japan's aid would not have increased newspaper circulation as much as the sensation caused by the islands' dispute; third, Russian journalists suspected that Japanese assistance was motivated by the ambition to get back the islands; and finally, the assistance did not reach every Russian citizen. This was not their business, but someone else's.

Our budget for PR was limited, but this was not a serious obstacle. PR cannot solve political problems: it is only one component of diplomacy. If more money becomes available, however, it should be used for extensive publication and translation of books on Japan and for broadcasting Japanese films on TV.

What Is Hampering a Mutual Understanding between the Peoples of Japan and Russia?

Japan and Russia were at the forefront in the confrontation between Asia and European colonialism. Both countries were never in alliance and did not learn from each other. They waged war three times during the twentieth century (Russo-Japanese War, the Japanese invasion of Siberia, and the Russian occupation of Manchuria). Therefore, their differences came to the surface easily, and the negative memory of wars still lingers in the minds of the elderly.

However, both countries were always a large factor in each other's diplomacy (except for the postwar years, when Gromyko neglected Japan), and their political and economic relations are rather deep, despite stereotyped perceptions. Probably because of this, their mutual images are not unequivocal, but multilayered, a mixture of positive and negative images. The Soviet annexation of the four islands, the brutal occupation of Manchuria by the Soviet army, and the internment of 600,000 Japanese left a negative imprint in the minds of Japanese over 60, and yet it is this generation that has a strong attachment to Russian literature, Russian folk songs, and (for some of them) Marxism. Most Russians hold in high esteem the modern technology and well-maintained traditional culture of Japan (Russian intellectuals are very familiar with modern

Japanese literature) and moral code of the samurai, and yet those same people are critical about Japanese "servility" and lack of humor, discrimination toward women, and the cruelty of Japanese soldiers during the war. The most visible component depends upon the generation, education, age, profession, gender, and region of the respondent. Simplistic generalizations should be avoided.

Several opinion polls were published about the Russian perception of the Japanese. They indicate the following general tendency. While the elderly and people of lower income and educational levels tend to be less interested in Japan, the general feeling toward Japan is positive, marred only by Japan's territorial claim. Knowledge about Japan is not too out-dated: most people consider Japan to be a technologically advanced country and not quite "Asiatic" in a negative sense of that word. Not many people realize, though, that Japan is now the number two economic power in the world. Interest in Japan is greater in Moscow and the Far East than in other regions: if Muscovites are more interested in culture, in the Far East the economy is more important.

However, misunderstandings carried over from the past still remain. Many people continue to believe that Japan is a country where the emperor is the ruler, where the income gap is large, and where the people are diligent and protective of their own dignity, but disingenuous toward foreigners. Russians' view on the territorial question with Japan varies, depending on each poll. Since this is a highly politicized issue, an objective poll might be impossible.

All in all, the Russian peoples' understanding of Japan is no worse than in the United States and Europe. In view of the consciously conducted negative propaganda against Japan in the past, for example the samurais' "treacherous attack" on Port Arthur, this is a fairly good basis for the future. Credit should be given to people like Vsevolod Ovchinnikov and Vladimir Tsvetov, and many others, who, despite the pressure from the Party, dared to bring the latest knowledge on Japan to the Russian people. Nevertheless, the perception gap between both peoples is immense. Misunderstandings arise, in my view, from the following factors.

Firstly, Russian intellectuals associate themselves with Western civilization. Some of them, therefore, take a wary attitude toward Asia, an inherent factor in Western colonialism. Those Russians feel frustrated by their own economic failure and thus close their eyes all the more to the reality in Asia. The Japanese are no better. Proud of their economic success, they neglect the cultural splendor of Russia. A childish game of "Who is better?" is apparent.

Secondly, the perception of power is much different in both countries. For the Japanese, power can be only economic and they are told that power means responsibility for the welfare of the entire world. For Russians, power comes from the size of territory, abundant natural resources, and military might. For them, power means the capacity to impose their will on other nations. Therefore, both countries very often fail to consider each other a true power. Lacking strategic and cultural interest, the Russians tend to value most Asian countries only from an opportunistic, mercantile viewpoint. Many Russians interpret Japan's motive on the territorial issue as mercantile, an interest in fishing and in meager mineral resources. This is a reflection of their own attitude toward Asia and Japan.

Thirdly, a difference in the policy-making process augments misunderstanding. For Russians, politics have supremacy over everything. Their decision making is dynamic and top-down, sometimes neglecting legal cohesion and financial, economic feasibility. Exceptions to laws and regulations are frequently made for political convenience. Japanese decision making is usually bottom-up. Precedence, legality of decisions, availability of financial resources, accountability to the Parliament and the press, all are meticulously perused before a decision is made and interested parties' voices are incorporated in any decision. For the Japanese, not only politics but also economics and legality are important. It is difficult for them to make exceptions for political convenience; a lengthy consensus-forming process makes their decision slow and incremental, instead of dynamic. One Russian paper named it the policy of a "bookkeeper."

This difference brings about misunderstanding. The legacy of Marxism and the cold war still lingers in the minds of some Russian leaders and journalists. In analyzing things, they tend to presuppose a malicious intention or conspiracy on the part of a partner. They, therefore, overlook such factors in Japanese policymaking as rivalry among interested ministries, pressure from the Parliament, and social opinion, opting instead to attribute all negative factors to a conspiracy. For example, in October 1993, Russian nuclear waste dumping in the Japan Sea caused an uproar in Japan. Some Russian journalists took this as an intentional anti-Russian maneuver instigated by the Japanese government.

Fourth, many Russians still consider Japan a highly centralized state, where economic activity is planned and controlled by the government. (The Russian communists use this as an argument as to why Russia should return to a planned economy.) They believe that if one politician gives an order, then economic aid and private direct investment will rush from Japan into Russia. They do not know that the allocation of budgets is subject to severe scrutiny, and that Japanese companies will listen to the government only when they find benefit in doing so.

Most Russians are not yet accustomed to a market economy way of thinking. This is why they still believe it is possible to play Japan against Korea or China in trade. They often tell the Japanese that if they wait too long, the Koreans and Chinese will take all trade with Russia.

Fifth, wars between Japan and Russia are interpreted in a totally different way. For the Japanese, the Russians were always aggressors (forgetting about the Siberian invasion and the battle in Mongolia in 1939), and for Russians, the Japanese were always to blame (unaware of the historical facts at the end of World War II). Thus, both are all the more tenacious in insisting on their cause in the islands issue. Russians cannot understand why the tiny islands matter to the Japanese, and the Japanese are infuriated by the negative reaction of the Russians to their demand.

Lastly, the Russian perception of the Japanese is still marred by negative stereotypes: the Japanese are collectivistic, lacking individuality; women are discriminated against; such national traits can never change, etc. When our Embassy issued materials about postwar economic reforms in Japan, several Russian officials shrugged their shoulders, saying that Japan's example was not useful to them, because the Japanese national character was totally different from theirs. Such stereotypes take their toll on the younger generation, too. They tend to dislike Japan as collectivistic, closed, and heavily regulated by the government. American movies, in which Japanese are depicted as odd, exotic, and inhumane creatures, are very often aired on Russian television. Kung fu movies are taken as representative of Japanese culture, leaving a distorted impression about the Japanese. Some new Russian businessmen are assertive and cynical. They neglect and deny everything that does not bring them a quick profit. I was once shocked in Yekaterinburg to encounter a young businessman, who bluntly stated that he was not interested in doing business with the Japanese because "they are incongenial and slow in business."

This is a real problem. It results from a lack of real contacts with the Japanese and not from outdated stereotyped images. Stereotypical perceptions of the Japanese are also sometimes strengthened as a result of contacts with Japanese individuals, some of whom look, in the Russian eyes, insufficiently responsive, imaginative, and humane.

What Should and Could Be Done?

PR is not omnipotent. PR alone cannot retrieve the islands. The effects of PR efforts, if any, could be nullified overnight by one careless, negative statement by a politician of either country. Moreover, the Russians are historically suspicious of official PR, domestic or foreign. They feel that they have been so often deceived by beautiful slogans and statements. Therefore, in convincing Russians to solve the territorial issue with Japan, the benefit of doing so should be well explained and understood by the Russians.

This does not mean necessarily to offer a large amount of money. What is most important is to correct the impression that Japan will not help Russia as long as the territorial issue is not solved. Not the money, but the heart matters. For example, Moscow University Business School, under the auspices of our Embassy, has been conducting free courses for schoolteachers on the market economy. In these four years, about one thousand teachers have gone through this three-month course. It is highly appreciated by the teachers. They are eager to convey accurate knowledge about a market economy, and about the problems of the Russian economy, to their students, who believe that a free market equals the laws of the jungle.

Efforts to convince people remind one of election campaigns. People cannot be persuaded by mere words. If they do not see future benefits for themselves, they will not vote. Therefore, both the Japanese and the Russian governments should endeavor to create conditions in which the Russian people will see benefits in improving ties with Japan and in solving the territorial issue. PR should be continued with a priority, however, on building the image of Japan as Russia's friend.

Japanese-Russian relations used to be one of the "frontiers" of rivalries between European colonialism and Japan's surging power. Much enmity was engendered because of this. But today we live in a totally different world. Animosity that originated during the course of our past history must be terminated once and for all by the development of that history.

NOTES

1. However, this euphoria did not last long. As a rivalry among Yeltsin's entourage became apparent at the end of September 1991, skepticism about an overrepentant attitude became apparent in the Supreme Soviet and the conservative press. President Yeltsin, thus, had to reiterate his position on the territorial question with Japan in his open appeal to the Russian Supreme Soviet in November 1991. This appeal, however, did not draw much public attention.
2. This was not the first, however. In December 1990 the Japanese Government had already pledged $100 million of credit and 1 billion yen of grants for humanitarian aid. In November 1990 the Japanese government donated 2.6 billion yen to the WHO for saving those who had suffered from the Chernobyl nuclear power plant accident.
3. It took, thereafter, about two years for both governments to determine which products should be imported from Japan using these loans. This delay, too, tempered the effect of the package.

CHAPTER 17

Nihonjinron and *Russkaia Ideia*: Transformation of Japanese and Russian Nationalism in the Postwar Era and Beyond

Tadashi Anno

ONE OF THE MOST CONSPICUOUS DEVELOPMENTS in the intellectual history of both Japan and Russia since the 1960s has been the resurgence of discourse on the "nation" and its alleged "uniqueness." In Japan, concern for questions of democracy, peace, and socialism that had characterized the intellectual scene of the early postwar period (1945–60) was replaced since the 1960s by growing preoccupation with economic growth, and with the "uniqueness" of Japanese culture.[1] The 1970s witnessed a veritable explosion of *nihonjinron* (theory of Japanese uniqueness), a popular to semi-academic body of literature that described and analyzed various aspects of Japanese culture, usually in favorable, rather self-congratulatory terms. While *nihonjinron* has come under increasing scrutiny and criticism since the 1980s, it has had an enormous impact on the Japanese society, including politics, business, popular consciousness, and scholarship.[2]

At around the same time, a more quiet, yet no less interesting intellectual ferment was taking place in the USSR. In the first decade of the post-Stalin period (1956–66), a "neo-Leninist" tendency dominated the newly vibrant world of Soviet intellectuals.[3] While highly critical of Stalin, neo-Leninists expressed the belief that the USSR could realize the ideals of socialism by correcting the Stalinist deviations and by going back to Leninist principles. However, from the mid-1960s, neo-Leninism began to give way to new schools of thought, of which Russophilism was among the most important.[4] Borrowing many elements from nineteenth-century Slavophilism and other currents of "original" Russian thought (*russkaia ideia,* or the Russian idea), the Russophiles extolled the virtues of the Russian people and their culture. Despite ups and downs, Russophilism has since become an important trend in Russian intellectual life.

World politics after the collapse of communism seems to be characterized by the uneasy coexistence of the single universalistic ideology of liberalism and a host of particularistic ideologies. *Nihonjinron* and *russkaia ideia* are two of the most significant examples of particularistic ideologies that populate the global intellectual landscape in the post–cold war era. As such, they deserve careful study. The phenomenon of *nihonjinron* and *russkaia ideia* raises two major issues of both theoretical and practical significance. First, what are we to make of the persistence and resurgence of particularistic national ideologies in an increasingly globalized world? Are these ideologies temporary aberrations explained by transient factors? Or are they deeply rooted in the cultural makeup of the two countries? Second, what is their likely impact on the political developments in the two countries and the world outside? Are they simply manifestations of nostalgic yearning for the past, which have little impact on actual political processes, or should they be taken seriously—as a threat to global liberalism, or as precursors of a multicultural, postliberal era?

In an effort to explore these questions, this essay compares and contrasts *nihonjinron* and *russkaia ideia* in the light of the historical development of nationalism in the two countries. Given the drastic contrast in the historical trajectories of the two countries in the postwar period, a comparative analysis of national ideologies of Japan and Russia might seem pointless. However, a long-term historical comparison reveals many parallels between the two countries, especially with respect to the problem of formulating national identities under the impact of the more advanced civilization of the West.[5] The comparison is especially pertinent because after the cold war, Japan and Russia are likely to occupy intellectual positions somewhat closer to each other than they used to during the cold war era. Despite the continuation of drastic contrasts in the political and economic conditions of the two countries, a similar debate between liberal universalism and national particularism has been taking place in the two countries, and the parallels are often striking.

I begin in the first section with a general consideration on the nature of nationalism and its relationship with "national ideologies." In the second section, I provide a comparative sketch of the development of nationalism in Japan and Russia as a historical background for the analysis of the postwar period. In the third section, I proceed to the analysis of *nihonjinron* and *russkaia ideia*. The essay concludes by returning to the theoretical and practical questions raised above.

Nationalism and National Ideologies: A Conceptual Discussion

Both *nihonjinron* and *russkaia ideia* may be viewed as "national ideologies," which are expressions of nationalism in the broad sense of the word. Nationalism is best understood as a historically specific type of "collective ideology," a phenomenon that is common to "communities," or groups bound together by emotional ties.[6] As Emile Durkheim, Ferdinand Tönnies, and others have noted, not all groups are bound together by interests alone, contrary to the assumption often made by theorists of rational choice. Some groups are bound together also by the emotional needs of individuals. The emotional needs that form the basis of group-identification of individuals may be broadly categorized under two headings: the search for continuity and security, and the search for recognition. A sense of continuity and security is central to our sense of personhood. Without a sense of continuity and security, our lives would be a meaningless succession of events unrelated to each other. But this is not enough. Individuals want their lives to be not only coherent, but also to be meaningful and worth living. Identification with a group can answer both of these emotional needs. Our sense of continuity is dependent on the continuity not only of what is within ourselves, but also of what surrounds us. Individuals often develop emotional attachment to the surroundings with which they are familiar. These surroundings become part of individuals' "way of life" that gives them a sense of continuity and security. Thus, identification with a collectivity can be an important guarantor of the individual's sense of continuity and security. Furthermore, recognition as a valued member of a group can give individuals a sense of meaning, and allows individuals to vicariously transcend the limitations of their existence through linkage with the greater lineages of the collectivity.[7]

When individuals are "identified" with a collectivity, the latter becomes an "extension" of the members' individual "selves." When this happens, two consequences follow. First, the collectivity, as an extension of individual selves, turns into a "we" that must be distinguished from outsiders. Like individuals, this collective "we" demands autonomy and self-determination. Second, individual members wish "their" collectivity (nations in this case) to be managed in such a way as to satisfy their needs for recognition and security. In other words, they want their nation to be recognized and respected in the world, while maintaining the continuity of its traditions.

The aspiration for autonomy, continuity, and recognition of the national collectivity, then, is the main driving force of nationalism. It can be expressed in a variety of forms. Nationalism can spur practical action in search of autonomy (independence movement), continuity (preservation of cultural monuments), and recognition (membership in the club of "great powers"). It can be expressed in symbolic forms (flags, anthems, tombs of unknown soldiers). In addition to these, nationalism also generates "national ideologies," or verbal discourses typically concerning the distinctive characteristics and "missions" of a particular nation. *Nihonjinron* and *russkaia ideia* are examples of national ideologies in this sense. National ideologies can be expressed in mythological, religious, metaphysical, or quasi-scientific terms, depending on the worldview upon which they are based. Whatever their specific forms, national ideologies present an interpretation of the world that is convenient for nationalist aspirations. As such, they are ideological manifestations of nationalism.

While all nationalists want autonomy, continuity, and recognition, the specific aspirations of nationalists vary, depending on domestic and external conditions. To the extent that nationalists wish to preserve the continuity of "national traditions," nationalist aspirations are shaped by the cultural and institutional legacies of the nation. However, the orientation of nationalism is not determined by domestic traditions. The aspiration of nationalists for recognition can be satisfied only within an international context. What nationalists must do to gain recognition for their nation varies, depending on the "cognitive-normative framework" that informs the international system (such as "Enlightenment" in the eighteenth century, "liberalism" in the post–cold war era), and on the "reference groups" in comparison with which the nation wishes to gain self-respect. The historical development of nationalism in Japan and Russia, including their most recent manifestations, can be best compared and understood in the light of changing domestic and external conditions.

Historical Evolution of Japanese and Russian Nationalism

On the Periphery of China and Byzantium

Any discussion of the development of modern nationalism in Japan and Russia must take into consideration the fact that these two countries formed their distinctive national traditions on the periphery of great classical empires: China and Byzantium.[8] Both countries entered the "historical" (or literate) stage of development by borrowing basic elements of civilization (such as religion, system of writing, law, and art) from these civilizations. In both cases, an initial period of intense borrowing from the "lender" civilization gradually gave way to a period of cultural "indigenization," a process that generated distinctively "Japanese" or "Russian" cultural elements, and the awareness of such distinctiveness. This awareness became the basis of later national ideologies. In both Japan and Russia, two types of nascent national ideologies emerged, one centered around the emperor, and the other focusing on indigenous cultural sensibilities.[9]

A major difference between nascent national ideologies of Japan and Russia derived from their relationship to "historical religions." In Russia, Christianity was relatively successful in wiping out the preexisting pagan beliefs, despite the persistence of "double belief" (*dvoeverie*) among the common people. For this reason, national ideologies in Russia tended to build upon the "universalistic" belief system of Orthodox Christianity. The imperial authority of the tsar was justified by his mission to defend and spread Orthodoxy, while the distinctiveness of native Russian culture has most often been defined in terms of Christian virtues such as universal love and humility.[10] By contrast, the introduction of Buddhism and Confucianism to Japan did not lead to eradication of native beliefs. On the contrary, foreign influences led to the systematization of preexisting native beliefs into the independent national mythology of Shintoism.[11] The authority of Japanese emperors (*tenno*) derived from this mythology. Discourses on "distinctively Japanese" cultural sensibilities have also derived their inspirations from native traditions going back to the era before Buddhism and Confucianism.[12] The dependence of Japanese national ideologies on an "archaic" religion has imparted a parochial character to Japan's national ideologies.

The Impact of the West

The rise of modern Western civilization since the late fifteenth century had a decisive impact on the development of nationalism in the non-Western world. By virtue of military power and cultural appeal, "the West" became the most important reference point for non-Western nationalists. Having developed on the periphery of great classical empires, both Japan and Russia found themselves on the periphery of a new international order dominated by the West. In this new context, elites in both countries faced a similar dilemma between continuity of national traditions and the need to emulate the West and to be recognized as a major player in world politics. However, the response to this dilemma differed, due to the differences concerning the two countries' "positions" in the world, and the cultural impact of Westernization.

The first difference between Japanese and Russian nationalism has to do with their external orientations. Ultimately, this difference derived from the difference in the fate of China and Byzantium. Japan remained on the "periphery" of Chinese civilization well into the nineteenth century, when the Western impact reached Japan. Partly because of her peripheral position within the Chinese world order, Japan was able to respond effectively to the Western impact, and to transform herself into a "modern state" earlier than her Asian neighbors.[13] For this reason, nationalists in modern Japan had two points of reference against which to articulate their nation's identity: the West and the rest of Asia. Japanese national identity has been defined in this "triadic" context. By contrast, the fall of Byzantium in 1453 left Muscovite Russia as the natural "center" of the Orthodox world. Consequently, nationalists in modern Russia had only one point of reference. The attention of modern Russian nationalists has focused on the cursed question of "Russia and the West."

This difference between triad and dyad had a major consequence on the external orientations of Japanese and Russian national ideologies. Since elites in the non-West typically suffered from an inferiority complex vis-à-vis the West, a major function of national ideologies was to compensate for this sense of inferiority. In Japan, this was accomplished most often through "manipulation of reference groups." That is to say, Japanese nationalists compensated for their feeling of inferiority vis-à-vis the West by claiming that Japan was more "civilized" than the rest of Asia. The famous national slogan of modern Japan, *datsu-a nyu-o* (exit from Asia, entry into Europe) succinctly summarizes this strategy. This strategy was not available to Russian nationalists, who grappled with the question of national identity in a dyadic context.[14] Furthermore, unlike nationalists of the colonial areas, Russian nationalists could not extricate themselves from the sense of inferiority by blaming Russia's misery on external "oppressors." For this reason, national ideologies in Russia typically resorted to the third strategy of "transvaluation," or the "sour grapes argument." From Slavophilism to Soviet-Russian nationalism, Russian nationalists have typically compensated for their sense of inferiority by insisting that Western grapes are sour, and that "true" delicacy can be found in Russia.[15]

The second major difference between modern Russian and Japanese nationalism concerns the focus of nationalism. In an attempt to consolidate their domestic social privileges, the ruling elites of Meiji Japan and Imperial Russia invented remarkably similar ideologies (the "family state" ideology of Meiji Japan, and the "Official Nationality" of Russia under Nicholas I). These ideologies placed the emperor squarely at the center of the national community, and sought to prop up the traditional social order by linking the agrarian communities with the emperor by means of quasi-familial ties.[16] However, the ideology proved to be more effective in Japan than in Russia. The difference is explained by the impact of cultural Westernization on the two countries.

In Russia, cultural Westernization of the elite since the eighteenth century, coupled with the regime's hostility toward mass education, created a deep cultural gap between the elite and the masses. The Orthodox Muscovite tsars now became Christian emperors, intermarried with royalties of Western Europe, and led the process of Russia's Westernization. During the eighteenth century, when Russia achieved major successes in Westernization, national ideologies of Russia emphasized Russia's proximity to the West,[17] and the Westernized elite was understood to be the core of the Russian nation. However, the French and Industrial Revolutions drastically changed the international context, and, as a result, Russia emerged in the nineteenth century as a country of political "reaction" and economic backwardness. The deterioration in Russia's international position led Russian nationalists to search for an alternative measure of values according to which Russia would emerge in a more favorable light. At this juncture, the common people (*narod*) of Russia emerged as a new, alternative focus of Russian nationalism. This new "populist" brand of nationalism claimed that the common people were the true depository of "Russian" virtues, and thereby criticized the "isolation" of the Westernized elites from the people. Thus, populist nationalism gave nationalist credentials to the revolt of the masses against the elite.

In Japan, by contrast, the process of cultural Westernization was much less divisive. Due to great geographical and cultural distance, the stream of Western cultural influences came into Japan in a relatively controlled, steady flow. Moreover, new influences from the West were disseminated relatively quickly to Japan's internal peripheries through the system of universal education. Consequently, the cultural gap between the elite and the masses was much smaller in Japan than in Russia. Furthermore, Japanese nationalists felt less need than their Russian counterparts for an alternative focus of nationalism, because they could satisfy their nationalist aspirations by resorting to manipulation of reference groups. For these reasons, modern Japanese nationalism had a single focus: the emperor. In the 1930s, Japanese nationalists did attack the urban, Westernized elements in Japan for being "un-Japanese." However, in Japan, agrarian populism justified itself not in the name of the people, but of the emperor.

The Revolt against the West

The late nineteenth century witnessed the culmination of the expansion of the West. While Western dominance over the rest of the world was most directly based on military and industrial prowess, it was also supplemented by the appeal of Western ideas. In the late nineteenth century, liberalism and the idea of "progress" served as the "cognitive-normative framework" of the international order. Elites in relatively backward countries by and large accepted this framework, and sought to improve the position of their country within the existing international order.[18] World War I and the Great Depression dealt a decisive blow to the liberal, Eurocentric order of the nineteenth century. The crisis of the international order derived in part from a changing power balance, but it also reflected a grave crisis of Western civilization as a whole. In this context, nations and peoples that had harbored grievances against the dominance of the West began an open revolt against the West, mobilizing antiliberal ideologies to legitimize their claims.[19] In both Japan and Russia, the interwar period witnessed the rise to power of radical, antiliberal regimes that combined a high degree of domestic regimentation with a revisionist external policy. However, the relationship between the revolt against the West and traditional nationalism differed considerably between the two countries.

In some ways, Leninism was a successor to the "populist" version of Russian nationalism—for Leninism combined the claim of superiority of Soviet Russia over the capitalist West (transvaluation) with the populist theme of antipathy toward the Westernized elites of tsarist Russia.[20] However, it would be a mistake to regard Leninism as just another version of traditional Russian nationalism. In pursuit of their ideological vision, the Bolsheviks were ready to sacrifice the three sacred symbols of traditional Russian nationalism: the tsar, the peasant commune, and the Orthodox Church. The destruction of old nationalist symbols culminated in the 1928–34 period, when collectivization of agriculture proceeded simultaneously with the Cultural Revolution. Denouncing tsarist Russia as a "prisonhouse of peoples," the Bolsheviks pledged to build a brotherhood of nations where all would enjoy equal rights. In relation to the outside world, the Bolsheviks called for an alliance of the Western proletariat and of the oppressed peoples of the global periphery against imperialism. In all these respects, Leninism broke decisively with traditional Russian nationalism. It is true that elements of Russian nationalism found their way into Bolshevik ideas and policies, especially after the triumph of the doctrine of "socialism in one country." Under Stalin, the fusion of "Marxism-Leninism" and Russian nationalism became quite obvious. However, throughout the Soviet period, elements of Russian nationalism in the official ideology were harnessed to the left-wing notion of proletarian internationalism. Thus, the relationship between Leninism and traditional Russian nationalism remained discordant.

By contrast, in Japan, the revolt against the West was carried out under the ideological banner of traditional nationalism, especially its imperial mythology. The *kokutai* ideology had acquired the status of an official doctrine in 1890, and it was inculcated into the masses through primary and secondary schools. But until the early 1930s, the government was run not according to this "exoteric" dogma (*kenkyo*), but according to the rules of constitutional monarchy, which was the operative or "esoteric" ideology (*mikkyo*) shared among the elite, who received higher education.[21] The basic orientation of government policy was still characterized by *datsu-a nyu-o*. However, when the relationship between Japan and the West became strained in the 1930s, the pro-Western elements committed to the esoteric ideology were cast aside, and the new militarist regime came to power, seeking to mobilize the resources of the entire nation around the traditional imperial mythology. Domestically, the militarist regime emphasized traditional values such as loyalty to the emperor, filial piety, and agrarian virtues. In external policy, the notion of the "Greater East Asian Co-Prosperity Sphere" was justified as an extension of the family-state principle.[22] This is not to say that there was no tension between militarism and traditional nationalism. The centralizing impulse of the imperial state and "state Shintoism" conflicted with the traditional localist sentiments. Moreover, the rise of the quasi-Marxist ideology of "rational planning" in the 1930s in the bureaucracy horrified the traditionalists. However, overall, it was clear that Japan revolted against the West under the ideological banner of traditional nationalism. This difference between Japan and Russia had a significant consequence for the development of nationalism in the postwar era.

Transformation of Nationalism in the Postwar Period

In both Japan and Russia, the revolt against the West ultimately failed, and in the postwar period, the two countries faced the task of "reincorporation" into the liberal international order. While radical reforms have been carried out in both countries, assimilation into the international order has not been complete. Each time, a period of "liberalization" and "opening up to the West" has been followed by a period of "nativist" intellectual reaction. In both Japan and Russia, we may discern two such cycles of assimilation-indigenization. Obviously, however, nationalism in Japan and Russia developed in a quite different manner, reflecting the contrast in the domestic and international conditions of the two countries. These differences, in turn, derived from the consequences of World War II. I will compare below the cycles of assimilation and indigenization first, and then the ideological contents of *nihonjinron* and *russkaia ideia.*

Two Cycles in the Politics of National Identity

Japan, Cycle One (1945–91). In Japan, defeat in World War II initiated a period of radical liberalization under the allied occupation. During the first three years of its rule, the occupation authorities pursued the goal of radical demilitarization and democratization. Since the *kokutai* ideology had led the nation into abject defeat and material hardships, the new ideals of "peace and democracy" were accepted as eagerly as Hershey's chocolates and other relief goods. Although the beginning of the cold war led to a conservative turn in occupation policy, the intellectual dominance of the "democratic enlightenment" continued for about 15 years. Since Japanese nationalism became closely bound up with the discredited militarism, traditional Japanese culture came under an all-out attack by leading "progressive intellectuals," such as Maruyama Masao, Otsuka Hisao, and Kawashima Takeyoshi. While the occupation forces had signed the death warrant for the *kokutai* ideology, these liberal intellectuals felt that this was not enough. In alliance with Marxists, they called for a veritable "cultural revolution" in Japan.[23]

This aroused a vigorous reaction on the part of the conservatives. Japanese politics in the early post-occupation period was characterized by a series of highly ideologized confrontations, pitting the progressives, who sought to complete the "democratic revolution," against the restorationists, who sought to reverse at least part of the postwar reforms. The struggle came to a head in the Anpo crisis of 1960. While the progressive camp failed to prevent the renewal of the U.S.-Japan Security Treaty, the restorationists realized that their agenda did not enjoy the support of the public. The end result was a defeat for both the progressives and the restorationists, and the rise of a moderate conservative tendency. Unlike the restorationists, the "moderate" conservatives accepted the basic framework of the postwar constitutional order, and instead focused on economic growth. The Ikeda cabinet, with its low profile ideological posture and its Income Doubling Plan, epitomized the victory of moderate conservatism.

The "progressive camp" of the 1945–60 period was in fact an alliance of liberal and Marxist intellectuals and a broad segment of the public, which was weary of war and self-sacrifice, and which appreciated the democratizing reforms of the postwar period. While the intellectuals and the broader public were united in their support of postwar reforms, the radical goal of cultural revolution was not shared by the public. When the Japanese economy entered a period of rapid growth, the public became less concerned with the ideological and political agenda of the progressives, with the important exception of pacifism. In this new environment, the progressive intellectuals' persistent attack on the "feudal, backward character" of Japanese society became both less convincing and more irritating.[24] The stage was thus set for the emergence of *nihonjinron*. From the 1960s, the discourse on Japan's national character began to flourish, and a narrow stream of publications turned into a massive torrent, containing some well-known best-sellers.[25]

In the 1960–91 period, moderate conservatism defined the framework for Japanese politics, and *nihonjinron* provided a tacit ideological support for this framework. Initially, *nihonjinron* was not a deliberate ideology. Japan's postwar consensus on economic growth was an expression of cultural self-effacement of a nation faced with the discrediting of its traditional culture. The rise of *nihonjinron* came only after economic growth restored the self-confidence of the Japanese in their cultural traditions. However, once it emerged, *nihonjinron* was quickly picked up by the conservatives in support of their position. The celebration of the centennial of the Meiji Restoration in 1968 is a clear example. After a period of crisis surrounding the two oil shocks, the self-confidence of the Japanese people in their nation reached its peak in the 1980s, when Japan emerged as an economic superpower. Prime Minister Nakasone was particularly active in appealing to the Japanese sense of national pride.[26] In the second half of the 1980s, elements of *ni-*

honjinron influenced the thinking of business leaders, politicians, and scholars far beyond Japan's borders.

Russia, Cycle One (1953–85). Russia's postwar history is very different from Japan's. The victory in World War II led to consolidation of the revolt against the West, and the Soviet xenophobia reached its peak in the final years of Stalin's rule. The first postwar cycle of assimilation-indigenization started with the death of Stalin. Khrushchev's "secret speech" at the Twentieth CPSU Congress in 1956 initiated a period of liberalization, which lasted until the mid-1960s. The extent of liberalization under Khrushchev was of course limited, and one can hardly speak of assimilation into the liberal international order. Nonetheless, intellectually, the 1956–66 period was characterized by the proliferation of relatively liberal, universalistic ideas.[27] This period was also similar to Japan's 1945–60 era in its neglect and attack on national cultural traditions. During this period, Khrushchev's antireligious campaign led to the closure and physical destruction of a number of churches.[28] As in postwar Japan, intellectuals became a major protagonist for the cause of liberalization. However, their relationship with the political establishment was quite different. While progressive intellectuals in Japan sought to organize a mass movement for democratic change, Soviet intellectuals did not have this option. Instead, they sought to "enlighten" the political leaders and the people around them.[29]

Since liberal Soviet intellectuals hoped to bring about social change by influencing political leaders, the ouster of Khrushchev was a major blow for their cause. The Siniavskii-Daniel' trial of 1966 marked the beginning of confrontation between the intellectuals and the regime. The Prague Spring of 1968 was a traumatic event for the progressive intellectuals, for it showed that the revolution was not only sick, but was dead for all practical purposes.[30] By the end of the 1960s, the liberals had been either silenced or forced to go underground. As the liberals retreated, Russophiles gathered forces. The destruction of churches and other cultural monuments under Khrushchev galvanized the Russophiles, and by the mid-1960s, several important Russophile movements emerged.[31] Having crushed the democratic movement, the regime turned against the "excesses" of Russophilism in the mid-1970s. By that time, however, Russophiles had made a significant impact on the Soviet intellectual scene through both legal and *samizdat* publications.

Moreover, the attitude of the regime toward Russophilism was not entirely hostile. Some nationalists were tolerated, and continued to publish legally in newspapers (especially *Sovetskaia Rossiia*) and journals (*Molodaia gvardiia, Nash sovremennik,* etc.). From the mid-1970s to 1985, one part of the Russophiles led an underground existence, while another part enjoyed a cozy symbiosis with the regime. However, not all was well with the regime. While Khrushchev fervently believed in Leninism, after the Prague Spring it became difficult even for Party elites to take the ideals of communism seriously. The regime's uneasy symbiosis with nationalism and the spreading corruption were symptomatic of the creeping ideological crisis of the regime. Furthermore, the policy of counterreform proved to be self-defeating. By the early–1980s, the Soviet system found itself in a deep crisis.

Russia, Cycle Two (1985-). The second cycle of liberalization, initiated by Gorbachev, went much further than the first, both due to the systemic nature of the crisis, and due to the recognition of the bankruptcy of communism. The 1987–92 period may be characterized as a period of "liberal-democratic enlightenment." Liberal intellectuals again stepped into the political limelight. Starting from an assault on the crimes of Stalinism, liberal intellectuals proceeded to criticisms of Lenin and Marx. Nor did they stop there. Liberals such as Yurii Afanas'ev and Leonid Batkin, much like Japan's postwar progressives, found the roots of Russia's problems in deep-seated historical traditions, which they assessed in starkly negative terms.[32] During this second cycle, however, liberalizing reforms acquired a social basis going far beyond the intellectuals; the masses and the political leaders themselves played crucial roles in the political process. A broad coalition of liberal intellectuals, reformist politicians, and masses catapulted liberals led by Yeltsin to a position of power. In postwar Japan, the radical reforms were carried out by the Occupation authorities, while the conservative Japanese government accepted them. In Russia, by contrast, liberals themselves came to power and carried out radical economic reforms, hoping to transform Russia into a "normal, civilized country" in a matter of months. The first half of 1992 may be regarded as the culmination of liberal enlightenment.

However, the perestroika years also witnessed the mobilization of conservative Russophiles. The general liberalization of public life allowed Russophiles to organize and to spread their influence.[33] Liberals' criticism of Russian history and culture irritated the sentiments of Russophiles.[34] From 1987 onward, a multitude of Russophile organizations of different stripes began to appear. At the intellectual level, too, a revival boom of long-suppressed works by prerevolutionary and émigré Russian thinkers took place, and *russkaia ideia* reentered Russian intellectual and political discourse.[35] In Russia during cycle two, the mobilization and resurgence of traditional nationalism took place much more quickly than was the case in postwar Japan. One reason for the relatively quick mobilization of conservative nationalists has to do with the fact that in Russia, traditional nationalism was not as discredited as it was in postwar Japan. Because of the ambiguity in the relationship between Leninism and Russian nationalism, Russophiles could shrug off Leninism as a "Western" disease that infected innocent Russia in 1917. Yet, on the other hand, the resurgence of nationalist forces gained momentum from the fusion of communism and nationalism. Faced with the rising tide of liberalism and of separatist nationalism in the union republics, conservative communists moved closer to the Russophiles, seeking an alternative legitimating ideology in Soviet-Russian nationalism. Also, as the communist regime weakened, Russophiles shed off their oppositional character, and increasingly focused on opposing the liberals and separatists.

In the perestroika years, the rise of conservative nationalism was dwarfed by the upsurge of liberal Westernizers. However, the dominance of liberal Westernizers lasted only a few years beyond the collapse of the USSR. The quick dissipation of the reformist impulse may be attributed to two factors. First, the economic difficulties that accompanied the reform were blamed on the liberals, and this undermined mass support for the liberal reforms. This was in sharp contrast to postwar Japan, where the material hardships were associated with the last years of the war. Second, the cause of liberal reformism was from the start tainted by the loss of the empire. After the December 1993 Duma elections, most political forces, including Yeltsin himself, moved "rightward" and appropriated for themselves much of the rhetoric originally brought into currency by the conservative nationalists. This does not necessarily imply that the political program of the "national patriots" enjoys wide support among the population. But it seems clear that by the mid-1990s Russia entered a new period of searching for a distinctively Russian solution to the problems she faced. In 1995, a programmatic statement of the pro-Communist "Spiritual Heritage" movement predicted that "from now on the struggle among various political forces to claim for themselves the most precise and true expression of *russkaia ideia* will become the most important element in the struggle for power in Russia."[36] They were not off the mark. In July 1996, Yeltsin himself appointed a commission to create a "Russian national idea" that could serve as an integrative force for the country.[37]

Japan, Cycle Two, (1991-). In the second half of the 1980s, the Japanese seemed to be confident of their "unique" culture as never before in modern history. Having achieved the status of an economic superpower, it seemed that Japan had solved once and for all the problem of national identity that had vexed her throughout modern history. Japan's mounting trade surplus and financial power seemed to augur a new age in which Japan could play a leading, or even a hegemonic, role in the global economy. In retrospect, however, the talk of Japanese hegemony proved to have been as overblown as Japan's asset markets. The collapse of the latter in 1991 initiated a new period of economic malaise and intellectual self-doubt.[38] *Nihonjinron* is in retreat, and, once again, calls are being made to transform the Japanese society in a liberal direction. This time, however, the keynote of reform has been the themes of market and antibureaucratism, rather than an abstract ideal of democracy and "subjectivity." This time, the crusade for liberalization is led by business leaders and technical specialists (economists and some political scientists) rather than by philosophically oriented intellectuals. As of this writing, Japanese public discourse seems to be dominated by the themes of "liberalization." If there will be another period of "reaction" and "indigenization," the period has not begun, nor do we know what it will look like.

Nihonjinron and *Russkaia Ideia* Compared

Both *nihonjinron* and *russkaia ideia* are particularist national ideologies that arose in the context of Western dominance. As such, both purport to show the "uniqueness" and even superiority of native culture. Both ideologies have been constructed in part as an antithesis to "materialistic rationalistic individualism" of the West.

Thus, they share some basic claims about the distinctiveness of the nation. First, concerning the relationship between humans and the natural environment, both Japanese and Russian authors have claimed that their culture places a higher value on "living in harmony with nature" than does Western civilization.[39] Second, concerning the principles of social organization, both *nihonjinron* and *russkaia ideia* emphasize the centrality of a distinctive brand of collectivism.[40] Third, with respect to religious-philosophical culture, both Japanese and Russian authors have contrasted the nonrational, nonlogical mode of thinking characteristic of their nation with Western rationalism. However, despite these similarities, there are important differences between contemporary *nihonjinron* and *russkaia ideia,* concerning their external orientations, modes of discourse, and relationship with the state. These differences derive from the external and domestic conditions of the two countries, and from historical contingencies.

As explained above, nationalists in modern Japan have defined the identity of their country in a triadic context, and they most often resorted to the strategy of "exit from Asia, entry into Europe." In the interwar period, frustrated nationalist sentiments, coupled with fragmentary domestic political dynamics, propelled Japan onto a collision course with the West, and Japan's national ideology turned against the West. However, after World War II, military expansionism became totally delegitimized in Japan, and this removed a major source of conflict between Japan and the West. Also, the expansion of communist power to Eastern Europe and to China redefined the boundaries of the "East" and "West," and Japan was incorporated into the "Western," "free" world. As Japan remained the single successful case of economic modernization in Asia, it seemed to "exit" from Asia both politically (capitalism rather than communism) and economically (rich rather than poor).[41] The pro-American foreign policy of the moderate conservatives was in effect a rerun of the old scenario of *datsu-a nyu-o.* Like the Meiji and Taisho theorists of "fusion of Eastern and Western civilizations," postwar *nihonjinron* authors took pride in Japan's modernization, rather than boasting of having built a civilization separate from and hostile to the West. In other words, *nihonjinron* was a particularist icing on the cake of "successful modernization."

By contrast, Russian national identity continued to be defined during the Soviet period in the context of the dyad of Russia and the

West. Indeed, the victory of Marxism-Leninism deepened the gulf between the two, and soured Russian attitudes toward the West. True, some Russophiles won admirers in the West by courageously resisting the Soviet system. However, from the start, the oppositional stance of the Russophiles coexisted with a degree of mistrust of the West, which intensified in the years of perestroika and liberal reforms. Today, Russians must define the identity of their nation in a context more troublesome than in the nineteenth century. If nineteenth-century Russians suffered from an inferiority complex vis-à-vis the West, they were quite certain of their superiority vis-à-vis Asia. Today, Russia has been outstripped economically by some of her Asian neighbors. While there are advocates of moderate Russophilism such as the academician Dmitrii Likhachev, anti-Western "national patriots" speak with a much louder voice in contemporary Russia.

Nationalism is defined not only by its external orientation, but also by domestic cultural traditions. Postwar nationalists in Japan and Russia faced the difficult task of defining the distinctiveness of the nation at a time when institutions central to the nation's traditional identity were either lost or severely challenged. In Japan, the war had discredited the official nationalism, which focused on the emperor, and which was based on a mythological worldview. Other building blocks of traditional national identity (rural communities and traditional families), too, had disappeared due to postwar reforms and economic growth. Postwar *nihonjinron* authors responded to this challenge by shifting the focus of attention from concrete institutions to value orientations that supposedly persist among the Japanese people, and by constructing a quasi-scientific discourse on this basis.[42] Another important effect of the war was the total discrediting of militarism. In sharp contrast to prewar Japanese nationalists, most *nihonjinron* authors have shied away from advancing positive political programs.

In Russia, too, many of the traditional building blocks of national identity had been lost by the 1960s. Gone was the Romanov family and so were the peasant communes. As the only remaining pillar of traditional nationalism, the Orthodox Church has become a major focus of contemporary Russian nationalism. However, the Church's subservience to the state has made the institution suspect in the eyes of more spiritually inclined nationalists. Less tainted than the Orthodox Church was the religious-philosophical discourse on

Russia's destiny and her world-historical mission, which was launched by the Slavophiles. This tradition, based on a romantic-idealist worldview, was the core of nonofficial Russian nationalism in the nineteenth century.[43] The impact of this tradition has been so profound that, even today, discussion on Russia's national ideology is dominated by a religious-philosophical discourse. While *nihonjinron* authors have sought to justify their claims by empirical evidence (with varying degrees of sloppiness), discussion of the distinctiveness of the Russian nation has largely remained on the level of philosophy of history.[44] Romantic-idealist philosophy may lift up our minds, but it is unlikely to be useful for dealing with practical issues of politics and economy. While pledging allegiance to the values of Russian religious philosophy, contemporary Russophiles seem to base their political programs on a combination of great power politics (which was never quite discredited in Russia), protectionist economic policy, and some vague reference to socialist ideals, such as "power to the people." Hence, contemporary *russkaia ideia* shows a curious combination of romantic nationalism and *Machtpolitik,* a pattern often associated with prewar German nationalism.

Comparison between *nihonjinron* during Japan's "cycle one" and *russkaia ideia* in Russia's "cycle two" shows that *russkaia ideia* has been a more troubled national ideology than *nihonjinron* has been. The explicit power-political orientation of many Russian nationalists certainly makes *russkaia ideia* more worrisome to the outside world than a bout of narcissism caused by economic success. In domestic politics, too, *russkaia ideia* faces a bigger immediate challenge than does *nihonjinron.* While ethnic Russians occupy a numerically more dominant position (85 percent) in the Russian Federation than they used to in the USSR, the ethnic diversity of Russia makes the parochial national ideologies politically more dangerous than in Japan. Liberal forces within Russia have searched for a more civic definition of Russian idea—*rossiiskaia ideia,* rather than ethnic *russkaia ideia.* So far, however, liberal ideals have not been able to surround their rationalistic reasoning with a mythology that could appeal to the emotions of the people.

Yet, *nihonjinron* is by no means trouble-free. Due to a long history of isolation, Japanese discourse on national character still seems to suffer from excessive parochialism and antilogicism.[45] Also, one might as well ask if *nihonjinron* would also take an anti-Western turn if it reemerges in the near future. To the extent that

Japan's membership in the Western world was based on the communist-capitalist division, the collapse of communism weakens Japan's ties to the West. Also, economic development of East and Southeast Asia has made Japan's "exit" from the region less obvious. To a certain extent, the triadic context in which the Japanese have defined their national identity is changing. So far, the Japanese government has shown no sign of heeding the Malaysian leader Mahatir Mohamad's call to "return to Asia." Given Japan's dependence on trade with countries outside the Asian region, "turning away from the West" or "return to Asia" would be a senseless policy with prohibitive costs. Nonetheless, the possibility cannot be excluded that increased friction in Japanese-Western relations will add a dash of bitterness to Japan's national ideology.

Liberalism and Nationalism after the Cold War

I wish to conclude this essay by going back to the question raised at the outset: What are the theoretical and practical significance of *nihonjinron* and *russkaia ideia?* Given the unprecedented influence and authority of liberalism in the post–cold war world, the resurgence and persistence of collectivist national ideologies such as *nihonjinron* and *russkaia ideia* may seem puzzling. From the liberal point of view, it is tempting for reformers in Japan and Russia and for their friends abroad to theoretically dismiss these ideologies as intellectually vacuous "atavisms" that are attributable either to the "backward" cultures of particular countries, or to the cynical machinations of minority elites. If so, the prescription is clear: to create a liberal individual capitalist order by breaking the grip of illiberal cultures and institutions, and to build a truly "rationalized" world on a global scale.

However, Japanese and Russian history in the postwar era seems to suggest the practical futility of such an approach. While there is an increasing consensus that some sort of liberalism should be the basis of a viable international order, a unitary understanding of liberalism may well prove to be self-defeating. Moreover, uncritical assumption of global applicability of liberal individual capitalism contains a dangerous theoretical trap, which has to do with the fundamental contradiction between liberalism and the nation-state. Liberalism requires that individuals be treated on the basis of their personal merits. By contrast, nation-states (be they constituted according to civic or ethnic principles) treat individuals differently on the basis of their citizenship. Truly individualistic liberalism can only be cosmopolitan, and any nation-state, however liberal its national ideology, is of necessity parochial. In a world divided into nation-states, even universalistic doctrines can easily degenerate into self-righteous collective ideologies that shore up the pride to the members of the collectivity and deny it to outsiders. To make matters worse, even messages with genuinely cosmopolitan intent are often interpreted by the recipients through the prism of national parochialism. Cosmopolitanism is a lofty ideal, but it is an ideal unlikely to be realized in the foreseeable future. The revolutionary developments in global communication networks have not restored the humanity to the condition of unity before the Tower of Babel. For better or worse, the humanity remains divided into different national communities bound together by the emotional force of collective identities. So long as this is the case, we have no choice but to muddle through, accepting the existence of a multitude of national ideologies, and attempting to find and increase the areas of common understanding among them.

Yet, if the liberal individualist crusade has its pitfalls, the dangers of openly collectivist nationalism could be even greater. Nations are intractable things. Once formed, they demand self-government, and often prefer foolish and inept self-government to wise and efficient foreign rule. While this in itself may be an expression of the human search for dignity, the history of Japan and Russia alone provides enough evidence of how the search for national dignity can lead to tragic political consequences, especially when national collectivism is not counterbalanced by meaningful guarantees of individual freedom. One cannot deny that each nation (and each cultural subgroup within the nation) has its own cultural distinctiveness. However, lopsided insistence on the "uniqueness" of the nation serves no purpose except vainglory, and it is likely to be counter productive not only from the point of view of practical interests, but also from the point of view of dignity of the nation. Proponents of *nihonjinron* and of *russkaia ideia* should make far more effort to formulate and express their ideas in a way that is less parochial and more comprehensible to the outside world.

One possible way to overcome the parochial features of national ideologies and to turn them into a broader and more accessible discourse is through comparisons. In this regard, a comparative analysis of *nihonjinron* and *russkaia ideia* is more than a matter of purely academic interest. Such an exercise may in fact be essential, if we do not wish national ideologies to become contagious emotional pollutants that add toxic fume to the already overpolluted atmosphere of international life.

NOTES

1. Few good general works on postwar Japanese intellectual history exist as yet. Among them are Najita Tetsuo, et al., eds., *Sengo Nihon no seishinshi: sono saikento* (Tokyo: Iwanami, 1989); Takabatake Michitoshi, *Toron sengo Nihon no seiji shiso* (Tokyo: San'ichi shobo, 1977).
2. For surveys of *nihonjinron,* see Yoshino Kosaku, *Cultural Nationalism in Contemporary Japan* (New York: Routledge, 1992); Minami Hiroshi, *Nihonjinron no Keifu* (Tokyo: Kodansha, 1980); For critical assessments of *nihonjinron,* see Tessa Morris-Suzuki, "The Invention and Reinvention of 'Japanese Culture,'" *The Journal of Asian Studies,* Vol. 54, No. 3, (August 1995), pp. 759–80; Befu Harumi, *Zoho ideorogi to shite no Nihon bunkaron* (Tokyo: Shiso no kagaku sha, 1987); Peter Dale, *The Myth of Japanese Uniqueness* (New York: St. Martin's Press, 1986).
3. For an excellent analysis of Russian (or Russified) Soviet intellectuals in the post-Stalin period and of various intellectual currents, see Vladimir Shlapentokh, *Soviet Intellectuals and Political Power: The Post-Stalin Era* (Princeton, NJ: Princeton University Press, 1990). See also Boris Kagarlitsky, *The Thinking Reed: Intellectuals and the Soviet State from 1917 to the Present* (London: Verso, 1988).
4. For the emergence and development of Russophilism since the mid-1960s, see Shlapentokh, *op. cit.;* John Dunlop, *The Face of Contemporary Russian Nationalism* (Princeton, NJ: Princeton University Press, 1983); *idem, The Rise of Russia and the Fall of the Soviet Empire* (Princeton, NJ: Princeton University Press, 1993); Alexander Yanov, *The Russian Challenge and the Year 2000* (Oxford: Basil Blackwell, 1987); Walter Laqueur, *Black Hundred: The Rise of the Extreme Right in Russia* (New York: Harper Collins, 1993); James P. Scanlan, "Interpretations and Uses of Slavophilism in Recent Russian Thought," in Scanlan, ed., *Russian Thought after Communism* (Armonk, NY: M.E. Sharpe, 1994), pp. 31–61; Tim McDaniel, *The Agony of the Russian Idea* (Princeton, NJ: Princeton University Press, 1996).

5. Cyril Black, et al., *The Modernization of Japan and Russia* (New York: The Free Press, 1975).
6. The discussion on the basis of "collective ideologies" cannot be fully developed in this essay. For a more extended discussion, see Anno Tadashi, "Collective Identity as 'Emotional Investment Portfolio': An Economic Analogy to a Psychological Process," in Rudra Sil and Eileen Doherty, eds., *Beyond Boundaries?: Disciplines, Paradigms, and Theoretical Integration in International Studies* (Albany: SUNY Press, 2000).
7. This was a central function of what Robert Bellah has called "primitive" and "archaic" religions—religions before the advent of "historic" religions, such as Buddhism, Christianity, and Islam. In primitive and archaic religions (such as Shintoism), the unit of salvation was not individual persons, but collectivities, such as families, tribes, or peoples. The revolutionary significance of "historic" religions was that they opened up the way for personal salvation not confined to any particular group. See Bellah, *Beyond Belief: Essays on Religion in a Post-Traditional World* (New York: Harper & Row, 1970), pp. 20–50.
8. For an excellent comparison of Chinese influence on Japan and Byzantine influence on Russia, see Marius Jansen, "On Foreign Borrowing," in Albert M. Craig, ed., *Japan: A Comparative View* (Princeton, NJ: Princeton University Press, 1979), pp. 18–48.
9. In Russia, the theory of the "Third Rome" and the notion of "Holy Russia" represented the imperial and popular strands of national ideology. One can observe a similar dichotomy between imperial mythology (*kokutairon,* or "theory of national polity") and a discourse focusing on distinctively Japanese cultural sensibilities.
10. See Michael Cherniavsky, *Tsar and People: Studies in Russian Myths* (New Haven, CT: Yale University Press, 1961). It is true that the close linkage between Russian nationalism and Orthodoxy has transformed the latter into a rather parochial, "national" religion. Nonetheless, it is also true that the intrinsically universal characteristic of Orthodox Christianity has given a universalistic bent to Russian nationalism.
11. *Kojiki* (or Chronicles of Ancient Times), edited in 712, is the earliest existing text of Japanese imperial mythology, which held that the emperors are the descendants of the Sun-Goddess. Buddhist monks attempted in the eighth and early ninth centuries to devalue native deities in comparison with Buddha. However, by the mid-ninth century, they made a compromise with Shintoism by arguing that Shinto deities are "manifestations" of Buddha and other Buddhist deities in Japan. This theory of "body and manifestation" (*honji suijaku*) has

allowed Buddhism and Shintoism to coexist peacefully. See Kasahara Kazuo, ed., *Nihon shukyoshi,* Vol. 1 (Tokyo: Yamakawa, 1977), pp. 144–50.

12. Motoori Norinaga, the greatest of the National Learning scholars, pointed to aversion to logos and to verbalism (*kotoage*) as a central feature of the "Japanese way." Contemporary theorists of *nihonjinron* often argue that the Japanese have an extraordinary ability to communicate nonverbally among themselves (*haragei,* or *ishin denshin*).
13. Since Japan was on the periphery of the Chinese World Order, Japanese elites of the Tokugawa period were less committed to the "great tradition" of Confucian China than were elites of Qing China or Yi dynasty Korea. For this reason, it was relatively easy for Japanese elites to shift their "model civilization" from China to the West. On this point, see Sato Seizaburo, "Response to the West: Korean and Japanese Patterns," in Albert Craig ed., *op. cit.* (fn. 8), pp. 105–29.
14. Russian elites of the nineteenth century did have a sense of superiority vis-à-vis the Asians, and they occasionally resorted to the same compensatory strategy. However, in general, Asia was not a valid point of reference. As the Populist V. P. Vorontsov explained, "Russia belongs to the family of civilized nations. . . . This means that her needs and the forms of their fulfillment are measured not against her own backward culture, but with those forms which Western Europe developed and put into practice." See Vorontsov, *Sud'ba kapitalisticheskoi Rossii* (St. Petersburg: M. M. Stasiulevich, 1907), p. 194.
15. Since Russian nationalists wanted their country to be recognized by the West, they typically appropriated ideas and principles developed in the West (such as "freedom" and "progress"), and insisted that those ideas were realized in Russia better than in the West. Thus, even in revolt, Russians wanted to "join" the West and be recognized as part of "civilized" Europe. The Bolshevik Revolution was in a sense a culmination of the development of this theme of "Russia as the truer West." However, the defeat of revolution in Europe dashed the Bolsheviks' hope to construct a socialist "common home of Europe," and thus widened the psychological distance between Russia and Europe. It is interesting to note that the first collection of articles published in 1921 by the "Eurasianist" émigré intellectuals was entitled *Iskhod k vostoku,* or "exit to the east," an exact opposite of *datsu-a nyu-o.*
16. On the "family-state" ideology, see Richard Minear, *Japanese Tradition and Western Law: Emperor, State and Law in the Thought of Hozumi Yatsuka* (Cambridge, MA: Harvard University Press, 1970).

On "Official Nationality," see Nicholas V. Riasanovsky, *Nicholas I and Official Nationality in Russia, 1825–1855* (Berkeley, CA: University of California Press, 1959).

17. Nicholas V. Riasanovsky, *A Parting of Ways: Government and the Educated Public in Russia, 1801–1855* (Oxford: Oxford University Press, 1976); Liah Greenfeld, *Nationalism: Five Roads to Modernity* (Cambridge, MA: Harvard University Press, 1992).
18. Certainly, there was no shortage of critics of the theory of liberal progress. However, in the late nineteenth century, the dominance of the West was so incontestable that criticisms tended to take defensive-particularistic forms. That is to say, critics maintained that the theory of liberal progress was not applicable to their own country, without challenging the structure of the international order. Examples include the notions of *Sonderweg* (original path) in Germany, *samobytnost'* (originality) in Russia, and *wakon yosai* (Japanese spirit, Western learning) in Japan. Even open critics of the existing international order (e.g., socialists) did not question that any changes to the international order must be brought about by the "leading" nations of Europe.
19. For a broad comparative discussion of this phenomenon, see Geoffrey Barraclough, *An Introduction to Contemporary History* (Hammondsworth: Penguin, 1964), pp. 153–98.
20. For a "nationalist" interpretation of Leninism, see Mikhail Agursky, *The Third Rome: National Bolshevism in the USSR* (Boulder: Westview, 1987).
21. Kuno Osamu and Tsurumi Shunsuke, *Gendai Nihon no shiso: sono itsutsu no uzu* (Tokyo: Iwanami, 1956), pp. 132–34.
22. "Joining" of new nations into the "Co-Prosperity Sphere" was explained as an "adoption" of children into a family headed by the emperor. See Gordon M. Berger, "Ajia shin-chitsujo no yume," in Sato Seizaburo and Roger Dingman, eds., *Kindai Nihon no taigai taido* (Tokyo: University of Tokyo Press, 1974), p. 212.
23. The historian of political thought Maruyama Masao kicked off the discussion with his incisive analysis of the *kokutai* ideology, "The Logic and Psychology of Ultranationalism," (*Sekai,* May 1946). The economic historian Otsuka Hisao called for a Japanese equivalent of the Reformation (which he considered a precondition for the establishment of a real "civil society") in his "Moral Bases for Modernization" (1948). The jurist Kawashima Takeyoshi subjected the "familial structure of Japanese society" to harsh criticism in a book of that title (Tokyo: Gakuseisha, 1948).
24. For a more detailed discussion of this process, see Aida Yuji, *Nihonjin no ishiki kozo: fudo, rekishi, shakai* (Tokyo: Kodansha, 1972),

pp. 181–86; Tsujimura Akira, *Sengo Nihon no taishu shinri: shimbun, seron, besutosera* (Tokyo: University of Tokyo Press, 1981).

25. Between 1946 and 1978, about 700 titles were published in the *nihonjinron* tradition. Of these, an astonishing 25 percent was published during the 1976–78 period. Peter Dale, *The Myth of Japanese Uniqueness* (New York: St. Martin's Press, 1986), p. 15.
26. Nakasone combined the theme of Japanese "uniqueness" with a call for "internationalization" and "neoliberal" economic policy.
27. Vladimir Shlapentokh identifies neo-Leninism, technocratism, and liberal socialism as the dominant ideological tendencies among Soviet intellectuals in the 1960s, and points out that all of them were universal, scientific, and Western in orientation. Shlapentokh, *op. cit.* (fn. 3), pp. 149f.
28. John Dunlop, *The Faces of Contemporary Russian Nationalism,* pp. 29–31.
29. Progressive intellectuals in the USSR were skeptical about the role of the masses in politics. Soviet history seemed to suggest that involvement of "the people" in history could engender violence, anarchy, and disorder. See Shlapentokh, *op. cit.,* pp. 164–71.
30. Boris Kagarlitsky, *The Thinking Reed,* pp. 199–201.
31. This included not only the clandestine All-Russian Christian Union for the Liberation of the People (VSKhSON), but also a multimillion-member voluntary society for the preservation of cultural monuments.
32. For Afanas'ev, Russia represented "an exhausted form of 'Eurasian civilization' which combines 'Buddhist and Byzantine Christian' elements, and which needs to be completely rejected in favor of the contemporary Western model." Dunlop, *The Rise of Russia,* p. 114. More recently, Egor Gaidar has made a similarly negative assessment of Russian history, emphasizing the lack of private property and despotic character of governance as persistent features of Russian history. See Gaidar, *Gosudarstvo i evoliutsiia* (Moscow: Evraziia, 1995).
33. To some extent, Gorbachev had to co-opt the "liberal" segment of Russophiles to prevent his conservative opponents (such as Egor Ligachev) from playing the Russophile card. See John Dunlop, *The Rise of Russia,* p. 14.
34. In a manner reminiscent of postwar Japanese nationalists, Aleksandr Prokhanov complained about liberals' attacks on Russia and things Russian. "Efforts are being made," lamented Prokhanov, "to instill an inferiority complex in Russians . . . a rigged trial is being staged of Russian history and the Russian character." Prokhanov, "The Tragedy of Centralism," in Alexander Dallin and Gail Lapidus, eds., *The Soviet System in Crisis* (Boulder: Westview, 1991), p. 348.

35. Robin Aizlewood, "The Return of the 'Russian Idea' in Publications, 1988–91," *Slavonic and East European Review,* Vol. 71, No. 3 (July 1993), pp. 490–99.
36. *Sovremennaia russkaia ideia i gosudarstvo* (Moscow: Obozrevatel', 1995), p. 42.
37. After a year of deliberation, the commission produced a rather nebulous report that failed to provide a positive definition of the Russian (*rossiiskaia*) national idea. Yeltsin has apparently instructed a separate group of "experts in different structures of power, including the Presidential Administration and the government, and independent experts in political sciences" to work on "a new ideological program for the country's development" (reported by Interfax, September 23, 1997).
38. In addition to economic malaise, another factor undermining the post-1960 synthesis was the withdrawal of tacit U.S. support for LDP rule. It will be recalled that radical reformism in postwar Japan was frustrated by the conservative turn in U.S. occupation policy, which was a direct response to the cold war. With the end of the cold war, and with the mounting economic frictions between the two countries, U.S. policy turned visibly against the moderate-conservative position of the LDP. Under this new condition, pro-American foreign policy and conservatism on domestic sociocultural issues came to conflict with each other.
39. See, for instance, Ito Shuntaro, *Hikaku bunmei to Nihon* (Tokyo: Chuo koron, 1990); O. D. Kurakina, *Russkii kosmizm kak sotsiokul'turnyi fenomen* (Moscow: Moskovskii fiziko-tekhnicheskii institut, 1993).
40. Russian nationalists from Slavophiles onward have routinely referred to the Orthodox principle of *sobornost'* (conciliarity) as a distinct organizing principle characteristic of the Russian society, integrating individual freedom with collective harmony. *Nihonjinron* authors, too, have emphasized the theme of "collectivism" in various guises. According to the influential view of Hamaguchi Esyun, the principle of *kanjin-shugi* (contextualism) underlies the mode of human relations in Japan. In his view, Japanese sense of "personhood" is not defined in terms of an unchanging and self-contained "individual," but with respect to each specific context. Hamaguchi Eshun and Kumon Shumpei, eds., *Nihonteki shudan shugi* (Tokyo: Yuhikaku, 1982).
41. Sato Seizaburo, "Bakumatsu Meiji shoki ni okeru taigai ishiki no sho-ruikei," in Sato and Dingman, eds., *Kindai Nihon no taigai taido,* p. 30.
42. Precursors of quasi-scientific discourses on the distinctiveness of Japan in the prewar era include Watsuji Tetsuro, who pioneered the

literature on geographic and climatic influence on Japanese culture known as *fudoron,* and Nishida Kitaro, a philosopher whose synthesis of German idealism and Zen Buddhism has influenced many *nihonjinron* authors.

43. In fact, the term *russkaia ideia* usually refers to this discursive tradition.
44. Exceptions to this generalization include Kasianova's study of Russian national character, and the study by Sushchii and Druzhinin of geographical influence on Russian culture, which is reminiscent of Japanese *fudoron.* See Kseniia Kasianova, *O russkom natsional'nom kharaktere* (Moscow: Institut natsional'noi modeli ekonomiki, 1994); S. Ia. Sushchii and A. G. Druzhinin, *Ocherki geografii russkoi kul'tury* (Rostov-na-Donu: Izdatel'stvo "SKNTs VSh," 1994). As in Japan, this more empirical discourse on "national character" has precursors. For instance, Lev Mechnikov advanced interesting ideas about the influence of geographical and climatic factors on Russian culture, which became a central theme of the theorists of Eurasianism in the 1920s. The famous émigré sociologist Pitirim Sorokin did a series of studies of the Russian national character in a manner similar to many *nihonjinron* authors. Some of these are collected in Sorokin, *O russkoi natsii—Rossiia i Amerika—Teoriia natsional'nogo voprosa* (Moscow: AKIRN, 1994).
45. Murakami Yasusuke has contrasted the "hermeneutic" mode of thinking in Japan with the "transcendental" thinking of those cultures that were more profoundly influenced by "historic religions." In Murakami's view, this hermeneutic mode of thinking is better suited for mutual understanding of cultures than Western conceptions of "transcendental justice." Whatever the merits of Murakami's critique of transcendental justice, it seems evident that the Japanese version of hermeneutic thinking must undergo a significant redefinition if it is to serve as a medium of cross-cultural understanding. See Murakami, *An Anti-Classical Political-Economic Analysis: A Vision for the Next Century* (Stanford, CA: Stanford University Press, 1996), chapter 12.

CHAPTER 18

Japan and Russia: Great Power Ambitions and Domestic Capacities

Gilbert Rozman

JAPAN AND RUSSIA ARE GREAT POWERS WITH UNBALANCED standing in the world order and an unfulfilled quest to return to "normalcy." This quest embraces two goals: to make domestic adjustments compatible with desired global responsibilities, and to shape international relations that enhance the country's role as a balance or, if need be, a sidekick to the world's foremost power. They have shared the experience of fallen powers and now are searching for international support to boost their own standing. The two countries matter for each other in at least three ways: (1) as symbols to each other of arrogance and lack of respect for legitimate great power aspirations; (2) as complementary economies with potential to contribute to both regional and national long-term needs; and (3) as parallel cases in some respects and contrasting cases in others in the struggle to adjust national ambitions and domestic capacities to suit the new world order that is taking shape.

During the half century from 1945 to 1999, Japan and Russia faced a similar challenge: to readjust great power ambitions in line with changing state capacities, economic development needs, and international expectations. Although the exact timing differed, the basic dilemma was similar: each country overreached, made an abrupt reversal of course, and then began to search for a path to normalcy. Japan made giant strides forward in reducing excessive ambitions through a spurt of far-reaching reforms, but it encountered renewed problems in the 1990s both in normalizing its global ambitions and in shrinking its state regulation in order to reignite economic dynamism. In contrast, Russia procrastinated each time that reforms rose to the fore until in the late 1980s and 1990s a monumental task loomed before it. Before long it was left with the remains of a shattered state in abject decline while grasping for "normal" power politics. The long-term need for these great powers, which simultaneously started in the 1860s rushing to catch up and were anxious to do so again, to align their international and domestic policies, bore striking similarities. Comparisons demonstrate both common patterns and different outcomes.

Comparisons of Japan and Russia have lost what little popularity they had. Japan presents a success story of management efficiency, family stability, and state harmony. Russia has fallen into a quagmire of enterprise incompetence, family breakdown, and civil disorder. Japanese have lost any interest in borrowing from Russia, a nation viewed negatively both for individual character and for ability to manage its own affairs and to deal with other countries in fairness and justice. Russians deem the Japanese experience too far removed from their own, expecting little from either a study of Japan's methods or a reliance on Japanese investments and multinational corporations. In defiance of these presumptions, this chapter finds value in direct comparisons of Japan and Russia as great powers in the midst of fundamental transformations in identities and social structures. This value is not, as some anticipated for a few decades after the war, to guide Japan domestically toward socialism and pacifism, and only secondarily is it, as others argued in the late 1980s and early 1990s, to suggest to Russia how it may model its own transition. The lessons to be learned serve above all social scientists interested in identifying improved ways for the great powers of the world to understand each other and to cooperate to harness a common set of forces of transformation. Because normalization of Russo-Japanese relations has been delayed by conflicting images of each other's great power standing, lessons from comparisons may build public understanding for diplomacy.

Comparisons of Japan and Russia/ the Soviet Union may be of increased value if we combine two perspectives and three periods. The perspectives are: (1) domestic social reform; and (2) worldview. The periods are: (1) the response to the collapse of the old order—in Japan from 1945 to 1952 and in Russia from 1991 to 1999; (2) the high tide of confidence in an existing model of development and world influence—in Japan from 1985 to 1992 and in Russia from 1970 to 1977; and (3) the acceleration of debate about reform—in Japan from 1993 to 1999 and in Russia from 1987 to 1991. Although comparisons may seem unwieldy because the order of periods differs in the two countries, the exact timing of the collapse should not obscure our vision of the long-term interest in reform. Moreover, if for some purposes it would make sense to treat the model of the 1930s as Japan's high tide of confidence, this paper argues that because of a shared international environment shaping reforms in the 1980s and 1990s, there are also benefits from treating both countries in the same time period. While each country has reason to look back, two of the three salient periods refer to the most recent decade. Evidence from mutual perceptions reveals, too, how in the second half of the 1990s, national identities influenced readiness to compromise necessary for a breakthrough in bilateral relations.

For analysts of comparative studies and international relations, Russia and Japan share four striking characteristics. First, they were non-Western latecomers to modernization able to accelerate economic development in the late nineteenth century and again for long periods in both the first and second halves of the twentieth centuries.[1] Second, they aspired to utilize their economic modernization to become hegemonic great powers repressing their neighbors and opponents in their own society, but with shocking suddenness found their plans dashed and then had to grapple with reemergence as "normal countries." Third, they faced the challenge of decentralization and reconstruction of social capacities from below both because of the way they attempted to catch up as latecomers and because of the transformation of global development in the information age. Fourth, they experienced a rude awakening to the fact that what only a few years earlier had been trumpeted as the supreme achievement of modern civilization was an unsustainable way of organizing even their own society. In the spectrum of societies, parallels between Japan and Russia create conditions unusually conducive to comparisons.

Japan experienced the failure of its great power ambitions and old model of domestic development in 1945. It lost its empire, suffered from a sharp fall in its economic capacity, and had to content itself with a reduced global role. Although the collapse of the Soviet Union did not come from military defeat, many of the consequences from 1991 were similar. Russia's experience in the 1990s bears many similarities to Japan's almost half a century earlier. Yet, for some purposes, one can consider Japan's efforts incomplete and point to the 1990s as a renewal of the reform process. One can also consider Russia's efforts of the 1990s as a delayed reform process that in a more balanced model of modernization and global integration would have begun approximately half a century earlier. This process remains incomplete; a long time may be required to reconcile great power ambitions to diminished state capacities. Thus, in both cases incomplete reform contributed to a revival of the reform process.

In the last decade of the twentieth century the common challenge for Japan and Russia is to channel great power aspirations into a strategy that enables the nation to compete effectively in the world. This means coping with internal conditions such as aging populations and youth materialism and external ones such as competitive science and technology and integration into an emergent Northeast Asian region. Both countries are searching to identify or define a national idea, debating decentralization as a means to stability or efficiency, questioning the balance of relations with two other great powers (the United States and China), and reexamining the relative weight of group loyalties and individualism. Of course, Japan has a record of success over many decades and Russia has yet to emerge from a massive collapse of a failed system. Comparisons must not trivialize this acute difference. The purpose of identifying both similarities and differences is to study common processes of interest to social science and international relations theory as well as to suggest ways in which one country can learn from the experience of the other and encourage mutual understanding for better relations.

The Response to the Collapse of the Old Order

In the aftermath of unconditional surrender to end a devastating war, and the collapse of the Soviet Union and the communist system to conclude a failed social experiment, eras of massive reform began. Both Japan from 1945 and Russia from 1991 faced uncertainty about what would and should be saved from the old order. For the populace as a whole, subsistence economics took priority as many became apathetic to politics.[2] Whatever purges of officials may have been initially contemplated were soon attenuated by the urgency of priorities related to economic reconstruction, social stability, and national strength in a threatening milieu.

Recovery depended heavily on the outside world led by the United States in both cases. That power encouraged economic dismantling on a scale that threatened stability. In order to put democracy on a sound footing, preference went to breaking up monopolies and stimulating small-scale businesses. But the short-term results caused much concern. The economic situation worsened and remained poor for over five years, at least until stabilization took center stage as the nation's priority. The Dodge plan in 1949–50 concentrated on austerity, just as did the Chubais tightening of government spending in 1996–97.

Another similarity was the arrogance of those who attempted to implant an alien ideology without respect for the cultural heritage of the country. Douglas MacArthur's belief in the efficacy of Christianity and in the civilizational immaturity of Japan reflected a clash of two civilizations, but even in Russia, where products of the same civilization remained in charge, faith in sweeping away the old ways did not mesh with popular psychology. The United States served as a model in many respects, while also becoming a symbol of a breakdown of authority and various abuses in the name of democracy that brought popular revulsion. It was insufficient to view Japan as a feudal society stuck in an earlier stage of history or Russia as a socialist society that had taken the wrong path, each of which could now become normal by following an enlightened foreign model at a more advanced stage. The power of freedom as an accelerant in historical transitions was overrated. Indeed, reactions against "cavalier attacks" on the old system through wholesale introduction of the Anglo-Saxon variant of a "superliberal model of a market economy" led some Russians to turn toward a Japanese, more managed type of market.[3] The need to build on an existing foundation was underestimated.

The geopolitical stakes were very high in Japan in the late 1940s as the Soviet Union was succeeding in spreading communism, including to China, and they were high in Russia in the mid-1990s as China was rising as a global power. If the Soviet Union could have benefited from the undermining of authority in Japan or if a half century later China could solidify a strategic partnership with Russia, then the United States and the West would suffer perhaps their most serious reversal of modern times. The United States came to recognize each threat and shifted course. This weakened the force of reform. In the case of Japan, conservatives shared the fear of a communist threat from the Asian mainland and from within. The Korean War consolidated this common sense of danger. Nationalism returned in league with U.S. nationalism. In Russia the threat to a diaspora under possible siege and the threat to sovereignty in Chechnya gave rise to a different focus for nationalism, driving Russia and the United States apart. But the fear of isolation had many sources: NATO expansion, Islamic fundamentalism, the rise of China, economic self-destruction, etc. The struggle to join Russia's visions of danger and salvation to the West's agenda remained unresolved in 1999, especially during the back-to-back wars of NATO in Yugoslavia and Russia in Chechnya.

Japan retained its emperor and looked back to a much earlier history in search of an authentic national identity. Russians also searched in their history for symbols of continuity and legitimacy. After three-quarters of a century of communist rule and without a symbol such as the emperor, this was a more difficult task. Three directions vied for people's attention in Russia: (1) pre-1917 history led by the Eastern Orthodox Church and state authority (*derzhavnost'*); (2) Soviet history symbolized by the Russian Communist Party that continued to entice roughly one-quarter of the population, as indicated by elections; and (3) the West as the most successful alternative in the outside world, both in the eighteenth and nineteenth centuries when it had served repeatedly as Russia's model and in recent times when it stood as Russia's rival against which it was always measured. Efforts to popularize a fourth model based on an Eastern variant of development in the late twentieth century, whether Japan, China, or a less obvious case, did not gain a large following as of 1999. Given the confusion over all choices, however, they reinforced the idea that a mixed variant is possible without succumbing to the Western model.

In retrospect, the reengineering of Japanese society after World War II is deemed successful, while that of Russian society in the 1990s remains problematic. For Japan, however, some of the success was based on temporary solutions well suited to one age but not resilient in the 1990s. And for Russia much of the initial failure can be attributed to more acute problems than in Japan, contributing to a slower and more complex transition. Some of the contrasts appear clearly in differing approaches to three common challenges: decentralization, finding a national idea, and integration with the West.

In carrying out decentralization, Japan in 1945 had a great advantage over Russia in 1992. Each country had spent three-quarters of a century under a centralized model of development and faced the necessity of strengthening local and community initiative. But during this time-frame Japan modernized with a market economy, while the Soviet Union imposed a command economy, complicating its changeover. Moreover, Japan started with a tradition of local autonomy before the 1870s, which Russia lacked before 1917 and especially before 1861. If hesitation to carry decentralization very far and the reversal of some late-1940s reforms was to catch up to Japan by the 1990s, the system that operated for four decades led to high levels of order and efficiency. In 1999, Russians continued to quarrel over the inadequate division of labor between Moscow and local administrations. There were too many of the latter, roughly twice the number as existed in Japan, which, meanwhile has been debating ideas for consolidating its prefectures.[4] Local governors could get away with criminality well beyond what fiscal and judicial authorities tolerated in Japan. Indeed, the *nomenklatura* system, by rewarding loyalty and hypocrisy more than competence, nurtured a second economy that made it easy to divert power in the course of decentralization to criminal gangs. And the dispersed geography of Russia makes cross-border integration a more essential feature of transformation than in Japan 50 years ago or even today, when it is much discussed. If the Soviet legacy of rejecting the existing world order was deeply entrenched seven decades after the Bolshevik Revolution, Japan's hostility to that order had lasted a much shorter time and could be overcome with the help of other elements of the old order that had survived. Cross-border economic ties were easier for the Japanese to embrace.

In addition to benefiting from a market economy, Japan did not have to struggle with resolving issues of nationality, rebuilding hierarchies of authority, and training dedicated professional elites. Order did not prove to be problematic. While swiftly and completely grasping the meaning of military defeat, Japanese did not have to look far for the means to advancement in the new era.

Japanese did not agree at once on a national idea to guide their country. Many gravitated toward the ideal of pacifism and neutrality. If this had prevailed, Japan would have limited its dependence on the United States and given itself more room to maneuver among the other great powers. Renunciation of war and offensive armaments, nuclear and nonnuclear alike, were seen as means to gain moral authority as an independent force. But Japan's government, big business, and conservative forces settled instead on a national idea focused on economic catch-up. The goal recalled the guiding philosophy of the Meiji era, but had narrowed to a rich country without a strong army. Once again citizens were warned of a test of Japan's national will in a dangerous international environment that required sacrifice. In this context, as Haruki Wada argues, a symbol of infringed sovereignty through unjust seizure of territory served a useful purpose.

Russians also searched for a national idea in the ebb tide of their post-Soviet existence.[5] They could not abandon their military pride, however, after living for four decades as a military superpower and collapsing from within rather than from unconditional surrender and foreign occupation. Protective of a Russian diaspora scattered to the south and west and fearful of regional separatism linked to ethnic nationalism within its new border, Russia tried to sustain its armed might despite budgetary collapse. This proved to be a losing battle, as the Chechen war in 1994–96 offered graphic evidence of the armed forces' deterioration at an alarming rate. Since overspending on the military was, perhaps, the principal cause of economic imbalance, continued attachment to this force as the nucleus of the national idea boded poorly for reform. Yet, the second Chechen war demonstrated the popularity of using the military to boost national pride.

An economic alternative failed to garner support as a national idea not only because of longstanding preoccupation with military might as the foremost source of national power but also because of a lack of self-confidence and trust in other countries. Russians had little reason to believe that they could produce industrial products competitive on global markets. After four decades of failed economic reforms, they could scarcely imagine success in such essential changes as creating responsible management and fostering market competition. Even grasping the advantages of foreign investment in natural resources and production assets proved nettlesome. Russian sources repeatedly blamed other countries for nefarious plans to take advantage of their country's weakness,[6] rarely acknowledging the seriousness of assurances that only a prosperous Russia could satisfy other nations of its democratic and peaceful intentions.

In the mid-1990s, in order to prove that it was a responsible internationalized society, Japan needed to broaden its national idea from a passive orientation geared toward expanding exports to an active leadership role ranging from absorption of foreign products and investments to peacekeeping and conflict resolution to cultural tolerance of foreigners and their customs. For Russia the need was even more urgent to find a cultural component to a new national idea. Efforts to uncover one in pre-Soviet history—religion, state authority, literary tradition, etc.—had aroused much discussion, but little sense of confidence. Despite the fact that unanticipated ethnic strife of the past decade had soured many on a model of ethnic diversity, copying Japan's focus on homogeneous traditions as seen in the literature on *nihonjinron* could only lead to further division inside Russia and a destabilization of efforts to achieve a degree of reintegration with most of the former Soviet republics. Of course, Russia still had unparalleled territory and natural resources as well as some scientific achievements second only to the United States. Perhaps, these could become the core of a national idea centered on catching up through, first, extensive development and selective high technology and second, division of the country into distinct zones each to be integrated into a multinational region—Europe, Northeast Asia, and Southwest and Central Asia. Doubtless, apart from a catch-up mentality, Russia's new national idea would scarcely resemble Japan's postwar model.

Japanese became so obsessed with integration into the West that they routinely referred to their country as part of the West. This did not mean that intense efforts did not proceed to retain economic autonomy, by limiting foreign investments and imports, and cultural distinctiveness, by textbook, media, and citizenship controls, but they did not much interfere with the drive in exports, security, and knowledge to draw closer to the United States and Western Europe. Russians found integration into the West more problematic. Despite the optimistic rhetoric under Gorbachev of joining the common European community, Russians remained ambivalent about virtually all types of integration. They gave priority to economic and security cooperation with the "near abroad," comprised of Central Asia and the Caucasus as well as Slavic territories formerly within the Soviet Union. It should have followed that nearby areas in central and southwestern Russia led in economic recovery and cross-border integration. In fact, these areas showed little promise of early recovery. Integration with the West focused on Moscow, St. Petersburg, and Russia's northwest, while ties between the Russian Far East and Japan, South Korea, and Alaska or the Pacific Northwest as well as Northeast China could also signify a linkage via Northeast Asia.

The High Tide of Confidence and Russo-Japanese Relations

In the early and mid-1970s a confident Soviet leadership missed a chance to improve relations with Japan on terms that could have advanced its own domestic reform and global standing. Despite the logic of turning to another Asian great power during the high tide of the Sino-Soviet split and taking advantage of détente with the United States to improve ties with its allies, Moscow under Leonid Brezhnev chose another course, as explained by Peter Berton in chapter 4. Misinformation about Japan reinforced this decision for the Russian populace, as did an arrogant worldview contrasting Soviet might to Japanese frailty.[7] In the late 1980s and early 1990s, as shown in chapter 6 by Nobuo Shimotomai, a confident Japanese leadership hesitated to make bold concessions in order to upgrade relations with Russia. Although eager to raise its overall global standing in line with its economic might and cognizant of the remarkable pace of U.S.-Soviet reconciliation, Tokyo demanded too high a price for an early breakthrough. Incomplete recognition of the forces of change in the Soviet Union and of what it would take for Japan to assume a leadership role in a changing global system contributed to the delay. In each case, hesitation exacted a price domestically in the evolution of a well-rounded worldview as well as internationally in the shift to a balance in great power relations.

After a decade of indecisive economic management reforms and talk of shifting from an extensive model to an intensive one, Russia could have turned to Japan around 1970 to find a model of effective management under strong state guidance, to cooperate in investing heavily in the Far East as an impetus to transform this area in line with the dynamism already spreading through East Asia, and to diversify international relations to allow for more options. Instead, Moscow dismissed Japan as a country of little consequence.

The Soviet Union accelerated the militarization of its Far East and the exploitation of the area's natural resources with maximum dependence on the center for consumer and industrial goods and minimal investment in local infrastructure.

Russian writings on Japan in the 1970s reflect utter incomprehension of Japan's rise as a great power. This contributed to the poor state of relations that Hiroshi Kimura describes in chapter 5. To be sure, as Semyon Verbitsky explains in Chapter 14, a streak of admiration appeared in accounts of the cultural legacy that Japan was preserving and in observations on daily life. A certain fascination with Japan, beyond that for any other non-Western country, was spreading. But efforts to debunk the "economic miracle," to vilify domestic politics, and to denigrate Japan's international stature intensified.[8] Furthermore, at the same time as Soviet leaders abandoned interest in management reform that had begun under Khrushchev and still seemed to be gathering steam in the mid-1960s, they showed no interest in Japan's employment system that already had aroused envy in many capitalist countries. If the reform momentum had not been stifled by the Brezhnev leadership, Japan could have emerged as a model for state-enterprise coordination, workplace loyalty, and affirmation of the enterprise as the nucleus of the society—themes for which Japan was winning world renown and that Russian socialism claimed as high priorities.

Through 1973, Japan was searching for additional sources of raw materials and energy, leading to much discussion of investment projects in Siberia and the Russian Far East. It was not yet counting on relations with China as the gateway to the Asian continent. And it held hope that in the spirit of détente Russia would agree to a compromise on the territorial dispute, even for a few moments interpreting Leonid Brezhnev's response at the 1973 summit with Tanaka Kakuei as consent, before being told that the Soviet leader had just been clearing his throat.[9] Having only recently regained Okinawa from the United States, Tokyo had reason to hope that the symbols of postwar abnormality would largely disappear and it could proceed to solidify its position as the world's second capitalist economy and a rising great power. Instead, it had to wait another 15 years before relations with the Soviet Union showed signs of improvement.

If Japan lost little from this impasse, Russia paid a huge price. Its economy stagnated, the Russian Far East became further mired in a dead-end exchange with central Russia that saw growth rates plummet, and Russia remained isolated from fast-paced global restructuring. Moreover, it alienated Japanese public opinion as Tsuyoshi Hasegawa demonstrates in Chapter 15. Yet, Japan's situation started to change for the worse in the late 1980s. As much domestic industrial production became uncompetitive, Japan became more dependent on Asia. Plans to "reenter Asia" accelerated, but at the same time as the rise of China beckoned to Japanese investors Chinese leaders took a firm stand against the kind of leadership role that Japanese were seeking. The Chinese crackdown following June 4, 1989, gave impetus to a more distant attitude by China, and six years later the commemoration of the fiftieth anniversary of the end of the Japanese occupation of China came amidst a cooling in bilateral relations. With China indicating opposition to Japan's goal of becoming a permanent member of the United Nations Security Council, the message was clear: Japanese diplomacy needed more leverage in great power circles.

If in its high tide of confidence Russia showed scant regard for the economic miracle in Japan that aroused interest elsewhere in the world, Japan in its own peak of confidence about 15 years later seemed rather indifferent to the upheaval in Russia that mesmerized the world.

Japanese thinking concentrated on the territorial problem, neglecting the global implications of Soviet transformation and the potential for Japanese-Russian partnership in economic development inside Russia including the Russian Far East. When times were good with ample supplies of raw materials and energy from global sources and rapid increases in Japanese exports as trade surpluses persisted, Russia just did not seem to matter. Although late in the 1980s Japanese sources showed more recognition of the import of events in the Soviet Union, they seemed to matter mostly for their impact on keeping in step with U.S. global leadership.

In 1987–91, writings on Japan in Russia became more accurate and informative. One taboo after another was broken. In the same period, coverage of the Soviet Union in Japan became more variegated. While some forces worried that the resolve of the Japanese public to stand firm on negotiations over normalization would slip, the majority recognized that only full understanding of ongoing global developments of this magnitude would allow a democratic society to weigh various options carefully. But the information gap did not disappear despite the efforts noted by Akio Kawato in Chapter 16. On the Russian side as late as 1996 few had yet awakened to the fact that Japan was earnest about reaching a breakthrough in relations and investing heavily in the Russian Far East. Although an article in the Russian press by Shigeki Hakamada in the fall of 1996 forcefully argued this position,[10] few took notice. Meanwhile, Japanese opinion followed the troubles and tribulations of the emerging Russian state with some attentiveness, but showed little interest in accepting a large role in finding a solution as Japan's international responsibility. Indeed, Japanese analysts bemoaned the fact that dislike or indifference to Russia complicated efforts to improve relations.[11] In Chapter 13 Hakamada observes the outcome of these mutual misperceptions. On both sides symbols of arrogance, rudeness, or unfairness blurred the image of the other side. Russian behavior was more provocative, lending more substance to Japanese symbols.

The Acceleration of the Debate about Reform

The Japanese debate about reform began gradually. In the mid-1980s, Prime Minister Nakasone embraced the goal of educational reform, and then the Maekawa Report called for structural reform to stimulate domestic demand. In the first half of the 1990s, most attention turned to political reform, both to change electoral districting and to reduce the impact of corruption in electoral financing and pork-barrel contracts. With the consolidation of the LDP's hold on power after several years of divided coalition government and the persistence of economic sluggishness, a more radical notion of reform known as the "big bang" drew attention. This symbolized a fundamental reordering in favor of smaller government, greater individualism, and further globalization.

Observers were divided in their assessments of state capacity to realize the "big bang." On the one hand, for decades the Japanese state had surrounded itself in an aura of omnipotence. It was credited with a master plan for catching up economically, an industrial policy that guided industries in their rise and fall, and social engineering that undergirded a homogeneous society steeped in conformism. On the other hand, failure of state reforms, one after the other, reinforced critics' charges that while ministries protected their only bailiwicks, no central government power could reach across these lines. Cozy deals with vested interests left local governments inflexible and the central government incapacitated.

Such ambivalence about state capacities did not indicate any kind of breakdown such as has existed in Russia in the mid-1990s. Nor did they suggest the degree of rigidity or criminality that kept market forces from operating in most areas of Russia. But they did testify to the fact that Japan too faced threatening competition from the promised economic openness under the new WTO regulations. It also felt increasingly vulnerable before the upsurge of competition in Asia, especially the rapid rise of Chinese exports. When the Japanese economy plunged deep into recession in 1998, the urgency of reform intensified.

After reaching for firmer global recognition as a great power in the late 1980s and the beginning of the 1990s, Japan had quieted its claims following the collapse of its bubble economy and the weakening of its domestic political leadership. Whereas at the G-7 summits, during the flux when the cold war was ending and the Soviet Union was collapsing, Tokyo pushed to leave its individual stamp, in the G-7 and G-8 meetings of the later 1990s it seemed content to work closely with Washington with little fanfare. There was less distance between the positions of Tokyo and Washington on great power relations. Essentially, Japan had shifted toward the U.S. positions on vigilance before China's military rise, and accommodation before Russia's economic instability and struggle for democracy. On the basis of a reaffirmation of the Security Treaty and close ties to the United States in great power relations, Japan was groping for new assertiveness in its own international relations.

Russia presents an opportunity to Japan just as Japan does to Russia. This is a point argued not only by Georgi Kunadze and Konstantin Sarkisov in chapters 9 and 12, but also by many of the Japanese authors. A breakthrough in normalization with Russia, including a leading role in the development of the Russian Far East, would be likely to serve at least five objectives for Japan: (1) to wean Russia away from a one-sided partnership with China and toward a balanced triangle of great powers; (2) to integrate Russia and especially its vulnerable Far East into the world economy, strengthening the prospects for stability in the region; (3) to upgrade Japan's global political standing by demonstrating leadership on an important matter and earning Russian goodwill as well as continued backing for Japan's proposal to become a permanent member of the UN Security Council; (4) to give a boost to decentralization and regional balance in Japan by spurring development in Hokkaido and along the Sea of Japan; and (5) to encourage North Korea, South Korea, and China to join in the cooperative development of the Northeast Asian region in a manner reassuring to global investors and markets. If these results could be achieved, this would not be a panacea for either Japan's or Russia's problems. But especially for Japan's identity as a "normal" country exerting leadership in its own region, the uplift could be substantial. To achieve this, however, Japanese must choose between the position that the centerpiece in their negotiations with Russia is never to forget the fundamental territorial question, and the position that both sides must now establish an environment to advance a political resolution.[12]

For Russia, a breakthrough in relations with Japan could pay even richer dividends. In the second half of 1992 and 1993, as Russians became enamored of a "Eurasian" identity to reduce a sense of dependency on the West, policymakers turned more to China than Japan. Since then, as the Sino-Russian relationship has risen to a strategic partnership and been treated by many as equivalent to the Russo-U.S. relationship, there have been worries inside of Russia as well as abroad that Russia's choices of countries such as China, India, and Iran to balance the West fail to serve Russia's national interests effectively. Although often seen as part of the West, Japan represents diversification and economic cooperation to meet the needs of the Far East. With Japan's assistance, the Presidential Program for the development of the Russian Far East and Trans-Baikal, announced in April 1996, could gain a huge boost. In addition, some models for industrial restructuring with Japanese assistance could be selected. But to reach an agreement Russians must question whether the primary purpose of a multipolar world is to check the United States and the West or whether Japan is a potential partner in multipolarity that serves mainly another goal.[13] Many of the authors of this book have noted how difficult it has been for Russians to come to this recognition. Sumio Edamura in Chapter 8 places this in diplomatic perspective while Tadashi Anno in Chapter 17 interprets it in historical comparative perspective

Idealistic appeals for Russo-Japanese cooperation are nothing new. Much of the literature on the "Sea of Japan rim economic sphere" (*kan Nihonkai keizai ken*) that reached a high point from

1991 to 1995 holds up tantalizing promises for what can be accomplished through such cooperation. But such appeals seldom are buttressed with realistic analysis of actual circumstances in the Russian Far East, including rampant criminality and corruption, privatization favoring former *nomenklatura* rather than genuine entrepreneurship, laws and tax obligations that defy international standards, a lack of receptivity to normal forms of business management, etc. Goodwill from Tokyo and a decision in Moscow to reach a political deal in no way ensure that Russia will treat business in the Far East as an opportunity to reassure the world community of its readiness for entering the global economy rather than as a means to enrich a few cliques and to prove once again that Russia can stand up to a foreign threat. At the end of 1999, however dim hopes were for the "Sea of Japan rim," a political breakthrough with Moscow would be bound to accelerate arguments that the obstacles are vanishing.[14]

In the early 1970s, Russia, not Japan, was the big loser from the failure to normalize relations and work together for economic development. In the late 1980s and the start of the 1990s, Russia again lost a lot more than Japan when negotiations made little progress. Although some observers blame Japan for not providing enough assistance in 1992 to 1996 when Russia was beginning the post-Soviet transformation, in retrospect it seems clear that such assistance would largely have been wasted and would not have cemented close ties. The burden continues to lie with Russia to set its own house in order. It would, of course, be easier to bear that burden if the payoff in foreign investment and close cooperation offered hope to the Russian people.

The Russian debate about reform quieted after the outcry against shock therapy. Even in the electoral campaign for president in 1996, the leading candidates said little specific about such fundamental questions as the creation of free economic zones, the means to attract investments to the Russian Far East, the Tumen river area development project, passage of a production sharing agreement, how to respond to proposals from China on ways to increase economic cooperation, etc. In the election campaign for the State Duma of late 1999 such specifics were again missing. Russia needs a renewed debate about reform not on the basis of abstract preferences, but in response to concrete proposals that show the Russian people how they are likely to benefit.

The Sino-Russian border dispute that for a quarter century seemed to block normalization was resolved to the satisfaction of leaders in both countries by a demarcation agreement of 1991, ratified in 1992, that allowed for the transfer of small amounts of land while setting aside three islands for future negotiations. Although some Russians vocally objected to the completion of the border demarcation in the eastern section in 1997, it has gone forward. Following this precedent, Russia should be able to reach a compromise with Japan. China has built on its agreement to strengthen its ties to Russia and solidify its great power claims. Japan could do the same with the possible added bonus of forging a stronger economic relationship with Russia than China has managed to do. Japanese need not be concerned that the Clinton administration is so eager to see Russo-Japanese ties improved that it is deemphasizing its backing for Japan's territorial demands,[15] since emphasis on the advantages of improved relations is a logical step toward a short-term compromise. If China has sought leverage against the United States and Japan to resist unipolarity, Japan may prefer to gain leverage against China more than the United States, while promoting a single global economic system. Its notion of multipolarity is likely to accept a much higher degree of cooperation to address world problems than confrontation to prevent one country or a group of countries from exercising leadership.

Russo-Japanese relations and comparisons are best seen in the context of the two strategic triangles of Sino-Russian-Japanese relations and Russo-Japanese-U.S. relations, or for some purposes as part of the quadrangle of Sino-Japanese-Russian-U.S. relations. The rise of China as a great power critical of the U.S.-led world order and of a regional order in which Japan exerts a strong influence encourages the United States to support closer Russo-Japanese relations and encourages Japan to solidify ties with Russia as well as the United States. China is driving Japan and Russia closer together. This does not mean that Russo-Japanese ties are targeted against China. Rather this indicates that in the shadow of a strong, rising power, its principal neighbors find an advantage to consolidating their own ties, maximizing their ability to work together.

For both Japan and Russia, a breakthrough in relations, with all that implies, would be a decisive step toward achieving the goal of "normalcy." It would do a lot to clarify each country's great power ambitions, raising Japan's in a healthy manner focused on assuming responsibility for global problems, and channeling Russia's toward integration without sacrificing multipolarity. Growing recognition that the two countries can become partners with common values in a multipolar but integrated world order suggests the importance of great power identities.[16] In neither case would a breakthrough in diplomacy solve domestic problems, but it would have the potential to give a boost to redefining center-local relations, to economic development, and perhaps even to political forces in the center amenable to cooperation.

The positive spirit of the Krasnoyarsk summit of November 1997 offered a taste of what might follow from a new stage in relations. Russia accepts Japan's right to become a permanent member of the United Nations Security Council and regards the U.S.-Japan Security Treaty as a positive force for stability. Japan pledges to support Russia's economic transformation more actively after backing Russia's entry into APEC. Yet, the momentum for normalization remains fragile, and both economic and political forces have been conspiring to undermine it. The sudden outbreak of the Asian economic flu left investors more cautious. If in July 1997 Hashimoto's speech about improving ties with Russia was partly directed at Japanese enterprises hesitant to invest, the prospects were much lower just six months later as the Russian economy was tottering anew and especially after August 1998 when Russia flirted with default and changed its economic course. Meanwhile, exposed Japanese creditors will be less likely to assume large risks. Already normal in most respects, Japan may decide that it has little to prove in assuming a special burden to assist Russia. But it is precisely because Russia remains at a crossroads far from normalcy and Japan has the potential to make a difference that it may agree to shoulder a large responsibility. In the process, Japan would be making a statement about completing its own transition.

As Hakamada informs us in chapter 13, the political impetus toward normalization of Japanese-Russian relations all but collapsed after the summit of November 1998. Japan has awakened to the fact that Russia is not serious about any territorial compromise, and Russia is now aware that the Japanese remain fixated on that goal as the purpose for improving relations. The world is threatened when the deadline for the countdown to the year 2000 passes with another downturn in the relations of two of the great powers, with negative consequences for each of the two countries domestically and for the emerging world order. During the cold war, periodic breakdowns in Japanese-Russian relations may not have caused much damage, but a recurrence at the start of the twenty-first century bodes badly for stabilizing the world in the face of numerous new threats. The principal lesson of our review of the past half century is to warn that both sides and the other great powers as well must learn from the lessons of repeated missed opportunities and misperceptions to make a concerted and realistic effort to set Japanese-Russian relations on a positive course. Before the momentum of Krasnoyarsk dissipates completely, national leaders and public opinion must grasp the larger significance of this bilateral relationship and nurture it. The burden on the Japanese side is, above all, patience. This does not mean abandoning territorial claims, but it does require putting them in a new context. The burden on the Russian side is integration. Only by tempering great power ambitions and acceding to global forces of integration can Russia achieve the level of normalcy essential to attract Japanese support. Through Japanese demonstrations of patience and goodwill and Russian policies welcoming integration and trust, a new era in bilateral relations may at last begin.

NOTES

1. Cyril E. Black, et al., *The Modernization of Japan and Russia* (New York: The Free Press, 1975).
2. Toshi Nishi, *Unconditional Democracy: Education and Politics in Occupied Japan 1945–1952* (Stanford: Hoover Institution Press, 1982), p. 63.
3. A. I. Kravtsevich, "Iaponskii opyt: uroki dlia Rossii," *Iaponskii opyt dlia rossiiskikh reform,* No. 6, 1996, p. 5.
4. Gilbert Rozman, "Backdoor Japan: The Search for a Way out via Regionalism and Decentralization," *Journal of Japanese Studies,* Vol. 25, No. 1, Winter 1999, pp. 3–31.
5. Timothy McDaniel, *The Agony of the Russian Idea* (Princeton: Princeton University Press, 1996).
6. Gilbert Rozman, "The Crisis of the Russian Far East: Who Is to Blame?" *Problems of Post-Communism,* Vol. 44, No. 5, September/October 1997, pp. 3–12.
7. "Moscow's Japan-Watchers in the First Years of the Gorbachev Era: The Struggle for Realism and Respect in Foreign Affairs," *Pacific Review,* Vol. 1, No. 3 (1988), pp. 257–75.

8. B. N. Dobrovinskii, "Ekonomika: vialyi i neustoichivyi rost," A. I. Ivanov, "Vnutripoliticheskaia obstanovka v Iaponii v 1978 g.," N. N. Nikolaev, "Nekotorye problemy vneshnei politiki Iaponii," *Iaponiia 1979: Ezhegodnik* (Moscow: Nauka, 1980), pp. 5–23, 24–46, 47–64.
9. Gilbert Rozman, *Japan's Response to the Gorbachev Era, 1985–1991: A Rising Superpower Views a Declining One* (Princeton, NJ: Princeton University Press, 1992), p. 118.
10. Shigeki Hakamada, "Rossiia i Iaponiia sposobny poniat' drug druga," *Nezavisimaia gazeta,* October 1996, p. 5.
11. "Nichiro kokumin 'kataomoi,'" *Asahi shimbun,* November 30, 1992, p. 3.
12. Kimura Hiroshi, "Wasurete naranu kihon na ryodo," and Hakamada Shigeki, "Seiji ketsudan unagasu kankyo tsukuri o," *Sankei shimbun,* August 9, 1997.
13. Sergei Kortunov, "Potential'nye soiuzniki Rossii: Moskve est' na kogo operet'sia v mnogopoliusnom mire," *Nezavisimaia gazeta,* March, 1, 1996.
14. Ogawa Kazuo, "'Kan Nihonkai' no koryu sokushin o," *Nihon keizai shimbun,* July 15, 1997.
15. Fujimura Kano, "Hoppo ryodo mondai de Nihon shiji kara kotai suru Beikoku," *Foresight,* July 1997, pp. 34–35.
16. "Kachikan koyu suru ryokoku," *Sankei shimbun,* July 17, 1997.

Index